# WORKING WITH SUBSTANCE USERS

# Working with Substance Users

## A Guide to Effective Interventions

George Allan

First published 2014 by
PALGRAVE MACMILLAN

Palgrave Macmillan in the UK is an imprint of Macmillan Publishers Limited, registered in England, company number 785998, of Houndmills, Basingstoke, Hampshire RG21 6XS.

Palgrave Macmillan in the US is a division of St Martin's Press LLC, 175 Fifth Avenue, New York, NY 10010.

Palgrave Macmillan is the global academic imprint of the above companies and has companies and representatives throughout the world.

Palgrave® and Macmillan® are registered trademarks in the United States, the United Kingdom, Europe and other countries

ISBN 978-1-137-27804-3      ISBN 978-1-137-27805-0 (eBook)

DOI 10.1007/978-1-137-27805-0

This book is printed on paper suitable for recycling and made from fully managed and sustained forest sources. Logging, pulping and manufacturing processes are expected to conform to the environmental regulations of the country of origin.

A catalogue record for this book is available from the British Library.

A catalog record for this book is available from the Library of Congress.

Typeset by Cambrian Typesetters, Camberley, Surrey

# Contents

*List of Illustrative Material*                                              ix
*Introduction*                                                             xiii
*Acknowledgements*                                                          xvi
*List of Abbreviations*                                                    xvii

**PART I   Context and Theory**

**1   Defining and Experiencing Substances**                                 **3**
The language maze                                                            3
Central concepts                                                             4
Experiencing drugs                                                          8
Substances: the central nervous system and the liver                       8
Commonly encountered substances                                            9
The individual and the environment                                         14
Concluding comments                                                        16

**2   What Is a Substance Problem?**                                       **17**
A superfluous question?                                                    17
Substances: different drugs, different risks                               19
The individual: some people run greater risks than others                  21
The environment: risks to users                                            24
Social consequences and the harm to others                                 24
Models for making sense of risks and harms                                 25
Concluding comments                                                        27

**3   Why Do People Develop Substance Problems?**                          **29**
Individual pathology or social forces?                                     29
Sociological theories: it's cultural forces that count                     31
The disease model and genetic theories: some people are
    different                                                              35
Learning theories: much the same for everyone                             39
Psychoanalytical theories: substance problems as symptoms                  43
Gateway theory                                                             45
Substance problems as choice                                               46
Integrated approaches; the bio-psycho-social model                         47
Concluding comments                                                        49

**4** **Cultural Trends; Social Control** **50**
Cultural influences on use 50
Social control: various options 52
Judging effectiveness 56
Substances in the UK since 1960: a shifting scene 57
Concluding comments 66

**5** **Why and How Do People Change?** **67**
Behaviour change 67
Unassisted recovery 68
Triggers and the maintenance of change 71
The cycle of change 75
Concluding comments 77

**PART II** **Interventions in Practice**

**6** **Effective Interventions, Competent Practitioners,**
**Successful Services** **81**
What makes the difference? 81
How do we measure success? 82
Controversies, controversies 83
Interventions 86
Practitioner skills in context 89
Successful services 95
Concluding comments 99

**7** **Assessment and Care Planning** **100**
Assessment: context and principles 100
The processes of assessment 101
Assessment: covering the ground 104
Care planning 114
Concluding comments 119

**8** **Motivational Interviewing** **121**
Motivation: the key to the door of change 121
The essence of motivational interviewing 123
The practice of motivational interviewing 125
Concluding comments 130

**9** **Harm Reduction; Less Intensive Treatment; Brief**
**Interventions** **132**
Different but connected 132
Harm reduction 133
Less intensive treatment 139
Brief interventions 140
Concluding comments 142

**10   Pharmacological Treatments**                                          **144**
Pharmacotherapy: a central intervention for some              144
The purposes of pharmacotherapy                                     145
Opiates                                                                        146
Alcohol                                                                        149
Psychostimulants                                                            151
Benzodiazepines                                                             152
Nicotine                                                                       153
Vaccines                                                                       153
Concluding comments                                                      154

**11   Interventions: Specific Approaches**                              **155**
The foundations of effective interventions                         155
Cognitive behavioural therapy (CBT)                                 156
Mutual aid groups and self-help resources                        163
Controlled drinking                                                         168
Working with stimulant users                                           173
New psychoactive substances and club drugs                     176
Concluding comments                                                      177

**12   Relapse Prevention, Endings and Follow-up Care**             **178**
Perspectives on relapse                                                   178
Relapse prevention using CBT methods                              182
Endings and follow-up care                                              187
Concluding comments                                                      188

## PART III   Specific Populations

**13   Psychological Distress and Substance Problems**             **193**
Dual diagnosis: an unhelpful term?                                   193
The links between psychological distress and substance
    problems                                                                   193
Co-occurring problems, multiple difficulties                       196
Prevalence                                                                     197
How services are provided                                                197
Assessment, care planning and interventions                     199
Concluding comments                                                      204

**14   Children Affected by Parental Problems**                         **206**
Children affected                                                            206
Children affected: the role of substance problems practitioners   210
Concluding comments                                                      215

**15   Significant Others: Adults**                                          **216**
Significant adults                                                           216
Drugs and alcohol: the impact on significant adults             217

Significant adults: assessment                                             219
Significant adults: care planning and interventions                       220
Significant adults: supporting the substance user                         223
Concluding comments                                                       224

**16 Young People: Substance Use and Substance Problems**      **226**
Young people's substance use                                              226
The structuring of services                                               230
Engagement, assessment and care planning                                  232
Interventions                                                             235
Concluding comments                                                       239

**17 Offenders and Other Involuntary Service Users**           **240**
Voluntary and involuntary                                                 240
Engagement                                                                241
Employee policies                                                         242
Substance problems and the criminal justice system                        244
Intervention with involuntary service users                               248
Concluding comments                                                       250

*Appendix:* Validated Questionnaires                                      252
*References*                                                              257
*Index*                                                                   275

# List of Illustrative Material

## Figures

| | | |
|---|---|---|
| 3.1 | Factors influencing patterns of substance use | 48 |
| 5.1 | The cycle of change | 76 |
| 6.1 | The tiering of services | 98 |
| 7.1 | The treatment process | 101 |
| 7.2 | Treatment within the recovery journey | 111 |
| 12.1 | Stages of relapse and relapse avoidance | 182 |
| 16.1 | Care pathways | 232 |

## Table

| | | |
|---|---|---|
| 2.1 | Thorley's framework applied to cocaine and crack | 27 |

## Activities

| | | |
|---|---|---|
| 1.1 | Defining a substance problem | 7 |
| 2.1 | Defining problematic use | 27 |
| 4.1 | Would harm reduction work for nicotine? | 58 |
| 4.2 | Alternative regulation of cocaine | 63 |
| 5.1 | Personal experience of change | 72 |
| 5.2 | The cycle of change | 77 |
| 6.1 | More definitions | 85 |
| 6.2 | A substitute for alcohol? | 89 |
| 7.1 | The welcoming gesture | 102 |
| 8.1 | Types of question | 127 |
| 8.2 | Analyse the processes of motivational interviewing | 130 |
| 10.1 | The dilemma of vaccines | 154 |
| 11.1 | Introducing recovery options | 168 |
| 11.2 | Controlled drinking | 170 |
| 12.1 | Planning to avoid relapse | 186 |
| 12.2 | Follow-up systems | 188 |
| 13.1 | Service coordination | 199 |
| 16.1 | Young adolescents and substances | 227 |

## Case illustrations

| | | |
|---|---|---|
| 2.1 | Do they have a problem? | 18 |
| 3.1 | Labelling | 34 |

| | | |
|---|---|---|
| 3.2 | Classical conditioning | 40 |
| 3.3 | Applying theory in practice | 48 |
| 4.1 | How do strategy and control impact on the individual? | 65 |
| 5.1 | Olly and the unanswered questions | 68 |
| 5.2 | Resolving cognitive dissonance | 70 |
| 6.1 | When the alliance is not there | 90 |
| 7.1 | The emergency appointment | 102 |
| 7.2 | Assessment in practice | 113 |
| 7.3 | Care planning | 118 |
| 8.1 | Unhelpful interactions | 122 |
| 8.2 | An example of motivational interviewing | 128 |
| 9.1 | Harm reduction | 138 |
| 9.2 | Less intensive treatment | 140 |
| 10.1 | Alcohol detoxification | 151 |
| 11.1 | Cognitive appraisals | 157 |
| 11.2 | A CRA action plan | 163 |
| 11.3 | A controlled drinking programme | 172 |
| 12.1 | Seemingly irrelevant decisions | 180 |
| 12.2 | Mapping environmental risks | 184 |
| 12.3 | A big breakfast relapse prevention plan | 185 |
| 13.1 | The problem of compliance | 196 |
| 13.2 | Co-occurring problems | 204 |
| 14.1 | Parental problems | 212 |
| 14.2 | Engaging with the issue of children's welfare | 215 |
| 15.1 | Substance use and family dynamics | 219 |
| 15.2 | Dilemmas for family members | 222 |
| 15.3 | A daughter's drug problem | 224 |
| 16.1 | A problem emerges and then subsides | 230 |
| 16.2 | A challenging situation | 233 |
| 17.1 | Engagement | 243 |
| 17.2 | Intervening through the criminal justice system | 249 |

## Boxes

| | | |
|---|---|---|
| 1.1 | Misuse: a loaded term | 8 |
| 1.2 | New psychoactive substances | 13 |
| 2.1 | Comparing the harms | 19 |
| 2.2 | Heroin administration: a hierarchy of risk | 22 |
| 3.1 | Jewish people and alcohol: swimming against the tide? | 32 |
| 3.2 | The founding of Alcoholics Anonymous | 36 |
| 3.3 | The Oriental flush | 38 |
| 3.4 | Abuse and the development of substance problems | 45 |
| 4.1 | The law of unintended consequences | 53 |
| 4.2 | Prohibition: an unmitigated disaster? | 56 |
| 4.3 | Misuse of Drugs Act 1971 | 59 |
| 4.4 | An alternative model for cannabis regulation | 62 |
| 5.1 | Self-efficacy: a critical component | 71 |

| | | |
|---|---|---|
| 5.2 | Factors precipitating change | 72 |
| 5.3 | Why do some people avoid treatment services? | 74 |
| 6.1 | Does methadone work? | 88 |
| 6.2 | The use of manuals: a good idea? | 94 |
| 7.1 | Motivation: not something to be assessed | 101 |
| 7.2 | Confidentiality | 103 |
| 7.3 | Dangers in withdrawal | 108 |
| 8.1 | Motivational interviewing: are there ethical concerns? | 124 |
| 8.2 | Key questions in motivational interviewing | 128 |
| 9.1 | User and peer involvement | 135 |
| 9.2 | Tobacco and harm reduction | 138 |
| 9.3 | Working with cannabis users | 139 |
| 10.1 | Agonists and antagonists | 146 |
| 10.2 | Heroin prescribing: back to the future | 147 |
| 10.3 | Physical dependency: more than one substance | 152 |
| 11.1 | The 12 steps | 165 |
| 12.1 | Key questions when service arrangements change | 187 |
| 13.1 | Cannabis and mental health | 195 |
| 14.1 | Pregnancy | 209 |
| 14.2 | Managing professional conflicts | 210 |
| 14.3 | Adult services: limits, dilemmas and confidentiality | 213 |
| 15.1 | Siblings of young substance users: hidden hurt | 218 |
| 15.2 | Diversity | 220 |
| 15.3 | Mutual aid groups for significant adults | 222 |
| 16.1 | The tier model of services for young people | 230 |
| 16.2 | Transitional arrangements: a cause for concern | 236 |
| 16.3 | Consent to treatment | 237 |
| 17.1 | Drug–crime connections: some statistics | 245 |

# Introduction

## Who is this book for?

From self-help books to academic papers, from texts exploring social policy to memoirs recounting experiences of substance use, drugs, alcohol and tobacco have a rich and varied literature. Where does this book fit in? As awareness has grown that substance problems permeate the caseloads of all social and health practitioners, so has the need to ensure that accessible guides to practice are available. This book has been written for all who come in contact with people with substance problems in their working lives – social workers, probation officers, support workers, psychologists, health practitioners, youth workers and the like. Although practitioners in these various professional roles will approach people experiencing difficulties from different perspectives, the knowledge and skills needed to intervene effectively are the same for all. Practice is similar in the various countries that make up the United Kingdom but there are legislative and policy differences. To ensure its relevance throughout the UK and beyond, the material has not been tied too closely to any one country. The book has been written for practitioners and for undergraduate and postgraduate students undertaking specialist modules. However, it is hoped that it will also be read by some people experiencing problems themselves, or their relatives, to help shed light on what engaging with treatment entails and to give them hope that their lives can change for the better.

## What does this book cover?

Practitioners will be most interested in the application of effective interventions. However, it is difficult to make sense of these without a grounding in the theories as to why people develop problems and an understanding of the wider social and cultural contexts which shape substance use, both harm free and problematic. This book tries to do justice to these themes. It is divided into three sections:

- **Context and theory.** Chapters 1 to 5 cover information about substances, the nature of problematic use, theories as to why people experience difficulties, the cultural setting and methods of control, and perspectives on why people change.
- **Interventions in practice.** Chapters 6 to 12 explore assessment, the main interventions and relapse prevention. Motivational interviewing, harm

reduction, CBT, pharmacotherapy, mutual aid groups and working with stimulant users are described.

- **Specific populations.** This section, chapters 13 to 17, considers the implications of problematic use for other people, both adults and children. It also addresses working with people with co-occurring psychological distress and substance use, adolescents and involuntary service users, including offenders.

While it might be desirable for readers to work through the book from start to finish, it is acknowledged that busy practitioners and students tend to seek out information as the situation demands. To this end, an effort has been made to present the material in an accessible way. Given the often complex and ambiguous nature of research findings, this has been a challenge. I hope I have done justice to the work of others.

Much is known about substances and their use but a great deal continues to perplex us too. Disagreements continue to rage as to why people develop problems, what the outcomes of treatment should be and how best to help people. To an outsider, the substance problems field must sometimes seem to be populated by warring tribes! Controversial issues, such as controlled drinking and the meaning of 'recovery', are addressed. The book is not, however, a polemic and the reader is encouraged to consider the evidence before drawing conclusions.

This book is about addiction, but it is not only about addiction; substance problems occur in many forms.

## Terminology and case studies

Clarification of the terminology used is needed.

- 'Practitioner' is used to describe anyone working in a formal capacity with a person with a substance problem or his/her relatives.
- 'Service user' denotes any person who is involved in 'treatment'.
- 'Substances' and 'drugs' are terms used synonymously, except when the latter is employed to differentiate other psychoactive substances from alcohol and tobacco.
- 'Interventions' and 'treatment' are used interchangeably.
- Substances are no respecters of gender. In recognition of this, 'he' and 'she' are used in alternate chapters, except where gender-specific issues are being addressed.

Some of the case studies are fictitious and some are based on real, but anonymized, scenarios. The introduction of 'I' or 'a colleague' differentiates the latter from the former.

## A plea

Historically, many professional groups and their associated training courses paid little heed to substance issues. This is changing very much for the better.

What is lacking, however, are opportunities to practise the hands-on skills needed before engaging with people experiencing difficulties. This book comes, therefore, with an appeal to course organisers and those designing undergraduate and post-qualifying training to build in significant space for rehearsing assessment, motivational interviewing, relapse prevention and the other skills essential to effective engagement. Proficiency only comes with practice supported by skilled mentors.

# Acknowledgements

This book has benefited greatly from the constructive criticism of a number of people. I would particularly like to thank Vicky Allan, Alastair Logan, Kenny Malcolm, David Ryder and others who gave advice but did not want to be named. The following people and agencies helpfully responded to queries: Carlo DiClemente; Tim Stockwell; Ron Roizen; Robin Room; Addiction Northern Ireland; ASH; Crown Prosecution Service; DrugScope; MindWise; Wales Alcohol and Drug Helpline. I also very much appreciate the advice and encouragement I received from Lloyd Langman, Helen Caunce and India Annette-Woodgate at Palgrave. Thanks also to Linda Auld and Caroline Richards for technical editing.

BMJ Publishing Group Ltd. for Box 8.2 'Key Questions in Motivational Interviewing' from Stephen Rollnick et al 'Motivation Interviewing' in *British Medical Journal* (2010);

Carlo C. Diclemente for Figure 3.1 'Factors Influencing Patterns of Substance Use', available at http://www.casat.unr.edu/docs/Addiction_Change.ppt, for figure 5.1 'The Cycle of Change', also available at http://www.casat.unr.edu/docs/Addiction_Change.ppt;

Guilford Publications Inc. for Figure 12.1 'Stages of Relapse and Relapse Avoidance' from G. Alan Marlatt and Dennis Donovan *Relapse Prevention* 2nd edition (2005);

Narcotics Anonymous UK for Box 11.2 'The 12 Steps' from 'The 12 Steps of Narcotics Anonymous' available at http://12step.org/steps/narcotics-anonymous.html;

Royal College of Psychiatrists for Figure 16.1 'Care Pathways' from *Practice Standards for Young People with Substance Misuse Problems* (2012), www.rcpsych.ac.uk;

The World Health Organisation for 'The Alcohol Use Disorders Identification Test' from Thomas F. Babor et al *The Alcohol Use Disorders Identification Test: Guidelines for Use in Primary Care* 2nd edition, http://whqlibdoc. who.int/hq/2001/WHO_MSD_MSB_01.6a.pdf, accessed 29/08/13.

# Abbreviations

The following abbreviations have been used throughout:

| | |
|---|---|
| ACMD | Advisory Council on the Misuse of Drugs |
| CBT | cognitive behavioural therapy |
| CMHT | community mental health teams |
| DTs | delirium tremens |
| EMCDDA | European Monitoring Centre for Drugs and Drug Addiction |
| GBL | gammabutyrolactone |
| GHB | gammahydroxybutyrate |
| NICE | National Institute for Health and Care Excellence |
| NRT | nicotine replacement therapy |
| NTA | National Treatment Agency for Substance Misuse |
| OST | opioid substitution treatment |
| UKATT | UK Alcohol Treatment Trial |
| WHO | World Health Organization |

## Note: Access to National Treatment Agency (NTA) documents

The NTA was absorbed into Public Health England in 2013. Guidance and reports on the NTA website are scheduled to be transferred by 2014 to the PHE website or placed on the National Archive's website or similar.

# PART I

# Context and Theory

# CHAPTER 1

# Defining and Experiencing Substances

## KEY THEMES

- It is important to use language precisely as it influences both how we view people experiencing difficulties with substances and society's efforts to devise strategies to reduce the harms.
- Dependency and addiction are central to our understanding of substance problems but are difficult to define. Many concepts surrounding substance use remain contentious.
- Psychoactive substances can be categorised by their different effects on the central nervous system.
- Phenomena such as tolerance, withdrawals and overdose can be explained to a great degree, but not entirely, from a physiological perspective.
- The chemical properties of a drug alone do not account for how a person experiences it. This is predicated on a complex interaction between the individual, the environment and the substance itself.

## The language maze

Addiction and dependence are difficult to define but, as concepts, they tend to mould our understanding of what problematic use of substances is. In the public mind, substance problems are often synonymous with 'addiction', but this is an example of language shaping – and limiting – our perception because people can experience problems with substances, irrespective of whether they are addicted or not. The term 'alcoholic' is used to describe the dependent drinker, a person who appears unable to stop when he starts and who uses most of the time. This stereotype has come to define what problem drinking is, thus minimising the risks inherent in bingeing or regular heavy use. Two examples illustrate the problem. I remember Mitch Winehouse, the father of the singer, Amy, saying that, initially, he was not overly worried by his daughter's heavy alcohol use. He did not think she was an 'alcoholic' as she did not drink all the time – a good example of how a word can influence understanding. At that time, for Mitch, a drink problem constituted persistent, dependent use and no other pattern. In a similar vein, Ward, Henderson and Pearson (2003, p. 30) describe how a group of care leavers dismissed concerns about their drug use by measuring this against the idea of 'addiction': 'Addiction was the point of reference that many of these young people used in defending the extent to which they used drugs, justifying their continuing use on the grounds that they were *"not addicted"*.'

The problem is not confined to how people make sense of their own or other people's use on an individual basis. The drinks industry has a vested interest in presenting Britain's alcohol problem as residing with a small minority of irresponsible or 'problematic' drinkers rather than being a wider public health issue involving excessive consumption by a significant proportion of the population. Such a view can then influence political decisions regarding what measures should be put in place to reduce the harms.

Words used to define specific concepts within the substance problems field have spilled over into common parlance to refer to unrelated ideas. Thus we have the media describing politicians as 'being in denial' over the outcome of their policies. Within the disease model, 'being in denial' is a characteristic which 'alcoholics' are deemed to possess – a controversial concept; however, we think we know what it means. Problems with language can become absurd. Detoxification refers to a specific process of ridding the body of poisonous substances and is used primarily to refer to alcohol and drugs. What are we to make of a company advertising 'corporate detox solutions' and a book entitled *Detox your Finances: The Ultimate Book of Money Matters for Women* (Trueman, 2009)? It is little wonder that concepts, which are both difficult to define in the first place and contentious within the substance problems field, become further muddied through imprecise use.

Words can reinforce stigma which, in turn, may militate against a person's recovery. 'Junkie' conjures up the idea of a hopelessly dependent individual living a squalid existence in a shadowy subculture with nothing to contribute to society. The phrase 'person with a drug problem' invokes a very different image. A junkie is not one of us, a person with a drug problem is.

If we are to make sense of substance use and substance problems, we need to use language with care.

## Central concepts

### Drugs, addiction and dependence

Drugs are consumed in most societies. Vast, complex industries, both lawful and illicit, surround their production and marketing. They are used for medical and recreation purposes. They can be defined by their effects on the central nervous system or by their legal status. But what are they? Gossop argues that cultural significance and methods of use are as important as chemical properties when struggling to define 'a drug', a notion he considers to be a 'social artefact' (Gossop, 2007, p. 2). Most people would agree that heroin is a drug, but when it comes to solvents, the response might be 'in particular circumstances only'. In respect of the non-medical use of substances, we are primarily referring to those which are psychoactive, in Edwards' words 'mind-acting'- they alter mood and cognitive functioning (Edwards, 2005, p. xvii).

Even this is unsatisfactory; steroids may affect mood but that is not why people take them.

If the concept of a drug proves hard to pin down, *addiction* and *dependence* present even greater difficulties. Addiction is commonly used as a pejorative word to describe an unhealthy preoccupation. Dependence is often used to mean the same thing. However, there are two separate but overlapping phenomena at work here:

- **Physical dependence.** Persistent, heavy consumption of some, but not all, substances leads to adaptions in the functioning of the central nervous system. When this occurs, more of the substance is needed to achieve the same effect: this is *tolerance*. If the person then stops using abruptly, the central nervous system reacts until it has readjusted to the absence of the drug: this is *withdrawals*. Raistrick, Heather and Godfrey (2006, p. 128) argue that 'physical addiction' can be a confusing term for these processes of neuroadaption but it is hard to find another phrase that makes the concept clearer. What is important is that physical dependence is a physiological process which anyone who takes certain drugs will experience if he consumes regularly and heavily. Psychological factors need not come into the equation. For example, a person prescribed morphine to control pain over a period will become physically dependent and withdrawals will occur if he suddenly stops; however, he may feel no desire to use beyond wanting to ward off the discomfort of withdrawal. With regard to tolerance, it is not the case that heavy users simply consume ever-increasing quantities. After a period of escalating consumption, a person tends to find a dose level which he then maintains (Gossop, 2007; West, 2006). For example, a regular smoker will stick to approximately the same number of cigarettes a day or a dependent drinker the same amount of alcohol. Both psychological and physiological factors may be at play here. With regard to physiological factors, a ceiling on the capacity of the individual's nervous system and liver, and balancing changes in the neurotransmitters, lead to a particular baseline of use.
- **Psychological dependence.** Here the person experiences a feeling of needing to take the substance irrespective of whether physical dependence is present. Many people exhibit mild psychological dependence, an example being wanting a few drinks to cope with social occasions. At the other extreme, psychological dependence can be experienced as a preoccupation with substance taking, involving overpowering feelings of being unable to cope without using and overwhelming cravings.

The jazz great Charlie Parker (undated), who had serious difficulties with heroin, neatly encapsulated these different facets of dependence: 'They can get it out of your blood but they can't get it out of your mind.'

It is the combination of psychological and physical dependence which we tend to call 'addiction'. Problems with defining addiction led the World Health Organization (WHO, 2013a) to replace it with the concept of the *dependence syndrome*:

A cluster of physiological, behavioural, and cognitive phenomena in which the use of a substance or a class of substances takes on a much higher priority for a given individual than other behaviours that once had greater value. A central descriptive characteristic of the dependence syndrome is the desire (often strong, sometimes overpowering) to take psychoactive drugs (which may or may not have been medically prescribed), alcohol, or tobacco. There may be evidence that return to substance use after a period of abstinence leads to a more rapid reappearance of other features of the syndrome than occurs with nondependent individuals.

The WHO (2013a) then suggests that a diagnoses of the syndrome can be made if a person displays three or more of the following characteristics at the same point in the previous 12 months: a desire to use; problems of control; withdrawals; tolerance; disregard for alternative activities; continuing to use despite problems.

This certainly captures a pattern of substance use distinguished by fixation with drug taking and an apparent inability to exercise restraint. However, it does not solve all the difficulties of definition. West (2006, p. 174) notes that addiction is a 'social construct' with 'fuzzy boundaries' and so, too, is the WHO concept of a dependence syndrome. Three characteristics and a cut-off point of one year are arbitrary. An individual diagnosis is involved, a medicalized approach, which divorces a person's behaviour from its social context which, to some degree, determines whether it can be considered 'abnormal'. The definition does, however, avoid suggesting that dependence is always problematic. This is important. While in most cases it will be, what is a problem depends on whose perspective is taken. A person who smokes cannabis daily to relieve the pain and spasms of multiple sclerosis might meet the WHO diagnosis of dependence but he might view use as being highly beneficial rather than a problem.

Although no solution is without difficulties, for the sake of simplicity we will use the term 'dependence' in preference to 'addiction' in this book. It will be used in line with the broader WHO definition above rather than its more rigid diagnostic interpretation.

However dependence is defined, it does not include other patterns of use such as bingeing or heavy consumption, short of dependence, which can bring a range of problems. This is the difficulty discussed at the start of this chapter. Another category introduced by the WHO (2013a) can help us here: that of 'harmful use': 'A pattern of psychoactive substance use that is causing damage to health.'

The World Health Organization includes both physical and psychological problems in this definition, along with possible detrimental social repercussions. While not a formal diagnostic category, the WHO (2013b) also notes that use can be 'hazardous', a pattern of substance taking with a heightened risk of physical, mental or social harms occurring. By introducing the concepts of harmful use and hazardous use, the WHO is emphasising that problematic substance taking is not limited to issues of dependency.

ACTIVITY 1.1

**Defining a substance problem**
Before reading Chapter 2, complete the following sentence:

A substance problem is  . . . . . . . . . . . . . . . . . . . . . . . . . . . . . . . . . . . . . . . . . . . . . . . . . . . . . . .

## Some other definitions

Many concepts in the substance problems field are ambiguous or contentious: examples include controlled drinking, recovery and harm minimisation. These, and the controversies surrounding them, are explored in future chapters. The following is an attempt to pin down some other common concepts.

**Abstinence** means refraining from use. It is usually applied to desisting from one drug only. A drinker who is abstinent may still smoke.

An overwhelming desire to use is described as **craving**. Cravings can have a physiological dimension, as experienced in withdrawal, and psychological aspects. Some people describe overwhelming desires to use, even after lengthy periods of abstinence. Whilst cravings can occur for no apparent reason, places, people or objects associated with past use can be triggers.

The disease model suggests that those who are addicted display distinct characteristics: one of these is **denial** (see Chapter 3). The dependent person is considered to be oblivious to what is patently obvious to those around him, namely that his use is out of control and is the source of other problems in his life. Denial is a controversial concept. Behavioural psychologists argue that what is interpreted as denial is often a defensive response to unwanted criticism or hostile questioning, rather than a characteristic of people with substance problems (Miller and Rollnick, 2013).

**Detoxification** is ridding the body of a psychoactive substance.

A bewildering array of new substances has become available in recent years. Many of these mimic the chemical composition of traditional drugs. Often called 'legal highs', **new psychoactive substances** is a better description since a number of them are not legal. Some, however, are not new.

**Polydrug use** describes the habit of either using two or more substances together or separately but on a regular basis.

**Recreational use** describes taking a substance in a non-dependent, 'as and when' basis; the user feels in control. Recreational use is not necessarily harm free.

**Relapse** is a return to use following a period of abstinence. It can also denote the reinstatement of problematic use after a person has controlled his substance taking in a harm-free way.

**Volatile substances** is a generic term for hydrocarbons whose vapour can be inhaled. They are contained in numerous everyday products.

## Experiencing drugs

How a drug is experienced is unique to the individual. Alcohol depresses the central nervous system. However, a person, having drunk a couple of glasses of wine, will feel and behave very differently relaxing with friends compared to sitting next to a feared superior at a formal dinner. One person may have a tendency towards exuberance after drinking, whereas another may become argumentative. These differences reflect a complex mix of biochemistry, physiology, learned behaviour, expectation and the influence of past and present environments. Zinberg (1984) categorises these as 'drug, set and setting'. Incidentally, modern thinking about 'treatment' suggests that a person needs to address these three domains (the substance, the individual's responses and the barriers and reinforcers in the environment) if recovery is to become a reality. Before we explore this further, it is important to consider aspects of the chemistry of psychoactive substances.

### BOX 1.1 MISUSE: A LOADED TERM

Misuse [or abuse] is the term frequently applied to any use of substances which are illegal or which are consumed in a risky manner. In government documents, use of drugs subject to the Misuse of Drugs Act 1971, unless taken as prescribed, is referred to as 'misuse'. However, drinking alcohol is not considered to be misuse unless it is consumed in potentially harmful ways. The word 'misuse' suggests that there is a consensus regarding what is acceptable and unacceptable use of substances. As this is far from the case, the words *misuse* and *abuse* are not used in this book.

## Substances: the central nervous system and the liver

Substances affect the central nervous system in various ways. Shapiro (2010) classifies drugs as:

- depressants
- drugs which reduce pain
- stimulants
- drugs which alter perception (hallucinogens).

Depressants and drugs which reduce pain are often grouped together and volatile substances are sometimes considered as a separate category. To complicate matters, a number of substances have effects which do not allow for easy classification: cannabis is a depressant which alters perception; ketamine presents a particularly complex range of effects.

In whatever way substances are ingested, they all enter the brain via the blood stream and are eventually eliminated from the body. In the brain, drugs work by interfering with the balance of the natural processes of the central nervous system. The cells in the central nervous system (neurons) communicate with each other via an electrochemical process which sees chemical messengers (neurotransmitters) fired from one cell across a small gap (the synapse) to a receiving cell (receptors). In this highly complex system, different sets of neurons have different functions geared to protecting the survival of the organism and its species. Neurotransmitters make the receiving cell more or less likely to activate, thus stimulating or inhibiting certain processes. In some circumstances, a proportion of neurotransmitters will be reabsorbed back into the neuron which fired them (a process called reuptake). Some drugs mimic the effects of neurotransmitters, thus enhancing their effects as they latch on to available receptors for that neurotransmitter. Other drugs prevent reuptake, thus increasing the amount of that neurotransmitter available.

Alcohol and cocaine provide contrasting examples of how aspects of the system work. Gamma-aminobutyric acid (GABA) is a neurotransmitter which dampens activity within the system. One characteristic of alcohol, among many, is that it binds onto the GABA receptor, hence its depressant effect. Cocaine acts in a different way. Dopamine is responsible for the pleasurable feelings linked to eating and sex, among other things, and cocaine increases the amount crossing the synapse by preventing its reuptake in the neuron which fired it, along with the reuptake of other neurotransmitters. Because of the complex and diverse actions of any particular drug in the central nervous system, the desired effects often come with unwanted side effects.

Substances can be removed from the body via breath and sweat but the key organ is the liver, in which they are broken down by enzymes for the purposes of excretion.

## Commonly encountered substances

### Depressants

Alcohol and the so-called minor tranquillisers, along with gammahydroxybutyrate (GHB and GBL) and barbiturates depress the central nervous system. Their use tends to facilitate relaxation, with increased dosage leading to reduced motor control, resulting in staggering and slurred speech, and diminished mental performance.

**Alcohol** initially depresses the centres in the brain controlling inhibition, which explains why euphoria and feelings of excitement can accompany ingestion of what is a depressant drug. Heavy drinkers often seek treatment for the low mood generated by their substance use. Alcohol has no current medical applications. Used in significant quantities over a period of time, it is associated with a wide range of health problems including various types of cancer, heart disease, cirrhosis of the liver and alcoholic dementia.

The prescribing of **barbiturates**, once common for anxiety and insomnia, is now rare because of the risks they present. In particular, the line between therapeutic dose and overdose is quite fine. They are not readily available on the black market.

Prescribing of **benzodiazepines**, the most common of the minor tranquillisers, reduced the use of barbiturates in the late 1960s. Diazepam (also known by the defunct brand name Valium), chlordiazepoxide (Librium), nitrazepam and temazepam are examples of these. Initially they were seen as wonder drugs, providing a problem-free route to controlling anxiety and insomnia. The fact that overdose only occurs at very high levels was a particular attraction. It was only after their therapeutic use had become established that it became evident that physical dependence and associated withdrawals are an issue, along with reduced effectiveness after fairly short periods of use. In addition, when taken with other depressants, as they often are, risk of overdose is increased. Benzodiazepines are usually taken orally but some can be injected or ground down and snorted.

**Gammahydroxybutyrate** (GHB) and its sister, gammabutyrolactone (GBL), which is metabolised into GHB when ingested, are normally taken orally in liquid, capsule or powdered form. GHB acts as a sedative and anaesthetic. Initial euphoria and reduced inhibition can lead, with increased dose, to nausea, convulsions, breathing problems and coma. The intoxicating effects of GHB can be quite long lasting. Physical dependence can occur.

The term **volatile substances** covers a very wide range of hydrocarbons which give off inhalable vapour. Many everyday products, such as adhesives, cleaning fluids, petrol and butane (lighter fuel and the propellant often used in aerosols), contain such substances and are cheap and readily available. The effects, which are similar to being intoxicated on alcohol, are short lived. Reduced inhibition, elation and dizziness may be followed by a hangover. Users can experience hallucinatory effects. The small number of deaths associated with volatile substances have occurred through accidents following use, suffocation when inhaling from plastic bags or from the effects on the heart. Long-term use can lead to health problems, with dependence being psychological rather than physical.

## Pain-reducing drugs

Depressants tend to have an anaesthetic effect, as anyone who has injured himself after drinking will know. However, drugs which are used routinely in Western medicine to control pain, generically classed as analgesics, are usually categorised as a separate group.

**Common analgesics,** such as aspirin and paracetamol, do not lead to physical dependence; however, their ability to reduce discomfort may lead to compulsive use. In this book, the term **opiates** is used as the collective term for drugs which act within the central nervous system in a similar way to morphine. Strictly speaking, **opiates** are derived from the poppy and **opioids** are their synthetically produced cousins. Contrary to popular myth, opiates are relatively safe drugs. Pharmaceutical heroin taken daily in controlled doses and ingested with care will lead to physical dependence but not to the damage to the organs wreaked by excessive alcohol use. Many of the harms linked to heroin come from how it is used and from illicit supplies. Morphine, codeine and heroin are examples of opiates, whereas methadone and pethidine are synthetically produced. Heroin, which is the most potent of the opiates in its pure form, is semi-synthetic, as is dihydrocodeine. Ingestion of heroin leads to pleasurable feelings of euphoria, warmth and being at ease, a state in which discomfort and troubles melt away. Motor control remains, although a person will become drowsy as the dose increases. Heroin can be injected, sniffed or heated and the vapour inhaled ('chasing'). Methadone is slower acting, longer lasting and produces less euphoria than heroin. Methadone is available in oral and injectable forms. Opiates are associated with tolerance and physical dependence.

### Stimulants

A wide range of drugs stimulate the central nervous system, including many of the new psychoactive substances. Stimulants increase heart rate and blood pressure and can affect respiration. Most stimulants energise, thus increasing alertness and reducing fatigue; however, the desired effects of some are very short lived. Some stimulants create physical dependence and some do not. Certain stimulants are used for medical purposes: cocaine as an anaesthetic in ear, nose and throat surgery; methylphenidate (Ritalin) for attention deficit hyperactivity disorder; bupropion to support smoking cessation and as an antidepressant.

Smoking **tobacco** delivers nicotine very rapidly to the brain where it both stimulates and depresses, which explains its ability to arouse and relax the user. Its effects are short lasting, encouraging repeat dosage. Tolerance and physical dependence develop readily. While nicotine does have potentially negative implications for the cardiovascular system, it is its delivery through tobacco smoke, which contains an assortment of toxic compounds, which is the chief culprit in terms of heart disease, stroke, cancers, emphysema and numerous other health problems. Tobacco can be smoked, snorted (snuff) or chewed. Snorting or chewing tobacco also increases the risk of various cancers.

**Cocaine**, in powder form, is snorted or injected whilst crack, a refined form of the drug which comes in small 'rocks', is normally smoked. Use produces intense but short-lived feelings of euphoria, excitability and increased confidence. Repeated use is common but tends to be followed by the 'come-down', which produces the opposite experience to initial ingestion, namely exhaustion, irritability and depression. Heavy users can experience chest pains and convulsions along with high levels of anxiety and paranoid episodes. Death through stroke or heart failure has been recorded. Longer term users risk developing cardiovascular problems and damage to the nasal membranes if the drug is snorted. Chronic use leads to a reduction in euphoric effects (Small et al., 2009). Smoking crack can harm the lungs. The physical come-down and distressing mental states experienced after persistent use are of a different order to heroin or alcohol withdrawals. Cocaethylene is a unique substance which is only produced when alcohol and cocaine combine in the liver. Its effects are longer lasting than cocaine and it is thought to increase the risk of heart attack, although much has yet to be learned about it (Alcohol Academy, 2010).

Unlike cocaine, which is derived from a plant, **amphetamines** (speed) are synthetically produced stimulants. Amphetamine can be sniffed, injected or taken orally; methamphetamine (crystal meth), a close relative chemically, can be smoked. The effects of amphetamines are not unlike cocaine. Increased energy and feelings of excitement can turn to discomfort and anxiety; low mood and exhaustion may follow. The amphetamine high lasts considerably longer than the cocaine rush. A type of psychosis, which includes paranoid feelings and hallucinations, can follow bursts of heavy consumption but this usually disappears following cessation of use. The body becomes tolerant to frequent use.

**Ecstasy** (3,4-methylenedioxymethamphetamine or MDMA for short) tends to combine the typical stimulant energy surge, along with some initial discomfort after ingestion, with a mild hallucinogenic experience and feelings of wellbeing and empathy for others (feeling 'loved up'). Well-publicised risks include both dehydration and excessive consumption of water to counteract this. Ecstasy is taken in tablet or capsule form and the effects can last for some hours; a mild come-down can follow. While tolerance can develop, it is unclear how far physical dependence can (Degenhardt, Bruno and Topp, 2010), although people tend not to use it often enough for this to be an issue. There is uncertainty as to whether ecstasy use has long-term implications for mental functioning (DrugScope, 2009a).

**Caffeine** is taken by most people on a daily basis, without thought, in tea, coffee and many soft drinks. Extremely heavy consumption, which is rare, can lead to a variety of physiological effects similar to other stimulant drugs. Caffeine's ability to enliven and ward off fatigue is prized. Stomach irritation, insomnia and its potential to exacerbate anxiety do not make it completely harm free.

### Hallucinogens

Many drugs alter perception as well as mood, at least to some degree: indeed this is one of the attractions of substance taking. However, the main effect of hallucinogens is significant distortion of reality.

When thinking about hallucinogens, **LSD** (D-lysergic acid diethylamide), with its psychedelic associations, is one of the first drugs to come to mind. Tolerance develops very quickly, to the point where consumption has little effect unless the person stops using for a period. LSD does not, however, create physical dependence. The LSD experience, which can last up to 12 hours, is unpredictable. Feelings of bodily detachment, heightened hues and illusory episodes, when colours appear as sounds and sounds are 'seen', can make for a pleasurable adventure. The archetypal 'bad trip', characterised by fear and confusion, is, however, a very different matter. Distressing 'flashbacks' can occur long after last use of the drug. Dissociation from reality has led to accidents but deaths through overdose are almost unknown. It is likely that a small number of users will experience mental health problems connected to use (Shapiro, 2010).

While various **mushrooms** can provide hallucinogenic experiences, the most commonly used in the UK is the Liberty Cap. The active ingredient is psilocybin, the positive and detrimental effects of which are similar to, but less intense than, LSD, and of shorter duration. Mushrooms can be eaten, cooked and consumed with food or brewed as tea. The Liberty Cap can upset the digestive system. Tolerance builds rapidly but psilocybin does not create physical dependence.

The most widely used illicit substance is **cannabis** (Home Office, 2012b). It is a central nervous system depressant with hallucinogenic properties which comes in leaf or resin form of different strengths. It can be smoked or eaten. Feelings of relaxation and detachment may be followed, at higher doses, by altered perception. Use can precipitate panic attacks. Regular heavy consumption can lead to tolerance and physical dependence with associated withdrawals symptoms, but these are relatively mild (Ryder, Salmon and Walker, 2001). There is an association between cannabis use and mental health problems (see Chapter 13). As cannabis is often used with tobacco, it is difficult to isolate its effects on the respiratory system but long-term use is likely to increase the risk of harm. There is considerable interest in the therapeutic potential of cannabis and an oral spray derived from it is available in the UK to relieve spasticity in multiple sclerosis sufferers.

**Ketamine** is not easily categorised. A powerful anaesthetic, it is used for this purpose in medicine and veterinary work. It is also used to reduce pain. Ketamine can be swallowed, snorted or injected. Stimulation, feelings of bodily detachment and hallucinogenic effects make for an experience not unlike LSD, although its effects are shorter lived. Panic and feelings of confusion can also occur; muscles can become rigid, inhibiting movement. Some users describe undergoing near death sensations called 'entering the K-hole'. Tolerance to ketamine can develop but dependence is psychological rather than physical. Shapiro (2010, p. 120) notes that anaesthetics increase the risk of choking on vomit. Ketamine's ability to distort reality brings the possibility that users will injure themselves and its analgesic effects lessen the likelihood that they will appreciate the seriousness of this. Heavy use can cause respiratory problems or cardiovascular failure. Longer term use is associated with serious bladder problems.

## Antidepressants

Antidepressants are prescribed for their mood-altering properties and treating conditions such as obsessive compulsive disorder and post-traumatic stress. Antidepressants work by influencing mood-enhancing neurotransmitters. Why, then, do they not figure among the drugs which people use for pleasure? The answer lies in their slow-acting nature, with some weeks passing before their effects are felt.

## BOX 1.2 NEW PSYCHOACTIVE SUBSTANCES

The European Monitoring Centre for Drugs and Drug Addiction (EMCDDA, 2012) recorded 164 new psychoactive substances in Europe between 2005 and 2011. Unsurprisingly, this deluge is proving a challenge to current methods of legal control and harm reduction and treatment services are uncertain how best to respond. Simply trying to keep up to date with what is available is a daunting task. These substances are marketed under a wide variety of names. They may not contain what it is suggested is in them. Sometimes purchasers are told they are buying more traditional drugs when they are, in fact, being given some new substance. Flemen (2013) advocates grouping drugs in families, thus linking these new substances with similar, but better known, compounds. This helps to make some sense of both the effects and the risks. In many instances the new drugs have been deliberately produced to mimic the effects of traditional substances in order to provide competitors to them or to circumvent the law. Synthetic cannabinoids, sold under brand names such as Spice and Black Mamba, are usually sprayed onto plant material for smoking. Methoxetamine is similar chemically, and in its effects, to ketamine. A number of new psychoactive substances are stimulants with mild hallucinogenic effects providing an experience similar to ecstasy. Examples of drugs which fall into this broad category include naphyrone, the cathinone family, which includes mephedrone (commonly known as miaow or M-cat), and the phenethylamines, one of the better known examples of which goes under the brand name Benzo Fury. The piperazines, such as BZP (benzylpiperazine), are stimulants and are also marketed as alternatives to ecstasy.

New substances can become established street drugs, mephedrone being a case in point, or may emerge briefly then fail to gain a niche in the market.

## Other considerations

This superficial tour of the more commonly used substances demonstrates the difficulties of neatly categorising the physical effects of drugs on the central nervous system. Drugs differ greatly in terms of how long they remain active for and the length of time they can be picked up in tests. Complexity increases when other dimensions are introduced to the equation. Although some people retain an allegiance to one 'drug of choice', mixing drugs is becoming more commonplace (DrugScope, 2009b). In broad terms, taking drugs with similar effects on the nervous system magnifies those effects. Taking drugs in different categories is much less predictable. The experience of the drug is also influenced by the method of ingestion. The route into the body can affect both the intensity of the experience and how quickly it starts. It hardly needs to be said that dose, the amount of the drug consumed, is also a central factor. Polydrug use and routes of ingestion will be considered more fully in Chapter 2 when we address the problems associated with use.

## The individual and the environment

So far, this chapter has considered drug use from a chemical and biological perspective. However, as has been noted, chemistry is only one variable in the experience of taking a drug. Zinberg's set (the attitudes, expectations and personal attributes which the individual brings to the equation) and setting (the environmental influences) are of equal importance (Zinberg, 1984).

The individual brings a number of factors into the reckoning. Smaller people are likely to feel the effects of a set amount of a drug more intensely than their bigger friends. Gender is relevant. As women have a higher proportion of fat to water than men, alcohol reaches the female brain in a more concentrated form so women become intoxicated more readily. Additionally, the female stomach and liver take longer to break alcohol down. Cirrhosis of the liver can develop in a shorter time period in women than in men. Opiates can interfere with the menstrual cycle. The body tends to tolerate substances less well with age. Ageing brings changes in the balance between lean body mass, fat and water which mean that substances are processed more slowly, arrive in the brain in more concentrated form or take longer to be eliminated from the system (Chau et al., 2008; IAS, 2013). These factors influence the experience of substance taking, which can become less rewarding. Biological changes go some way to explaining why older people drink less (Alcohol Concern, 2002).

Our mood and expectations are as relevant to determining how we feel and how we behave after use as the effects of drugs on the chemistry of the central nervous system. In one person, low mood may be lightened; in another, the same drug may deepen feelings of despair. Imagine two people injecting heroin together. The first one is pleased to have just acquired a good supply: the shot wards off the beginnings of withdrawals and the relaxing effects of the drug bring a sense of wellbeing. His friend is tired of a drug-using lifestyle but despairs of ever changing things. Any pleasurable sensations are offset by feelings of frustration and anger at what he sees as his continuing failure.

We learn not only how drugs are taken but what we can expect having taken them. Before we even try a substance for the first time, observing others will have taught us much about how we are likely to feel and how we should behave after using. Our own experimentation then builds on this so we begin to know what the experience will bring for us as individuals. As Edwards (2005, p. 6) says:

> Expectations psychologically transform the physical impact of the chemical into experiences which may include intimacy, elation, laughter, sexuality, fearlessness, creativity, a myriad good feelings, and then on the downside anger or rage, gloom or suicidal despair. The physical impact of the drug invokes and stirs all those possibilities but it is the individual's psychological interpretation of the impact that paints the colours of what then happens.

MacAndrew and Edgerton (cited in Social Issues Research Centre, 1998) describe how, historically, the traditional ceremonies of the Papago people of Mexico were characterised by cordiality and lack of aggressive behaviour despite the participants drinking cactus wine to a point of extreme intoxication. This contrasts sharply with what can be witnessed on any Friday night in the cities of the UK. Indeed MacAndrew and Edgerton (cited in Orford, 2001) conclude that behaviour following drinking in different cultural groups is so diverse as to suggest that expectation is more powerful than the chemical effects of alcohol. Expectation is thus a complex interweaving of the drug, the individual and environmental influences both past and current.

Culture and the environment impact on the individual both at the micro level (friends, family, social groupings) and the macro level (advertising, social norms, legislation). The immediate setting in which use takes place is a further influence on what the experience will bring. The cues are all there when we enter a pub and see our friends, drinks in front of them. Years of learning through personal experience dictate how we are going to feel and how we will behave.

## Concluding comments

This chapter has explored three separate themes:

- The importance of trying to use language precisely, despite the complexities of many of the issues involved.
- How drugs affect the central nervous system.
- How every experience of substance taking is shaped as much by the individual himself and the environment as by the chemical properties of the drug.

It was also noted that difficulties are not limited to people displaying a pattern of dependent use and we will consider more fully what constitutes a substance problem in the next chapter.

### RESOURCES

- WHO (2013b) *Lexicon of alcohol and drug terms.* www.who.int/substance_abuse/ terminology/who_lexicon/en/.
- The following provide good-quality information about drugs, their pharmacological effects and their street names:
  DrugScope: www.drugscope.org.uk/resources/drugsearch.
  Shapiro, H. (2010). *The Essential Guide to Alcohol and Drugs* (14th edition). London: DrugScope.
  Talk to Frank: www.talktofrank.com.

# CHAPTER 2

# What Is a Substance Problem?

- Substance use is associated with a wide range of problems and a preoccupation with addiction and dependence can restrict our understanding of risk.
- Drugs themselves can cause harm but much of the damage comes from how people use them.
- 'Significant others', both adults and dependent children, can experience serious problems related to a person's substance use.
- Substance use can affect the wellbeing of the wider community.

## A superfluous question?

'What is a substance problem?' may seem a superfluous question. However, our individual answers to this are likely to be influenced by socially defined notions of risk and our prejudices. Logic and evidence is often brushed aside when we consider the harms substance taking brings. Sometimes we see the problem as lying with the person and sometimes with the substance. Deaths from alcohol do not lead to calls for the introduction of prohibition, yet concerns regarding 'legal highs' do (North West Evening Mail, 2013). We tend to view how we use alcohol, not alcohol itself, as the problem; with illicit or new drugs we are inclined to see the substance as the source of the harms; this is despite it being a cliché to say that if alcohol were discovered today it would be made subject to the Misuse of Drugs Act.

In cultures which completely forbid substance taking, as Islam does, then any use is likely to be viewed as problematic. Prohibition tends to bring morality to the fore; we are prone to seeing the use of class A drugs as simply wrong. By way of contrast, rugby and mountaineering are generally seen as healthy activities, to be encouraged in the young, though both have their fair share of casualties.

'Addiction' can dominate our thinking, so that problematic use becomes primarily associated with 'alcoholics' and 'drug addicts' when, in reality, a great many problems are experienced by people for whom dependency is not an issue. In this chapter, we will look at what problems substance use can bring from various angles and at two models for making sense of the risks.

CASE ILLUSTRATION 2.1

**Do they have a problem?**

- Rajani (19) works as trainee personnel manager. She enjoys going to clubs at weekends where she drinks and takes cocaine and ecstasy if these are available. She gets quite intoxicated once a month or so. Following one such episode, she became pregnant and subsequently underwent a termination. Her lifestyle causes arguments with her parents.
- Cheryl (24) injects heroin three times a day. She lives in an area of social disadvantage with her son, aged four. She has debts and despairs that her life will never change but she does feel that she copes most of the time.
- Dave (52) is divorced. He has a pressurised job managing a sales team. He likes to relax most evenings in his local, where he is known for his entertaining company. He drinks around four pints a night. He never drives after drinking and alcohol does not interfere with his work.

Rajani, Cheryl and Dave are very different from each other but they are typical of particular types of substance users. Which of them do you think has a substance problem?

## The benefits of use

Any attempt to understand problematic use of substances must start with an acknowledgement that substances are consumed for their actual or perceived benefits. As well as their medicinal value, we prize psychoactive substances for the diverse rewards they bring. We take drugs to stimulate activity, brush away the cobwebs of lethargy, lighten depression, change perception and harden resolve. Substances can oil the wheels of conviviality and facilitate bonding in groups. We value these benefits and calculate that they outweigh the risks we run. The rewards are immediate, the potential harms may not occur and, if they do, it is often in a nebulous future. That regular bottle of wine helps us relax after a hard day and we forget about the heightened risk of cancers or liver damage. Cocaine will make the party go with a swing, and arrest or the development of a dependence are the last things on our minds. We tolerate the risks, and often continue to use when problems start to accrue, because we like the effects of substances and appreciate the other rewards they bring.

## Risk or harm

It is important to bear in mind the different notions of 'risk' and 'actual harm'. Sporadic use of ecstasy carries greater risks than drinking the odd cup of coffee but that does not mean that occasional ecstasy users will necessarily experience problems. As we noted in Chapter 1, the World Health Organization (2013b) draws this distinction between potential and actual harm by introducing the concepts of 'hazardous use' and 'harmful use'. Hazardous defines 'a pattern of substance use that involves the risk of harmful consequences'.

Harmful describes 'a pattern – that is causing damage to health'. Such damage can be mental or physical and may involve negative social consequences too.

### Identifying the sources of harm

Zinberg's insistence (see Chapter 1) that substance use can only be fully understood if equal weight is given to the influence of the drug, the individual ('set') and the environment ('setting') provides a framework for identifying the factors which shape risk (Zinberg, 1984). However, chemistry, the individual's characteristics, attitudes and experience and the context in which substance use takes place are difficult to disentangle.

## Substances: different drugs, different risks

### Physical health, mental wellbeing

In Chapter 1, we noted the potential physical damage which the more commonly used drugs can cause. The following provides examples of some of the health risks associated with three drugs:

> *Smoking tobacco*: lung cancer; heart disease; bronchitis; cerebral thrombosis; cancer of the throat.
> *Drinking alcohol*: gastritis; liver disease; various cancers; heart disease; neurological damage (Korsakoff's syndrome).
> *Snorting cocaine*: damage to the nasal membranes; respiratory problems; heart failure.

What is immediately striking is that we cannot consider the harmful effects of these, or other drugs, in isolation from the amounts consumed or the ways by which they are taken. Occasional moderate alcohol consumption will not lead to Korsakoff's syndrome; injecting cocaine, rather than snorting it, will bring an array of risks but it will not cause nasal damage. How the individual uses can be as important as the effects of the substances themselves; this is considered below.

Certain drugs are connected with immediate or longer term mental health problems, the effects of cocaine on mood and the possible link between cannabis and schizophrenia-like conditions in some people (ACMD, 2008) being examples (see Chapter 13). However, 'in some people' again forces us to look beyond the drug itself and consider factors related to the individual.

### BOX 2.1 COMPARING THE HARMS

Nutt et al. (2007) made a comparative study of the harms associated with a number of substances. A group of specialists used a risk assessment system to score these with regard to physical problems, dependence and social harms. Heroin, followed by cocaine, topped the list, with ecstasy a lowly eighteenth. Alcohol, at fifth, and tobacco, at ninth, were placed ahead of many substances subject to the Misuse of Drugs Act. This work stands as an attempt to dispassionately evaluate relative harms irrespective of public perception or legal status. Employing a similar scoring method, Nutt, King and Phillips (2010) further developed the indicators to more fully address the harms to others. The conclusions drawn from this second exercise were that heroin, crack cocaine and methamphetamine, in that order, present the greatest risks to users whilst alcohol is the drug causing most harm to other people, followed by heroin and crack.

Trying to apply logic is not necessarily welcome. When Professor Nutt (2009) suggested that the risks associated with ecstasy were less than the dangers of horse riding, he was roundly condemned by the Home Secretary of the time (Guardian, 2009). His arguments contributed to his dismissal from the chairmanship of the Advisory Council on the Misuse of Drugs (ACMD).

## Quality control or lack of it

The quality of illicit drugs makes their use something of a lottery. It is a popular myth that dealers regularly use poisonous materials as bulking agents; it is hardly in their interests to kill their customers! 'Cutting' agents used tend to be drugs with similar effects as the substance being sold (for example, caffeine or paracetamol) or inert materials such as sugars. Toxic materials may, however, be present. A lack of quality control means that sudden increases in purity can lead to overdose. Infections due to contamination are an ever-present possibility, an outbreak of anthrax among heroin users in Scotland in 2009–10 being one example with particularly devastating consequences. The plethora of new psychoactive substances means that those willing to experiment may not even know the likely effects of what they are about to take.

## Withdrawals

Unpleasant though they can be, withdrawals can be managed, but with some substances specific risks need to be addressed. Withdrawals are not purely a matter of chemistry. Some people appear to suffer more than others and psychological factors may affect how withdrawals are experienced. Reassurance and explaining to the person what will happen during withdrawals can lessen the unpleasantness of the experience (Gossop, 2007). In a fascinating study, Light and Torrance (1929) undertook an experiment which involved stopping the administration of morphine to a group of addicted men suddenly. As well as finding that withdrawal effects were different for different participants, they observed what they called the 'emotional' aspects of withdrawal. For some of the men, psychological discomfort appeared to precede physical symptoms of withdrawal. One participant, who demanded morphine prior to the end of the experiment, was given, unbeknown to him, an injection of sterile water. He immediately fell asleep. They linked this to what has been described as the 'needle habit' whereby a simple prick of a needle appears to reduce withdrawals for some people. A similar phenomenon was witnessed by a colleague of mine. A street drinker was experiencing the severe shaking and discomfort of alcohol withdrawals. The man was given a can of lager by a friend and, the moment he released the ring pull, the symptoms subsided. Withdrawals do appear to be a complex amalgam of both the physical, as the central nervous system readjusts to the absence of a chemical to which it has adapted, and the psychological (expectation). The physiological aspects do, of course, have to be managed.

Opiate withdrawal is rarely dangerous (Edwards, 2005); however, withdrawal from certain depressant drugs is: these include alcohol, barbiturates, benzodiazepines, gammahydroxybutyrate (GHB) and gammabutyrolactone (GBL). Death from seizures can occur during withdrawal from these drugs, so detoxification should always take place under medical supervision (see Chapter 10).

In withdrawal, the central nervous system tends to react in the opposite way to the effects of the drug concerned. Overstimulation of the central nervous system is the hallmark of withdrawal from depressant and pain-reducing drugs; by way of contrast, stopping using stimulants such as amphetamines and cocaine leaves the person feeling exhausted and despondent. As these substances do not create physical dependence in the same way as depressants, and withdrawals are of a different kind to those experienced with heroin or alcohol, what follows cessation is sometimes not defined as withdrawal at all. However, the physical and psychological consequences of a period of use should not be underestimated.

Withdrawals for nicotine are well known. They include irritability, insomnia, dry mouth, constipation, hunger and cold-like symptoms ('quitter's flu').

## The individual: some people run greater risks than others

A person's pattern of use – how much, how often, who with and in what way – is of greater importance in determining both the level and type of risk than the drug itself.

### Mixing drugs

Polydrug use, often with alcohol in the mix, is common. People may take different drugs together to achieve a particular effect or they may mix them simply because they are available. Whilst unpredictability is the hallmark of polydrug use, the usual outcome of using substances together which have similar effects on the central nervous system is to intensify these. Thus stimulants taken together put added pressure on the cardiovascular system; depressants ingested together tend to further flatten mood.

As a generalisation, mixing drugs which impact in different ways on the central nervous system tends to have a countering effect. Use of alcohol with ecstasy is often shunned because the former is deemed to compromise the positive feelings associated with the latter. In addition, the risks of heatstroke associated with using ecstasy while dancing are well known and alcohol, a diuretic, adds to this problem. Cocaine, amphetamines and the so-called energy drinks, with their high caffeine content, are used with alcohol to keep the depressant effects of the latter at bay, allowing the drinker to continue to party for longer: this increases the risks associated with intoxication. Speedball, the simultaneous use of cocaine and heroin, is attractive to some as it softens the 'jaggedness' of the stimulating effects of the former while limiting the sedative effects of the latter. This combination interferes with the heart rhythm with potentially fatal effects (Good Drugs Guide, 2013).

## Methods of ingestion

As has been noted, different methods of ingestion bring different risks. Substances can be drunk, eaten, sniffed, absorbed through the skin or the mucus membranes in the mouth, nose and anus. They can be inhaled or injected into veins, tissue or muscle. It should be noted that street drugs should never be injected into tissue or muscle and steroids and image-enhancing substances should never be injected into veins (see Chapter 9). A number of factors influence the decision as to how to take a drug including ease of administration, how the method used influences the experience and judgements as to risk.

Speed of delivery to the central nervous system and the intensity of the experience are dependent on the method of ingestion, inhalation and intravenous injection being particularly efficient in this regard. Smoking tobacco delivers nicotine to the brain extremely rapidly, hence the almost instantaneous stimulation. Nicotine patches, by way of contrast, lead to a more consistent, but slower, absorption. This may ward off withdrawals and remove the risks associated with smoking but it does not provide what dependent smokers enjoy.

Some people simply do not want to inject. First-time heroin users often 'chase' (inhaling the vapour) (Gossop, 2007). Curiosity may then tempt them to try injecting: this provides a more powerful 'rush' which, in turn, encourages people to continue with the practice. Injecting costs less than chasing because smaller quantities are needed to obtain the same effect. Regular injection into the veins in the arms may lead to their scarring and subsequent collapse. When this happens, people may use more dangerous sites such as tissue, muscle or less accessible veins (see Chapter 9).

## BOX 2.2 HEROIN ADMINISTRATION: A HIERARCHY OF RISK

- Chasing: not safe but safer than injecting.
- Injecting into veins in the arm: significantly greater risks than chasing.
- Injecting into skin or muscle or veins in places such as the groin or neck: very high levels of risk.

Physical dependence can follow both chasing and injecting. While overdose can occur and blood-borne viruses can be contracted using either method, the risks are much less when heroin is chased. Chasing involves no damage to veins but it can harm the lungs. Bacterial infection multiplies very readily in skin or muscle so these sites should never be used if injecting street drugs.

## Overdose

Overdose can occur with most drugs. The likelihood of it happening depends on the individual and the situation as well as the amount consumed. A young teenager might become seriously ill after drinking a quantity of alcohol which would lead to mild intoxication in a seasoned adult drinker. A first-time heroin user might die from quantities a regular user, with a high level of tolerance, could easily cope with. Mixing depressants, or depressants with pain-reducing drugs, is particularly dangerous. These drugs slow the activity of the medulla oblongata, the centre of the brain which controls the involuntary signals to the heart and lungs, and, if taken in sufficient quantities, completely compromise its functioning. Heroin tends to be seen as the major cause of death from overdose but a significant proportion of 'heroin deaths' involve the combination of that drug with similar-acting substances such as methadone, alcohol or benzodiazepines (National Statistics for Scotland, 2012). Benzodiazepines are an interesting case. If used on their own, very large quantities have to be taken to risk serious consequences (Edwards, 2005); however, they can readily tip the balance when ingested with other depressants.

Surprisingly, the environment can come into the picture. Tolerance is lowered, and death from heroin overdose is more likely, when people use in unfamiliar environments, a phenomenon Siegal (2001) attributes to Pavlovian conditioning. Focusing simply on the amount of a drug taken belies the complexity of the phenomenon of overdose.

## Innate and lifestyle risks

Genetic inheritance makes some people more vulnerable to developing substance problems than others (see Chapter 3).

Gender can also be a factor in the development of problems. Liver damage caused by drinking occurs more readily in women than men. Women's veins are less robust than men's and collapse may lead to their seeking out riskier injecting sites at an earlier stage.

Age, too, can play a part. The developing organs of adolescents are particularly susceptible to drug-related damage. There is also evidence that the likelihood of developing problems as an adult is increased when a person starts to use at a young age (Grant and Dawson; Robin and Przybeck, both cited in Sullivan and Farrell, 2002). Ageing affects the body's ability to process drugs.

Physical problems related to heavy substance use can be exacerbated by poor health, which in turn may be linked to a lifestyle unfavourable to physical fitness. A substance-using way of life can involve poor diet, lack of regular sleep and a failure to seek medical help when needed. A spiral of physical decline is created.

## The environment: risks to users

### Where people use

The environment in which a person uses can influence the level of risk. An adolescent sniffing glue alone in a wood is at greater risk than if she was doing the same thing along with others. Shapiro (2010) notes that the unpleasant aspects of a bad LSD trip can be lessened with the support of an experienced friend. Mention has already been made of the fascinating potential effect of the immediate environment on tolerance and overdose. What may be of little consequence in one situation can be of real significance in another. Smoking cannabis occasionally with friends may have few negative implications; doing this whilst driving will impair judgement.

### How cultural factors can shape problems

Culture influences use and is one of the factors which determines the extent and nature of the problems which emerge in a society. If substance use is widely accepted and excessive use is condoned, then more people are likely to experience problems. Governments are well aware of this and efforts to change cultural attitudes towards harmful drinking in the UK are based on this premise (Home Office, 2012a; Scottish Government, 2009).

The controls put in place by society to limit problems can also shape, to some degree, the types of problem that society will experience. The Royal College of Psychiatrists and the Royal College of Physicians (2000) suggest that if a society allows a substance to be widely available, then more people will use and the health problems associated with it will increase; however, if availability is severely restricted, then a black market and all its associated criminal activity will spring up.

A comparison of historical drinking habits in the UK and France demonstrates how culture shapes the type of problems a society experiences. The tendency of the French to drink wine throughout the day led to rates of liver disease in excess of those in the UK but little alcohol-related disorder. Binge drinking in the UK was associated with antisocial behaviour but fewer health problems. However, at the turn of the millennium, increasing consumption in the UK and decreasing drinking in France saw death rates from cirrhosis tending to converge (WHO, 2013c).

## Social consequences and the harm to others

Substances can reduce inhibition, both a benefit and a detriment. Substances do not cause inappropriate conduct, antisocial behaviour or risk taking but their loosening effects on inhibition can lessen control or serve to rationalise unwise or unacceptable actions. Relationships can become strained or be lost completely. Most people who use substances in detrimental ways do maintain employment, housing and the basic structures of normal living. Some, however, face unemployment, homelessness and isolation from family. Debt is a chronic problem for many, particularly those on low incomes who have a dependence on relatively expensive illicit drugs.

### Problems for the family

Stress, mental health problems, the skewing of relationships and aggression within the family are just some of the possible consequences for others of a person's substance use. The lives of partners, parents, siblings and friends can be blighted. The risks to children from parental use of alcohol or drugs are well documented. The dangers from tobacco smoke, too, cannot be excluded. Substance use has implications for pregnancy. These troubling issues are considered more fully in Chapters 14 and 15.

### Harms to wider society

From antisocial behaviour on the high street to blighted housing estates, from shoplifting to trafficking, crime and substance use are entwined (see Chapter 17). In the debates about drug control, a neglected area tends to be the links between use in one country and harms elsewhere in the world. Demand for illicit drugs fuels criminal activity on a global scale. It is a trade which pays for wars, supports corrupt governments and creates so-called 'narco-states' where black-market production and export is woven into the functioning of the body politic. Mexico provides an example. Since the end of the twentieth century, the trafficking of cocaine and other drugs through that country has led to a virtual civil war among the drug cartels themselves and between the cartels and the government. It can be argued that aggressive government action, along with the prohibition of cocaine, has not helped the situation. Nevertheless, consumers at the end of the supply chain, snorting cocaine in the clubs and bars of Britain, cannot absolve themselves of some responsibility.

It is not just illicit substances that pose uneasy questions about the relationships between countries. What of the trade in alcohol? In the controversy surrounding the passing of legislation in Scotland in 2012 to introduce minimum unit pricing of alcohol, there was no debate about the implications of exporting whisky around the world, particularly to the growing markets in the Far East.

## Models for making sense of risks and harms

We tend to say 'Does John have an alcohol/drug problem?' or 'Is John an alcoholic/drug addict?' when a more helpful question is 'What problems is John's drinking/drug use bringing to him or his family?' The emphasis shifts from diagnosing and labelling the person to the difficulties he is experiencing: it is these which he will ask practitioners to help him resolve. The two models we will now consider both adopt this focus and categorise the bewildering array of actual and potential problems outlined in this chapter in helpful ways. The theme of this chapter is that we should take the widest possible view of substance problems; we should not simply confine our interest to those associated with 'being addicted'. Roisen and Thorley take this stance too.

### Roizen's four Ls

Roizen (cited in Room, 1980) is associated with an uncomplicated schema categorising the areas of a person's life which may be affected by his substance use. This has come to be known as the 'four Ls':

■ Liver: any physical or psychological problems.
■ Lover: all relationship difficulties.
■ Livelihood: problems in the areas of employment, finance etc.
■ Law: conflict with the law.

This simple, but all-encompassing, framework allows the practitioner and service user to make sense of the impact of her substance use. The focus is on the individual but it is important that 'lover' is interpreted as also including the implications for those on whom the person's substance taking impacts.

### Thorley

Thorley (1980) based his model on alcohol but it is equally applicable to other substances. He takes a somewhat different perspective by categorising the different types of problems which can emanate from the following three patterns of use:

■ intoxication (the act of being drunk)
■ excessive consumption (regular, heavy consumption)
■ dependence (psychological and/or physical).

An individual may experience problems in one, two or all three of these domains. Thorley then links these three patterns of use to the problems they can bring under three headings: medical; social; legal. Social covers Roizen's 'lover' and 'livelihood'. Thorley argues that intoxication is not always problematic but excessive consumption of alcohol, because of its implications for health, almost always is.

Thorley's schema is not a rigid framework and potential harms can appear under more than one heading. Table 2.1 shows how it can be applied to cocaine.

The potential problems noted in Table 2.1 are just some of those associated with cocaine and crack use; of course, not everyone who uses will experience all of these. With alcohol, excessive consumption – that is, regular heavy drinking over a long period – can be differentiated from dependence. With the heavy episodic bingeing which is typical of many cocaine users, excessive consumption and dependence tend to merge.

Roizen and Thorley help us make sense of the risks faced by the weekend binge drinker and the dependent benzodiazepine user, the adolescent trying

**Table 2.1** Thorley's framework applied to cocaine and crack

|  | Intoxication | Excessive consumption | Dependence |
|---|---|---|---|
| Medical | Headache<br>Confusion<br>Respiratory/heart<br>problems<br>Overdose<br>Risks of mixing with<br>other drugs<br>Seizures<br>Paranoia | Nasal damage<br>Blood-borne viruses<br>Pregnancy – effects on<br>foetus<br>Anxiety/panic attacks/<br>paranoia<br>Mental health problems<br>Damage to coronary<br>arteries<br>Vein damage if injected<br>Smoking crack – lung<br>damage | Craving<br>Lengthy period of<br>dampened mood<br>following abstinence |
| Social | Aggression<br>Risk taking<br>Neglect of<br>responsibilities<br>Come-down/<br>exhaustion | Loss of sex drive<br>Lack of motivation<br>Employment problems<br>Relationship difficulties<br>Financial problems | Stigma<br>Social withdrawal<br>Severe financial<br>problems<br>Neglect of<br>responsibilities<br>Drug-using lifestyle |
| Legal | Misuse of Drugs Act<br>Driving offences<br>Anti-social behaviour | Misuse of Drugs Act | Misuse of Drugs Act<br>Offences to obtain<br>funding |

new psychoactive substances and the heroin injector. Their models steer us away from diagnosing people to concentrating on the problems they are experiencing and in what ways these might link to their substance use.

ACTIVITY 2.1

**Defining problematic use**
- Look again at your own definition of a substance problem in Chapter 1 (Activity 1.1). Would you alter this at all in the light of the current chapter?
- Consider again the cases of Rajani, Cheryl and Dave at the start of this chapter (Case Illustration 2.1). Have you changed your views about which of them has a substance problem? If so, why?

## Concluding comments

Perhaps our answer to the question 'What is a substance problem?' should be a simple one: it is any difficulty which use of substances is causing a person or those close to them. With this in mind, services provision in any given area should include options for people experiencing all types of problems; to be effective, social policy must include initiatives to reduce harms across the board.

## RESOURCES

- Nutt, D. (2012). *Drugs – Without the Hot Air.*
- Ryder, D., Walker, N. and Salmon, A. (2006). *Drug Use and Drug-related Harm: A Delicate Balance* (2nd edition).
- Zinberg, N. (1984). *Drug, Set, and Setting.*

# CHAPTER 3

# Why Do People Develop Substance Problems?

## KEY THEMES

- A number of theories attempt to explain why people develop substance problems.
- Some theories focus on the concept of addiction, whereas others seek to understand the causes of problematic use in its wider sense.
- Many theories reflect wider questions regarding the nature of human personality.
- The perceived inadequacies of individual theories have led to the emergence of the bio-psycho-social paradigm, an integrated model.
- The importance for practitioners is that interventions are based on these different theoretical perspectives.

## Individual pathology or social forces?

History teaches us that a particular theory as to why people develop substance problems will tend to take precedence for a period of time only to be swept to one side by a new paradigm. The disease model, which dominated thinking in the middle of the twentieth century, was elbowed aside in the 1970s by behavioural psychologists, who put the case that problematic use is essentially a matter of faulty learning. At the turn of the millennium, increasing knowledge regarding genetics and neurology threw the spotlight onto the roles of both heredity and the workings of the brain. This chapter will outline a number of these contrasting approaches without making claims to address every theory or cover all the variations within each conceptual framework. An understanding of the main perspectives, however, is essential for practitioners. This can help make sense of service users' experiences and enhance assessment while providing the theoretical underpinning for interventions. It is important to stress that the reasons why a person starts to use substances may not be the same as the reasons why he develops a particular pattern of use, problematic or otherwise, at a later stage.

The tendency among some theorists and the wider public is to take, as the starting point, the idea that there is something abnormal about people who develop problems with substances. They are, somehow, different from the rest of us. The focus is on individual pathology. This approach is also predicated on the assumption that there is a readily described syndrome, an agreed idea of what problematic use is, which leads us back again to the concept of addiction and the difficulties the very word presents. The presupposition is that addiction is definable, that there is a group of people who can readily be described as addicts and that we can discover what makes them as they are if only we search hard enough. Theories attempt to explain a particular phenomenon, but where that phenomenon is woolly and difficult to define, as addiction is, we run into difficulties. The following two people illustrate the problem:

- John (19) drinks heavily but only at weekends. He does this with friends whose level of consumption is similar to his and to that of many young men. Drinking for this group is fun. John gets regular hangovers and takes the occasional Monday off work. He has a criminal record for urinating in the street.
- Eric (40) drinks all the time and is currently physically dependent on alcohol. He was detoxed with medical assistance recently but relapsed within a few weeks. He has serious health problems and is unfit for work.

Both John and Eric are experiencing problems with alcohol, but why? Are John and Eric very different? Does Eric have a 'condition' that John does not? Is John's pattern of use one which he has chosen whilst Eric's is determined by forces over which he has little control? Does Eric's behaviour suggest some abnormality of personality while John is just doing what young men in our society do? In the future, will John become like Eric and, if so, why?

The water is further muddied by the same inconsistencies of approach which, it was argued, bedevil our understanding of what constitutes a substance problem (see Chapters 1 and 2). The concepts of the 'alcoholic' or 'drug addict' tend to dominate thinking. Such people are deemed to have personal deficits which make them as they are; the dependent smoker, on the other hand, is more likely to be seen as having acquired a habit by virtue of using a particularly addictive substance.

John Davies tells a story (Davies, 2006a). Undertaking research in a housing scheme characterised by high levels of disadvantage, he tried to identify a control group consisting of people who did not drink, smoke or use drugs; he could not find one. His conclusion was that either everyone on the estate was abnormal, a patently absurd suggestion, or the people who lived there were 'rationally – if perhaps unhelpfully – adapting to a set of circumstances in a way which many of us would'. This is a good example of the power of culture to shape the destiny of the individual.

The starting point of this chapter will, therefore, be sociological perspectives on problematic use before other frames of reference, which centre primarily on the individual, are considered. An attempt will be made to differentiate between those theories which try to make sense of why problematic use, in its widest sense, occurs and those which focus on 'addictive behaviour'. By definition, theories are all encompassing. To be credible they must explain all aspects of the behaviour under consideration. As we shall see, these single-perspective theories fail to meet this test. This has led to attempts to develop integrated theories amalgamating different fields of study. Perhaps attempts to find a grand theory are a chimera. We might best see current knowledge as providing a set of different prisms through which to view aspects of the complex question as to why some people develop problems with substances and some do not.

## Sociological theories: it's cultural forces that count

The importance of the social context to understanding why people develop problems with substances is eloquently put by Edwards (2005, p. 4): 'The play may put the spotlight on one actor, but to understand why he drinks we also have to look at the nature of the contemporary drama, who directs the play, the script, and the other actors on the stage.'

The work of sociologists can illuminate our understanding of problematic use of substances in a wide variety of ways. Initiation, the availability of substances, the influences of wealth and disadvantage, the implications of gender, norms and pressures within both wider society and subcultures can all shed light on the development of problematic use. In its various analyses of how individuals function socially, sociology often merges into psychology. Under the broad umbrella of sociology, the drug, the individual and the environment all have high degrees of relevance.

### Availability, the environment and social norms

It is axiomatic that the more available a substance is, the more widely it is likely to be used and, consequently, the greater the number who will develop problems. In societies where large numbers of people smoke, levels of smoking-related disease are high (Tobacco in Australia, 2013). When alcohol becomes more available, the harms tend to increase (Edwards et al., 1994). It is possible to conceive of a society where a particular substance is easily accessible and rates of problems are low, the Jewish community's use of alcohol being one (see Box 3.1), nevertheless this is exceptional. However, physical availability needs to be set in the context of other influences such as:

- *Affordability.*
- *Personal factors.* Principles and personal experiences encourage or inhibit use. As the Royal College of Psychiatrists and the Royal College of Physicians (2000) comment, just because glue is available in his garage does not mean that a middle-aged man is likely to sniff it.
- *Social reinforcement.* Wider cultural acceptance or disapproval of a substance and attitudes within a person's peer group will play their parts. Gossop (2007)

The fascinating case of the Americans in Vietnam demonstrates the power, and complexity, of environmental influences.

### The Americans in Vietnam: an epidemic which was stopped in its tracks

As the Vietnam War was drawing to a close, the authorities in the USA were facing a nightmare scenario. Ready availability of cheap substances, the terrible strains of war and the lack of social constraints in a foreign country made it unsurprising that drug use among the soldiers was commonplace. Some estimates suggested that up to 20 per cent were dependent on smoking heroin. What would happen when they arrived back on main street, USA? Under the guidance of Jerome Jaffe, America's first drugs czar, a plan was devised to test all troops and to detox those who were found to be positive before they boarded the plane home. As the environmental cues and reinforcers for their drug use lay in a foreign country, Jaffe believed that if the soldiers were clear of drugs before they returned home, they would be less likely to continue to use. He was right. Back home, some did use heroin from time to time but the number who returned to dependent use was much lower than might have been predicted (after three years around 12 per cent of previously dependent users). Certain factors were at play: for example, the heroin in Vietnam was primarily smoked, not injected, whilst much of the heroin available in the USA was unsmokable. Nevertheless the story of these veterans illustrates the capacity of the setting to influence behaviour (Edwards, 2005; Gossop, 2007; Zinberg, 1984).

## BOX 3.1 JEWISH PEOPLE AND ALCOHOL: SWIMMING AGAINST THE TIDE?

In most cultures, ready availability of alcohol and social approval of its use are linked to high levels of problems. Among Jewish people, the percentage of abstainers is comparatively low but so too are rates of problematic use. Orthodox Judaism supports the use of alcohol, particularly wine, but clearly prescribes when and how it should be used. Drunkenness is frowned on, apart from during one particular festival, and controlled use, for which the individual is held responsible, is strongly endorsed (Gossop, 2007). Compare these cultural norms with those of the UK population generally, where drinking at work or before driving is deplored but weekend excess is seen as normal. In the British Crime Survey, 74 per cent believed it was acceptable to get drunk occasionally (Millard and Smith, 2011). It is not hard to see why rates of problems among Jewish people are lower than the average. Interestingly, another factor may be at work. Research suggests that a gene variant which offers some protection against the development of alcohol problems is present in a proportion of Jews (Hasin et al., 2002). The same research, however, noted that immigrants to Israel from Russia, a country noted for heavy alcohol use, had higher rates of past problems than some other groups despite the gene variant. This provides a good example of the intertwining of individual and cultural factors.

### Affordability and social status

Affordability, the cost of a substance relative to disposable income rather than price per se, is one element of accessibility. Affordability can influence in various ways. High relative cost can discourage use and potential cost savings to the individual are sometimes used as a motivator for smoking cessation (Department of Health, 2013). There is significant evidence that sensitively applied increases in the relative cost of alcohol reduce a range of harms (Edwards et al., 1994). However, expense may lead to changes in the types of drugs used or how they are ingested. High cost can lead to, or exacerbate, poverty.

Use of alcohol is widespread and illicit drug consumption is not confined to the disadvantaged or to areas of deprivation; however, the latter are associated with higher rates of problems. Social and economic exclusion, particularly in inner-city areas, are risk factors. Lack of economic and social opportunities may encourage substance use, with people in such circumstances being more likely to be housed together in particular areas. When drug use in an area reaches a certain level, a drug market becomes established with all its attendant problems. The social reinforcers become embedded and, even when people want to escape, the opportunities to do so are limited and the challenges are enormous (ACMD, 1998; Royal College of Psychiatrists and Royal College of Physicians, 2000). Wilkinson and Pickett (2010, p. 70) make the case that income inequality is a factor in explaining why use of illicit substances is higher in some countries than others.

### Strain theory

Merton (1968) suggests that when a society places great emphasis on achieving particular aspirations, such as wealth and status, and the means of realising these are not open to everyone, strain occurs. Merton describes five possible responses to this disruption to the bonds between the individual and society (anomie): conformity, innovation; ritual; retreatism; rebellion. Three of these have relevance to substance use and problems:

- *Innovation.* Innovators pursue socially sanctioned goals but not by using the approved methods of achieving them. Some turn to crime as a method of obtaining wealth and status. Some people involved in the organised side of drug dealing, or the trade in contraband alcohol or tobacco, are exemplars of this response.
- *Retreatism.* People with low educational attainment and difficult social circumstances, feeling that they have no hope of clinging onto the ladder of advancement, may abandon both societies' goals and the accepted means of attaining these and withdraw into destructive behaviours, such as heavy substance use. People in this position may form a subculture with its hierarchies and social mores. The majority of the heroin-using population in the UK can be seen in this light.
- *Rebellion.* Rejecting societies' norms, rebels adopt different goals and novel ways of achieving these. Cannabis and hallucinogens in the 1960s can be

viewed as symbols of a subculture which espoused a fundamental reordering of the system.

## Gender and ethnicity

Use of drugs and alcohol are lower among women than among men (Home Office, 2012b; Office of National Statistics, 2012). Attitudes towards women's use of substances, social roles and physiological differences between men and women are relevant factors.

Alcohol and drug use varies between minority ethnic groups in the UK but, overall, tends to be lower than in the white population. Different preferences regarding methods of administration of certain drugs have also been noted. However, the high levels of stigma in some ethnic communities regarding substance use and problems makes gathering accurate data difficult (Beddoes et al., 2010a; Hurcombe, Bayley and Goodman, 2010).

## Labelling and stigma

Becker (1997) explores the consequences of labelling people who act in certain ways as deviant; his work can shed light on how the reactions of others can reinforce substance-using behaviour and how a person can emerge with the public identity of 'drug addict' or 'alcoholic'. Being labelled influences the subsequent career of the substance user. From time to time, we all act in ways which might be considered deviant by others, although we might not view our actions as such. If a person keeps this behaviour to himself, or within a small group of like-minded people, his identity as a citizen living as part of the mainstream remains intact. Lemert (1967) calls this 'primary deviance'. However, if the behaviour becomes known to the majority who consider it aberrant, the consequences can be profound with the person becoming defined primarily in terms of the behaviour (for example, 'drug addict'). He has now become a 'secondary deviant'. Others will react to him on the basis of the label and he is more likely to behave in line with it. Negative labelling also sets in train a process whereby the person becomes socially marginalised, forcing him further into a lifestyle in which the behaviour is likely to continue (see Case Illustration 3.1).

In addition, stigma, a product of labelling, is a major barrier for people attempting to reintegrate back into society following formal treatment for a substance problem (UK Drug Policy Commission, 2010a).

---

CASE ILLUSTRATION 3.1

### Labelling

Hassan (22) uses cocaine most weekends with close friends. He has experienced no problems and has no interest in other illicit drugs. He does not view himself as deviant. Following a conviction for possession, he is dismissed by his employer, a pharmaceutical company with a strict drug policy. Now viewed by others as a 'drug user', he has become a secondary deviant. His parents warn him that any further use will lead to his being asked to leave home, a threat his father follows through on finding a small quantity of cocaine in his room. Hassan moves in with a friend whose drug-using tastes are more catholic. Jobless and bored, Hassan tries other substances which are now readily available. Soon he finds that heroin use is becoming difficult to stop. With a conviction, work is hard to obtain and this, along with escalating use, unstable accommodation and drug-using peers, means that Hassan is slipping into a drug-using lifestyle. Stigma makes escape additionally problematic.

Consider someone you have worked with who had difficulties with drugs or alcohol:

- In what ways did the role of 'substance misuser' reinforce his/her behaviour?
- What were the implications of stigmatisation for this person?

Sociological theories underpin aspects of government strategies to reduce the harms at the population level. For the individual practitioner, an understanding of the importance of the impact of the environment on the maintenance of problematic use is critical to ensuring that efforts are made to help the person cope with, or alleviate, such pressures.

We will now turn to theories that view the development of problems as lying primarily in the make-up of the individual.

## The disease model and genetic theories: some people are different

The disease model and genetic theories suggest that those who are dependent are somehow different from the rest of the population. These are theories of 'addiction': the reasons why many people who are not dependent develop problems are beyond their scope.

### The disease model

The proposition that habitual drunkenness is not a simple matter of choice but rather a 'syndrome' was first put forward at the end of the eighteenth century by two physicians, Benjamin Rush in the USA and Thomas Trotter in Scotland. Trotter called this 'a disease of the mind' (Heather and Robertson, 1997, p. 21). Inevitably their ideas reflected a medical perspective. The disease model has been the most enduring of the theories of addiction. It was strengthened by the founding fathers of Alcoholics Anonymous and was the dominant paradigm in the mid twentieth century. It has been criticised on a number of grounds but remains the bedrock on which Alcoholics Anonymous and all 12-step approaches are built. The disease model has popular appeal and continues to be used to explain addiction to alcohol and to various illicit drugs; however, it is rarely used to account for dependence on nicotine.

BOX 3.2 THE FOUNDING OF ALCOHOLICS ANONYMOUS

In 1934, Bill Wilson, an American with a long-term dependent drinking problem, was hospitalised. There he experienced something of a spiritual revelation, the seeds of which had been sown earlier by an old school friend who had achieved abstinence through finding God. Feeling unable to control his drinking, Wilson decided to put himself into the hands of God and fearlessly face up to his own shortcomings. In addition, he came to believe that he had a mission to help others who had suffered as he had. He was also impressed by his psychiatrist's view that some people have an allergy to alcohol, a definable medical condition. Six months later, in Akron, Ohio, Wilson found that his ability to stay sober was being severely tested by the collapse of a business venture. 'When all other measures fail, work with another alcoholic' (Alcoholics Anonymous, 2001, p. 15) was becoming his dictum and, putting this into practice, he searched out another dependent drinker, Dr Robert Smith. These two men supported each other in maintaining sobriety and then sought out others to help: Alcoholics Anonymous (AA) was born (Alcoholics Anonymous, 2001; Stepping Stones, 2013).

The concept of alcohol problems promoted by the founding fathers of AA inevitably reflected their own experiences of heavy dependent drinking and their belief that they had a disease. Ironically, Bill Wilson died of smoking-related health problems (Hartigan quoted in Orange, 2013).

The precepts of the disease model are that:

- a minority of the population has a specific condition, often depicted as an allergy to alcohol or drugs;
- the condition is deterministic – all that is necessary for the disease to emerge is for the person with the syndrome to continue to use the substance;
- the condition is progressive and develops insidiously through various phases. If an individual continues to use, he will proceed down a slippery slope accruing physical and social problems until he reaches his personal 'rock bottom'. The condition is incurable but abstinence provides the ladder out of this pit, in which case a normal and satisfying life can be lived;
- loss of control is a key symptom: once the condition has developed, a person is unable to refrain from use once he has started;
- craving and denial are part of the syndrome;
- environmental factors are irrelevant; what is critical is the individual and his relationship with the substance.

Inevitably, attempts have been made to refine the disease model, among the most influential being E. M. Jellinek's work on alcohol. Recognising the diverse nature of problematic use, he developed the idea of five types of 'alcoholism', which he named after letters of the Greek alphabet. He considered that people in all five groups experienced problems but regarded only gamma and delta alcoholism as fitting with the concept of alcoholism as a disease.

Gamma and delta alcoholics are united in that they have undergone physiological changes which have led to the development of tolerance and withdrawal symptoms; they are different in that gamma alcoholics exhibit loss of control whereas delta alcoholics seem unable to desist from drinking at all. Jellinek considered that loss of control was central to the disease state but it is interesting to note that he was uncertain as to whether this resulted from excessive drinking or was inherent in the person with the condition. In Jellinek's typology, alpha alcoholism is relief drinking with associated problems, beta alcoholism is excessive consumption with consequences for health, and epsilon alcoholism is bingeing interspersed with spells of abstinence (Jellinek cited in Heather and Robertson, 1997 and in McMurran, 1994).

It is easy to criticise the disease model. Its advocates have failed to identify what makes alcoholics different from the rest of the population; couching this in general terms, such as asserting that alcoholics have 'an allergy to alcohol', is insufficient. This idea, and many of the other concepts inherent in the model, such as the slippery slope of addiction, can be seen as symbolising experiences rather than substantiating alcoholism as a disease. Jellinek's types can be viewed as categories describing clusters of behaviour as opposed to providing a scientific basis for the reasons why people develop difficulties. A further conundrum surrounds the idea of loss of control. The disease model holds to the notion that this will occur when the dependent person takes that first hit or drink. It is captured in the Alcoholics Anonymous slogan 'One drink, one drunk'. Paradoxically the model grants the person full control over whether he does have that first hit. Why loss of control should inevitably follow ingestion of a small amount of a substance is not adequately explained.

Despite such objections, the popularity of Alcoholics Anonymous and its sister fellowships attest to the disease model providing a framework which makes sense to many people experiencing problems. It has profound implications for both service provision and interventions by placing the concept of addiction centre stage and insisting that abstinence is the only solution.

## Genetics

While genetic theories might seem to be similar to the disease model, there are important distinctions. As we have seen, the disease model is deterministic. It suggests that there is an inevitability regarding what will follow if a person has the condition and continues to use. Genetic predisposition, by contrast, does not confer certainty but rather a greater likelihood than the average of a person developing problems. In addition, genetic theories do not exclude the influences of the environment or learning in the development of problematic use. As Saunders (1996) says, 'Any genetic predisposition is neither sufficient or necessary for drug addiction to occur.'

It has long been known that alcohol problems can run in families, which has, historically, led to polarised nature/nurture debates. In the light of twin studies, experiments with animals and the development of neurology, certain broad conclusions can be drawn, although much is still unclear:

- Genes can affect receptor sites or the processes through which substances are metabolised, the 'Oriental flush' being an example of the latter (see Box 3.3). Animals have been bred to be more, or less, sensitive to particular substances, thus demonstrating that resistance, or vulnerability, to the effects of drugs can be reinforced by genes. This suggests that genes may enhance the intensity of the drug experience, making the substance more desirable, or compound the side effects, making use less pleasurable. Some people may need to consume more to become intoxicated.
- Some genes may influence susceptibility to specific drugs, others to substance dependence more generally.
- Particular clusters of genes may determine certain personality traits which are associated with impulsiveness, substance taking, risk taking and antisocial behaviour. (Robson, 2009, p. 7; Uhl, 1995)

## BOX 3.3 THE ORIENTAL FLUSH

In the process of eliminating alcohol from the body, a toxic substance called acetaldehyde is formed which is then, in turn, broken down. Enzymes are involved in this process. Individuals can have variants of these enzymes which are all linked to differences in the same gene. Some of these variants allow acetaldehyde to remain in the system longer. This explains why Chinese, Japanese and Koreans, a significant percentage of whom have these particular enzyme variants, can feel unwell and experience facial flushing and accelerated heart rate after consuming quite modest amounts of alcohol. This reaction can, to some degree, discourage people from drinking in ways that lead to problems. On the downside, retention of acetaldehyde may also heighten certain health risks (National Institute on Alcohol Abuse and Alcoholism, 2007). While providing an example of the influences genes can exert, this response does not, however, inoculate Asian peoples from environmental pressures.

### Neurobiology and the maintenance of addiction

As has been noted, Jellinek was undecided as to why apparent loss of control occurs. Advances in neurobiology have led to investigation into the changes in the central nervous system which can occur through prolonged exposure to drugs, with loss of, or impaired, control and cravings being attributed to such changes. Once a dependency has been established such changes may make altering behaviour more difficult. Although much has still to be learned about these processes, some changes do appear to be reversible while others are not.

Our understanding of genetics and neurobiology is progressing rapidly and has sparked renewed interest in conceptualising addiction as a 'brain disease'. This has sometimes led the media to make simplistic suggestions that genes cause addiction. Our growing knowledge of the effect of drugs within the central nervous system and how this can be mediated by genetic predisposition may well lead to new pharmacotherapies and the possibility that different groups of people with problems should be channelled to different types of treatment. However, none of this lessens either the importance of the role learning plays or the influences of the wider environment.

Davies (2011) draws the distinction between the brain and the mind. As a riposte to those who see addictive behaviour as being primarily determined by neurological processes he says:

> there is a genetic and neurobiological basis ... for everything we do. But despite these underpinnings, we do not cross the street simply because our brains make our legs walk. We do so because Marks and Spencer is on the other side, and to the best of my knowledge neurones and chemicals don't have a strong desire to shop there ...

## Learning theories: much the same for everyone

The latter part of the twentieth century saw learning theories become the predominant explanation of problematic substance use, in academic circles at least, after behavioural psychologists had mounted a concerted challenge to the disease model. Early radical behaviourists, such as Watson and Skinner, were interested in investigating observable behaviour only (Gleitman, 1995); however, the cognitive revolution emphasised the importance of thought processes in shaping behaviour and merged these ideas with the earlier concept that learning is primarily a response to cues in the environment. What is striking about learning theories is that:

- They apply to everyone. Just as we learn to do any task well or incompetently, so we learn to use substances in safe or risky ways. The potential to develop substance problems is not, therefore, confined to specific predetermined groups of people; given the right circumstances, any of us can get into difficulty.
- Addiction is not a condition separate from other patterns of substance use with detrimental consequences; it is part of a continuum of possible learning outcomes.
- If we have learned to use substances in ways which cause us difficulties, we can teach ourselves, or be taught, to use in non-problematic ways. This opens up the possibility that, for some people, abstinence may not be the only therapeutic goal. Controlled use may be an option in certain circumstances.

We will consider now how the development of a substance problem can be explained by three theorists: Pavlov, Skinner and Bandura.

### Learning by association (classical or respondent conditioning)

Pavlov is famous as a founding father of behavioural theories but, as so often happens in science, he stumbled upon what has come to be known as classical conditioning by chance. A physiologist studying digestion, he won the Nobel

Prize for this work in 1904. He was undertaking experiments with dogs when he noticed that they salivated not only in response to food but also at the sight of the people bringing them food. His decision to investigate this phenomenon led to his famous experiment. Food was an unconditioned stimulus and salivation an unconditioned response. Pavlov then exposed the animals to a ticking metronome just before being given food (he tried various instruments). After this process had been repeated over a period, the dogs began to salivate at the sound of the metronome on its own. The sound of the metronome had become a conditioned stimulus and salivation on hearing it the conditioned response (Cherry, 2013; Gleitman, 1995). Heather and Robertson (1997) note the evolutionary importance of learning through association as the process involves learning to respond to cues which warn organisms of danger or signal that food may be available. In terms of substance use, the sheer number of potential cues in the environment leads to countless opportunities for embedding patterns of use and then reinforcing their continuation, as Case Illustration 3.2 demonstrates.

---

**CASE ILLUSTRATION 3.2**

**Classical conditioning**

Megan smokes occasionally at social events. A cigarette is the unconditioned stimulus and the pleasurable effects of nicotine the unconditioned response. She gets a new job and meets Gerry, a heavy smoker. He encourages her to join him for a cigarette at coffee breaks and after lunch. This ritual leads to certain times of the working day becoming the conditioned stimuli and these provoke a conditioned response (the desire to smoke). In addition, Gerry has begun to enter the equation. He, too, has become a conditioned stimulus, with his very appearance in the office triggering a feeling in Megan that it is time for a cigarette. Megan has become a regular smoker. This process can become more generalised with coffee and meals all becoming cues for smoking whether or not Megan is at work and whether or not Gerry is present. The widening of conditioned stimuli means that Megan's desire to smoke is subject to persistent reinforcement in numerous environmental settings. If Megan decides to stop smoking, she may find it easier to do if she finds another job.

Classical conditioning can explain why Megan smokes as much as she does and it can gives us pointers as to how certain links might be broken, thus helping her to stop smoking. It also sheds light on how the attractiveness of ritual can be as important as the substance use itself.

---

## Operant conditioning

The idea that the consequences of a particular behaviour influence whether it will be repeated or not is the core of operant conditioning, a theory forever associated with the work of B. F. Skinner (1953). Often experimenting with animals, he developed the central principle that if the organism receives a reward for acting in a particular way, that behaviour is reinforced. Conversely, if unpleasant consequences (punishment) follow an action, the organism is less likely to repeat it. Sheldon (2011, p. 109) succinctly describes operant conditioning as the idea that 'behaviour is a function of its consequences'. Reinforcement and punishment can be either positive or negative. The following provides a simple example:

Jenny drinks at social events. She enjoys the intoxicating effects of alcohol (positive reinforcement), and the reduction in inhibitions which come with drinking reduces her shyness (negative reinforcement). Positive reinforcement is the acquisition of something desirable, negative reinforcement is the lessening or removal of something which is unwelcome. These benefits lead Jenny to drink more heavily with the consequence that she is regularly sick at parties (positive punishment) and friends begin to invite her out less because of the embarrassment she causes (negative punishment). Positive punishment is the experience of something undesirable, negative punishment is the removal of, or failure to acquire, something which is considered to be beneficial.

Whether a behaviour continues or is extinguished depends on this balance between reinforcement and punishment. Given the unpleasant nature of withdrawals from certain drugs, the question might be raised as to why this positive punishment does not extinguish the drug-using behaviour. This can be explained in terms of the negative reinforcement: the rising tide of discomfort which occurs as levels of the drug in the system subside is immediately relieved by further consumption of the drug.

The likelihood of reinforcement embedding or maintaining a particular behaviour depends on variables such:

- how often the rewarding takes place;
- whether the reward occurs every time the behaviour happens;
- whether rewarding happens on a regular or irregular basis;
- the speed with which the reward follows the behaviour. (Sheldon, 2011)

The same is true for punishment.

Each cigarette is rewarding to a smoker and as long as the effects occur each time, the behaviour is maintained. If a smoker suddenly found that each cigarette he lit failed to produce an effect, he would probably persist for a while and then stop. If, however, some cigarettes provided nicotine and some did not, the smoker would probably continue to light up knowing that the reward would occur at some point. The mechanisms of reinforcement and punishment provide real challenges for health educators. Young smokers can be told that a high percentage of people who continue the habit will suffer poor health but this potential punishment, because it is so far in the future, will have limited impact. Messages based on more immediate punishments, such as being unattractive to the opposite sex, are more likely to have an influence.

## The introduction of cognition

Although poles apart, the early behaviourists and the psychoanalytical schools shared one thing: a lack of interest in conscious mental processes (cognitions). For the behaviourists, the mind was of little interest as its workings were beyond empirical investigation. For the psychoanalysts, conscious thoughts were not to be taken at face value; it was their underlying meanings which were of importance. Albert Ellis, Aaron Beck and others rebelled against what they considered to be the limitations of these theories, namely that they fail to take into account how thought influences mood and behaviour. Beck (1989), particularly, considered that thoughts precede how we feel and then influence how we act. Past learning leads to beliefs which, in turn, serve to maintain both helpful and unhelpful behaviours. The thought 'I can't get through the day without a cigarette' leads both to feelings of inadequacy and the pack being opened. 'I can manage' leads to optimistic feelings and success in abstaining. Bandura's great contribution has been to take behavioural and cognitive theories and the blend these together into what is known as social learning theory (Bandura, 1977). His work on self-efficacy – the idea that the successful completion of a task is linked to the belief that we can accomplish it – is of major therapeutic importance. The following are hallmarks of Bandura's work:

- Learning does not occur solely though interaction with the environment. Learning by modelling, watching how other people do things, is equally important. In his famous Bobo doll experiments, Bandura demonstrated how young children copied specific aggressive acts which they had seen adults carrying out at an earlier point in time (Bandura, Ross and Ross, 1961). Learning by modelling is more likely to occur when certain conditions are met. These include the behaviour being seen as appealing and the demonstrator being competent, having authority and being a person with whom the 'learner' identifies (Heather and Robertson, 1997). From this we can immediately see the importance of family, peer groups and the media in how the next generation learns to take substances. Before we even try a substance, we have a fairly good idea of how to ingest it, in what social circumstances it is usually taken, what effect it will have and how we are expected to behave following use.
- We can also learn through watching how others succeed or fail (vicarious learning). Such learning does not necessarily lead to our carrying out a particular action. A person who sees a friend injecting may judge the behaviour and its consequences to be undesirable.
- Cognitions are central to both modelling and vicarious learning. We repeat the behaviour at a later point having remembered what we have witnessed. This leads us to Bandura's ideas about internal cognitive constructs: we can symbolise what we have experienced and what we have observed. Our ability to recall and make sense of what we have seen enables us to then reflect on it and so predict the consequences of future actions (Bandura, 2008). We learn what to expect.

A woman I was working with told me how she experienced an overwhelming temptation to drink one night when she was feeling lonely and depressed. She said that she resisted this by thinking about how unwell she was after her last relapse and this strengthened her resolve to weather the storm. Her cognitive frameworks allowed her to both recall past experience and to test the likely outcome of drinking against this.

■ We shape the environment as much as the environment shapes our behaviour. Bandura (2008, p. 87) says of this reciprocal relationship, 'people are contributors to their life experiences, not just products of them'.

This is a more complex equation than that suggested by operant conditioning where the individual simply responds to the influences in the environment. Social learning theory also helps to makes sense of why, when our initial experiences of using a substance may not be particularly pleasant, we persevere. We see that others are gaining benefits and, if we persist, we hope these will come our way too.

In social learning theory the mechanistic processes that direct behaviour are offset by the ability of humans to reflect and to be guided by that reflection. The ability to exercise what Bandura calls 'personal influence' has been introduced into the mix. This is not free will in the uncomplicated, classical sense but rather one factor in the interaction between the individual with his cognitive capacity, behavioural factors and environmental forces (Bandura, 2008, p. 87). How we use substances is not a simple matter of choice, nor is it something which is completely out of our control.

Learning theories place particular emphasis on the interaction between the individual and the environment, with somewhat less emphasis on the substance. They go a long way to explaining why some people use in problematic ways and others do not. They help to make sense of problematic use in its widest sense of which addiction is but one facet. Both John's and Eric's behaviour can be interpreted using learning theories (see the beginning of this chapter). However, what we know of neurology and genetics suggests that, on their own, they do not provide a complete picture.

From a therapeutic point of view, cognitive and learning theories are of major importance. They underpin a number of the main interventions which are known to be effective with people with substance problems: motivational interviewing, cognitive behavioural therapy and various approaches to relapse prevention.

## Psychoanalytical theories: substance problems as symptoms

From a psychoanalytical perspective, the root cause of certain psychological and behavioural difficulties is failure to successfully negotiate normal developmental stages or resolve past problematic experiences. Difficulty with substances is a symptom which alerts us to underlying issues. In learning theory problematic use is an end in itself; in psychoanalytical theory it serves a function. Psychoanalytical theories tend to be developed from speculative interpretation of case material, thus making them less amenable to empirical evaluation.

In psychoanalytical theories, substance use provides relief from tension and distress. The present environment is of little relevance; what is of concern is how past experiences have led to unresolved conflicts for which current excessive substance use serves as a maladaptive response. This general theme has been interpreted from a variety of angles:

- At one stage in his career, Freud interpreted alcoholism as a failure to negotiate the earliest phase of development, the oral phase (Heather and Robertson, 1997). Kessel and Walton (1965, p. 78) suggest that many alcoholics display characteristics of helplessness and overreliance on others which the orally fixated person is deemed to exhibit.
- Levine (1995) cites Menninger's belief that alcoholism was a prolonged self-destructive act based on guilt linked to aggressive feelings.
- The critical nature of the infant–caregiver relationship in helping the former develop into a secure adult personality is the core of Bowlby's theories of attachment. Reading (2002) suggests that substances may help a person cope with difficulties which can be traced to a failure to successfully establish such early attachments. Turning to substances can also be seen as mirroring the infant turning to the adult caregiver for succour in times of distress.
- The linking of alcoholism to repressed homoerotic tendencies has long been a theme in psychoanalytical literature (Abraham cited in Levine, 1995, p. 157; Hopper, 1995).

These, and similar hypotheses, are difficult to validate; some may also seem quaint or even absurd. In Freudian terms, smoking can be interpreted as an oral activity. In 1948, 82 per cent of adult males in the UK smoked (ASH 2013). Are we to infer from this that the psychological development of most of these men was locked in the oral phase? It is more likely that the availability of cheap tobacco, in a culture which endorsed smoking, explains the phenomenon. Most ex-smokers have achieved abstinence without addressing deep-seated conflicts in the unconscious. However, that there is something amiss in the personality of the addict, as opposed to deficiencies of a biological nature, is an idea with a lengthy history. In addition, the concept of the addictive personality, a cluster of traits which leads a person to use different substances in compulsive ways or indulge destructively in various behaviours, has popular appeal. There is no doubt that there are people who, for example, smoke, drink and gamble; however, controversy surrounds attempts to isolate particular personality traits (Clark, 2011).

The use of substances to cope with the aftermath of traumatic experiences, such as war, bereavement or abuse, or the distress of mental health problems falls under the broad umbrella of psychoanalytical theories. Here the issue is not one of struggles in the unconscious, as the person is likely to be well aware of the source of his unhappiness. The principle, however, remains the same: the use of the substance is a secondary issue. Self-medication can provide solace, however temporary, through reducing pain or altering consciousness and this can lead to problematic use. 'Escape coping' has been used to describe the function heroin serves for many (Hammersley and Dalgarno, 2013).

The links between mental health and substance problems are well evidenced, although it is sometimes difficult to establish whether psychological distress precedes the development of problematic substance use or whether substance use precipitates this (see Chapter 13).

## BOX 3.4  ABUSE AND THE DEVELOPMENT OF SUBSTANCE PROBLEMS

Experience of sexual and physical abuse is a theme in the personal histories of many people with substance problems. In a review of the literature, Downs and Harrison (1998) conclude that childhood sexual or physical abuse is a risk factor for the development of substance problems. This is supported by other studies such as the examination by Rohsenow, Corbett and Devine (1988) of the link between sexual abuse in childhood and later substance use. McKeganey, Neale and Robertson (2005) describe significant levels of sexual and physical abuse among drug users in Scotland. Both men and women in sexual minority groupings have been found to have higher rates of substance problems than heterosexuals and this can be partly explained by experiences of sexual and physical abuse (Hughes et al., 2010).

In a study tracing the links between post-traumatic distress disorder and substance problems, Bremner at al. (1996) found that drugs with calming properties, such as alcohol, heroin, cannabis and benzodiazepines, tended to be favoured, rather than cocaine. Khantzian (1995, p. 213; 1997) speculates on the possible connection between the use of specific drugs and particular personality types or people who regularly experience unsettling emotions. He suggests that depressants provide release for people who over-control their feelings, whereas opiates dampen anger. He also considers that driven, ambitious people can experience fluctuations in mood and stimulants can help both to lift depression and enhance periods of high energy.

Edgar Allan Poe (undated) speaks for many who say that they take substances to deal with issues which trouble them:

> I have absolutely *no* pleasure in the stimulants in which I sometimes so madly indulge. It has not been in the pursuit of pleasure that I have periled life and reputation and reason. It has been the desperate attempt to escape from torturing memories ... from a sense of insupportable loneliness and a dread of some strange impending doom.

A major limitation of psychoanalytical theories is their failure to take into account the implications of the cultural contexts within which people take substances. The therapeutic implication of these theories is that the focus should be on resolving the underlying difficulties. If this is achieved, the presumption is that the problematic use of the substance will wither on the vine. However, there is not strong evidence that this happens unless the substance use is also directly addressed (see Chapter 6).

## Gateway theory

Gateway theory suggests that a step progression occurs whereby the use of a less problematic drug leads to the use of a more harmful one. It is often used as justification for not reducing the legal restrictions on drugs such as cannabis. Ironically, the opposite case can be made. By making some 'softer' drugs more readily available, greater splits in the market might occur thus lessening the likelihood of people buying from the same people who sell more harmful drugs. In addition, the Royal College of Psychiatrists and the Royal College of Physicians (2000, p. 65) suggest that using less harmful substances may satisfy a person's inclination to experiment and so reduce the likelihood of his trying drugs which present greater risks. Various processes might be involved in the step progression of gateway theory (Ryder, Salmon and Walker, 2001; West, 2006):

- The experience of one drug may increase the desire to use a more powerful one.
- If few problems are experienced with one drug, fear of using another that presents greater risks may lessen.
- A peer group supporting the use of one drug may accept the use of other substances. Here the effects of the drug are less important than the reinforcing nature of the social context.

The challenge of establishing the validity of gateway theories is one of proving cause and effect. People who start using heroin will almost certainly have prior experience of drinking but this hardly proves that the alcohol is a gateway to the former. Only a tiny percentage of drinkers become heroin users. Cannabis has attracted considerable attention as a possible gateway substance because it is the most widely used illicit drug. Proof that cannabis acts as a gateway to other drugs has proved elusive. Van Grundy and Rebellon (2010) suggest that there may be some effects but that these are short-lived, and sequential use may be equally dependent on social or other factors in people's lives. Gateway theory might also explain the progression to riskier ways of using, such as the step from smoking or snorting to injecting. One interesting issue for future consideration is whether the decline in tobacco smoking will lead to a reduction in cannabis use with the method of ingestion, smoking, being the gateway.

## Substance problems as choice

What is sometimes termed the 'moral model' (Clark, 2011) adopts the classical perspective that human behaviour is a matter of unfettered choice. A person will freely decide on a course of action after weighing up the benefits and disadvantages. This holds true even when a person's substance use is causing problems. A youth trying tobacco for the second time may decide that the kudos which follows lighting up outweighs the feeling of nausea he experienced the first time he smoked. A lifetime smoker may decide that satisfying a craving offsets any worries about a persistent cough. Both are exercising free will. Choosing to act in a particular way based on a rational calculation of outcomes is fundamentally different from the concept of mechanistic learning promoted by the early behaviourists. The rational choice model suggests that, while our options may be influenced by the environment, biology or the like, free will, the act of making decisions, is not compromised by these. Just as we choose to use substances, we can also choose to stop using them if they no longer suit our purposes; seriously impaired control is not an issue. With regard to excessive alcohol consumption, the rational choice model was widely held until the end of the eighteenth century when medicine began to develop as a discipline, followed by the sciences of human behaviour (Heather and Robertson, 1997; McMurran, 1994). If use of substances is entirely a choice, then society's response to problematic use, particularly when it affects others, will be to punish. Interestingly, the law in the UK is based on this premise but with qualifications. Intoxication is no defence in court and addiction is not accepted as a mental illness. However, when it appears that a person is having difficulty in controlling his use, a court may pass a sentence requiring the person to receive treatment. This paradox is a good example of our inability to decide what the causes of problematic use and dependence are and how far we are able to exercise control.

What are the therapeutic implications of the rational choice model? As decision making is central, helping a person to clarify his thinking at times when he is considering change would seem to be critical and motivational approaches might help with this. In addition, once a decision has been made to change, the person may need services, such as detoxification, to help carry this through.

## Integrated approaches; the bio-psycho-social model

What we have considered so far are various frames of reference, some overlapping and some at variance, some amenable to empirical evaluation and some less so; however, none by themselves adequately account for what is clearly a multifaceted phenomenon. This has led to the application of the bio-psycho-social paradigm to problematic substance use (Pycroft, 2010). This takes us back to Zinberg (1984) and his assertion that substance using cannot be understood unless we take full account of the drug, the individual and the environment. The bio-psycho-social paradigm also acknowledges that the balance of influences will be unique to each person. For one person, the impact of genetic weighting and the consequences of social disadvantage might be the most telling factors; for another, prior trauma and operant learning might be to the fore. These examples, of course, simplify what in each person is a highly complex mixture of predisposition, past experiences and learning, cultural and social contexts and the characteristics of substances themselves. Whether a person abstains, uses in a harm-free manner or develops difficulties is predicated on this balance of influences. Figure 3.1 shows how this interplay of factors influences the development of both harm-free and problematic use.

This holistic paradigm is becoming increasingly accepted, but whether it will stand the test of time has yet to be seen. Two key interlinked principles for working with people with substance problems have emerged from this strand of thinking:

- Interventions should be person centred. Engagement should start with what each individual brings and should respond to his unique circumstances.
- A menu of evidenced-based treatment options should be available and each person should be helped to decide which might suit him best.

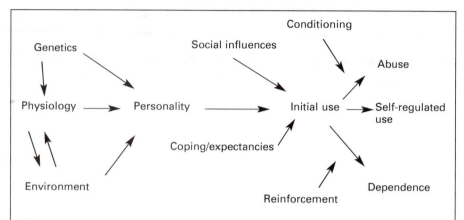

All of these factors can have arrows to initial experience and then to any or all of the three patterns of use. Most could have arrows that demonstrate linear or reciprocal causality as well.

**Figure 3.1** Factors influencing patterns of substance use
*Source*: DiClemente, C. (reproduced with permission)

**CASE ILLUSTRATION 3.3**

### Applying theory in practice

Leanne (24) never knew her father. Her mother, who experienced serious difficulties with alcohol, had a number of unfulfilling relationships with men, one of whom sexually abused Leanne. In her early teenage years life settled down somewhat and her mother's drinking subsided. Leanne discovered drugs when she was 14, smoking cannabis and taking various stimulants with a group of friends. She recalls enjoying the changes of mood these brought and appreciating the confidence in social settings which came with use. Taking drugs also gave her entry to a group of girls who enjoyed a high status among their peers because of their risk-taking behaviour. She describes these as good years.

When she was 18, her mother died and, finding herself isolated and depressed, she began taking drugs on a more consistent basis; however, she did manage to contain her use and completed a course as a hairdresser. Two years later she moved in with an older man who introduced her to heroin. Initially, she only smoked this occasionally. When this relationship ended, the only place where she could find a flat was in an area with high indicators of social disadvantage and a reputation for drug use. Having lost her job, and with a growing sense that she had always been a failure whom nobody cared for, she began to inject heroin on a daily basis. She felt it helped to calm her feelings and cope in an increasingly difficult situation.

- Which theories might explain why Leanne has become dependent on heroin?
- Are the theories which might throw light on why Leanne started to use drugs the same as those which might explain her dependence on heroin?

## Concluding comments

On hearing of the death of George Best, a famous football manager is reported to have said that we are not all equal in front of addiction, an astute remark. While no one is immune from developing problems with substances, certain factors increase the likelihood of difficulties occurring. These include genetic predisposition, learning, social circumstances, developmental difficulties and traumatic experiences. Whilst the potential impact of upbringing is well recognised, often too little weight is given to the wider cultural context in which substance taking occurs and its influence on individual behaviour.

### RESOURCES

- McMurran, M. (1994). *The Psychology of Addiction.*
- Orford, J. (2001). *Excessive Appetites: A Psychological View of Addictions* (2nd edition).
- West, R. (2006). *Theory of Addiction.*

# CHAPTER 4

# Cultural Trends; Social Control

## KEY THEMES

- What is considered to be problematic use and how best to reduce the harms differs between countries and shifts over time.
- Societies use both formal and less formal methods of control but these are often shaped as much by economics and perception as by evidence or logic.
- Successive governments remain ambivalent as to whether substance use and its consequences should be primarily a health matter or a criminal justice issue.
- Attempts by the state to lessen problems involve measures aimed at either reducing the supply or reducing demand or addressing specific harms.
- Practitioners should bear in mind that how services are structured and what treatment entails reflect, to a significant degree, current political priorities and social attitudes.

## Cultural influences on use

While we only have to open the Old Testament to see that attempts by the authorities to regulate the consumption of substances has a lengthy history (Judges, 13:4), what is considered to be problematic and how best to reduce the damage is continually shifting. These change over time and differ between cultures. Use of opium was perfectly acceptable in early nineteenth-century Britain; the unrefined coca leaf, a class A drug in the UK, is not subject to legal restriction in Bolivia. Tobacco use, once enjoyed by the majority, is rapidly becoming a subcultural activity. This chapter will consider what factors influence attitudes and what methods society uses to reduce the harms.

A series of forces within society account for how substances, and the problems they bring, are perceived.

### Accidents of geography

Humans discovered early on that fermenting fruit, along with certain plants and fungi, are powerful intoxicants. Beer and wine were produced in Middle Eastern societies long before Christ. The ubiquity of fruit ensured that alcohol was widely available whereas some other substances are only found in particular plants, which meant that their use, in early history, was circumscribed by geography. Records show that substances were used for medicinal purposes, as the centrepiece of religious ceremonies and, no doubt, for their 'recreational' value (Royal College of Psychiatrists and the Royal College of Physicians, 2000, p. 24). Nothing has changed! Whilst tastes and allegiances to particular substances do alter, cultures tend to feel most comfortable with the drugs with which they have a lengthy association, irrespective of the harms they may cause. This can be seen in the bond between Europeans and alcohol (beer and spirits in Northern Europe and wine in the Mediterranean countries) and the relationship the Andean countries have with the coca leaf. Protection tends to be afforded to such drugs whilst the arrival of novel or alien substances is marked by hostility or panic. It is not just conservatism which is at play here. Grapevines grow well under the warmth of the Mediterranean sun whilst coca thrives in the cool, bright conditions found in the foothills of the Andes. For centuries, individuals and societies have gained economic benefits from these accidents of geography and are unwilling to relinquish them. The export of 140 million cases of whisky a year (ScotchWhisky.net, 2012) is a major boon to the financial wellbeing of Scotland; so too is the growing of the opium poppy for the economy of Afghanistan. It is hard to argue that these are totally different in kind.

## Religion

Muslims proscribe the use of alcohol and drugs; Christians use wine as a potent symbol; native peoples of Mexico and the USA use peyote as part of their religious devotions. Religion is a strong thread in the tapestry of cultural attitudes towards substances, stipulating whether substances can be used and, if so, in what ways and whether intoxication is ever legitimate.

## Therapeutic value

From the earliest of times, the medicinal benefits of drugs have been exploited and there has long been a cross-fertilisation between the therapeutic and recreational use of substances. Opium derivatives are the major weapon in the control of pain in Western medicine and this is paralleled by the use of street heroin. LSD was employed as a tool in psychiatry prior to being subject to legal restriction following concerns about growing recreational use. Some drugs which are used for non-medicinal purposes are found to have medicinal value. Current research into the potential therapeutic benefits of cannabis is a good example.

## Fashion

Drugs, and how they are ingested, go in and out of fashion. Few take nicotine these days by inhaling snuff. The British Crime Survey (Smith and Flatley, 2011) suggests that ecstasy and LSD use declined significantly between 1996 and 2010/11, presumably due to changes in tastes in the dance scene.

### Rebellion

Substance use has a long association with both the rejection of prevailing norms and with more overt rebellion. With coffee's arrival in the UK in the seventeenth century came the coffee house as a hub of social intercourse. Fears that people were plotting the downfall of the state, as they enjoyed a novel drug, led Charles II to outlaw coffee houses, a move which popular outrage forced the state to abandon (Edwards, 2005, p. 56). In the 1960s, cannabis and hallucinogens had meaning beyond the pleasure to be derived from their use: they were symbols of an idealist counter-culture. Compare this with the rave scene 20 years later where drug use seems to have been purely hedonistic. Moral panics spring not only from the fear of unfamiliar substances but also from concerns that the subcultures which use them may undermine predominant values. Such panics can become intertwined with other social attitudes such as racism. Hoffman (1990) argues that moves to restrict opium in the USA towards the end of the nineteenth century were connected to negative attitudes towards Chinese immigrants at a time of economic hardship.

### Subcultures

Particular groupings may have specific drug preferences, whether it is Rastafarians with their beliefs about cannabis or Somali people in England and their tradition of khat use. Age, too, can be a factor, with older people being less likely to experiment with new substances. Drug use is higher among men than women (Home Office, 2012b). Compared to the white population, people of mixed race have higher levels of drug use and those in other ethnic groups exhibit lower levels of use (Beddoes et al., 2010a).

These, and other social factors, shape attitudes, extent of use and types of problems. This complex mix of forces faces governments trying to reduce the harms.

## Social control: various options

Governments both reflect the prevailing mood and attempt to influence it by delineating what is considered acceptable and unacceptable. There is a symbiotic relationship between cultural attitudes, problems and the initiatives a society takes to reduce the harms. Indeed, the very method of control is one factor influencing the nature of problems which a society experiences. If the state made possession or supply of tobacco illegal, the nation's health might improve as more people stopped smoking, but those who continued to smoke would become criminalised and the black market, with all its associated harmful activity, would expand. In this example, health problems or crime is our choice. Perhaps 'How do we rid ourselves of substance problems?' is the wrong question; 'What steps should we take to ensure the least harm to the greatest number?' may be a more realistic approach.

## How does the state try to exercise control?

Supply reduction, demand reduction and harm reduction are the three broad courses of action open to any government intent on limiting problems (Royal College of Psychiatrists and the Royal College of Physicians, 2000). In practice, of course, packages of measures tend to be put in place containing elements of all three.

## Supply reduction

When the substance is seen as presenting significant risks, then supply reduction measures aimed at reducing availability are implemented. We see a need to tightly control access to opiates, whereas we allow caffeine to be available without restriction in numerous products. Supply reduction may be more specifically targeted, as in the age restrictions placed on the sale and purchase of alcohol and tobacco. Supply reduction usually involves legislation and, to be effective, requires enforcement.

## Demand reduction

The focus of demand reduction is not the substance but the user. When it is thought that attitudes or habits are leading to particular difficulties, the state will implement measures to encourage people to use less or abstain. Drug education in schools, campaigns to highlight the health risks inherent in heavy drinking and taxation of alcohol and tobacco are examples of demand reduction measures.

## Harm reduction

When specific behaviours cause problems then measures aimed directly at these may be introduced. Drink driving legislation is a good illustration; its purpose is to reduce death and injury in particular circumstances, not to restrict access to alcohol or to encourage people to drink less overall. The ban on smoking in enclosed public places and the introduction of plastic beer glasses in venues with a history of violence are other examples. Treatment provision and services for people affected by someone else's substance use are harm reduction measures of a somewhat different kind.

BOX 4.1  THE LAW OF UNINTENDED CONSEQUENCES

As with all social policy initiatives, control of substances is subject to the law of unintended consequences. The black market in tobacco is an unwelcome by-product of high taxation, a demand reduction measure. Examining the complexities of achieving intended goals, Ashton (2004) describes how some educational and social skills training programmes aimed at young people actually increased substance use. Encouraging lifestyles considered to provide 'protection' may, in fact, do no such thing. Sport is widely believed to be a diversionary activity but one American study (Eitle et al. cited in Ashton, 2004) showed that young white males involved in school sport were more likely to drink as young adults. Involvement in American football actually increased the risk of a person developing problems, a phenomenon attributed to the influence of a powerful masculine subculture.

The history of opiates provides a case study of how measures to control the harms reflect changes in social context and values, perceptions of risk and alterations in patterns of use.

### Opiates from 1800 to 1960: from availability to restriction

In the first half of the nineteenth century, people had ready access to a veritable cornucopia of drugs of which opium was but one. The medical profession was in its infancy and people dealt with most health problems by using what could be readily bought from shop or travelling salesman. Use of opium, with its ability to reduce discomfort, was widespread; it was taken orally in pill or powder form. Laudanum, a mixture of alcohol and opium, was much beloved of some of the Romantic poets. Opium's addictive properties were known but its medicinal value overrode such concerns. Widespread acceptance began to be replaced by ambivalence as the century progressed. Driven by philanthropy and the need for a healthy workforce to power the Industrial Revolution, the wellbeing of the working classes became a political issue. Their substance-taking habits tended to provoke greater concern than those of their middle-class contemporaries. Lack of quality control was also an issue as adulteration of opium led to accidental poisonings and the use of opium products to sedate babies was seen as a serious problem (Berridge and Edwards, 1982; Royal College of Psychiatrists and Royal College of Physicians, 2000).

This led to vigorous debates between pharmacists and doctors about what levels of control should be introduced. The former were concerned that draconian measures would damage their businesses, an early example of the profit motive intruding into policy making. The outcome was the Pharmacy Act of 1868 which brought the sale of a number of drugs, including opium, under the control of registered pharmacists. The purpose of the Act was to manage, not to radically restrict, access to opium. It also gave the state and the developing health professions a central role in the control of drugs for the first time. The Act can be seen as both an attempt at supply control and a harm reduction measure.

The arrival of the hypodermic needle and the realisation that treatment with morphine could lead easily to physical dependence increased awareness of the risks of opiates; however, no further moves to curtail availability were deemed necessary. Heroin, an even more powerful semi-synthetic opiate, was first produced in 1874 and joined the range of medicines derived from the poppy. It relieved the toothache suffered by a future prime minister: "'Poor little man,'' wrote a friend of his family to the 16-year-old Winston Churchill

at Harrow School in 1891 .... "Have you tried the heroin I sent you ..."'
(quoted in Hutchinson, 1998, p. 167).

As other options became available, use of opiates declined as the twentieth
century approached. In addition, moral indignation had increased because of
Britain's role in the opium trade, a business which had led to two wars that
had forced China open its shores to the importation of opium to help fund the
empire in India; an epidemic in China followed (Berridge and Edwards, 1982;
Edwards, 2005).

At the beginning of the twentieth century, demand reduction was occurring
without any rigorous curtailing of availability. However, as is so often the case,
it was extraneous factors that changed the ground rules. A less relaxed atti-
tude permeated the United States, which pressed for international control of
drugs. The Hague International Opium Convention of 1912 committed the
nations that were party to it, including the UK, to introducing legislation to
control the manufacture and distribution of various drugs including opium. It
also enshrined the doctrine of limiting opium use to research and medical
applications (International Opium Convention, 1912). This obligation was
not immediately implemented in UK legislation but the Great War provided
further impetus for control due to concerns that cocaine, in particular, was
undermining the war effort. Regulations made in 1916 under the Defence of
the Realm Act laid down restrictions on opium and cocaine and placed drug
control in the hands of the Home Office. Finally, the Dangerous Drugs Act
1920 enshrined the principles of the Hague Convention in UK law. In less than
ten years a paradigm shift had occurred which set the foundations for modern
drug policy. Opiates had been readily available, with control and response to
problems being the domain of pharmacists and doctors; they now became
primarily a matter for the criminal justice system with supply reduction the
key strategy.

The story is not quite over. Doctors became concerned that they would no
longer be able to prescribe various drugs. The Rolleston Committee was established to explore where the line should be drawn in law. Rolleston's report in
1926 supported the view that addiction was a disease and that medical treatment for this should include maintenance prescribing of drugs, such as opiates,
where a patient found withdrawal impossible. Thus the so-called 'British
system' came into being with harm reduction at its core. Substance control
was a matter for the criminal justice system but prescribing drugs as a formal
treatment was legitimate. Substances then dropped off the agenda. The
number of dependent users was very low and was primarily made up of those
who had become addicted through being prescribed opiates for other conditions or who were professionals who had ready access (Edwards, 2005, p.
111; Royal College of Psychiatrists and Royal College of Physicians, 2000, p.
40). These people were not members of subcultures that threatened the social
order and their problems were easily contained. How things were to change
from the 1960s onwards!

This brief history provides an example of how restriction becomes seen as
being essential where none was previously thought necessary. It shows how, at
one point, harm reduction is the preferred approach and, at the next, demand

or supply reduction are felt to be more effective. It also illustrates how crises and the agendas of the powerful, whether they are professional groups, moral entrepreneurs, the United States or the Home Office, can influence policy as much as the actual risks inherent in the use of a drug.

Opiates were not the only substances taxing the Victorians. Temperance was one of the great reforming causes of the time but campaigners failed in their objectives in the UK. Their success in the USA was a fascinating experiment in substance control (see Box 4.2).

### BOX 4.2 PROHIBITION: AN UNMITIGATED DISASTER?

The United States' experiment with prohibition from 1920 to 1933 is often dismissed as a wholly negative experience but the reality was more complex. As demand did not disappear, organised crime found an ideal product; corruption permeated through civil and political life and left a legacy which is still felt today. What is often overlooked, however, is that per capita consumption decreased with consequent health benefits (Royal College of Psychiatrists and the Royal College of Physicians, 2000, pp. 194–5). Initially at least, there were reductions in some alcohol-related crimes and alcohol-related admissions to psychiatric hospitals fell (Blocker, 2006; Kerr, 1999). Death from liver cirrhosis reduced by almost 50 per cent (Edwards et al., 1994, p. 131). Declining public support and the government's need to raise revenues during the Depression sounded the death knell of this supply reduction venture. This interlude in American life is another example of how imposing severe restrictions can lead, on the one hand, to improvements in public health but, on the other, to a rise in criminal markets.

## Judging effectiveness

How do governments judge the effectiveness of the initiatives they take? It needs to be borne in mind that the objectives of social policies differ between substances. In the UK, a smoke-free country is the overall aim determined by the view that the dangers of tobacco demand no less; alcohol policy, by way of contrast, is based on the assumption that the desirable outcome is harm-free drinking. Key indicators of effectiveness are:

*Primary prevention*
- reduced supply
- reduced numbers starting to use
- reduced use at the population level
- reduced numbers developing problems

*Improvements in health*
- at a population level
- among those in treatment
- reduced mortality

*Reductions in crime*
- reduced illicit supply
- safer neighbourhoods/reduced antisocial behaviour
- reduced offending by people with substance problems

*Improvements in social functioning of people in treatment*
- stabilisation
- reduced homelessness
- reintegration into society (meaningful activity; employment; stable relationships)

*Reduction in harms to others*
- passive smoking
- domestic abuse
- risks to the wellbeing of children through parental/carer substance use

## Substances in the UK since 1960: a shifting scene

We will now consider how smoking, drug and alcohol policies have developed in recent decades.

### Tobacco: abstinence within a health framework

Amid the welter of statistics indicating the harmful impact of substances, it is easy to ignore the great success of smoking policies. The mounting evidence of harm was strongly endorsed by a famous epidemiological study by Dr Richard Doll and Professor Austin Hill in 1951 which confirmed the relationship between lung cancer and smoking. Because the health risks are indisputable, successive governments on both sides of the political divide have maintained broadly consistent strategies. The elimination of smoking is the objective. Prevention of uptake, backed by legal restrictions short of prohibition, has been a priority. Smoking is viewed primarily as a health issue. Despite some political opposition and lobbying, along with legal challenges by the tobacco industry, the direction of travel has received popular endorsement. Even the ban on smoking in enclosed public places, initially controversial, was introduced without problems of compliance (Department of Health, 2008a).

Supply reduction has been applied through measures such as raising the age of sale from 16 to 18 and banning vending machines.

Demand reduction measures have included increases in taxation above inflation and educational measures aimed at reinforcing public understanding of the risks including health messages on packaging. Advertising of cigarettes on television ended in 1965 and was eventually followed by an outright ban on tobacco advertising beyond the place of sale brought in under the Tobacco Advertising and Promotion Act 2002. Under the Health Act 2009 and the Tobacco and Primary Medical Services (Scotland) Act 2010, shops must ensure that tobacco products are not visibly on display. Further measures being considered include introducing plain packaging, thus removing one of the last opportunities to glamorise the product. A comprehensive demand reduction approach has, therefore, encompassed pricing, measures to reduce the attractiveness of smoking and initiatives to remove smoking from public consciousness.

A major harm reduction measure was the ban on smoking in all enclosed public spaces which was brought in throughout the UK. Its prime purpose was to eliminate passive smoking, the risks of which were becoming better known. European Union directives on tar levels are further examples of harm reduction initiatives. Pressure is mounting to consider banning smoking in vehicles both to prevent passive inhalation, especially by children, and as a road safety measure (ASH, 2012b). For those who smoke, cessation services including telephone quit lines, counselling, self-help packs and pharmacotherapies, such as nicotine patches and craving-reducing drugs, have been made available.

The cumulative impact of these measures has been to improve the nation's health. Smoking rates have declined sharply with the Office of National Statistics General Lifestyle Survey 2010 (Office of National Statistics, 2012) suggesting that 20 per cent of adults smoke, compared with 45 per cent in 1974. From a peak in the 1990s, numbers of regular smokers among younger teenagers halved by the end of the first decade of the twenty-first century (Health and Social Care Information Centre, 2012; Ipsos MORI, 2011). The decline in smoking has led to significant reductions in deaths from heart disease (Unal, Critchley and Capewell, 2003) and lung cancer (Peto et al., 2000). Bans on smoking in enclosed public places have been shown to improve the health of non-smoking staff in the hospitality industry, one of the main objectives of bringing in such a measure (Centers for Disease Control and Prevention, 2012). Given that deaths from smoking continue to outstrip those from drugs and alcohol by a wide margin, and that one fifth of adults smoke, it can be argued that the UK is still in the grip of a national epidemic, but an epidemic which is in serious decline. The challenge for the future is to discourage initiation among the young and to make inroads into lower socioeconomic groups where smoking rates are higher and which remain resistant to current measures (ASH, 2012c).

---

ACTIVITY 4.1

**Would harm reduction work for nicotine?**

Harm reduction approaches have focused on the effects of smoking on other people rather than on the smoker who, under an abstinence strategy, is faced with a choice of 'quit or die'. Nicotine is now available in smokeless forms such as e-cigarettes (electronic and tobacco-less) and oral tobacco pouches for those who cannot or do not want to stop.

- Should the government promote the use of such products to those who want to continue to use nicotine?
- Would such an approach reduce the harms or would it undermine current policies?

## Drugs in modern Britain: pragmatic prohibition

In the 1950s, a drug culture existed among some musicians and very small numbers of people continued to be prescribed opiates. Amphetamines were available with little restriction in the first part of the decade. None of this aroused significant concerns. The first stirrings of wider disquiet came with a growth in black-market amphetamines at the turn of the decade, but two factors catapulted drugs to the top of the political agenda, a position which they have yet to relinquish. The counter-culture of the late 1960s, with its use of substances – particularly cannabis and other hallucinogens – as symbols of rebellion changed the landscape, as did the bizarre prescribing practices of a handful of doctors. As the number of recorded heroin addicts grew, it emerged that this increase could be traced to a few London-based physicians who were prescribing at cavalier levels, with users selling on what they did not need. A harm reduction approach had become a source of wider supply, highlighting yet again the troublesome relationship between medical and non-therapeutic use. The government's response was to pass the treatment of drug users from individual doctors to new specialist clinics (Royal College of Psychiatrists and the Royal College of Physicians, 2000, pp. 44–6). The 'British system', a medical approach within a prohibitionist legal framework, was thus re-established in a slightly different form. Drug laws were consolidated in the Misuse of Drugs Act 1971, which remains the core legislation.

## BOX 4.3 MISUSE OF DRUGS ACT 1971

The following are the central features of the Act:

- Drugs subject to the Act (known as 'controlled drugs') are placed in three classes (A, B and C); these define the penalties which courts can impose for illegal possession for personal use or for cultivation, manufacture or supply to others. Supply offences attract higher maximum penalties than possession for personal use. The classes are intended to reflect the risks particular substances present.
- Regulations made under the Act place each controlled drug in one of five schedules which state who can legally possess that drug. Drugs in schedule 1 cannot be prescribed and a Home Licence is required before a person, usually a researcher, can handle them legally. Drugs in schedules 2, 3 and 4 can be held legally by those to whom they have been prescribed, along with various other restrictions. Drugs in schedule 5 can be bought from a pharmacy without prescription but it is illegal to then give them to someone else. Contrasting heroin with cannabis shows how the Act works in practice. Cannabis is a class B, schedule 1 drug, whereas heroin is a class A, schedule 2 drug. Cannabis cannot be prescribed whereas heroin can be.
- Under the Act, the police can stop and search anyone whom they suspect of possessing a controlled drug.
- The Act established the Advisory Council on the Misuse of Drugs, whose central role is to advise the government on drugs which are 'likely to be misused'.

Responsibility for legislation controlling drugs was retained by Westminster under the settlements which devolved powers to the constituent countries of the UK.

In an amendment to the Act in 2011, the government introduced Temporary Class Drug Orders, which allow substances that are not already controlled to be restricted for up to 12 months. The purpose of this change is to allow time to review the risks posed by the flood of new psychoactive substances before deciding whether they should be permanently controlled. Manufacture or supply of a drug subject to an order is illegal but simple possession is not, although the police have the power to confiscate.

Completely unpredictable events changed the landscape again. Following the Iranian revolution in 1979, some refugees brought their wealth out in heroin. This heroin was smokeable, thus more attractive to a wider range of potential users, and the method of ingestion was thought by some to be unlikely to lead to dependence; they were sadly mistaken (Royal College of Psychiatrists and the Royal College of Physicians, 2000, p. 52; Yates, 2002). A ready supply then coincided with the economic upheavals which ended many of the old heavy industries in the UK and left pockets of deprivation where young people were trapped without prospects. Serious outbreaks of heroin use erupted in various cities, some primarily involving smoking and others injecting. As Edwards (2005, p. 101) says: 'Where there is a large population which is poor and powerless, drug epidemics often seem to take root rather easily.'

Then HIV arrived. The prime concern became the prevention of the spread of the virus from minority communities into the wider society. With urgency and commendable pragmatism, the Thatcher government adopted a harm reduction strategy. Encouraging people to come off drugs became secondary to reducing needle sharing and encouraging people into treatment where methadone could be substituted for street heroin. Looking back, it is hard to grasp just how radical this idea was, but it worked. HIV rates among injecting drug users in the UK have remained low (NAT, 2013). However services, both state run and voluntary, orientated their provision towards injectors at the expense of a wider constituency of problematic users whose needs were different. The legacy of the swing to harm reduction has been the polarised debates about what 'recovery' should mean (see Chapter 6).

As the twentieth century drew to a close there was an increase in the popularity of cocaine, a second wave of heroin use, a menu of dance drugs and the ever-present cannabis. Different drugs appealed to contrasting social groups, with little connection between Ibiza holiday makers and people living in areas of urban deprivation. At this point, the government began to develop a more coherent strategic approach which prioritised integrated planning at government level, partnership working locally and the delivery of more coordinated and comprehensive treatment responses (HM Government, 1998). Strategy documents have been updated on various occasions since and, following devolution, have become the responsibility of the individual governments of the UK. The emphasis may be different between the four countries but the central tenets remain the same. New Labour came into power in 1997 with crime reduction and community safety as a priority; drugs were first and foremost a criminal justice issue once more. Blank (2002, p. 219) makes the point that the response to HIV and to drug-related crime focused on the effects on others, not on the wellbeing of users themselves, just as threats to the war effort drove changes in 1916. This emphasis on reducing crime by concentrating resources on getting class A drug-using offenders into treatment led to criticisms that the system was becoming skewed with other people with drug problems being afforded low priority (the Royal Society for the Encouragement of Arts, Manufactures and Commerce, 2007, p. 117). The implications for children of parental substance problems were also firmly placed on the agenda (ACMD, 2003; Scottish Executive, 2003a). The creation in 2013 of Public Health England with overall responsibility for the development of services for people with drug problems appears to signal a move towards substance issues being viewed primarily as a health matter again, at least in one part of the UK.

By the end of the first decade of the twenty-first century services had become more integrated and waiting times had been reduced, but the big issue had become recovery. A belief that too many people had become 'parked on methadone' with few opportunities to reintegrate into society switched the focus onto what treatment should entail. Should recovery mean cessation from all drug use including prescribed substitutes? Harm reductionists and those whom Ashton (2008) has called the 'new abstentionists' engaged in rancorous debate whilst government strategies (HM Government, 2010; Scottish Government, 2008) attempted to lay out a more aspirational direction for services without losing the gains that substitute prescribing had brought. What this means for practice is explored in Chapter 6.

Can the UK's pragmatic prohibition, with its emphasis on treatment and public health wrapped up in restrictive legal controls, be judged a success? HIV rates have remained low, treatment services appear to have become increasingly effective (NTA, 2013a) and the great majority of the population do not use illicit substances. At the start of the second decade of the twenty-first century, there are signs of modest declines in illicit drug use, albeit with some variations between substances (Home Office, 2012b; Scottish Government, 2012). However, on the debit side, hepatitis C is a problem, people with drug problems become enmeshed in the criminal justice system, efforts by the police and border agencies to reduce supply are only partially successful and drugs deaths remain high. Rates of use are greater than in most European countries (EMCDDA, 2013b). Is this a reflection of the UK's drug policies? Interestingly Holland, with a harm reductionist policy, and Sweden, with an abstinence model, are considered to be at opposite ends of the spectrum. Both have significantly lower levels of illicit drug use than the UK (EMCDDA, 2013a). What is, perhaps, telling is that the income differential between rich and poor in both these countries is considerably less than in the UK (European Commission, 2013; Wilkinson and Pickett, 2010, p. 71). Could it be that addressing income inequalities would have a greater impact than drug strategies and legislation?

### The legalisation debate

Fear of being branded 'soft on drugs' by a sensationalist press has left most UK politicians reluctant to debate the effectiveness of current methods of control. Despite calls from credible national and international groups, such as Transform and the Global Commission on Drug Policy, to consider alternative approaches, few countries have been prepared to apply fresh thinking. A simplistic narrative has become established: the status quo may be far from perfect but the alternative is a drug free-for-all. This fails to acknowledge that those calling for change are not advocating that drugs should be available at the corner shop. Most reformers are under no illusions; change would not eliminate problems but it might lessen them. As Rolles (2009, p. 10) says, 'Prohibition cannot produce a drug free world; regulatory models cannot produce a harm free world.'

It is unfortunate that open debate seems impossible; if illicit drug use continues to fall somewhat, it seems even less likely that this will take place.

### Alternative models

Society already operates a system with gradations of availability for different substances. These range from outright prohibition to unrestricted supply, with access to drugs for medical purposes or regulation and licensing, as for alcohol and tobacco, in between. Control, where this is felt necessary, is achieved by addressing a series of variables. These can include:

- *Production*: Cultivation; importation; manufacture.
- *The product*: Potency; form/method of use (pill; liquid; injectability); price through taxation.
- *Packaging*: Tamper/child proofing; information about risks; branding on packaging.
- *Suppliers and outlets*: Advertising; licensing; siting/density of outlets.
- *The user*: Age restriction; licensing the user; preventing sale to intoxicated people; place of use. (Rolles, 2009)

Applying this framework, it is easy to construct possible systems for the regulation of substances on an individual basis determined by their potential levels of harm (see Box 4.4). Under such a system, it is likely that controls on alcohol and tobacco would increase.

### BOX 4.4 AN ALTERNATIVE MODEL FOR CANNABIS REGULATION

| Production | Licensed growers at home/abroad |
| --- | --- |
| | Processed by state company (no market incentives) |
| Product | Standardised potency |
| | Leaf and resin |

| | |
|---|---|
| | Standardised price and taxed |
| **Packaging** | Plain (state company, no branding) |
| | Information about risk |
| **Outlets** | Licensed and limited in number |
| | No advertising. |
| **User** | Aged 21 or over |
| | Illegal to use in a public place |

Under the model outlined in Box 4.4 consumption of cannabis might increase and more people might suffer health consequences; however, this is by no means uncertain. Strategies to address Internet sales would need to be implemented. However, the advantages would be that:

- fewer people would be drawn into the criminal justice system and it would reduce, although not eliminate, the black market;
- producers would benefit from being part of a legitimate trade;
- state company and standardised pricing would remove market pressures to increase sales. Tax could be set at levels high enough to dampen demand but low enough to discourage an illicit market;
- revenues could be channelled into treatment services.

Different levels of restriction would be available for drugs which carry higher risks. Rolles (2009, p. 160) suggests that heroin might only be available by prescription, whereas certain opiates in pill form might be obtainable from pharmacies by users with a personal licence.

Other countries have experimented with less radical initiatives within the context of current international agreements. These include the cannabis cafes in Holland, heroin prescribing, injecting rooms and decriminalisation for possession. When judging such initiatives, it is important to be clear about what they are trying to achieve and how they fit into wider packages of control measures.

ACTIVITY 4.2

**Alternative regulation of cocaine**
Using the framework outlined above:

- Design a system for regulating cocaine based on the risks it presents.
- Note which harms might reduce and which might increase under your system.

### Alcohol: eyes off the ball

From the First World War to the 1950s the UK enjoyed, if that is the right word, unprecedented low levels of alcohol consumption (Heather and Robertson, 1997, p. 11). The period since then has been characterised by relaxation of the licensing laws, a marked reduction in price relative to incomes, aggressive marketing, a shift in habits from public house to home drinking and the availability of very cheap alcohol in supermarkets. A culture supporting drinking as an everyday activity and tolerant of intoxication took root. Preoccupation with illicit drugs meant that little attention was paid to all this until the end of the millennium brought the stark realisation that increasing per capita consumption was being mirrored by very significant rises in alcohol-related mortality and health problems (Plant, 2009): an entirely predictable outcome of laissez fair policies. Ironically, legislation relaxing control on availability in England and Wales (Licensing Act 2003) was introduced after concerns had risen up the political agenda. The strategy at this point was representative of much of New Labour's thinking: the focus was on addressing antisocial behaviour following drinking and irresponsible retailers, not on the health harms to the wider population (Light, 2010). Scotland led the way in shifting the agenda from crime to public health (Scottish Government, 2009). Limits on promotions such as happy hours and 'three for the price of two' offers in off-sales were banned and legislation allowing a minimum unit price to be set was passed, although the alcohol producers and some wine-producing countries within the European Union have mounted a legal challenge to the latter. In 2013, the Westminster government shelved plans to introduce minimum unit pricing in England and Wales.

Alcohol is our most popular drug, the one we have chosen to help us relax, facilitate conviviality and lower the barriers of sexual inhibition. And yet we remain ambivalent about it. As a US politician (Sweat, 1952) once aptly put it:

> If when you say whiskey you mean the devil's brew, ... that defiles innocence, dethrones reason, destroys the home, creates misery and poverty ... then certainly I am against it. But, if when you say whiskey you mean the oil of conversation ... which enables a man to magnify his joy ... and to forget, if only for a little while, life's great tragedies ...; if you mean that drink, the sale of which pours into our treasuries untold millions of dollars ... to build highways and hospitals and schools, then certainly I am for it.

This ambivalence makes consistent policy making difficult, as does the fact that moderate consumption is relatively harm free. Abstentionist messages regarding smoking are simple; advising the public that drinking is safe if certain limits are adhered to and specific situations are avoided, is much more complicated. Alcohol policy swings between the belief that greater availability will lead to a mature respect for a dangerous product to the view that such accessibility will simply lead to increased demand. There is a growing consensus that alcohol should not be treated like any other product and that the liberalisation of restrictions and the normalisation of drinking which took in the latter part of the twentieth century have not led to the desired outcomes. This perceived failure of policy is leading to renewed interest in pricing (demand reduction) and availability (supply reduction) as the levers for reducing the harms.

**How do strategy and control impact on the individual?**

Liam (26) joined the army as a teenager partly to escape an unhappy family life. A drinking culture existed in his unit but the structures of military life contained this. Following disciplinary offences, Liam was discharged from the forces when he was 21. Homeless and already a heavy drinker, he began to use various drugs. He drifted round the country, eventually receiving a custodial sentence for theft. In prison he started to inject heroin. Back in the community, binge drinking and now dependent on heroin, he was again homeless and stealing regularly to survive. Following an overdose, he decided to seek help.

Assume that Liam lives in the country where you are based:

■ What legislation and which government strategy document cover Liam's use of heroin?
■ What legislation and which strategy document cover his use of alcohol?
■ What are the objectives of the legislation and the main themes in the strategies?

## Emerging challenges

Trends in substance use keep on shifting. In the second decade of the twentieth century, a new and unpredictable landscape has thrown up a number of questions:

■ Will reductions in illicit drug use continue?
■ Will polydrug use, with alcohol part of the mix, become the norm?
■ Will the increase in the non-medical use of prescription painkillers seen in the USA (Miech et al., 2013) filter across the Atlantic?
■ What impact will the recession and changes to state benefits have? In developed countries, alcohol consumption tends to drop among heavy drinkers during recessions (Pacula, 2011). By way of contrast, recessions can lead to a fall in the price of illicit drugs and an increase in their use (Bretteville-Jensen, 2011), although other factors, such as the impact of exclusion on certain groups, may also play a part. This is what occurred in the recession of the early Thatcher years, although the financial collapse of 2008 does not appear to have led to similar increases in drug use.
■ How best should new psychoactive substances and Internet sales be controlled?
■ What are the implications of so-called 'smart drugs', which enhance cognitive functioning?
■ Will smoking continue to decline and increasingly become a symbol of class-based health inequalities?
■ How should services respond to this changing scene?

## Concluding comments

History teaches us that there are no easy answers. Epidemics of use sometimes seem to rise and then wither whatever the authorities do. Our appreciation of the benefits of substances is offset by our awareness of the problems they bring; this makes us ambivalent and fuels our uncertainties regarding restriction and control. However, our success in reducing the harms related to smoking shows that much can be achieved when:

- objectives are clear and based on the evidence of risk;
- consistent policies are pursued over time;
- equal priority is given to control and enforcement, prevention and treatment.

### RESOURCES

- Edwards, G. (2005). *Matters of Substance. Drugs: Is Legalization the Right Answer – Or the Wrong Question?*
- Rolles, S. (2009). *After the War on Drugs: Blueprint for Regulation.*
- Release. Information about UK drug legislation is available on the Release website at: www.release.org.uk/drugs-legal-advice.
- Royal College of Psychiatrists and the Royal College of Physicians (2000). *Drugs: Dilemmas and Choices.*
- Acts of the Westminster and devolved parliaments, including drug, tobacco and licensing legislation, is available at: www.legislation.gov.uk.

# CHAPTER 5

# Why and How Do People Change?

- To be effective, interventions must be based on what we know about human change.
- Change can occur surreptitiously or it can involve considerable conscious struggle.
- For many people with problems, change occurs without formalised help.
- Motivation is a fundamental issue.
- The 'cycle of change', a model which describes how people progress through various stages, remains popular. It has, however, been subject to criticism.

## Behaviour change

Helping a person to move on from problematic substance use involves working with the grain of human change. To understand this, we must consider certain questions:

- What spurs people to alter their behaviour?
- How do people enact changes?
- How do people maintain new behaviours?

To try to answer these, we need to learn from the dynamics of naturally occurring change and then use interventions which reinforce these processes.

As practitioners we tend to view problematic substance use from the perspective of our clients, a skewed sample. We work with people who have presented for treatment having failed to utilise their own resources to resolve their difficulties; research cohorts are often obtained from the same source. In addition, there is an inclination to exaggerate the importance of formalised treatment in promoting change. Treatment can save lives and help facilitate change but this must be put in the context of a bigger picture. Many people change their substance-using behaviour without any formal help. Those that do approach services will have made efforts to resolve their difficulties before, sometimes with temporary success. They will try to maintain a changed direction after treatment has ended. Some will engage with services for quite long

**67**

periods and some only briefly, but for everyone treatment is a transitory interlude in a longer journey. What goes on away from treatment is as important as what happens during it.

## Unassisted recovery

In a world where celebrities go into expensive clinics and the authorities exhort people to seek help, it is easy to overlook those who resolve their difficulties without recourse to significant levels of treatment or indeed any formalised interventions at all (Peele, 1983). Numerous studies (cited by Sobell, Ellingstad and Sobell, 2000) suggest that 80–90 per cent of smokers recover through a process of unassisted change. In a study by Sobell, Cunningham and Sobell (1996), the great majority of people who had experienced alcohol problems had resolved their difficulties without formal treatment, either through abstaining or through altering use, although those who had used services were likely to have experienced more serious problems. In popular mythology, heroin use invariably leads to either lengthy interventions or death; however, in reality it, too, has its share of the 'recovered without treatment' (Waldorf and Biernacki, 2008). However, as with alcohol problems, unassisted change is more likely to occur when a person's dependence is at a lower level and his social supports remain intact (ACMD, 2012).

---

CASE ILLUSTRATION 5.1

**Olly and the unanswered questions**

Olly's sister, a single parent, approached the service I was working for saying something had to be done about her brother. Having lost his job, he had moved in with her. She said his drinking set a bad example to her children and that she was finding his presence stressful. He left the house only to buy alcohol, spending much of his time watching television. He consumed around 30 units every day and was obviously physically dependent. He was polite but made it clear to me that he had little interest in discussing his drinking. He did say that he, too, was unhappy with the living arrangements and so I obtained forms for him to apply for social housing. After a few visits, we agreed that I had no further role.

Some months later, staff at the local hospital contacted me to say that Olly would appreciate a visit. I found him in good spirits. The hospital had detoxed him prior to emergency surgery for stomach problems and he hoped that I might chase up his housing application. This I did and, as luck would have it, he was able to move straight into a flat. I helped him to obtain furniture and he set about decorating his home. He also started to volunteer at a community centre. I visited Olly from time to time. He enjoyed a chat but never intimated that he wanted a therapeutic relationship. No relapse occurred and, when we decided to part company, he had been abstinent for nine months. The sum of the interventions was one detox and some practical help. I would love to know:

- What motivated Olly to change?
- Did he experience some kind of epiphany in his hospital bed or had he ruminated on the possibility of changing as he sat watching television? Had he a plan and was he waiting for an opportunity?
- What prevented him from slipping back into his old habits?

Change can occur slowly or quickly. It can happen as part of maturation processes or be triggered by changes in the environment; it can occur seemingly without planning or be the result of a carefully devised strategy.

### Maturation processes

The implications of ageing are central to any substance-using career and the phrase 'maturing out' is used to describe one of the processes through which use, problematic or otherwise, declines. At the population level, use of illicit drugs wanes as people reach their later twenties (Home Office, 2012b). The situation is more complex in respect of alcohol (Health and Social Care Information Centre, 2013a). Binge drinking tends to be highest among young adults but middle-aged people are the group most likely to consume above weekly limits. Consumption drops among older people.

As well as physical and psychological changes, ageing brings changing interests, different relationships, a reduction in risk taking and an awareness of mortality. Even some people with serious difficulties do appear to simply grow out of use. However, sometimes change occurs in a more dramatic fashion.

### Spontaneous and planned change

A colleague of mine was married to a renowned folk singer who had experienced serious difficulties with alcohol; she said that one day he simply stopped drinking without warning. A close friend describes how he planned to give up a 30-a-day cigarette habit by setting a date and then steeling himself for action. These provide different examples of how untreated change can occur. Ryder et al. (2001) argue that change is never wholly spontaneous but rather the culmination of shifts in the way people regard their substance taking. This is likely to be the case even when people undergo 'road to Damascus' experiences or take seeming spur-of-the-moment decisions. Peele (1983) uses Vaillant's metaphor of an egg to describe apparent spontaneous change. The chick may suddenly burst into the world but plenty was happening before that event. On one level, this tipping of the balance towards change can be explained by operant conditioning: the punishments linked to substance use have begun to outweigh the rewards. This does not, however, fully explain the more conscious calculations that often precede deliberate planning for change which social learning theory can make sense of (see Chapter 3). A negative experience of substance taking or a reappraisal of the risks can lead to a restructuring of the cognitive framework through which a person explains his substance taking to himself. The emergence of new perspectives that challenge previously held assumptions becomes a precursor to change. This process can cause cognitive dissonance, that uncomfortable state of mind where we find ourselves wrestling with two conflicting ideas or a discrepancy between our self-image and our behaviour (Festinger, 1957). To reduce this psychological discomfort, we will either defend our dearly held beliefs and maintain long-standing behaviours (the conservative impulse) or we set about changing them.

CASE ILLUSTRATION 5.2

**Resolving cognitive dissonance**

Kevin takes a variety of drugs but sees himself as very different from acquaintances who inject heroin. His self-image is of a person who takes 'softer' drugs socially. He tries heroin, likes it and finds that he is using quite regularly. He wakes one morning with the stark and uneasy realisation that either he has to stop using or he can no longer deny to himself that he is not 'one of them'. To reduce cognitive dissonance, he is being forced to choose.

## Motivation and ambivalence

Motivation, the desire to pursue goals through action, operates at various levels. At a basic level, the innate instinct to survive and maintain the species motivates people to eat, sleep and procreate. Such drives tend to remain stable. Physical dependence can create such stability too, with the person consistently prioritising substance taking to ward off withdrawals. At another level, motivation is unstable. One minute we convince ourselves that change is desirable, at the next we hesitate. We take steps to do things differently only to slide back into old ways. In our minds, the balance between the rewards of changing and the security of staying the same seesaws. We reduce cognitive dissonance by committing ourselves to action only to remember how much we enjoyed what we have just stopped doing. These fluctuations are summed up in one word: ambivalence. Ambivalence towards change is normal but it undermines motivation. We all experience it when facing major decisions. It is the reason why the course of change rarely flows in a straight direction. Change holds the promise of benefits but it is a step into the unknown which involves loss; it elicits our conservative impulses.

Understanding that ambivalence towards change is normal helps to make sense of the apparent reluctance of people with substance problems to act in ways which, to the observer, seem to be patently in their best interests. Change may bring better health, the promise of a job and avoidance of trouble with the law but it can also mean losing friends and good times. The rewards for altering are often longer term and motivation to change is easily compromised by the prospect of immediate positive reinforcement. A smoker may worry about potential health problems but the instantaneous rewards a cigarette brings take precedence. For some, change will mean the anxiety-provoking prospect of dealing with withdrawals. Where a person's identity is firmly bound up with a drug-using lifestyle, then a change in direction will entail a profound shift in his sense of self. It is little wonder that people vacillate at the door of change.

Helping people resolve such ambivalence as a precursor to change has led to the development of a key intervention, motivational interviewing (see Chapter 8).

## BOX 5.1 SELF-EFFICACY: A CRITICAL COMPONENT

Wanting to change is the starting point. Taking action to alter behaviour and then maintaining the new direction require motivation to be sustained. Bandura's work on self-efficacy, an individual's assessment as to whether he can carry through an enterprise successfully, is important here. Bandura (1998) argues that self-efficacy is strengthened when a person:

- demonstrates to himself that he can master demanding, rather than readily accomplished, tasks;
- receives realistic encouragement;
- acts to reduce any negative effects of emotional reactions to the challenge (for example, fear);
- sees others, particularly respected peers, successfully completing the activity in question.

People who approach services have attempted to change their substance use themselves without success and their self-efficacy is low. Many see themselves as failures in other areas of their lives. Strengthening self-efficacy is an essential element of therapeutic work. In addition, involvement in Alcoholics or Narcotics Anonymous, recovery groups or user involvement activities can provide people with role models who have put their own problematic use behind them.

## Triggers and the maintenance of change

Research has identified factors which can activate change (Blomqvist, 2002; Cloud and Granfield, 1994, p. 26; McIntosh and McKeganey, 2002; Saunders and Kershaw, 1979; Sobell et al., 2000; Stall and Biernacki, 1986). These may slowly enter a person's consciousness or they may precipitate a crisis. They can occur within the individual (intrapersonal), between the person and others (interpersonal) or in the person's wider environment (extrapersonal) (see Box 5.2).

## BOX 5.2 FACTORS PRECIPITATING CHANGE

| *Intrapersonal* | *Interpersonal* | *Extrapersonal* |
|---|---|---|
| Health concerns | Family issues | Legal problems |
| Religious motives | Social/relationship factors | Employment difficulties |
| Shifts in how substance | Marriage | Lifestyle changes |
| use is viewed | Fear of losing children | Alterations to living |
| Fears about consequences | | situation |
| Awareness of detrimental | | Financial problems |
| effects on other people | | |
| Embarrassment/traumatic | | |
| events | | |
| Negative self-image | | |
| Stigma | | |
| Desire for self control | | |
| Pregnancy | | |

### Sustaining change

Initial gains need to be maintained if fuller recovery is to occur. Some of the factors which precipitated initial action, outlined in Box 5.2, continue to be relevant. However, these shift from causing anxiety about use to positively reinforcing changed behaviour. Better health and improvements in employment and financial circumstances are all cited. Particularly important are supportive families or social groupings. For some, major changes in lifestyle or living situation are necessary; people may reject their substance-using networks completely and some move away (Blomqvist, 2002; Cloud and Granfield, 1994; Sobell et al., 2000). Interestingly, in a cohort researched by Cloud and Granfield (2001), it was those who had used illicit drugs, rather than people who had experienced alcohol problems, who went as far as relocating physically. Perhaps this is because those with alcohol problems have no choice but to deal with its ready availability wherever they are. For many, developing other interests becomes essential. Religion becomes important for some. The need to learn ways to prevent relapse, such as how to refuse substances and how to deal with cravings, also comes into the picture (see Chapter 12).

Two overarching and interlinked challenges face people struggling to put problematic substance use behind them: the necessity of building, and effectively utilising, 'recovery capital', and the need to re-establish positive self-regard through acquiring a non-using identity.

ACTIVITY 5.1

**Personal experience of change**
Consider a major change that has, at some point, taken place in your own behaviour or lifestyle:

- Did you plan this or did it occur without much apparent forethought?
- What intrapersonal, interpersonal and extrapersonal factors precipitated the change?
- Can the cycle of change (see below) be applied to your experience of how the change occurred?

### Recovery capital

A person's 'recovery capital' is the sum of his internal attributes and the resources in his environment which positively support change. Many of these have been outlined above. They can be divided into human capital (good health; self-efficacy; positive outlook and the like), physical capital (access to suitable accommodation; availability of constructive activities/employment; adequate income) and social capital (the support available from others; constructive relationships; learning from role models) (Cloud and Granfield, 2001). These elements are entwined. Human capital can be eroded by a lack of access to the basic physical requirements for living; conversely, strong personal assets make it more likely that a person will be able to find and keep a job or sustain relationships which support recovery. It is self-evident that recovery capital will vary greatly from individual to individual, with people living in situations of social disadvantage having less confidence to draw on the limited resources available in their environments. How often do practitioners see a person returning after a successful stay in a residential rehab to his old accommodation in a rundown estate where his substance-using friends are still living? Unless people are helped to both build and utilise recovery capital, the chances of maintaining change are lessened. The challenge for services is to address this wider frame of reference alongside specific interventions facilitating initial change.

### Re-establishing positive identities

McIntosh and McKeganey (2002) suggest that shifts in how people see themselves differentiate successful attempts to change from previous failed efforts. These authors use Goffman's concept of 'spoiled identity', a loss of self-respect in their own and other people's eyes, to describe how many of their cohort viewed themselves. The factors outlined above that can precipitate change were not enough on their own to lead to sustained recovery but, in McIntosh and McKenganey's words, 'acted as mirror to the self' (p. 51). Cognitive dissonance occurs as a person compares how he sees himself in the present with what he once was or would like to become. The feelings of dissatisfaction engendered then act as the catalyst for taking steps to build a new identity as a non-user. Kearney and O'Sullivan (cited by West, 2006, p. 72) suggest that a feedback loop may be established whereby small changes in behaviour lead to improvements in self-image; these, in turn, encourage the person to persist with the new behaviour. Building a new identity is achieved in different ways. Some choose to 'come out' as recovered or recovering and join self-help groups along with people in the same situation. Others prefer to build a new self-image which makes no reference to a substance-using past. Hecksher (2001) refers to Giddens' ideas when suggesting that the option taken, whether presenting oneself as an 'ex-addict' or maintaining a persona in which substance use is not the defining feature, can be explained by personal identity being the 'narrative' of how we make sense of ourselves.

It is worth noting that stigma is central to the notion of spoiled identity and this is socially mediated. McIntosh and McKeganey's group had been, in the main, opiate users, people about whom society has particularly negative feelings. The expense and illegality of opiate use increases the likelihood that users will act in ways which cause shame. This contrasts with smokers. Because smoking is not associated with problematic behaviour and because of its social acceptability, at least until the turn of the millennium, dependence on nicotine is less likely to invoke feelings of spoiled identity. The implications of stigma are complex. It can discourage people from using in the first place or it may reinforce a desire in people with problems to stop. Conversely, stigma stereotypes and isolates people, erodes self-efficacy and, through discrimination, erects barriers which prevent people from accessing physical capital such as employment or accommodation. Whilst accepting that moral pressure against smoking reduces consumption, Stuber, Galea and Link (2009) suggest that stigmatisation can have both positive and adverse consequences for existing smokers. Growing negative attitudes towards smoking will provide a rich field for research into the consequences of stigmatisation. From a policy perspective, stigmatising certain substance-using behaviours, but not the people involved, might be the desirable approach, a balance impossible to strike in the real world.

## BOX 5.3 WHY DO SOME PEOPLE AVOID TREATMENT SERVICES?

As has been noted, people modify their identities in various ways when moving away from problematic use. Major adjustments may be less necessary if a person has continued to maintain a sense of normality in terms of relationships, employment and the like, despite his substance use. How others view the situation is also important. In their study of middle-class people who had recovered without treatment, Cloud and Granfield (1994) found that the individuals concerned shunned the identity of 'addict', often hiding their previous substance use from the new social groupings they engaged with as they rebuilt their lives. This is a classic example of the avoidance of the role of secondary deviant (see Chapter 3); these people did not want their lives to be defined by one particular problematic behaviour. This cohort disliked self-help groups which held to the view that addiction is a life-long condition. In their meta-analysis of studies into natural recovery, Sobell et al. (2000) also note that a desire to avoid labelling was a factor behind a reluctance to engage with treatment. Other considerations included being unwilling to forego privacy, having poor opinions of treatment and believing that the problem was not serious enough to merit formal interventions.

## The cycle of change

The cycle of change (transtheoretical model) has been so influential that it has become, to a degree, accepted wisdom. Prochaska and DiClemente (DiClemente, 2005; Prochaska, DiClemente and Norcross, 1992) originally developed their ideas from work with smokers. Their model suggests that change involves people progressing through six distinct stages:

1 Precontemplation: the person either does not consider that he has a problem or has no immediate intention of addressing it.
2 Contemplation: the contemplator has yet to take action but has begun to give serious consideration to the need to do so. Ambivalence is the hallmark of people in this stage.
3 Preparation: the person has committed himself to the idea that action is necessary and is formulating a plan.
4 Action: the person alters his substance-using behaviour in significant ways and makes environmental and other changes that support this.
5 Maintenance: this is not a static phase but one where the person acts to sustain the changes made and to avoid relapse.
6 Relapse: a return to the previous behaviour.

The authors of the model abandoned their early notion that progression is linear, except in a very small number of cases. To accommodate relapse, they have represented the model visually as both a circle (see Figure 5.1) and a spiral. The relapser returns to an earlier stage, as often as not the precontemplation or contemplation modes. DiClemente (2005) stresses that relapse is not failure: many experience it and it should act as a spur to review what went wrong. He calls repetition of the process 'recycling'; this can occur a number of times before sustained change is achieved.

The model also includes 'processes'. These are the drivers which both motivate and facilitate movement through the stages:

■ Consciousness raising: through experience and knowledge, the person becomes increasingly aware of the nature of his difficulties.
■ Dramatic relief: the person articulates feelings about his problems.
■ Environmental re-evaluation: the person becomes more aware of the implications of his circumstances on his environment and those around him.
■ Self re-evaluation: the person appraises his situation in the context of his identity and values.
■ Self-liberation: with a commitment to take action, the person's self-efficacy is strengthened.
■ Reinforcement management: the person consciously rewards himself, or accepts positive reinforcement from others, for progress made.
■ Helping relationships: the person utilises supportive relationships.
■ Counter-conditioning: the person actively adopts strategies to neutralise the unwanted behaviour. Examples of this are learning relaxation techniques or ways of dealing with cravings.

- Stimulus control: by defining the circumstance in which risks increase, the person can learn avoidance techniques, refusal skills or rearrange his living situation to support changed behaviour.

It is suggested that the processes come into play at different stages in the cycle. Consciousness raising, dramatic relief and environmental re-evaluation are prevalent during the precontemplation and contemplation stages whilst reinforcement management, helping relationships, counter-conditioning and stimulus control tend to come to the fore during action and maintenance.

For practitioners, the cycle of change provides a relatively simple framework. It lays out the phases which people appear to pass through as they struggle to alter their behaviour and, by outlining what they may be experiencing during these phases (the processes), gives pointers as to what engagement with the person should focus on at any given point.

Criticism has been levelled at the cycle of change (Davidson, 2002; West, 2006). The idea that people move through discrete stages in a neat, sequential way has been questioned. Some people make radical changes without appearing to pass through the preparatory stages. It has also been suggested that helping a person to move from, say, contemplation to preparation is

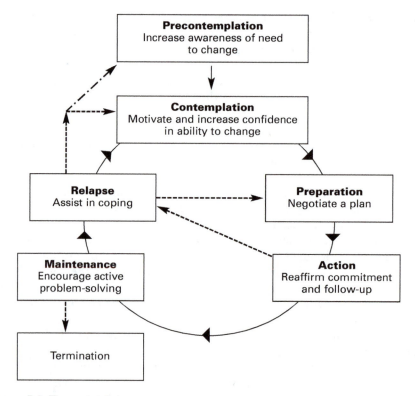

**Figure 5.1** The cycle of change

*Source:* DiClemente, C. (reproduced with permission)

not necessarily valuable in itself as no actual behaviour change has taken place. Indeed, basing the approach on this whole notion may postpone the point at which interventions more directly aimed at fostering action are offered.

Despite the criticisms, the popularity of the cycle of change suggests that it does strike a chord with practitioners and service users alike. Whilst its limitations indicate that rigid application should be avoided, it does provide a common-sense framework which brings together a number of key themes: motivation, ambivalence and commitment to change. It outlines factors which need to be addressed if change is to occur and be sustained. In addition, Prochaska and DiClemente's work is important historically. It underscored the normality of relapse and the importance of viewing this as an opportunity to address the issues again rather than a catastrophe. The normality of relapse has led to serious problematic use of substances being described as a 'chronic relapsing condition'; whilst true to a significant degree, this somewhat pessimistic mantra is one which the recovery movement is attempting to rewrite.

---

**ACTIVITY 5.2**

**The cycle of change**
Consider an aspect of your life which you would like to change.

- Where would you place yourself on the cycle of change?
- What do you need to do to make the change happen?
- What would help you maintain the change after it has occurred?

---

## Concluding comments

Interventions are effective when they nudge the processes of human change forward. Practitioners, therefore, should:

- help the person identify factors in his life which might trigger change and use these to strengthen motivation;
- view cognitive dissonance and ambivalence towards change as normal and work with these;
- capitalise if a crisis occurs;
- try to strengthen the person's self-efficacy;
- help the person to build his recovery capital;
- support the development of a new identity.

---

**RESOURCES**

- Cloud, W. and Granfield, R. (2001). 'Natural recovery from substance dependency: lessons for treatment providers'. *Journal of Social Work Practice in the Addictions*, 1 (1), 83–104.

- Connors, G., DiClemente, C., Valasquez, M. and Donovan, D. (2013). *Substance Abuse Treatment and the Stages of Change* (2nd edition).
- McIntosh, J. and McKeganey, N. (2002). *Beating the Dragon: The Recovery from Dependent Drug Use.*
- Prochaska, J., DiClemente, C. and Norcross, J. (1992). 'In search of how people change: applications to addictive behaviors'. *American Psychologist*, 47 (9), 1102–14.

# PART II

# Interventions in Practice

# Effective Interventions, Competent Practitioners, Successful Services

## KEY THEMES

- A range of indicators is used to evaluate whether interventions are effective.
- Research demonstrates that motivational interviewing, cognitive behavioural therapy, pharmacotherapy, relapse prevention and 12-step approaches can be effective, but not with everyone.
- A combination of interventions is more likely to lead to a positive outcome than one on its own.
- Controlled drinking and how recovery from drug problems should be defined remain controversial issues.
- Practitioner attributes and skills are factors in successful outcomes.
- What makes a good service is a somewhat neglected topic.

## What makes the difference?

I received Kayleigh's referral from a concerned health visitor. She was aged 20, a single parent with a three-year-old son, Ryan, and had been injecting heroin for two years. Along with a childcare social worker and a nurse from the substance problems clinic, I worked with her until I changed jobs two years later. During this time, Kayleigh was detoxed in the community but quickly relapsed. She was then stabilised on methadone and, after achieving abstinence following a slow reduction regime, was prescribed the opiate blocker naltrexone; she stopped taking this and again relapsed. At that point, Ryan was taken into care for a short period. I used motivational interviewing and relapse prevention techniques as the situation demanded, along with providing practical support. When I moved, Kayleigh was on a waiting list for residential rehab. Six years later, I met her in the street; she was pushing a pram. She had moved, married and obtained a part-time job; Ryan was doing well at school. She told me that residential rehab was not for her and, missing Ryan, she left early. Eventually she settled for methadone on a maintenance basis and, after three years, felt ready to slowly reduce. This time it all came together; she came off methadone and was now drug free.

What worked for Kayleigh? It would be tempting to suggest that time-limited methadone, motivational interviewing, relapse prevention and rehab all failed and that methadone maintenance was the answer. However, would maintenance have paid off at an earlier point or would she have continued to use on top? Did trial and error help her find what worked for her, with the cumulative effect of various interventions building a platform for a lasting solution? Perhaps maturation and external events, such as moving and a new relationship, were the overriding factors.

The effectiveness of individual interventions is often difficult to pin down. Kayleigh's case demonstrates again that dealing with a substance problem is often a journey, not an event. It underscores the need to judge outcomes on indicators additional to improvements in substance use; for Kayleigh, these included being able to provide more stable mothering, gaining employment and entering a secure relationship.

## How do we measure success?

The impact of interventions should be judged against three overarching outcomes:

- **Substance use:** safer consumption; reduced frequency of use; decreased consumption; abstinence.
- **Health:** improvements in physical health and psychological wellbeing.
- **Social functioning:** improved relationships; reduced offending; obtaining/maintaining employment; living in settled accommodation; reduced impact on relatives including children. (Gossop, 2006; Raistrick, Heather and Godfrey, 2006)

This holistic approach to effectiveness is important. Abstinence without health or social benefits leaves a person with an impoverished life. Surprisingly, what substance use outcomes are desirable remains the subject of disagreement, as we shall see when we consider the debates about controlled drinking and recovery.

### Gathering the evidence

Randomised controlled trials and meta-analyses have been used to draw conclusions about what works. However, the limitations of the methods used need to be taken in account:

- Most research is undertaken with treatment populations and these are unrepresentative of people with substance problems as a whole.
- Follow-up is often limited to relatively short periods, when recovery from problematic use may take a long time.
- Some interventions are more difficult to research than others. For example, each residential rehab is unique and therefore standardisation of treatment is not feasible.

- Recovery groups, self-selected and with fluid membership, present obvious challenges to researchers.
- In the best trials, resources are plentiful, caseloads are small and practitioners are highly trained. It is difficult to replicate such quality in everyday work.
- Much of the research has been undertaken in the USA, which raises the question of cross-culture applicability.
- The voice of the user is rarely heard.

Over and above such difficulties sit the issues of belief and principle which cannot be resolved by research (Ashton, 2012a). If a person maintains that methadone simply reinforces a drug habit, no amount of data demonstrating that it reduces crime and improves health is likely to persuade him of its value. In policy terms – and policy shapes what services are available – evidence is only one element. Political priorities and what politicians consider will be acceptable to their constituents come into play.

## Controversies, controversies

### Controlled drinking

In the mid twentieth century, the disease model was the dominant paradigm. For alcoholics, a return to harm-free drinking was considered impossible and the goal of treatment was invariably abstinence. D. L. Davies, a psychiatrist, followed up a group of dependent drinkers he had treated and wrote a paper in 1962 which noted that a small number, less than ten per cent, had returned to harm-free drinking. The furore that this caused was repeated when a major American study in the early 1970s (the Rand Report) again presented evidence that some people treated for alcoholism seemed able to return to normal drinking. The controversy reached its peak in 1982 when two researchers in the USA, Mark and Linda Sobell, were investigated, and exonerated, on charges of falsifying the results of research they had undertaken into the outcomes of a controlled drinking trial (Heather and Robertson, 1997). By then, some services in the UK were offering controlled drinking programmes.

The acrimony that surrounded this debate reflects two fundamentally different views of the nature of dependence on alcohol. Those who believed that alcoholism is a progressive disease rejected the findings of such studies, sometimes suggesting that the people who returned to harm-free drinking were not true 'alcoholics' (Heather and Robertson, 1981, p. 24). Behaviourists, on the other hand, expressed little surprise, arguing that if harmful drinking is learned it can be unlearned, at least by some people. This division remains today. Some services, along with Alcoholics Anonymous, are wedded to the view that abstinence is the only goal, whilst other services offer controlled drinking programmes as well as abstinence-orientated interventions. It is essential to stress that those who support controlled drinking as a legitimate treatment goal do not advocate it for everyone. Abstinence remains the desirable aim for those with more severe difficulties (see Chapters 7 and 11).

**Recovery wars**

In the early years of the millennium, a similarly acrimonious debate taxed the drugs field. White (2011) has divided this into two closely related controversies:

- Harm reduction versus abstinence.
- Whether 'recovery' can include those maintained on methadone or other pharmacotherapies.

Concerns about the health of the wider public drove the response to HIV, while New Labour's crime reduction agenda shaped that government's drug policies. Coaxing people into treatment and encouraging them to stay there for the greater public good took precedence; substitute prescribing, primarily methadone, supported these objectives. Less attention was given to helping people to 'recover', that is to say reintegrate into mainstream society. Whilst this criticism was undoubtedly valid, two opposing narratives emerged. Critics of harm reduction have tended to imply that it sanctions drug use and that policies have allowed people to become 'parked on methadone' with little hope of fuller rehabilitation. Supporters highlight evidence that harm reduction saves lives and reduces health and social harms. What recovery should mean became hotly debated. Wardle (2012) argues that harm reduction was still the main driver of drug treatment policy at the end of 2005 but by 2008 it had been swept aside and recovery had taken its place. As agencies rushed to rewrite their publicity documents to incorporate the new buzzword, it became increasingly clear that there was little consensus around what the emerging paradigm should mean in practice. Should recovery imply being drug free? Does drug free mean using no substances at all, even if some are causing the person little harm? Can a person who is functioning well on a prescribed substitute be considered to have recovered? In attempts to resolve these dilemmas, various definitions of recovery have been suggested such as:

- 'The process of recovery from problematic substance use is characterised by voluntary sustained control over substance use which maximises health and wellbeing and participation in the rights, roles and responsibilities of society.' (UK Drug Policy Commission, 2008, p. 6)
- '... a process through which an individual is enabled to move on from their problem drug use, towards a drug-free life as an active and contributing member of society. ... recovery is most effective when the service users' needs and aspirations are placed at the centre of their care and treatment.' (Scottish Government, 2008, p. 23)

What unites such definitions is a person-centred, forward-looking ethos which lays out an aspiration for people with drug problems to reintegrate as fully functioning members of society. Perhaps recovery should just mean 'wellbeing'. Such broad-brush definitions have not, however, united the field behind a single vision. Two distinct models sitting, somewhat uncomfortably, side by side have emerged:

1 The first might be characterised as 'hard recovery'. In this version, recovery means adding links to the existing chain of service provision. For people to recover, the practical building blocks must all be in place. Upstream activities, such as ensuring that accommodation is available, opening the doors to employment and helping a person to build social capital, must be added to harm reduction, stabilisation and therapeutic interventions.

2 What might be termed 'soft recovery' is a more radical but, as yet, untested vision. Formal services, while being required, become subservient to a peer-led movement involving mutual aid groups, recovery champions, recovery events and online communities. Recovery is said to be 'contagious' (Best, 2010); it thrives in neighbourhoods and not in the clinic. In short, it is a social phenomenon with parallels to empowerment movements such as Gay Pride.

These different perspectives are not mutually exclusive. Formal interventions can address issues which mutual aid groups cannot and the latter can provide the longer term peer support which is beyond the scope of mainstream services. A visible recovery movement can also help to challenge stigma. However, as of 2013, the volatility of the landscape is throwing up concerns:

- Opposition to substitute prescribing continues within some recovery thinking. This has led to certain mainstream services only using substitute prescribing as a short-term prelude to complete abstinence. Fears have been expressed that a 'methadone fits all' model is being supplanted in places by an 'abstinence fits all' model, with the risk that a return to illicit use beckons for those who are not ready (Drink and Drug News, 2011).
- The soft recovery paradigm is about addiction; it has little to offer those whose substance problems are not of that nature. In addition, mutual aid fellowships do not appeal to everyone, as the history of Alcoholics Anonymous demonstrates.
- A model which appears to support a speedier transition from formal treatment to cost-free self-help groups is bound to be attractive politically whether or not it is in the interests of all who have experienced problems.

The continuing growth of a vibrant self-help movement will extend the options and facilitate reintegration, but not if it is at the expense of evidence-based methods of promoting change.

---

**ACTIVITY 6.1**

**More definitions**

In not more than one sentence each, how would you define:

- harm reduction?
- recovery?

## Interventions

### What do we know about effective interventions?

Four broad principles emerge from the research:

- A number of interventions are known to work but these do not work with everyone.
- No single intervention stands out as being the most effective.
- A combination of interventions is likely to be more effective than one on its own.
- A positive therapeutic alliance between the service user and the practitioner will increase the likelihood of positive outcomes. (Gossop, 2006; Raistrick, Heather and Godfrey, 2006)

### Predicting outcomes

It is known that particular service user characteristics are linked to poorer outcomes. These include mental health problems, higher levels of dependence, limited social supports and a general lack of recovery capital (Best, 2010, p. 12; Gossop, 2006, p. 4). However, all practitioners will have experience of unpromising cases which turned out well, and service users, the outlook for whom appeared to be optimistic, who struggled to make progress. Predicting outcomes at the individual level is only helpful in so far as it can act as a guide to the intensity of interventions needed and range of services required.

### The main interventions

What follows is a summary of the interventions which research identifies as being the most effective. With some variations, they are applicable to all substances. How they are applied in practice is addressed in future chapters.

The Mesa Grande (Miller and Wilbourne, 2002), a meta-analysis of alcohol studies, and major reviews of alcohol treatments (Raistrick, Heather and Godfrey, 2006) and drug interventions (Carroll and Onken, 2005; Dutra et al., 2008; Gossop, 2006) identify the following as the key approaches:

- **Less intensive interventions.** Short-term inputs provided by specialist practitioners for people with lower levels of dependence can be effective; however, this level of engagement may be insufficient where problems are more deeply engrained. **Brief interventions** differ from less intensive interventions. These are very short, opportunistic sessions, undertaken primarily by non-specialist staff in a variety of settings, aimed at encouraging people at risk to reduce their consumption.
- **Motivational interviewing.** The purpose of this style of interviewing is to help the person to resolve ambivalence and enhance her motivation to change.
- **Pharmacotherapy.** Drugs can be used for various purposes including detoxification, substitution and craving reduction.

- **Cognitive behavioural therapy** (CBT). CBT covers a range of approaches which focus on changing unhelpful patterns of thought, altering behaviours and utilising positive reinforcements in the community. CBT is one of the main methods used to help people avoid, or deal with, relapse. **Relapse prevention** is sometimes categorised as an intervention in its own right. Interestingly, NICE (2007a, p. 17) does not recommend the routine use of CBT for people with drug problems, but the weight of evidence in favour (Carroll and Onken, 2005; Dutra et al., 2008) suggests that this should be reviewed.
- **12-step approaches.** Based on the disease model of addiction, the 12 steps are at the core of Alcoholics Anonymous and its sister fellowships. Alcoholics Anonymous rates poorly in the Mesa Grande but this has been questioned because the studies involved were limited to samples required to attend under court orders (Raistrick, Heather and Godfrey, 2006, p. 140). Some residential rehabs in the UK base their programmes on the model but 12-step therapies are rarely delivered on an individual basis in the UK.
- **Family work.** Relatives may be involved in two different ways, although these can overlap. Firstly, family members can be helped to cope with the practical and psychological difficulties which being close to a person with substance problems brings. Secondly, involving family members directly in the treatment of the person experiencing difficulties improves outcomes (Evans, 2010).

What will strike the reader is that different theories underpin some of the interventions which are found to be effective. This has led researchers to consider what commonalities link apparently contrasting treatments. The question changes from 'What works?' to 'What are the essential elements common to interventions which we know achieve better outcomes?' For example, it can be argued that what happens at AA meetings is grounded in behaviourism and that relapse prevention involves helping a person to identify risk situations and learn skills to deal with these, under whatever treatment banner it is located. Pycroft (2010, p. 107) suggests that what unites effective interventions is that they embody the 'core processes of change' (see Chapter 5). He notes, too, that the interventions chosen must make sense to the practitioner and the person with the problems alike. There is also growing interest in why some practitioners consistently achieve better outcomes than others, whatever intervention is used.

The reader will have noticed that insight-based psychoanalytical therapies are not numbered among effective interventions. The evidence does not support such approaches on their own for alcohol problems; however, the picture regarding people with heroin problems is less clear (McMurran, 1994, p. 126; Miller and Wilbourne, 2002). Platt, Husband and Taube (1990–91) suggest that the addition of psychoanalytical therapies to primary interventions for heroin users, such as substitute prescribing, may bring benefits. Psychoanalytical methods may help people resolve underlying difficulties which support their continuing use but it seems likely that these need to be combined with interventions dealing directly with the substance-using behaviour.

## BOX 6.1  DOES METHADONE WORK?

The controversies surrounding methadone led the National Treatment Agency for Substance Misuse (NTA) to commission an expert group to consider the place of opioid substitution treatment (OST) within a recovery model. In the UK, OST is methadone and, to a lesser degree, buprenorphine (Subutex). Reviewing the evidence (NTA, 2012a), the group concluded that people on OST:

- are more likely to remain in treatment;
- reduce their use of illicit heroin;
- are less prone to contracting blood-borne viruses;
- are less likely to experience overdose;
- commit less crime.

In addition, restricting OST to arbitrary time limits leads to poorer outcomes and increases the risks of the harms associated with a return to illicit consumption. OST offers opiate users an immediate, tangible option. This may partly explain why more drug users are in treatment than people with alcohol problems, despite the latter being a much larger group (NTA, 2012c).

The expert group also considered the limitations of OST. OST reduces heroin consumption but it does not impact significantly on the use of other substances. There is little information as to whether OST facilitates social inclusion. The group underlined the dangers of using other substances on top of substitutes and the heightened risk of death at the time of starting and ending OST. Also noted was the evidence that OST may not lead to people coming off the substitute itself. The relevance of the latter depends on whether abstinence from substitutes is considered an important outcome. Interestingly, William White, a champion of the recovery movement in the USA, dropped his original hostility towards methadone maintenance through contact with people who had reorientated their lives through its long-term use. For White (Bamber and White, 2011), 'recovery orientated methadone maintenance' is characterised by 'optimum dose stabilisation, remission of all substance use disorders and movement towards global health and community reintegration'.

The NTA expert group stressed that OST is insufficient on its own and best practice should involve:

- optimal prescribing levels;
- additional psychosocial interventions;
- interventions to address mental health difficulties;
- active support to help reintegration, including finding employment and engaging with community-based recovery activities including 12-step groups;
- supporting a person's desire to come off OST when she feels ready and her recovery capital is sufficient to support complete abstinence.

Opioid substitution treatment brings a number of benefits. The question, therefore, is not whether methadone and other substitutes work (that debate should now end) but how they can best be used to support a person to build a new life.

### Is matching the way forward?

As awareness grew that no single treatment could be identified as being the most effective, interest increased in the idea of 'matching'. Could it be demonstrated that people with certain characteristics, such as level of anger, readiness to change or ability to conceptualise, would fare better with particular interventions? The high point of this line of investigation was Project Match. In this major, and meticulously implemented, action research programme in the USA the participants, who had alcohol problems, were assessed against a wide range of psychological and other indicators. They were then randomly allocated to either motivational enhancement therapy or cognitive behavioural coping skills therapy or 12-step facilitation therapy. While all three treatments achieved good outcomes, what was highly surprising was that only a very limited number of matching effects were discernible (Project Match Research Group, 1997). Matching interventions to particular personality types has proved to be something of a dead end.

It would be unwise, however, to assume that matching in a more general way is irrelevant. Tailoring a treatment programme to ensure that an individual's particular difficulties, such as family or employment problems, are addressed is common sense and has been shown to improve outcomes (McLellan et al., 1997). In addition, the whole concept of tiering services to ensure that those with less ingrained problems are channelled to briefer, less intrusive interventions and those with more deep-seated and complex problems receive more intensive responses is a form of matching (see Figure 6.1 below). Further research is also needed to determine whether service users benefit from having practitioners who share similar attitudes and values.

ACTIVITY 6.2

**A substitute for alcohol?**
Unlike opiates, there is no substitute for alcohol to offer to people who are not ready for detoxification or who regularly relapse. What do you think the advantages and disadvantages of a 'methadone for alcohol' would be?

## Practitioner skills in context

Certain principles govern successful engagement.

### A positive therapeutic alliance

The ability to use therapeutic skills, such as motivational interviewing and relapse prevention, is essential but their effectiveness is dependent on their being grounded in a positive therapeutic alliance with the person. Empathy is the foundation of this. Whilst sympathy is an emotion that leads to indiscriminately taking a person's side, empathy is based on understanding. It is the ability to see the situation from the perspective of another even when we might not agree with her actions or her point of view. Empathy is a skill which can be honed. It demands the ability to listen and identify what is important to the person, but listening is not enough; the person needs to know that her perspective is understood and this is realised through summarising what she has said from time to time. 'Have I got this right?' or 'Tell me if I'm understanding correctly what you have just told me?' become precursors to a brief recapping of what the person has said. The summary must accurately reflect the person's viewpoint; the practitioner must avoid the temptation to reconstruct it from his perspective. The following is an example of summarising:

> *Tell me if I am getting this right, Carrie? You used quite a lot of cocaine on Sunday night and felt rough on Monday morning. You phoned work to say you would take the day as leave. Your boss has given you a warning. You are annoyed with her because you think this is unfair and she is getting at you.* [Pause – Carrie nods]. *Tell me a bit more about what happened on Sunday?*

Even though the practitioner may consider that her boss has a legitimate case, he is ensuring that the service user knows that he understand how she sees it. He is also giving Carrie the opportunity to comment if she feels he has misunderstood what she is saying. Having done this, he moves on.

In hardly needs saying that a therapeutic alliance cannot be established if a person sees a different practitioner each time he attends.

The spirit of the empathetic approach is well captured by William Miller (2005), the father of motivational interviewing:

> I got interested in this field on an internship .... Knowing nothing, I did what came naturally to me – Carl Rogers – and in essence asked patients to teach me about alcoholism and tell me about themselves .... I mostly listened with accurate empathy.
>
> There was an immediate chemistry – I loved talking to them and they seemed to enjoy talking to me. Then I began reading about the alleged nature of alcoholics as lying, conniving, defensive, denying, slippery, and incapable of seeing reality. 'Gee, these aren't the same patients I've been talking to,' I thought.

CASE ILLUSTRATION 6.1

### When the alliance is not there

Kenny (29) referred himself voluntarily for help with his drinking. Regular bingeing had led to loss of employment and a request by his partner to leave; he was now sleeping on a friend's sofa. During sessions with me, he spent much of the time describing how, when drunk, he went to his house to try to persuade his partner to take him back. I felt myself becoming increasingly frustrated with my inability to bring the discussion round to his drinking in any meaningful way and to help him see that his partner might view the situation differently. I began to feel uncomfortable with him. Kenny was charged with public order offences, received a community penalty and the case was transferred to a probation colleague, an older woman.

Nine months later, my probation colleague told me that Kenny's consumption was much reduced. He was renting a flat, working again and had accepted that his relationship was over. Maybe Kenny had picked up my unease or perhaps he had immediately warmed to a motherly figure. Whatever the reason, a therapeutic alliance had been established with the new practitioner where Kenny and I had none.

There is another lesson here. Sensing the futility of my efforts, I should have discussed with my supervisor the possible transfer of the case to another worker.

Have you found yourself in a similar situation? If so, how did you handle the case?

### Confrontation is normally counterproductive

Confrontation was once considered necessary in order to break down the denial that people with substance problems were presumed to possess in abundance. Modern psychology suggests that it is this very confrontation which leads to denial in the first place. The more we try to persuade a person to see things from our own viewpoint, the greater the likelihood she will react by defending her position (Miller and Rollnick, 2002). As the barriers go up, the therapeutic relationship is threatened. To avoid this in Carrie's case (see above), the practitioner might return to the issue of her employment in this way:

*You're angry with your boss. If you were in her position, tell me what you would have done.*

Here the practitioner is guiding Carrie towards exploring a different point of view without confronting her directly. She will probably stop and think about this, a very different response to her likely reaction if the practitioner had said: *Well Carrie, I think your boss was right to give you a warning, don't you?*

How to respond to resistance is a key technique of motivational interviewing (see Chapter 8).

### Practitioners earn trust

Trust is built on consistency and honesty. The practitioner needs to outline clearly the nature of her role, its limitations and the boundaries of confidentiality. Where appropriate, taking specific practical actions on behalf of a service user, such as contacting other agencies where appropriate, is tangible evidence of concern (Mayer and Timms, 1970). Inefficiency and, in particular, failure to carry through agreed actions may so undermine a relationship as to make it unrecoverable.

### People with substance problems: a dishonest group?

The disease model presupposes that denial is part of the condition and the wider public tend to view people with substance problems as a devious group. However, as the quote from Bill Miller above suggests, how people respond is, to a great degree, dependent on how we approach them. However, if honesty has consequences which a person thinks are against her best interests, she may not tell the whole truth – and being honest about substance use often does have consequences. Consider two scenarios. Graham (50), a divorced man with no family ties, binges on alcohol. Concerned about his health, he has sought help. He is perfectly open with his practitioner about the frequency and extent of his consumption: he has no reason not to be. April (28), a single mother of two pre-school children, also binge drinks. She was referred for specialist help by a social worker who is concerned about the impact of her behaviour on her children. April, too, wants to stop doing what she is doing but, fearful that the state may remove her children, she has every reason to play down the extent of her drinking. It is what most of us would do.

With each new case, the first question the practitioner should ask herself is: 'Given the role I am playing and the authority I have, how does this person view me?' Answering this will go a long way to understanding how the service user will present her situation to us. Shameful feelings about relapse or concerns about letting the practitioner down can also be behind an unwillingness to disclose the full picture. This problem can also occur with substitute prescribing. If the agency sets strict rules about illicit use on top of opioid substitution treatment, game-like behaviour may occur. The service user, worried that her script will be removed, will not be honest and the practitioner may not really want to know: hardly a constructive scenario (Exchange Supplies/The Alliance, 2004).

### It's the service user's agenda

The parameters of the agenda will be determined by the situation, but the agenda itself must belong to the service user. Change will not occur unless the person herself both wants it to happen and owns the processes of achieving it. This is a central principle of goal setting (see Chapter 7). The boundaries of engagement might be a court order with a condition to undertake drug treatment, but how this is accomplished should belong to the person. Individualisation is paramount. It is not for practitioners to provide limited options or specify solutions; it is our job to provide a menu of opportunities and then act as a guide. In a film exploring people's experiences of drug treatment, one service user expressed amazement when he finally came across a service where the staff said to him 'What do you want?' rather than telling him what he was going to be given (Exchange Supplies/The Alliance, 2004).

### Types of question

Different kinds of questions serve different purposes and confidence in using these come with training and practice.

**Closed questions.** These restrict responses to 'yes', 'no' or to limited factual answers.

The following are examples of closed questions:

- 'Can you give me your address, please?'
- 'Did your last binge cause you problems?'

If the person replies 'yes' or 'some' to the latter question, then the practitioner must ask a further question if he wants to find out more. Closed questions are not, therefore, useful for exploring an issue. They are, though, an essential tool for checking the accuracy of information and they do let a person know that a particular topic is a legitimate one for discussion. However, closed questions put the service user on the spot by forcing her to take a definitive position. This can be counterproductive, as the following example demonstrates.

Brian had been abstinent for a period but has relapsed since his last appointment. He is ashamed and in two minds as to what to say to his key worker. Consider his possible responses to these two questions:

> *Practitioner*: 'Hello Brian, have you managed to stay off cannabis since we last met?'
> Faced with this closed question, Brian is forced to decide quickly whether to admit or deny that he has relapsed. If he denies it, he is unlikely to retract later and the rest of the session will be unproductive.

> *Practitioner*: 'Hello Brian, how have things been since we last met?'
> With this question, things are left open. Brian can start talking in general terms. If he alludes to things being difficult, the practitioner can tentatively probe in ways which will feel less threatening to him; admission may then be easier.

**Open questions.** The second question to Brian is an example of these. They start with words or phrases such as 'how', 'tell me about', 'what' or 'why'. It is not possible to answer open questions with 'yes' or 'no'. The service user is obliged to reflect on the situation and respond on her own terms. Open questions encourage people to divulge how they feel about, or view, the situation; they are the main technique for exploring issues.

**Leading questions.** By planting seeds, these guide the person in a specific direction. 'If you stopped smoking cannabis, Brian, what would be the benefits?' is a leading question. It assumes that stopping cannabis use is desirable but it also leads Brian towards exploring what he might gain. Because they can include assumptions, leading questions should be used with care. Encouraging Brian to consider what life without cannabis might be like could strengthen his motivation to change or he might simply list possible benefits because that is what the questioner expected him to do.

It is important to note that children and certain vulnerable adults are susceptible to agreeing with leading questions even when what is said is not true. For this reason, queries such as 'Your father hit you after he was drinking, didn't he?' should never be used when responding to a disclosure of abuse (Department for Education and Skills, 2006).

### Keeping the door open

If it is obvious that the person has reservations about discussing an issue, it is useful to make it clear that she can return to it at any time. Before changing the subject, the practitioner might say:

*I appreciate that you don't want to discuss this now, but if you do decide you want to in the future then that's ok.*

### Optimism but realism too

An important skill is treading the fine line between optimism and pessimism. A person's situation may present seemingly intractable difficulties but she will soon pick up any practitioner negativity. Holding out hope and praising positive steps, however small, will support self-efficacy. On the other hand, unwarranted optimism, based on limited progress or short-term change, can be dangerous. It may lead to a case being closed too early or the risks to other people going unrecognised. Where domestic abuse or child protection is an issue, healthy scepticism is warranted. Improvements need to be acknowledged while priority continues to be given to arrangements to ensure the well-being of vulnerable third parties.

### Attitudes towards halting progress

Sensitivity is required regarding speed of progress and relapse. In the previously mentioned film exploring service users' views, people described how practitioner attitudes towards relapse can compound feelings of low self-esteem (Exchange Supplies/The Alliance, 2004). One person suggested that relapse of any sort should prompt the practitioner to review what is being offered rather than attributing failure to the service user. The most constructive response may be: *What do we need to do differently to help you avoid this in the future?* Here the practitioner is reaffirming in a positive manner that the way forward lies in a partnership with the person.

It is a human response for us, as practitioners, to credit progress to our exceptional skills and ongoing problems to the inadequacies of the service user. Needless to say, such illusions should be rapidly dispelled!

### BOX 6.2 THE USE OF MANUALS: A GOOD IDEA?

Manuals, which guide the change process through a series of steps, have been developed. They can promote programme integrity, ensuring that an intervention is followed through consistently and remains true to its theoretical base. It is not clear, however, how far stringent adherence to a manual increases the likelihood of a positive result. Research by Luborsky and O'Brien (cited by Raistrick, Heather and Godfrey, 2006, p. 48) found that with specific interventions, such as CBT, close compliance with the manual improved outcomes. However Ashton (2005b) notes that a study by Miller involving motivational interviewing suggests that rigid compliance with a manual can prevent the practitioner from adapting responses to the individual service user. In short, the manual may compromise the therapeutic alliance. When manuals are used, perhaps some flexibility in application, without undermining the principles of the intervention, should be the rule.

In addition to structured manuals, packs and workbooks are available which contain assessment, motivational and relapse prevention exercises. These often utilise graphs, process mapping tools or the like; they can help structure engagement and enable the person to explore her situation from a variety of angles. Practitioners should not impose the use of these on people as some may find them patronising. Trying out one or two with the person will soon clarify if she feels comfortable with their use.

## Successful services

### The importance of culture

The influence of agency culture tends to be underplayed. Ashton (2005a, 2011) and Ashton and Whitton (2004), reviewing various studies, identified measures which agencies can take to encourage engagement, boost rates of retention in treatment and improve outcomes. These include:

- providing staff training;
- ensuring that premises are adapted to confidential counselling;
- developing close relationships with other agencies. Staff need to know how their project fits into the mosaic of services in their area. In a well-functioning agency, practitioners recognise when to refer a person on and when to work in tandem with other providers. Where people have more serious difficulties, multi-agency working is likely to be the norm;
- ensuring clarity of mission and role;
- working to eliminating waiting lists, which can lead to low service uptake, by ensuring rapid access to simplified assessments and a triage system. People can then either be signposted to the most suitable service or be provided with some level of initial intervention;
- establishing systems of personalised reminders about appointments, along with offers of further sessions when people have failed to attend. Modern communication systems can help facilitate this. Such messages should be tailored to the person and express optimism about the value of further engagement;
- addressing the problem that transport causes for some people. Where transport cannot be provided, pre-paid vouchers are preferable to reimbursement;
- improving access through flexible opening hours;
- undertaking home visiting, particularly when people have multiple difficulties. Obviously staff safety is a consideration when putting arrangements in place;

- routinely following up service users after treatment has ended (see Chapter 12).

Outcomes are also improved where there is good staff supervision, including constructive feedback, and where individual practitioner outcomes are monitored (Department of Health (England) and the devolved administrations, 2007). Filming practice or role playing is a powerful tool for facilitating reflection. Service user involvement initiatives can provide constructive criticism of an agency's performance.

Triage systems now operate in parts of the UK and significant reductions in waiting times for drug services have been achieved. However, much remains to be done to improve provision in line with all these findings.

## Particular communities

A number of factors act as barriers to engaging effectively with special and minority groups. People in these communities may feel doubly stigmatised. They will be reluctant to approach mainstream services if they think these are orientated primarily to the needs of white, heterosexual men, the dominant group with substance problems. Except in the case of women, planning and commission services can be hampered by a paucity of research, with little being known about the extent and nature of problematic use in certain communities. It is also essential for service planners to take into account the fact that special and minority communities are, themselves, heterogeneous. Key questions include how best to reach these groups, whether separate or integrated services should be provided and how to ensure that practitioners and services are 'culturally competent'.

In respect of black and minority ethnic communities, Khan (2002) considers that responses based primarily on cultural differences are essentially racist as this approach assumes that individuals' substance use can be defined primarily on racial grounds; it ignores the shifting nature of cultural groups and focuses on ethnicity, as opposed to other characteristics such as socioeconomic status. He argues that what is important is 'not to deliver a culturally appropriate service but an individually appropriate service that takes account of the full humanity of the client, including culture and heritage'. Embedding this principle into models for delivering services to all groups is a major challenge.

## Women

Specific provision is needed for pregnant women and may be necessary for those involved in sex work but all services should be structured to ensure that women's needs are met. Particular concerns for women are stigma, fear regarding possible repercussions in respect of their children if they approach services and the implications of being the victims of domestic abuse. Potential barriers which services should address include:

- opening times;
- childcare; solutions include ensuring access to childcare in the community, the provision of crèches, the option of home visiting and arranging transport;
- insecurity; women-only spaces or times should be considered;
- reluctance to engage; outreach can make connection with the hesitant. (Becker and Duffy, 2002)

Do women-only services or offering women same-sex counsellors improve outcomes and are such options necessarily attractive to women? Thom and Green (1996) suggest that no firm conclusions can be drawn. Mixed-sex groups may be unappealing to women and same-sex counsellors may be more appropriate for women who have been subject to domestic violence (Jarvis, 1992 and Connors et al., 1997, cited in Raistrick, Heather and Godfrey, 2006). As women may be more willing to discuss certain issues with other women, it would seem good practice to ask each service user what her preference is with regard to practitioner gender. The same holds true for men.

One suggestion which has implications for therapeutic orientation is that women respond to an empathetic style of counselling, whereas men find a utilitarian, problem-solving mode more helpful (Fiorentine, Nakashima and Anglin, 1999).

### Lesbian, gay, bisexual and transgender (LGBT) people

While use varies markedly between different communities within the LGBT population, consumption of alcohol, stimulants and other drugs associated with the club scene is known to be high among certain subgroups (Beddoes et al., 2010b). Factors that are relevant to the extent of substance taking among LGBT people include:

- the stress which being part of a stigmatised minority entails;
- problems of coming to terms with, and managing, identity issues;
- clubs and bars being the focus of social life for many;
- the use of substances to facilitate sexual intimacy and the associated health risks, particularly HIV. (Eliason and Hughes, 2004; Keogh et al., 2009)

With all service users, practitioners need to be aware that sexual orientation may be an issue and that some people may want to start the process of coming out within the security of a therapeutic relationship. Again, taking services to the minority group, rather than expecting their members to come forward, is essential. In this regard, existing specialist health initiatives provide a vehicle for engagement with LGBT people on their substance-taking habits.

### Black and minority ethnic (BME) communities

Stigma, lack of knowledge of the options and inadequate service provision mean that BME communities are likely to be under-represented in treatment populations (Hurcombe et al., 2010; UK Drug Policy Commission, 2010b). In addition, practice is unlikely to be effective unless it is informed by an understanding of culture and heritage. To achieve this, the NTA (2009) emphasises the importance of local needs assessments for ensuring that services are able to respond to people from BME communities, although planning can be hampered by the reluctance of some groups to acknowledge that substance problems exist in their midst. Services need to be able to respond to the variety of minority communities in a particular area and the nature and extent of use in those groups. In addition to stigma, potential barriers to engagement which need to be addressed include language issues, diverse cultural attitudes towards substances, religion and differences in how minority groups deal with personal problems. Outreach is seen as important in both engaging the difficult to reach and advertising the availability of services (NTA, 2009). As for other minority populations, debates continue as to the value of creating specialist services.

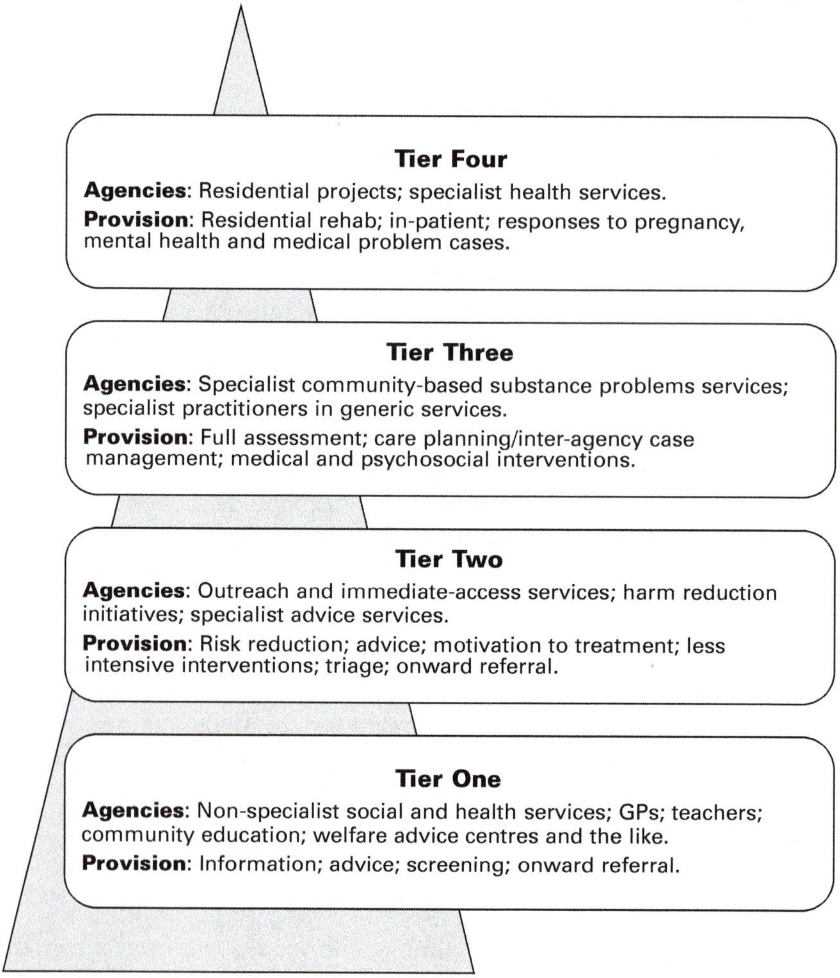

**Tier Four**

**Agencies**: Residential projects; specialist health services.
**Provision**: Residential rehab; in-patient; responses to pregnancy, mental health and medical problem cases.

**Tier Three**

**Agencies**: Specialist community-based substance problems services; specialist practitioners in generic services.
**Provision**: Full assessment; care planning/inter-agency case management; medical and psychosocial interventions.

**Tier Two**

**Agencies**: Outreach and immediate-access services; harm reduction initiatives; specialist advice services.
**Provision**: Risk reduction; advice; motivation to treatment; less intensive interventions; triage; onward referral.

**Tier One**

**Agencies**: Non-specialist social and health services; GPs; teachers; community education; welfare advice centres and the like.
**Provision**: Information; advice; screening; onward referral.

**Figure 6.1** The tiering of services

## A stepped approach to service provision

Although the structural arrangements for providing services vary from area to area and in different parts of the UK, local commissioners tend to use the National Treatment Agency's tiered model as a blueprint (NTA, 2002). The tiers broadly define levels of treatment intensity and complexity; they are not rigid demarcations. The same agency may offer services at different tiers. Where tiered arrangements work well, the individual is rapidly directed to the service appropriate to the level of her difficulties. For the tier system to function effectively, all parties must know what other agencies offer, seamless referral systems must be in place and harmonious operational relationships between services need to exist. As Figure 6.1 shows, services for the great majority of people with more serious difficulties lie in tier three. Close links between specialist substance problems agencies and the providers of 'wraparound' services, such as housing and access to training and employment, is essential if people are to move beyond the narrow confines of treatment.

## Concluding comments

Despite the controversies outlined in this chapter, we do know which inventions are most likely to help people to change. We also know that the nature of the relationship between practitioner and service user is as important as these interventions. The context within which individual practitioners operate is a telling factor too. Supportive agencies bolster practitioner competence and a client-centred culture retains service users. However, it remains true that many are unable to make constructive use of what is currently provided; there is much yet to learn.

### RESOURCES

- DANOS. The Drug and Alcohol National Occupational Standards describe the skills and knowledge and skills required by practitioners: www.skillsforhealth.org.uk.
- Drug and Alcohol Findings produces easily read digests of research into all aspects of working with people with substance problems. The Drug and Alcohol Matrices provide rapid access to key documents: http://findings.org.uk/.
- Exchange Supplies/The Alliance (2004). *Substitute Prescribing: The User's View* (DVD). www.exchangesupplies.org/. In this excellent short film, a group of service users, in addition to describing their experiences of methadone, give their insightful views into what makes an effective practitioner and good service.
- Gossop, M. (2006). *Treating Drug Misuse Problems: Evidence of Effectiveness.* www.nta.nhs.uk.
- Raistrick, D., Heather, N. and Godfrey, C. (2006). *Review of the Effectiveness of Treatment for Alcohol Problems.* London: www.nta.nhs.uk.
  (NB: Material on the NTA website is scheduled to be transferred by 2014 to the PHE website or placed on the National Archive's website or similar.)

# CHAPTER 7

# Assessment and Care Planning

## KEY THEMES

- Assessment is a continuous interactional process and not an event.
- Assessment should include the positive factors in a person's situation as well as the risks and difficulties.
- Assessment should include the implications of the person's substance use for those who are dependent on him.
- Care planning is the person's own statement of how he would like his life to be and what needs to happen to realise this.

## Assessment: context and principles

Assessment is an ongoing process of gathering information, structuring it and making sense of it in order to inform decisions about the actions necessary to maximise [a person's] potential. ... This process assumes the sharing of information where the law, practice and policy allows or requires it. It identifies and builds on strengths, whilst taking account of risks and needs. (Scottish Executive, 2004)

This definition succinctly describes the elements of a good assessment. Information gathering is central to assessment but it is not assessment itself. Assessment is drawing out from this information the main risks and unmet needs; this allows an action plan to be formulated. Assessment should identify the issues and difficulties for the person and those close to him which:

- have influenced and are supporting the current use of substances;
- have occurred because of the pattern of use. (Keene, 2010, p. 169)

Assessment is likely to be a collaborative process involving other individuals and services. Whilst the problems a person is facing need to be addressed, it is the positive elements in his life, his personal and environmental capital, which will support changed behaviour and the emergence of a different identity.

Assessment, care planning and interventions are interlinked. The care plan, informed by the issues prioritised in the assessment, lays out what changes a person needs to make to reach his goals. Interventions then become the tools

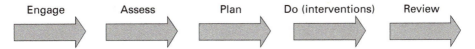

**Figure 7.1** The treatment process

the person uses to implement these changes. The process should be an evolving and flexible one, with regular reviews ensuring that altered circumstances and additional information are taken fully into account (Figure 7.1).

Open questions are the primary mode of encouraging the service user to explore what is of concern to him. They can be used to guide the person towards particular issues whilst creating space for him to expand on his responses. Closed questions are used by the practitioner to obtain factual information and to check that she has understood what the person has said (see Chapter 6).

### The starting point

Assessment is an interaction played out between the practitioner and the person with the problem. Whilst the practitioner will have a loose script to follow, the service user will be making judgements as to whether the person sitting opposite is listening and can help. As we saw in Chapter 6, the role the practitioner plays can influence what the service user is prepared to divulge. Early resistance needs to be understood in this context; patience and care with the timing of introducing sensitive topics, such as domestic abuse or the implications for children, is needed. Assessment is not divorced from intervention; it may be appropriate to use motivational interviewing and discuss harm reduction from the earliest stages.

### BOX 7.1  MOTIVATION: NOT SOMETHING TO BE ASSESSED

Because ambivalence is normal and motivation fluctuates, it is impossible to assess the latter in anything but the broadest terms. We also know that the interaction between the practitioner and the person can strengthen commitment to change. Together, these factors suggest that telling a person to return when he is motivated is not an acceptable response to a request for help (Sellman, 2010). Thorley (1980) gets to the root of the matter when he says: 'for the patient to come to the doctor's surgery shows he is motivated about something'.

The practitioner's task is to discover what that 'something' is and to utilise it as a building block for change.

### The processes of assessment

The circumstances of initial engagement will dictate how it should be handled. The prearranged appointment allows time for the issues to be considered in depth whereas the unplanned, and often time-limited, interview needs to simply focus on immediate risks (see Case Illustration 7.1).

---

**CASE ILLUSTRATION 7.1**

### The emergency appointment

Arnie (57) comes in off the street seeking an urgent appointment with the duty worker at an alcohol agency run by a voluntary organisation. He wants help because his daughter, with whom he lives, is threatening to evict him unless he stops drinking. With time at a premium, the practitioner must concentrate on identifying the immediate issues as Arnie sees them, along with any obvious concerns about third parties. Arnie is 'motivated about something' but it is not his drinking, it is his fear of homelessness. If this crisis can be averted temporarily, then Arnie may think that it is worth his while to return for a fuller assessment. If, at the same time, the practitioner can check that the situation is presenting no immediate risk to his daughter, so much the better.

This particular situation highlights a common feature of initial engagement: the problems substance use is bringing are the spurs for action, not the use of the substance itself.

---

## Triage

The National Treatment Agency for Substance Misuse (NTA, 2006a) suggests that immediate access and generic services should use triage, a response falling between brief screening and full assessment. Identifying the extent and seriousness of current risks and problems allows the practitioner to decide immediately whether to follow this up with a brief intervention, with a fuller assessment or with a referral on to a more appropriate agency.

## The importance of the welcoming gesture

What helps to facilitate engagement is explored in Chapter 6. Uncertainty, anger, anxiety, shame and ambivalence are just some of the feelings that most service users will be experiencing on first arrival at a service. The friendly receptionist, the appointment started on time, the welcoming handshake, the offer of water, the bright and soundproofed interview room, all these help lessen feelings of distress and let the person know that he is valued. First impressions can be the difference between the person returning and being lost to treatment.

---

**ACTIVITY 7.1**

### The welcoming gesture
Consider a service which you have been involved with.

- How far does it meet the welcoming gestures test?
- What additional measures might facilitate the process of engagement?

## A collaborative exercise

When the case is uncomplicated and the person is experiencing lower levels of dependence, only one practitioner may be involved. However, when the situation is complex and issues such as physical dependence, homelessness, domestic abuse or mental health problems are present then assessment, care planning and interventions will be collaborative exercises. The practitioner needs to identify what other organisations are, or have recently been, involved with the person. Contact with these facilitates assessment and establishes the multi-agency network. The single shared assessment has been introduced in most areas. This allows agencies to work to the same protocol and ensures that the service user does not have to repeat his history with each agency involved.

In addition to inter-agency collaboration, seeking the involvement of other people in the person's life, such as partners, parents and the adult children of older substance users, can enhance the assessment. They can confirm or contradict information given, put the problematic behaviour in its wider historical and current contexts and identify factors which reinforce or weaken the substance use. Where possible, partners should be involved in care planning. If a partner does not support the goals a service user wants to achieve, tensions in the relationship are inevitable. There is another side to the involvement of relatives. Contact with them provides the opportunity to determine whether they need help for themselves to cope with the stresses which close involvement with a person with a substance problem often brings (see Chapter 15).

## BOX 7.2 CONFIDENTIALITY

Confidentiality policies should be given to service users in hard copy. While it is beyond the scope of this book to address the legal situation in detail, in broad terms the guidance is that information should not be shared without the person's consent except where there are clear grounds to believe that the person poses a serious risk to himself or to the safety of others. For example, if a child is at risk then the police or social services must be advised even if the service user objects or cannot be contacted; consent should not be sought when to do so would put a third party in greater danger.

Most service users see the value of the agencies with whom they are involved liaising on a regular basis and it is desirable that all parties attend reviews. When a service user expresses doubts about sharing information with relevant parties, then the reasons for his concerns should be fully explored.

Possession of most substances controlled under the Misuse of Drugs Act 1971 is illegal unless they have been prescribed. It is sensible, therefore, for practitioners to warn drug users that information divulged about illegal activities may have to be passed on to the police. They should be cautioned to think carefully before disclosing from whom they have bought drugs and the details of how they fund their use if this involves criminal behaviour.

### Assessment tools

There are two types of assessment tool. The first is the agency's own document or the single shared assessment used in the area. In addition to allowing full factual information about the person to be gathered, such forms cover past and present substance use, physical and mental health issues, offending behaviour, details of significant others, childcare responsibilities and the like. They usually provide space for the person's views to be documented along with a separate section for the care plan, future reviews and the recording of outcomes. Such forms, which may be computerised, are usually designed to facilitate the collection of statistical information.

The second type of tool is the validated questionnaire, used in addition to the assessment form, to analyse specific issues such as patterns of use or dependence. A typical tool involves the service user answering questions, often by ticking responses on a grid, and then these are scored. Brief training is needed before using some of these questionnaires and it is important to understand the purposes and limitations of each of them. The results obtained from validated questionnaires should be used to complement the service user's views and the practitioner's judgement, not replace them. AUDIT and SADQ-C are provided as examples of these questionnaires for use with people who drink (see the Appendix).

### Structuring the assessment interview

Assessment forms should not be allowed to intrude. It is difficult to establish a therapeutic alliance when the focus is a piece of paper or a computer! One way of avoiding this pitfall is to schedule a period at the end of the interview for form filling. A note pad can be used to jot down 'memory joggers' as the person tells his story and the practitioner probes key areas. Use of the form at the end of the session allows for recapping, an important method of letting the service user know that he has been understood; it also provides the opportunity to clarify any issues. The first interview should identify the key issues and any immediate risks so that urgent actions, a type of 'temporary care plan', can be agreed. It is unlikely that one interview will provide enough information to complete a full assessment. It may be necessary to approach other services involved, contact relatives or ask the person to monitor his use over a period of time.

## Assessment: covering the ground

Having established why the person has sought help at that point, and having tried to put in place immediate harm reduction measures (see Chapter 9), a more detailed assessment can begin.

### The pattern of use and its consequences

The starting point is the nature and extent of current use:

- *What substances are being used?* The person is likely to speak about the drug which he feels is causing him the most problems. The heroin user concerned about an impending court case may say nothing about heavy alcohol consumption. The drinker whose partner is threatening to leave may not raise his erratic use of prescribed painkillers. The complete jigsaw needs to be pieced together.
- *How often does the person use?* Is the pattern consistent daily use or bingeing? Depending on the drugs used, this will give early clues as to whether physical dependence may be an issue.
- *How much does the person use* (see below)? How are the substances ingested? The answers will point up immediate risks.
- *Does the person use alone or with others* and what are the safety implications of this? The solitary heroin user will be more at risk of dying if overdose occurs but is less likely to share injecting equipment.
- *Has overdose occurred in the past* and, if so, what were the circumstances and what drugs were involved?

It is best not to assume that the picture which emerges will be wholly accurate. Harris (2007, p. 83) notes that the accounts which people give of their use are often subject to considerable bias. Self-image, fear of stigmatisation or concerns about the consequences of accurate disclosure can influence what a person decides to reveal. In certain circumstances, people may not know how much they have been taking. For example, significant periods of an alcohol binge may be beyond the person's recall. However, when asked, he may feel obliged to give an estimate of use, however inaccurate. Diaries, available in hard copy or via the Internet, have a part to play here. Used over a period of time, these allow amounts, triggers and circumstances of use to be logged.

While a clear account of current use allows harm reduction and stabilisation measures to be put in place, the twists and turns of a person's substance-using history is needed before the care plan can be drawn up. Mapping can be used to plot use over time against significant life events, along with periods of harm-free use or abstinence. What influences escalations or declines in use can give pointers to both what puts the person at risk and what the prerequisites for reducing problems are.

Thorley's framework can be used in visual form to link the problems a person is experiencing to his pattern of use (see Chapter 2).

### Causes

People are often keen to explore why they have developed problems. This can help to identify possible contributing factors, such as past abuse, trauma or loss, which can act as barriers to change unless they are addressed. Whilst it is essential that such issues are included in the care plan, attempting to pin down with any certainty the reasons why a particular individual has developed a problem can be a fruitless exercise. We make sense of our lives by creating narratives out of experience and by attributing meaning. If a person is asked why he has a problem with substances, he will tend to identify external factors such as stress, a difficult childhood or distressing events. He is less likely to assign responsibility to personal choice. It is rare that a practitioner will hear someone say, 'I simply let a pleasurable habit take over my life'. It is also the case that a person may give different reasons to different audiences (Davies, 2006b; Harris 2007, p. 84). For a person who adheres to the disease model, there is a ready answer to the question 'Why am I addicted?'; for others, it brings the opportunity to explore possible contributing factors.

## Assessing amounts

**Alcohol** consumption is calculated in 'units'. Different drinks have different strengths, measured by the percentage of alcohol by volume [ABV].
    One unit is equivalent to:

1/2 pint of beer or lager at 3.5 per cent ABV
1/3 pint of ordinary cider or stronger beer at 5 per cent ABV
Single measure of vodka or whisky (25 ml–1/6 gill)
2/3 of one standard glass of wine (125 ml)

The 'unit' content of any drink is calculated by multiplying the volume by the ABV and dividing by 100 (1000 if the volume is in millilitres).

*Examples*:
    Bottle of wine 75 cl x 12 per cent = 900 ÷ 100 = 9 units
    Can of strong lager 440 ml x 9 per cent = 3960 ÷1000 = 4 units

As of 2013, the government recommended that consumption for adult males should not regularly exceed 3–4 units a day for adult males and 2–3 units per day for females. Guidance also suggests that a person should have a minimum of two alcohol-free days a week; an alcohol-free period of 48 hours should follow a heavy drinking session; and that drinking should be completely avoided if a woman is pregnant or trying to conceive (House of Commons Science and Technology Committee, 2011; NHS, 2013).
    Measuring the quantity of **illicit drugs** is impossible without professional analysis. 'Cutting' increases with the distance from the source of importation and droughts caused by policing activities and poor harvests affect purity. There is evidence that the purity of many drugs fell in the first decade of the millennium and it has been suggested that this may be one of the reasons for the rise in polydrug use (Daly, 2009). On occasions, drugs marketed as one substance have been found to be something completely different.
    Drugs are often sold in denominations such as 'bags', 'wraps', 'tabs' or 'scores' rather than by weight. Ounces or grams may be used when selling by weight, with suppliers tending to under-sell.

**Heroin** is usually sold in bags, either by monetary denomination (e.g., a £10 or £20 bag) or in fractions of a gram (1/4 g; 1/2 g).

Cocaine is usually sold as a powder in 'wraps' of 1/2 or 1 gram.

Freebase/crack cocaine is sold in small individual lumps ('rocks'). Freebase cocaine can also be bought as a paste.

Amphetamine is usually sold in clubs or on the street in small quantities wrapped in magazine-type paper. These 'wraps' nominally contain a gram and are sold by monetary value. If bought from a dealer, amphetamine is usually sold in fractions of an ounce.

Cannabis is normally sold in 'scores' or ounces or fractions of either. A 'score' is approximately 1/4 oz (7 g). Working out how much a person is using is difficult because it depends on how much he/she puts in a 'joint' and whether it is smoked with others.

Drugs which come in powder form are sometimes sold in the plastic container inside Kinder eggs, with one egg containing approximately 3.5 grams.

Other indicators, such as how often a person uses and how much he pays, can provide as useful a picture as the amount itself. Price volatility, however, makes cost an unreliable guide.

New psychoactive substances present a challenge, as it is often unclear what actual drug the person has used, let alone how much has been consumed. Flemen (2013) suggests that when a person seeks immediate help, concerned about the effects of what he has taken, it is better to discuss how he is feeling rather than spend time trying to establish what drugs might be involved. Temperature, pulse rate, perception and other signs will indicate what action should be taken.

For those not working in specialist services, local drugs agencies will have information about trends in price and purity in the area, along with what new psychoactive substances are popular.

Amounts are, of course, only one dimension in the complex equation of the individual, the substance and the environment. Someone using an eighth of a gram of heroin a day may be experiencing more difficulties than someone using one gram.

### Physical health and mental wellbeing

While not all people presenting at services will have health problems, many do. Some of the health problems associated with different substances are outlined in Chapter 1. All service users, except perhaps younger people with short substance use histories and no obvious physical issues, should be encouraged to get a health check. Permission to liaise with the GP and other health professionals involved should be sought. A liver function test is the starting point for determining whether there is damage which indicates that abstinence from alcohol is desirable. Drug users are at risk of hepatitis B and screening for this and vaccination is highly desirable. A diagnosis of hepatitis C or HIV is a life-changing event. Specialist counselling will precede testing so that the person knows what the implications of such a diagnosis are. Poor diet, failure to deal with injuries or infections and other types of self-neglect should also be included in the assessment.

Attention should be paid to particular issues during the assessment of women. Female veins are less robust than those of males and so women may graduate to riskier sites earlier on in their injecting careers. Women are susceptible to alcoholic liver problems at an earlier stage than men. Some drug-using women supplement their incomes through sex work, as do some men. This brings a range of health risks along with the prospect of being subject to violence.

Screening for psychological distress should be routine (see Chapter 13). However, teasing out whether mood disorders, cognitive impairment or paranoid episodes indicate underlying psychiatric problems or are the consequences of the substance taking can be difficult to do whilst use continues. It is important to establish whether there is a history of self-harm, attempted suicide or psychiatric treatment.

Psychological distress can be a particular issue for older people, with alcohol and the cavalier use of prescription drugs being used to deal with isolation, depression and loss of role.

## Sexual and reproductive health

Reductions in the numbers of unwanted pregnancies and the spread of blood-borne viruses are public health priorities; so too is encouraging those already affected by the latter into treatment. Because opiates can interfere with menstruation, women may assume, incorrectly, that pregnancy will not occur. Assessment should include these issues as appropriate. Contraceptive advice should be a routine part of work with both women and men. If a woman with a substance problem is pregnant then special arrangements, outlined in local protocols, should be enacted (see Chapter 14).

## Physical dependence

A core consideration is whether a person is physically dependent on a substance. Not all substances lead to physical dependence and associated withdrawal, but this can be an issue with certain depressants and drugs which reduce pain. Adaptation within the central nervous system lies on a continuum and so there is no simple demarcation line between not being and being physically dependent. Practitioners should explore the possibility that a person is physically dependent on more than one substance.

## BOX 7.3 DANGERS IN WITHDRAWAL

Seizures, and even death, can occur in withdrawal from the most commonly used depressants, alcohol and the benzodiazepines. Gammahydroxybutyrate (GHB), gammabutyrolactone (GBL) and barbiturates present similar risks, although the latter are rarely encountered. Medical advice should always be sought before a person tries to come off these drugs.

A level of neuroadaption and increased tolerance occurs when a person drinks regularly but, for most people, this does not reach a level where physical dependence becomes an issue. For **alcohol** withdrawals to occur, heavy daily consumption needs to have taken place over a significant period of time. Withdrawals can also occur following binges that last for a week or more, particularly if such bingeing is the person's normal mode of use. Alcohol withdrawals tend to start between six and eight hours after the last drink and are characterised by sweating, agitation, dry retching and shaking. These symptoms peak and then tend to subside after around three days, although agitation or disrupted sleep patterns may continue for some months. Some people experience visual or auditory hallucinations. Complications include seizures and DTs (delirium tremens), both of which carry a risk of death. If a person has experienced these before, he is more likely to experience them again. Seizures can occur some days after stopping drinking. The phrase 'DTs' is often mistakenly used to describe 'the shakes' which occur with simple withdrawal when, in fact, delirium tremens is a condition of an entirely different order. DTs begin two or three days after the last drink with the person becoming disorientated and delusional. In ordinary withdrawals, the person is aware of who and where they are; the person experiencing DTs is not.

When a person is planning to stop drinking, the practitioner must judge whether he is likely to experience serious withdrawals. He may display symptoms of withdrawal during interview. The person's description of his pattern of drinking will provide clues, as will asking certain questions such as:

- *How do you feel first thing in the morning?* Agitation, sweating, sickness and craving are tell tale signs.
- *Do you take a drink to reduce the discomfort?*
- *Can you only sustain short periods, perhaps less than a day, without alcohol?*
- *Have you experienced seizures or DTs in the past?*

Validated tools, such as the SADQ-C, can help here (see Appendix). The point at which medical supervision of detoxification becomes essential is considered in Chapter 10.

With daily use, physical dependence on heroin develops quite quickly. **Heroin** withdrawals can last longer than alcohol withdrawals and are equally unpleasant, but they do not present the same risks. Managing heroin withdrawals can normally be undertaken safely without medical supervision, although health service involvement is essential if a person has serious physical or psychiatric problems. Miscarriage can follow rapid cessation of use, so a dependent female who is pregnant should always seek medical advice. In addition to cravings and psychological distress, a person withdrawing from heroin will experience restlessness, a runny nose, an inability to sleep, stomach cramps, diarrhoea and muscle and joint pain. Starting up to 12 hours after last use, symptoms are at their most intense after two or three days and fade over the next ten days, although some people experience a general lack of wellbeing for some months. With methadone, withdrawals begin around 30 hours after last ingestion. The distressing symptoms of opiate withdrawal mean that detoxing without additional help is very difficult for many to achieve. As for alcohol, a clear picture of the person's pattern of use and a few judicious questions will determine what the person is likely to face if he stops.

**Benzodiazepine** withdrawals may not start until a few days after cessation of use, or longer, and can last for several weeks. **GHB/GBL** withdrawal symptoms tend to start quite soon after last ingestion.

The management of withdrawals is addressed in Chapter 10.

### Assessment and the cycle of change

In Chapter 5, it was suggested that the cycle of change should be used as a broad guide. Applied in this way, it can help shape the care plan and signpost the most appropriate interventions. For example, for the precontemplator, motivational interviewing may be a suitable starting point; for the person struggling in the maintenance phase, relapse prevention will be the likely approach. In addition, it is not advisable to use motivational interviewing when a person, having committed himself to a specific course of action, is in the preparation, action and maintenance stages (Ashton, 2005b) (see Chapter 8). Gauging where a person is on the cycle can, therefore, be important.

A *precontemplator* may suggest that he does not have problems with substances. If this is the case, he will make statements such as: 'My parents keep getting at me about my drinking, but I don't drink more than my friends.' However, a precontemplator may acknowledge that he has difficulties but express little current interest in addressing these. A person who smokes might say:

'I should stop but I can't think about it with this pressure at work.'

A *contemplator*, while not yet ready to commit to change, will express uncertainty and ambivalence:

'Perhaps I should stop smoking but I've failed when I've tried before.'
'When I go out on Saturdays I tell myself I won't take cocaine but I always seem to end up doing it.'

By way of contrast, a person in the *preparation* stage will articulate clarity of purpose:

'I'm fed up with this. I'm going to stop using.'
'I have worked out a plan to quit smoking when I go on holiday.'

### Personal and environmental capital

Assessment should consider the factors which support or hinder recovery. These include:

- abilities and interests
- relationships with family and friends
- social setting and peer groups
- accommodation
- qualifications and employment history
- financial circumstances.

Exploring a person's skills, positive experiences and preferences not only acknowledges that he is much more than his problem with substances, it also identifies the foundations on which he can build once the situation has stabilised. The person's environmental capital, the sum of the beneficial influences in his surroundings, is of equal importance (Best, 2010). Secure accommodation, adequate income and the consistent support of non-using friends and family support the recovery process (ACMD, 2012). Employment or involvement in constructive activities are strong indicators that the person still has a sense of identity beyond the role of problematic user: they are valuable personal capital. Constructive activity includes the ability to parent in a consistent manner.

For many who seek treatment, the absence of such resources is a major barrier to maintaining engagement or sustaining any changes made. The assessment needs to identify these deficits and the care plan should include ways of rebuilding this capital. The importance of considering this wider dimension cannot be overemphasised. As was suggested in Chapter 5, for those with more serious difficulties treatment episodes may be necessary but they are transitory phases in a much longer process (see Figure 7.2). What resources the person can both call on and build in his life are what will help sustain progress in the long term.

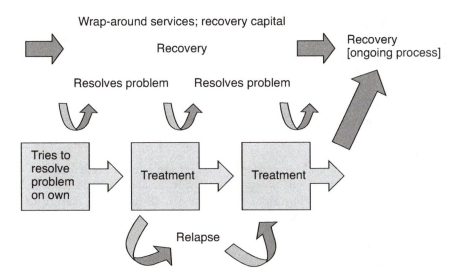

**Figure 7.2** Treatment within the recovery journey

## Significant others

Earlier in this chapter, the importance of involving significant others, such as parents or partners, in assessment was noted. The implications for them, and for any children involved, are considered in Chapters 14 and 15. Suffice to say that gathering information regarding relationships and considering risks to others is a central part of assessment. When a service user has responsibilities for children, the wellbeing of the latter becomes the highest priority.

## Domestic violence and offending

Domestic abuse, ranging from bullying and systematic control to serious sexual and physical aggression, can occur in all forms of relationship; it may be carried out by women against men or against parents by substance-using offspring. It is, however, most commonly perpetrated by men against women and, for ease of description, it will be considered in this context. A substance user may abuse his partner or a woman with a drug or alcohol problem may be the victim of aggression. Victim and perpetrator may both have difficulties with substances. For some women, problematic use of drugs or alcohol is a response to past ordeals or a way of coping with a current harrowing situation. There is evidence from general population studies and research into cohorts involved with both substance problems and domestic violence treatment services that domestic abuse occurs in a significant proportion of relationships where substance use is an issue (Galvani, 2012, p. 114).

The issue of domestic abuse should be broached as a standard part of the substance problems assessment. The principles of best practice include the following:

- The service user should be told that the issue is raised with everyone who comes to the service.
- The subject should never be introduced when the person is accompanied.
- If a person discloses that she has been abused, she should be encouraged to identify options which might help; prescribing a course of action should be avoided.
- Information about specialist services should be provided, along with practical support to access these.
- If abuse is an issue, safety will not be improved if substance use alone is addressed.
- The practitioner should not offer to contact the alleged perpetrator.
- If the person admits to behaving aggressively, he should be listened to in a way which avoids giving any impression of collusion. The nature of the disclosure and local policies will dictate what action the practitioner should then take.
- Family or couples counselling is not an appropriate intervention. (London Borough of Camden, 2007)

Domestic abuse is an issue which needs to be approached with circumspection and with careful consideration given to timing. Simple, everyday language should be used since people may find terms such as sexual or domestic abuse confusing (Jarvis et al., 2005, p. 27). Closed questions are direct questions and can send a strong signal to the person that it is quite permissible to speak about the subject. However, they can put the person on the spot before she is ready to discuss the issue.

The practitioner might prepare the ground in the following way:

*Lots of problems can occur when drugs/alcohol are an issue in a family. Sometimes violence can occur so we ask everyone about this. We will come back to this later when you have had a think about whether there is anything you would like to talk about.*

The person can also be led gently towards the topic:

*Practitioner*: You have told me about the pressures at home. What about your relationship with your partner?
*Service user*: Not bad. Sometimes we argue.
*Practitioner*: What does arguing mean for you?
*Service user*: Well, we fight a bit, you know.
*Practitioner*: Fight can mean a lot of things.
*Service user*: No more than other couples.
*Practitioner*: This is a very sensitive issue, I know, but we ask everyone who comes here this. We raise it to try to ensure their safety and so that they can get help if need be. Has he ever hurt you?
*Service user*: Not hurt like that, no. But he shouts at me all the time and tells me what to do. Sometimes he threatens me.
*Practitioner*: Would you like to talk about this a bit more?

Substance problems practitioners and their counterparts in domestic violence services will not normally be specialists in each other's disciplines and so it is important that local protocols covering assessment, referral and case management pathways are in place.

The person may have a history of offending. In certain situations involvement in criminal behaviour is the reason for referral and raising it will present no problems. When this is not the case, it may also be an issue that provokes shame and a reluctance to disclose. Service users need to be aware that an admission of offending which has not been the subject of police investigation cannot be kept confidential.

> **CASE ILLUSTRATION 7.2**
>
> **Assessment in practice**
> Earlier in this chapter, we considered a case where a crisis triggered help seeking (see Case Illustration 7.1). The following shows how a fuller assessment of Arnie's and his daughter's situation might develop.
> Arnie's AUDIT score was 25 (see Appendix) and his responses to the questions four to six suggested a high level of physical dependence. Contact

with his daughter (Mary) gained enough information to confirm that the agency he had approached, the community alcohol service run by a voluntary organisation, was an appropriate one to take the case forward (triage). An assessment appointment followed which Mary attended with him. A fuller picture began to emerge:

- Arnie had always been a heavy weekend drinker. A painter and decorator by trade, Arnie had not worked for three years following an industrial accident which left him unable to sustain full-time employment. His wife died shortly after this.
- Bored and depressed following his bereavement, he moved in with his daughter, a divorcee. A pattern of daily drinking emerged, with a half bottle of vodka and three cans of super lager becoming the norm (28 units).
- Mary's threat to ask her father to leave had provoked a crisis and Arnie's positive attitudes suggested that he was entering the preparation phase.
- Although Arnie had exhibited no serious behavioural difficulties, Mary was becoming increasingly worried about his deteriorating health. She had not been sleeping, had taken time off work and was embarrassed to invite friends round. She felt that she could not cope for much longer.
- Positive elements identified were Arnie's willingness to address the situation, Mary's support and his skills as a decorator, which he might use again in the future.

At this assessment interview, the immediate concerns identified were Arnie's health and the impact of the situation on Mary. Arnie was advised not to attempt to stop drinking suddenly and given the reasons why (provision of factual information).

An interim care plan, covering a fortnight, was formulated with the goals of:

- *gauging the implications* of Arnie's drinking more fully. Arnie agreed to keep a diary of his drinking, to attend two appointments with the agency and to arrange to see his GP with a view to assessing his physical health. He also agreed to try to reduce his daily consumption by a few units.
- *ascertaining what support* Mary might find helpful. One appointment was arranged for Mary on her own.
- *holding a meeting* with Arnie and Mary, at the end of the two-week period, with a view to drawing up a full care plan.

## Care planning

Contact with other parties and further investigation may mean that assessment will take more than one interview. If the care plan cannot be drawn up quickly, some steps to help the person may need to be taken in the meantime. Certain interventions may, therefore, start during the assessment process.

## Interventions during assessment

In addition to harm reduction measures (see Chapter 9), providing information can be an appropriate part of assessment. This should include giving details of the nature of the service and, when relevant, information about other agencies or projects for family members. Some service users are well informed about the drugs they use and the risks they run but others can be surprisingly ignorant. The process of assessment presents opportunities to find out how much the person knows and to provide information directly or give the person leaflets. When it is clear to the practitioner that the person is ambivalent about engagement, a motivational style of interviewing during the assessment may be relevant (see Chapter 8). Responding to issues as they emerge makes assessment an interactional process.

## The principles of care planning

The NTA (2006a) defines care planning as 'a process for setting goals based on the needs identified by an assessment and planning interventions to meet those goals with the client'. The plan should be both practical and aspirational. The person will only be motivated to reach the goals in the plan if he has set them himself. This is true for both voluntary and involuntary service users. Individualisation and ownership are the rule. Practitioners inform, advise and guide; service users decide. Care plans should be tested to ensure that they meet the **SMART** criteria (NTA, 2006b):

Specific: plans should be explicit, easily understood and written in plain English.
Measurable: a person can only monitor his own progress if the outcomes in the plan can be measured. A vague goal such as 'reducing risk' does not meet this yardstick, whereas an objective such as 'never using diazepam along with methadone' does.
Agreed: while the plan should belong to the person, it needs to be acceptable to all the agencies involved. In some situations, it will need to meet the approval of partners or other family members.
Realistic: the goals must be achievable within the time frame set. Care should be taken to ensure that the person does not take on too much too quickly. Longer term aspirations should be acknowledged but put on hold until immediate priorities have been addressed.
Time limited: a date for review should be scheduled.

Most agencies have standardised care planning forms and these are often incorporated into assessment documents. The service user should sign the plan and be given a copy of it.

When a number of services are involved, it is important to ensure that roles and responsibilities are clearly delineated. A lead professional can facilitate case coordination. When the assessment indicates that a partner or parent requires help, then a separate care plan for the significant other is required.

Where serious tensions exist between the person with the substance problem and a significant other, it may be appropriate for the latter to be allocated to a different practitioner. In such circumstances decisions as to whether joint work is desirable can be taken after the partner or parent has been given help to address the issues she faces (see Chapter 15).

Every effort should be made to adhere to the plan but flexibility should be built into the system, with reviews being brought forward if necessary.

## Harm reduction

When harm reduction is understood as a response to risks – any risks and not just those associated with opiate use – it takes on a much wider meaning and much of the controversy surrounding it evaporates. Evaluation of risk should be an ongoing activity throughout the life of a case. It should be on the agenda at every review and issues of concern should be addressed in each updated care plan (see Chapter 9).

## Choice of substance use goals

Some people in the preparation phase will be clear what goals they want to pursue. Others will be uncertain, particularly if they feel confused or daunted by the prospect of major change. 'Does this mean I can never drink again?,' said in an anxious tone, is often the response to a discussion about trying to stop drinking. Agreeing time limits breaks the process into steps which the person can manage. The answer to the question becomes: 'You said that you want to stay abstinent for the next few weeks, let's see how you feel after that.' A teenager might not agree with her youth justice worker to stop taking stimulants but she might agree to avoid them on her next night out. 'Short term' and 'manageable' become the watchwords for goals in the early stages.

Possible goals for people with **alcohol** problems are abstinence, controlled drinking or reduced consumption. Raistrick, Heather and Godfrey (2006, p. 24) suggest that when a person opts for abstinence this should be automatically accepted whatever his level of problematic use. Whilst a small number with more serious difficulties do return to harm-free use (see Chapter 6), abstinence is the rational goal for people with longer term, entrenched patterns of dependent drinking. Continued drinking is also inadvisable if anyone has alcohol-related health problems. There is support for the idea that a period of complete abstinence (one to three months) is desirable before a person with an alcohol problem decides what longer term goal he wants to pursue (Booth, 2006; Riastrick et al., 2006, p. 25; Scottish Council on Alcoholism, 1983). This has the benefit of breaking past patterns and allowing health to improve, whilst creating a space for reflection.

For people with shorter histories of problematic use, controlled drinking may be an option. Controlled drinking is not simply reduced consumption, although this is bound to be part of it; it is adopting a mode of drinking which no longer leads to problems the person was previously experiencing. Controlled drinking, with the discipline it demands, is not an easy option.

Assessment for controlled drinking is considered in Chapter 11. Reduced alcohol taking, by way of contrast, is drinking less, although harm may still be occurring. A practitioner may believe that a person's best interests would be served by pursuing a goal of abstinence or controlled drinking; however, if he is not ready to consider these, moderating consumption or bingeing less often are obviously desirable first steps.

For **opiates,** the options are stabilisation on a prescribed substitute, followed by maintenance or reduction. More immediate detoxification is also a possibility, but for this to be successful it is essential that the person is well prepared for a life without drugs and that his environment is conducive to this aim.

Pharmacotherapies for alcohol and opiate detoxification and the management of the processes are addressed in Chapter 11.

Controlled use of **stimulants** is extremely difficult and, as pharmacological substitution is rarely used, abstinence is the only realistic long-term goal (see Chapters 10 and 11). However, reduction in consumption and harm minimisation are first-step goals for those unwilling to contemplate complete cessation in the short term.

### Addressing the supporting issues

The care plan will also include actions to address the practical and personal problems identified in the assessment such as:

- past trauma and abuse
- domestic violence
- mental health problems
- debt
- accommodation problems
- relationship difficulties.

Helping to resolve these issues is likely to necessitate the involvement of various 'wraparound' services.

### Residential rehab

While most residential rehabs provide abstinence programmes, a small number provide very specialist services such as permanent care for street drinkers who are allowed to continue to consume within limits. The NTA (2012c) states that residential rehab is the appropriate option for some people but that the quality of projects is variable, early drop-out is common and significant numbers subsequently engage again with community-based programmes. In an analysis of the research comparing residential and community-based treatment, Ashton (2010) concluded that it was not possible to say that one was superior to the other but that residential rehab has particular value for people with the most serious difficulties.

Some rehabs are based on behavioural principles, others on the 12 steps. Some have religious affiliations. A number only take people who have been detoxed before admission, whereas others provide detoxification or manage its final stages if reduction has taken place before admission. Some offer shorter stays and others take residents for up to a year. It is important that a person considering residential rehab has accurate information about the nature of the programme and the establishment's ethos so that he can make an informed choice; a prior visit is essential. A person who finds personal disclosure in group situations trying will find it difficult to adjust to the residential setting. Most rehabs are based on the premise that abstinence from all substances, not just the one that has caused the person difficulties, is the aim. People likely to be considered most suitable include:

- those who have tried and persistently failed to make use of use of community-based options;
- those with complex or multiple problems which the chosen project has the expertise to deal with;
- those whose social circumstances are so disadvantageous that progress is unlikely if they remain in the community.

The last of these criteria underscores the importance of planning for discharge from the outset. Unless the living situation the person returns to is conducive to recovery, the gains made in rehab will be lost.

---

CASE ILLUSTRATION 7.3

**Care planning**
The following continues the case study outlined in Case Illustrations 7.1 and 7.2 above.

Arnie's SADQ-C score was 32 (see Appendix) and his diary noted shaking and sweating each morning, which subsided following an early drink; it was clear that he would suffer serious withdrawals if he stopped rapidly. The GP said that initial tests suggested some liver issues. She agreed to arrange detoxification in the community if the alcohol service offered ongoing support. Mary had attended a family support group and found this helpful.

On the basis of this, the following care plan was drawn up.

**Arnie**
*Goals:*

- Achieve abstinence.
- Restructure routine and develop constructive activities to support this.

*Actions agreed:*

- Try to reduce consumption by two units a day until a community detox can be arranged.
- On the morning the detox starts, avoid drinking completely and ensure that there is no alcohol in the house.
- Cooperate with the medical staff supervising the detox.

- Keep two appointments a week with the community alcohol practitioner prior to the detox to discuss changing routines.
- Keep twice-weekly appointments with the practitioner for the three weeks after the detox for support and to look at options for filling time.
- Following the detox, visit the project's 'dry' social club to see if he likes it.

**Mary**
*Goals*:

- Stress reduction.
- Support for Arnie.

*Actions agreed*:

- Continue to attend the family support group.
- Ask for individual counselling if she feels she needs this.
- Assist with the detox as advised by the medical staff.

Arnie gave permission for all parties to liaise as needed. Plan to be reviewed after six weeks.

Assume that Arnie detoxed successfully and then remained abstinent. Devise a care plan for Arnie and Mary which might be drawn up at the six-week review, ensuring that it meets the SMART criteria.

## Concluding comments

At its core, an effective assessment meets two simple criteria:

1 It identifies risk and unmet needs in respect of the person and those close to him.
2 It is carried out in a manner which encourages the person to continue to engage with the help-seeking process.

The care plan then lays out how the person wants to address the priorities identified in the assessment and interventions become the tools for achieving the goals set. With the practitioner as guide, the service user should own the process.

### RESOURCES

- Against Violence and Abuse. This is a national voluntary organisation supporting practitioners and policy makers dealing with domestic and sexual abuse. Its website contains a range of resources: www.avaproject.org.uk.
- DrugScope. Information about the purity and cost of street drugs is available in the FAQs section of the DrugScope website: www.drugscope.org.uk.

- Exchange Supplies. The following guides for service users can be purchased in hard copy or accessed free of charge from the Exchange Supplies website. www.exchangesupplies. org:
  Preston, A. (undated). *The Methadone Handbook* (11th edition).
  Preston, A. and Malinowski, A. (undated). *The Detox Handbook* (8th edition).
  Preston, A. and Malinowski, A. (undated). *The Rehab Handbook* (4th edition).
- National Treatment Agency for Substance Misuse (2006). *Care Planning Practice Guide.* London: National Treatment Agency: www.nta.nhs.uk/uploads/nta_care_planning_ practice_guide_2006_cpg1.pdf. (NB: Material on the NTA website is scheduled to be transferred by 2014 to the PHE website or placed on the National Archive's website or similar.)
- Skills Consortium. The Skills hub section of the Skills Consortium website provides links to numerous online treatment guidance documents and manuals: www.skillsconsortium.org.uk/skillshub.aspx.

# CHAPTER 8

# Motivational Interviewing

- Motivational interviewing is a staple intervention.
- The purpose of motivational interviewing is to help resolve ambivalence and prepare a person for change. As such, it is only appropriate at particular points in the cycle of change.
- It is effective but not more so than other interventions known to help reduce substance problems.
- Its application involves the practitioner adopting a particular orientation and learning specific skills.

## Motivation: the key to the door of change

In Chapter 6, the idea that motivation is a static personality trait was discarded in favour of the view that it is primarily a response to perceived or actual rewards. We are motivated to act if doing so is to our advantage. How we view such benefits, along with our beliefs regarding whether we are capable of taking the steps necessary to acquire them, may remain stable but, as often as not, they fluctuate depending on situation and mood. When faced with a major change, we often become ambivalent, vacillating between finding the rewards of altering our situation attractive and worrying about what we will lose. We become immobilised, unable to move on. This is a phenomenon all of us will have experienced. A trigger will set a substance user thinking about change, only for the risks that this entails to undermine her growing resolve. Val wants to give up heroin. She feels that she cannot go on living a life of petty crime, debt and general aimlessness. She arranges to see her GP. On the morning of the appointment, a sense of panic envelops her. Will she have to abandon her friends? How will she cope? Does it mean that she will have to stop using cannabis too? She reaches the surgery door, pauses, and then turns away. If Val's ambivalence towards change can be lessened and the belief that she can take the necessary steps to alter her situation strengthened, major obstacles will have been removed. The purpose of motivational interviewing is to help a person resolve such internal conflicts and nudge herself towards preparation for change. For some people it elicits change too.

### William Miller and the basis of motivational interviewing

Although some people arrive at services committed to change, many come but then seem determined to resist 'treatment'. Why is this? Ambivalence towards change is sometimes only part of the answer. The ethos of the service can also strengthen resistance. People may reject the label of addict that the process seems to be applying to them (Miller, 1983) or they may feel that they are being forced to subscribe to particular goals or philosophies. This is what William Miller, the father of motivational interviewing, believed when he started his work in the 1970s.

Miller was disturbed by what treatment for people with alcohol problems in the USA often entailed at that time. Many practitioners who adhered to the disease model maintained that little could be done to help people until they reached 'rock bottom', or that their apparent denial needed to be confronted by aggressive means. Miller's view was that the latter was sometimes unethical and often counterproductive. If someone tries to persuade us of something, then our natural reaction is to marshal the counter-arguments. If a practitioner lists the reasons why a person with a substance problem should change, then the latter will often respond with the case for continuing to use. This, for Miller, steeped in the cognitive behavioural tradition and the work of Carl Rogers, was the cause of denial; it was the product of confrontation, of attempts to impose solutions onto other people, rather than an innate characteristic of problem drinkers. Miller (White, 2012) also dismisses the idea that reaching some sort of personal rock bottom is needed before change can occur: 'It's not that people need to suffer severely; it's that they need to decide.'

Motivation to change is strengthened when a person envisages a future that is more fulfilling than the present and believes that she can reach it. A person must persuade herself that change is both desirable and possible; someone else trying to convince her will be counterproductive: 'it should be the client and not the counselor who voices the arguments for change' (Miller quoted in White, 2012).

Motivational interviewing is founded on this central precept.

CASE ILLUSTRATION 8.1

**Unhelpful interactions**

As practitioners, it is all too easy to fall into the traps which Miller identified. Consider this interaction between a young offender and his probation officer following the former's arrest for public order offences and possession of cocaine:

> *Practitioner:* Darren, you were drinking before you were arrested, weren't you?
> *Darren:* Yes, but not a lot.
> *Practitioner:* You only get arrested after you have been drinking, don't you?
> *Darren:* [long pause] It was only a few drinks with my mates. The police were harassing us, that's why I got angry.
> *Practitioner:* You're going to have to do something about your drinking.
> *Darren:* I don't have a problem, I'm not an alki.

*Practitioner:*You said that you would like to go to college, but this will make
   things harder.What are you going to do to prevent this happening again?
*Darren*: I'll stop drinking.
*Practitioner:*Well, avoiding going out on Friday nights would be a start.

It is easy to sense the probation officer's frustration. He sees a young man
with potential who repeats a destructive behaviour. Confronting Darren with
what is glaringly obvious to those around him should convince him of the need
for change; yet Darren is far from persuaded. He has a view of what happened
that Friday night which he has not had the opportunity to express. First, he
argues against the demand to address his drinking and then, with a complete lack
of conviction, he agrees in order to end the conversation. Closed and narrow
questions, and an accusatory tone, means that the interaction has taken place
solely on the probation officer's terms with Darren owning nothing of the
agenda. From time to time, most of us fall into this trap of trying to impose
change, with predictable consequences.Yet, despite glossing over the role drinking
plays in his difficulties, Darren has ambitions. Motivational interviewing may be a
way of helping him to explore for himself the advantages of changing.

Motivational interviewing can help precontemplators, such as Darren (Case
Illustration 8.1), to make the links between their substance use and the difficulties they are experiencing. It can strengthen the resolve and self-efficacy of
contemplators such as Val (see above). There is an argument, therefore, that
this chapter should have been included before care planning. However, motivational interviewing is as applicable to the person who has slipped back into
the contemplation stage following relapse as it is to the precontemplator or
contemplator engaging with services for the first time.

## The essence of motivational interviewing

Miller describes motivational interviewing as a 'collaborative, person-centred
form of guiding to elicit and strengthen motivation for change' (Miller and
Rollnick, 2009). This strengthening occurs through articulation. If we say that
we believe something, we are more likely to believe it; if we state that we are
going to do something, we are more likely to actually do it. In everyday parlance, 'we talk ourselves into it'. Encouraging a person to build on self-motivational statements is a central part of motivational interviewing. Miller (White,
2012) was greatly influenced by Carl Rogers but, whilst motivational interviewing is 'person centred', the questions and responses used do guide in ways
that Rogerian counselling does not.

Motivational interviewing is not an intervention applied by a practitioner
to a person; it is a communication style with a particular purpose. It is 'not a
packageable 'programme' to be lifted off the shelf' (Ashton, 2005b, p. 30);
indeed when manuals have been used, rigid adherence to these has been found
to undermine the need to react flexibly to service users' responses (Ashton,
2005b). It is a way of relating to people but it also requires certain skills. These

skills need to be learned and then practised under supervision if a high level of competence is to be gained (Miller and Rollnick, 2009). In some ways, motivational interviewing runs counter to our natural responses to people in distress. Faced with another's unhappiness and the question 'What should I do?', our inclination is to prescribe the course of action we think will reduce the suffering. Practice is needed to suppress this tendency.

Motivational interviewing is a time-limited mode of working, normally used over a couple of sessions. As we shall see in Chapter 9, it can be employed in brief opportunistic interventions where the interaction may last for as little as ten minutes or so. It is widely applicable: used at the right time, it can benefit the Friday night cocaine user as much as the person with a long-term heroin habit. It has been used as a stand-alone approach both in treatment trials and with people with less engrained difficulties. However, for those with more entrenched or complex problems, the commitment to change engendered by motivational interviewing is a necessary step prior to other interventions coming into play.

### How effective is motivational interviewing?

Whilst the central purpose of motivational interviewing is to prepare the ground for change, research shows that it can also influence behaviour and increase the likelihood of participation in other types of interventions for both drug and alcohol users (Gossop, 2006, p. 10; Raistrick, Heather and Godfrey, 2006, p. 95). Motivational approaches score well in the Mesa Grande (Miller and Wilbourne, 2002). There is, however, no evidence that motivational interviewing is superior to other interventions known to be effective (Smedslund et al., 2011). In two major alcohol trials (Project Match Research Group, 1997; UKATT Research Team, 2005), motivational interventions achieved positive but broadly similar outcomes to the very different treatment modalities with which they were compared. The use of motivational interviewing has spread beyond the substance problems field and smoking cessation initiatives. It has been employed extensively with offenders (McMurran, 2009); it has been used with people with gambling problems and those with a range of health-related issues where behaviour change is desirable (exercise; eating disorders; treatment compliance) (Britt, Hudson and Blampied, 2004).

### BOX 8.1 MOTIVATIONAL INTERVIEWING: ARE THERE ETHICAL CONCERNS?

Miller and Rollnick (2002, 2009) have rebutted the potential charge that motivational interviewing could be used to manipulate people against their will. Unlike pharmacotherapy, for example, when the doctor will ask the person whether they want to take a particular drug, the practitioner is unlikely to say that she intends to use a motivational approach. However, she might start the session with a sentence such as, 'Your view of your situation probably changes from time to time; it might be useful for us to discuss this.' Miller and Rollnick argue that the process of developing discrepancy is not about creating a conflict between the practitioner's views and the service user's values but about helping the person resolve the dichotomy between her behaviour and her aspirations or between two sets of values which she, the service user, already holds. The practitioner is not, therefore, imposing beliefs on the person or trying to get her to act against her will. Nevertheless they counsel caution when:

- what the person wants is different from what the practitioner thinks is best for her;
- when the outcome is in some way advantageous to the practitioner personally;
- when the practitioner's role confers coercive powers.

An open discussion about roles and values can lessen any difficulties.

## The practice of motivational interviewing

Careful attention to what a person is saying will help to identify where she is on the cycle of change and whether motivational interviewing should be considered. Some people approaching services are already committed to change and resolving ambivalence will not be an issue. Examples of the types of statements precontemplators, contemplators and people in the preparation stage say are given in Chapter 7.

### When motivational interviewing is not the right approach

Through heightening ambivalence, motivational interviewing tries to bring the person to the point where she commits herself to change. Once the decision has been taken, the preparation stage starts. This is the care planning phase with its focus on helping the person to formulate goals and address the practical steps needed to achieve these. With ambivalence resolved, or at least greatly reduced, a plan is mapped out. Logic suggests that using motivational interviewing at this point, and also when the person has begun to take action, will heighten ambivalence again. The person will, once more, mull over the gains that change might bring, contrasting these again with the costs of altering her behaviour. The attractions of substance use will come back into the equation and commitment to change may weaken. Research suggests that this is, indeed, what can happen (Ashton, 2005b). Motivational interviewing is not, therefore, an appropriate approach when a person is in the preparation, action or maintenance stages. It may, however, become the right tool following relapse if the person has reverted to precontemplation or contemplation modes.

It has also been noted that continuing to pursue a motivational approach when it becomes clear that the person remains ambivalent or is uninterested in changing is counterproductive (Ashton, 2005b).

## The four principles of motivational interviewing

Miller and Rollnick (2002) outline these as follows:

**Express empathy.** Empathy (see Chapter 6), the ability to listen with acceptance and let the person know that he has been heard (reflective listening), underpins motivational interviewing. So too does awareness that ambivalence is to be expected. The practitioner may not agree with the person's perspective but through reflective listening demonstrates that the agenda belongs to that person.

**Develop discrepancy.** Developing discrepancy involves the person contrasting the benefits of remaining the same with the gains that change would bring. Motivation can be enhanced by helping the person to become more aware of how her current situation compares with how she would like her life to be. Miller and Rollnick (2002, p. 38) stress that this is about personal aims and values rather than the service user identifying the extent to which she needs to change her behaviour to achieve her goals. It is important that the person does not become overwhelmed by dwelling on what she has to do, rather than on how she would like to be.

**Roll with resistance.** Despite the practitioner trying to avoid presenting the case for change, the ambivalent person will, from time to time, resist the direction the dialogue is taking. She may play down the extent of the difficulties use is causing or say that she feels unable to do anything about her substance taking. As directly challenging such views is likely to lead to intransigence, the practitioner should maintain the principle of avoiding arguing by trying to get round the blockage. Reframing what the person has said becomes the technique for doing this.

The following is an example of a direct challenge which fails:

> *Service user*: I only take cocaine a few times a month.
> *Practitioner*: Don't you think that's quite often?
> *Service user*: No, not really – you should see some people I know.

Reframing might dismantle the barrier:

> *Service user*: I only take cocaine a few times a month.
> *Practitioner*: You don't use that often but tell me about any problems you have experienced when you have been using.

**Support self-efficacy.** Motivational interviewing stresses personal responsibility, choice and the service user's ownership of change. By doing so, it aims to strengthen self-efficacy, the belief the person has that she can change.

---

**ACTIVITY 8.1**

**Types of question**
Note down the purposes of closed and open questions. List five words or phrases which:

- a closed question might start with;
- an open question might begin with.

(Types of questions are considered in Chapter 6.)

---

### Eliciting self motivational statements (change talk)

Verbalising the desire to change is fundamental. McMurran (1995) says that the practitioner should only expect the service user to make self-motivational statements in cautious and hesitant ways; clear statements expressing determination to change are unlikely. 'I might be able to cut down my drinking' or 'I could think about stopping using coke' are examples of what to expect. The following strategies encourage people to make self-motivational statements:

- Using open questions. These allow the service user to explore the issues for herself. Leading questions can help direct the person into particular areas.
- Asking the person to describe the positives and negatives of the behaviour in question and the advantages and disadvantages of changing. This process heightens discrepancy. Additional techniques include asking the person what the worst outcome might be if she does not change and following this by asking her to consider the best outcome if she does alter her behaviour. Another option is to encourage the person to describe how she would like life to be in six months' time.
- Acknowledging the benefits the current problematic behaviour brings. This it is likely to lead the person to consider the adverse consequences.
- Asking the person to score, on a scale from one to ten (where ten is the highest), how important change is for her. When the response is given, the practitioner can ask why the score was not lower and then what it would take to nudge it higher. With this last question, it is important that the person selects actions which are achievable.
- Encouraging the person to expand on any self-motivational statements.
- Where appropriate, providing factual information about issues raised or services available.
- When resistance occurs, reframing.
- Summarising. This is another technique for ensuring that the person knows she has been listened to. It also allows the practitioner to check that he has interpreted correctly what has been said. (Clinical Training Institute, 2013; McMurran, 1995)

## BOX 8.2 KEY QUESTIONS IN MOTIVATIONAL INTERVIEWING

- What changes would you most like to talk about?
- What have you noticed about …?
- How important is it for you to change …?
- How confident do you feel about changing …?
- How do you see the benefits of …?
- How do you see the drawbacks of …?
- What will make the most sense to you?
- How might things be different if you …?
- In what way …?
- Where does this leave you now?

Reproduced from S. Rollnick, C. Butler, P. Kinnersley, J. Gregory and B. Mash (2010), 'Motivational Interviewing', *British Medical Journal*, 340, c1900. Reproduced with permission from BMJ Publishing Group Ltd.

### CASE ILLUSTRATION 8.2

**An example of motivational interviewing**

Although Darren's continued offending is a disappointment (see Case Illustration 8.1 at the beginning of this chapter), it presents a potential trigger for change if his probation officer can exploit the opportunity. With motivational interviewing, the session might develop as follows:

*Practitioner:* Tell me what happened, Darren, when you were arrested. (*An example of an open question*)

*Darren:* The police were getting at me again – they're always harassing us.

*Practitioner:* They were harassing you again. (*An empathetic statement. The probation officer is not condoning Darren's behaviour but he is acknowledging his point of view.*)

*Darren:* Yes, whenever I am out with my mates, it's always the same.

*Practitioner:* Can you tell me a bit more about the situation?

*Darren:* We were on our way home on Friday, late on. We weren't doing anything. I just told them not to stop us. [Darren getting a bit angry]. I just had a few drinks, I am not an alki!

*Practitioner:* You told them not to stop you. What had you been doing beforehand? (*The practitioner almost certainly has a picture of a fairly intoxicated Darren shouting abuse at the police. He does not, however, challenge Darren's version of events but acknowledges how the latter sees it and then shifts the focus. An example of rolling with resistance.*)

*Darren:* We'd been in the pub playing pool but I wasn't drunk.

*Practitioner:* You were going home with your mates after a few drinks. When the police stopped you, you objected. You thought it wasn't fair. (*Summarising*)

*Darren*: [Nods].

*Practitioner*: What does a few drinks means for you and your mates? (*An example of an open question leading in a particular direction*)

*Darren*: Four or five lagers – it was Friday night.

*Practitioner*: You enjoy Friday nights. (*Acknowledging the benefits*)

*Darren*: Yeah. I get fed up during the week hanging about with nothing to do. We play pool and have a laugh, sometimes go to a club.

*Practitioner*: Tell me about the cocaine.

*Darren*: It was nothing, just a little Charlie.

*Practitioner*: Mixing alcohol and cocaine is interesting. It produces cocaethylene. The only place it occurs is in the human body after taking booze and coke together. It is toxic and can damage the heart and liver. (*Factual information presented without additional comment*)

*Darren*: [Remains quiet, thinking about this statement].

*Practitioner*: It seems to me that Friday night is the only time you have some fun. (*Again acknowledging the benefits*)

*Darren*: Yeah, if it wasn't for the trouble. My dad thinks I won't get into college now. (*Darren responds to the positive view of Friday nights with the negative experience it has involved. A very tentative self-motivational statement.*)

*Practitioner*: Is that the worst outcome for you if things don't change? (*This is a closed question but it also reframes what has been said by linking difficulties to possible change.*)

*Darren*: Yes, and ending up in prison.

*Practitioner*: What would be the best outcome? (*Heightening discrepancy*)

*Darren*: Getting to college and getting the police off my back.

*Practitioner*: You've been thinking about college for a while. What do you think your life would be like if you do get a place? (*Again trying to heighten discrepancy*)

*Darren*: Something to do; something to get out of bed for; new friends; help me get a job (*Examples of self-motivational statements*). I get really fed up at times.

*Practitioner*: What do you think would help you get to where you want to be? (*Another example of an open, leading question*)

*Darren*: Staying out of trouble, for a start.

*Practitioner*: Any ideas about how to do that?

*Darren*: Maybe drink a bit less. (*A tentative self-motivational statement*)

*Practitioner*: You enjoy Friday nights, they're good fun. What happens, though, is getting in the way of your ambition to go to college and learn a trade. You're wondering whether you could get the police off your back if you drank a bit less. Is that how you see it? (*Summarising with some reframing*)

*Darren*: I suppose so, yeah.

Open questions and a lack of criticism have created a person-centred environment. The agenda is Darren's but his probation officer has his hand gently, but firmly, on the tiller. The result is they are moving together in a particular direction. Unlike the scenario at the beginning of the chapter, the practitioner is not pushing against Darren. At the start of the interview, Darren was in the precontemplation stage; motivational interviewing has brought him to the point where he is, rather hesitantly, contemplating change. Nothing dramatic has occurred. Darren is unlikely to stop going out on Friday nights or declare that abstinence from alcohol or drugs is his immediate aim. However, he is now acknowledging that his use of substances is an issue to be considered. He is likely to have started to experience ambivalent feelings and the next step will be to help him resolve these by encouraging him to tip the decisional balance towards change.

In this case illustration, we can also see some of the processes which Prochaska et al. (1992) suggest promote movement through the cycle of change:

- *Consciousness raising*: Darren is beginning to think about how his behaviour might be holding him back.
- *Dramatic relief*: He has expressed feelings about being stuck in a rut.
- *Self re-evaluation*: Darren is becoming aware of how he lives now and what he might become.

ACTIVITY 8.2

**Analyse the processes of motivational interviewing**
Look at one or two of the short films demonstrating motivational interviewing which are available on YouTube. Note examples of the application of the four principles and the techniques of motivational interviewing as they occur. How successful do you think that the practitioners are at:

- expressing empathy?
- avoiding confrontation by rolling with resistance?
- elaborating on self-motivational statements?

## Concluding comments

Used at the correct points in the counselling process, motivational interviewing is a key weapon in the armoury of well-evidenced interventions. It is used increasingly widely but to apply effectively what is as much an orientation as a technique demands training and practice under supervision. The next challenge is to ensure that these are available to more practitioners.

### RESOURCES

- Latchford, G. (2010). *A brief guide to Motivational Interviewing*. Describes the principles of motivational interviewing and its application in health settings. Available at: www.psychmap.org/uploads/Motivational%20Interviewing%20brief%20guide.pdf.
- Miller, W. and Rollnick, S. (eds) (2013). *Motivational Interviewing* (3rd edition).

- Psychotherapy.net. A commercial site marketing a range of DVDs demonstrating the practice of motivational interviewing and other interventions relevant for use with people with substance problems. www.psychotherapy.net.
- Substance Abuse and Mental Health Services Administration (US) (1999). *Enhancing Motivation for Change in Substance Abuse Treatment.* Comprehensive Web-based guidance on the practical application of motivational interviewing. Available at: www.ncbi.nlm.nih.gov/books/NBK64967/.

# CHAPTER 9

# Harm Reduction; Less Intensive Treatment; Brief Interventions

- Harm reduction, less intensive interventions and brief interventions are separate but overlapping.
- Harm reduction can be used as both a first stop and an ongoing intervention for both drug and alcohol problems.
- Less intensive interventions can be effective, particularly where problematic use is not engrained.
- Brief interventions involve non-specialist practitioners in a variety of settings engaging, opportunistically, with large numbers of people whose use may be problematic or potentially harmful.

## Different but connected

It is important to clarify how the terms 'harm reduction', 'less intensive treatment' and 'brief interventions' are applied here as they are open to different interpretations.

- **Harm reduction** is used in its widest sense as encompassing any measures put in place specifically to reduce risks.
- The term **less intensive treatment** describes short-term, structured approaches delivered by specialist practitioners to people who have sought help for difficulties they are experiencing.
- The phrase **brief interventions** is used to describe short, one-off inputs undertaken opportunistically or as part of wide-scale screening initiatives by non-specialist staff in a number of settings. Brief interventions last from a few minutes up to half an hour and their purpose is risk reduction in the general population.

In the literature, the term 'brief interventions' is sometimes used to describe either the second or the third of these concepts. The names and definitions used here are those suggested by Raistrick, Heather and Godfrey (2006, p. 79).

# Harm reduction

Harm reduction as a distinct entity emerged as a response to controlling the spread of HIV in the 1980s. It developed initially with a focus on people who inject and it has become indelibly associated with substitute prescribing, needle exchanges and the like. Harm reduction approaches have been extended to other substances and other methods of ingestion but it is still seen principally as applying to drugs rather than alcohol and tobacco. Keene (2010, p. 87) argues that 'harm minimization', 'treatment' and 'help with other problems' can be viewed as discrete activities demanding somewhat different approaches dependent on the context. Such differentiations can encourage practitioners to be clear about what the objectives are in any given situation but Keene acknowledges that these different activities do often take place at the same time. A less distinct and more holistic view will be taken here: one that considers that harm reduction encompasses any practical steps taken by a person to lessen the risks connected with his substance use or associated way of living. As such, it is as much about helping someone with an alcohol problem to avoid eviction as it is about clean syringes.

## Harm reduction: the evidence

As service provision reorientates to accommodate the recovery agenda, there is a risk that the classic harm reduction measures of needle exchange and safer injecting advice will be downgraded. Should this occur, the consequences would be serious. Based on extensive reviews of the evidence, the NTA (2012a) and NICE (2009) support the use of opioid replacement therapy and needle exchanges respectively as key measures for reducing harm. Telling evidence of the health benefits of harm reduction for people who inject can be found in international comparisons of HIV rates. In Russia, where harm reduction is not state policy, 37 per cent of injectors were HIV positive in 2011 (England: less than 2 per cent) and in Greece and Romania rates have risen sharply as investment in harm reduction has been cut (Judge, 2012). Hepatitis C remains a problem but rates in England are lower than in most developed countries (NTA, 2010).

A meta-analysis by Ritter and Cameron (2006) endorses the use of needle exchange and outreach but notes that evaluation of harm reduction initiatives for non-injecting methods of administration, alcohol and tobacco is limited.

## Harm reduction in practice

Harm reduction can:

- increase the safety of a person who continues to use;
- act as a first-stop intervention to prevent further harms occurring while a person decides what longer term goals he wants to pursue;
- be one component in a package of interventions: an element factored into the care plan throughout the treatment journey.

At societal level, harm reduction is a major strand of government policy, with the ban on smoking in enclosed public places, drink-driving legislation and alcohol licensing law being prime examples.

On an individual level, risks directly connected to both how substances are consumed and the consequences of use should be considered with all who approach services, even if contact is limited. The person can then be:

- given factual information about the issues identified;
- helped to take particular actions to lessen the actual or potential harms;
- signposted to specialist facilities such as needle exchanges and contraceptive or debt advice services.

In addition to its application in formal treatment, harm reduction underpins brief interventions and outreach work on the street, at dance events and at music festivals.

What follows regarding safer use comes with a note of caution: it is an overview. Practitioners giving advice about particular substances are advised to obtain fuller information. Detailed advice on injecting should only be given by people trained to do so.

### The value of information

Giving factual information is an essential component of harm reduction. As was noted in Chapter 7, it should not be assumed that people are well informed about the substances they use. Face-to-face discussion can be supplemented with leaflets or by pointing people to reliable Internet sites.

### Consumption

An obvious step which a person can take to protect his health is to use less often or reduce the amount consumed on any given occasion; reduced consumption also decreases the problems which can accompany intoxication and lessens the risk of overdose. Reviewing a typical session with the person, or his use over a period, can help him to become more aware of the risks and identify ways of cutting down. These include:

- starting later in the day;
- buying limited quantities;
- consciously pacing use;
- with alcohol, sipping rather than gulping, avoiding the round system and interspersing alcoholic drinks with soft drinks.

It is safe for people who are dependent on those drugs which are dangerous in withdrawal to reduce by small amounts in a staged way over time as long as they know that they must not stop suddenly (see Chapter 10). Keeping a diary can be a useful awareness-raising and self-monitoring tool. Except when a person is physically dependent on a substance which is dangerous in withdrawal, he should be encouraged to have regular breaks from use.

### Preventing overdose

In the European context, levels of drug deaths remain high in the UK (EMCDDA, 2013c). A number of factors are known to increase the likelihood of overdose (Baldacchino, 2012; Siegal, 2001):

- Injecting drugs. Encouraging ingestion by other methods will reduce, but not eliminate, the risk.
- Mixing drugs, particularly with alcohol.
- Loss of tolerance having recently left prison. Returning to use after a period of abstinence is a particularly risky time.
- A history of overdose, especially in the previous six months.
- Using alone.
- Using in an unfamiliar environment.
- Having mental health difficulties or having experienced a recent traumatic event.

Baldacchino also notes that being in treatment lessens the likelihood of overdose. It is important to raise awareness of these risks in the context of the individual's pattern of use and encourage potential changes in behaviour. Whilst there is a tendency to associate overdose primarily with opiate use, it can also occur with various other substances, including alcohol.

### BOX 9.1 USER AND PEER INVOLVEMENT

User and peer involvement can extend from inputs to service planning through to running recovery projects. It is essential that people recruited for such tasks are trained and well supported. People who have experienced problems themselves bring credibility and can access hard-to-reach groups. They have been utilised in a variety of ways in harm reduction schemes such as:

- designing leaflets;
- blood-borne virus education;
- initiatives to discourage initiation into injecting;
- outreach at dance events and festivals;
- take-home naloxone programmes. When injected, naloxone immediately counteracts opiate overdose. Easy to administer, naloxone is being made available to drug users and their relatives in many parts of the country.

### Methods of ingestion

The dangers of **injecting** are well documented. A practitioner whose main task is to engage with the psychosocial aspects of a person's drug use should be able to screen injecting practices and give general advice on risk. However, if a person is involved in particularly dangerous procedures, it is highly advisable that he discusses the issues with medical staff or trained practitioners in needle exchanges. Injection always presents risks but harm reduction advice can be summarised as follows:

- Keep areas around sites clean. Use a medical swab before injection but not afterwards as alcohol keeps the wound open.
- Avoid dangerous sites. In no circumstances should arteries be used. If an artery is hit, blood loss may occur very quickly; aneurisms can form and blocked arteries can lead to gangrene. The safest vein is in the inside of the elbow. Veins, however, can scar, narrow and collapse, leading people to use places that present much greater risks. Women's veins are less robust than men's and damage can occur more quickly. The groin is a site of particular concern. Here veins, arteries and nerves run close together and depth makes accurate injection difficult. Other high-risk sites include the hands, back of the legs, feet and ankles; the neck, breasts and penis are particularly dangerous.
- To avoid blood-borne viruses, never share injecting equipment; this includes filters, spoons, water containers and tourniquets. New needles, syringes and filters should always be used. However, people should also be given instructions as to how to bleach clean equipment, although this provides no guarantee of safety.
- Use the smallest needles possible, except when groin injecting or using steroids.
- To reduce the risk of fungal or bacterial infections, never inject street drugs into muscles or tissue.
- Prepare heroin using citric acid or vitamin C (ascorbic acid) and not vinegar or lemon juice as these can cause fungal infections. Vitamin C is the best option. As little citric acid or vitamin C as possible should be used as acid damages the vein. Citric acid and vitamin C are provided by needle exchanges in small packets, a quarter of which should be used and the rest discarded.
- When using heroin, pick any paracetamol out of the spoon and dispose of it. Paracetamol is often added to heroin as a bulking agent; it does not dissolve in citric acid or vitamin C. Adding more citric in an attempt to dissolve it risks further damage to veins and surrounding tissue.
- Do not inject pills or capsules. These contain additional compounds which can speed the collapse of veins when injected. If people do inject these, the powder should be dissolved thoroughly and then drawn into the syringe through a filter.
- Be aware that the anaesthetic effects of cocaine mean that the pain caused by inefficient injecting may not register.
- If veins are seriously damaged, chasing heroin or administering it rectally are options.
- Inject steroids only into muscle. The top of the arm, thigh or buttock muscles are the sites which should be used. However, some performance

and image-enhancing drugs, such as human growth hormones and tanning agents, are injected subcutaneously in the stomach area. Steroids and image-enhancing drugs should never be injected into veins.

- Seek medical advice for bleeding or discoloured skin or if an area around an injection site is hot, painful or red.
- Dispose of equipment safely. (Birmingham Drug and Alcohol Action Team, 2012; Malcolm, 2013; Preston and Derricot, 1999)

Injectors, those whose use suggests that they may progress to injecting and people who snort drugs should be encouraged to be screened for, and vaccinated against, hepatitis A and B. Partners and people who live with injectors are also priority groups for hepatitis B vaccination. Improvement in treatments for blood-borne viruses underscores the importance of early diagnosis and the value of promoting testing.

**Snorting** risks the spread of blood-borne viruses if bank notes or tubes are shared. Damage to the nose can occur and amounts can be difficult to control. Harm can be reduced by:

- ensuring the powder is as fine as possible;
- flushing out the nose after use;
- never sharing equipment. (Substance Create, 2013a)

Over time, **swallowing** substances can damage the stomach and other organs. Because absorption via the stomach takes time, a person may take a dangerous amount whilst waiting for the effects to start. People using this method should:

- eat before use;
- take a small amount and await the effects;
- dilute drugs which come in liquid form and which can damage the throat, GHB and GBL being examples. Some other drugs which come as liquids – amyl nitrite (poppers) being a case in point – should never be taken orally as death can follow. The vapour of poppers is inhaled. (Know the Score, 2012; Substance Create, 2013b)

**Smoking** drugs such as heroin and crack is preferable to injecting them and injectors who are not willing to stop should be encouraged to adopt this method of ingestion. Smoking reduces the risk of blood-borne viruses and overdose but does not eliminate them. The harm reduction mantra that no paraphernalia should ever be shared holds as true for crack pipes, foil tubes and the like as it does for injecting equipment. Long-stemmed glass crack pipes avoid the toxicity which can come from using plastic bottles, soft drinks cans and similar self-made equipment.

## BOX 9.2 TOBACCO AND HARM REDUCTION

As all smoking is potentially damaging to health, smoking strategies across the UK advocate abstinence. Reduced consumption of tobacco is, however, included in NICE guidance (2013) as preparation for complete cessation. Methods suggested include delaying the first cigarette of the morning, setting non-smoking periods and increasing the times between cigarettes, along with the use of alternative methods of delivering nicotine such as gum or patches. It will be interesting to see if e-cigarettes become popular for maintenance as opposed to providing a bridge to abstinence. Snus, a type of tobacco contained in a pouch, is placed under the upper lip. It is illegal in the UK but not in Norway and Sweden. Although it is not harm free, Gartner et al. (2007) suggest that if people who smoke switched to snus, there would be considerable health gains. It has the potential, therefore, of being a harm reduction measure for people unable to quit. However, e-cigarettes and snus could have unintended consequences, such as acting as a gateway to smoking for non-smokers.

### Substitute prescribing

For opiate users, substitute prescribing is a central harm reduction measure (see Chapters 6 and 10).

### Sexual and reproductive health

Contraceptive advice and guidance on avoiding sexually transmitted infections are routine harm reduction measures.

### Reducing other harms

Problems which are the consequence of use, rather than the risks of use itself, should also be addressed. Indeed, the person may see these as immediate priorities and it may be these that motivated him to seek help. Steps to prevent homelessness, loss of employment or financial problems reaching crisis point can be critical to stabilising the situation. Practitioners should ensure that any health problems are addressed and that the person is exercising adequate self-care, including eating regularly. For isolated older people with chronic substance problems, the provision of home care services can ensure that basic needs are met. Risks to significant others are addressed in Chapters 14 and 15.

### CASE ILLUSTRATION 9.1

**Harm reduction**

Robbie (aged 18) has approached the substance problems agency you work for. His father has threatened to throw him out of the home because of his drug use. Robbie has a girlfriend but he cannot stay with her. He says that his substance use has been increasing. He chases heroin three or four times a week and has injected it twice. He also binge drinks and uses benzodiazepines.

- Identify potential risks in this situation.
- What immediate steps would you encourage Robbie to take in order to reduce these?

## Less intensive treatment

When a person has a low level of dependence on a substance and associated difficulties are not severe, then less intensive treatment may be appropriate. Such people may actively seek out treatment but they may also be identified through opportunistic screening and want to address the concerns raised more fully. Less intensive treatment involves a maximum of four counselling sessions and is delivered by substance problems workers or generic practitioners with a special interest.

Reviewing the evidence in respect of alcohol problems, Raistrick, Heather and Godfrey (2006) suggest that partners should be involved in less intensive treatment where possible and that the following approaches can be effective:

- Assessment and full advice.
- CBT delivered in a condensed form.
- Brief marital therapy.
- Motivational interviewing.

The interventions are similar, therefore, to those used for more intensive work but they are tailored to a limited number of sessions.

### BOX 9.3 WORKING WITH CANNABIS USERS

Gossop (2006) notes that research into the effectiveness of interventions for cannabis dependence shows mixed outcomes and also that it is unclear whether brief or intensive interventions are the most appropriate. Because cannabis is often the secondary drug of concern when people present for treatment, there is a risk that the problems it is causing for them will be neglected. Interventions are similar to those used with people experiencing difficulties with other substances. There are no particular pharmacotherapies for cannabis users but symptomatic prescribing may be used in withdrawal (Copeland, Frewen and Elkins, 2009).

There is strong evidence supporting the effectiveness of less intensive treatments for people with alcohol problems (Raistrick, Heather and Godfrey, 2006). For people with drug problems, the evidence is less conclusive (Gossop, 2006); however, this finding should not be interpreted as suggesting that less intensive treatments have no place in the armoury of interventions for problematic drug use. Those approaching immediate access services for help with lower-level problems with stimulants or cannabis may not want lengthy engagement. People can be encouraged to consider more intensive programmes if there is a subsequent lack of progress or if it becomes clear that the extent of their difficulties merits this.

The principle of encouraging the person to set goals for himself holds true for less intensive treatment. Many may want to reduce the harms through moderation, rather than abstinence, but the latter should be supported if that is the person's choice. Moderating illicit drug use, of course, does not remove the risk of arrest. Follow-up is as relevant to less intensive work as it is to more comprehensive treatment, particularly as this can help to identify people who would benefit from accessing longer term support.

---

**CASE ILLUSTRATION 9.2**

**Less intensive treatment**

Gary approached the substance problems service where I worked. He was concerned that his alcohol consumption was accelerating and that his health would suffer; his partner had also expressed such fears. He drank on five evenings a week in a pub after work. Consumption on drinking days averaged about five pints of lager (around 50 units a week). This, along with an AUDIT score of 15, confirmed that he was right to believe that he should make changes. He did not describe any withdrawal symptoms and considered his health to be good. He said that his drinking had only increased over the past year and he put this down to boredom. We discussed units, how alcohol is metabolised in the body and the risks that heavy drinking entails; I gave him an alcohol information leaflet. We considered options for the coming week. He decided to go home straight after work and avoid drinking completely for a couple of weeks to break his pattern. At the next appointment he said that he had achieved this goal and that he and his partner had discussed going out more often together. He had decided to drink only at weekends and never more than six units in a day. We set a further appointment for a month later. Prior to this, Gary phoned to say that he did not think that another meeting was necessary. Apart from a couple of week-night evenings, he had stuck to drinking at weekends only and his consumption was now within national guidelines. He said he would phone if he felt he needed a further appointment.

Gary was in the preparation stage when he approached the agency. In addition to wanting to talk over what action he might take, seeking help was a way of reinforcing his determination.

---

# Brief interventions

The purpose of brief interventions is to deliver very short inputs to people who are not specifically seeking treatment but who would benefit from reducing their consumption or the risks they face. Building on existing skills, practitioners in a wide range of settings can be trained to engage with very large numbers of people in what has been called a 'structured conversation' (NHS Scotland, 2011).

## Drinking

Brief interventions have been used as part of government drives to reduce alcohol-related health harms. The main objective is to encourage people to decrease their consumption rather than to abstain. Mass screening is used in various healthcare settings to identify people whose drinking is hazardous or beginning to become harmful and a brief structured interaction follows. Brief interventions can also be used opportunistically; for example, a youth worker might apply the methods with a binge-drinking adolescent. Raistrick, Heather and Godfrey (2006) emphasise the importance of offering onward referral where a pattern of dependency exists; fuller responses are also needed when additional problems are identified such as mental health difficulties or serious debt. An analysis of the evidence shows that brief interventions reduce consumption in the target group of at-risk drinkers (Raistrick, Heather and Godfrey, 2006). These gains are maintained for significant periods, although booster inputs may be advantageous.

Once a person has been identified through simple discussion or using a tool such as AUDIT (see Appendix), the structured conversation can be facilitated by using the **FRAMES** approach (Miller and Sanchez as described by the National Institute on Alcohol Abuse and Alcoholism, 1999):

- Feedback. The practitioner discusses with the person the specific risks his pattern of use presents, including any links with health problems.
- Responsibility. The practitioner emphasises that change lies with the person taking responsibility for making decisions and exercising control.
- Advice to change. Specific advice is given to the person to make changes.
- Menu of ways of making changes. The practitioner outlines methods by which changes can be accomplished such as setting limits, drinking on fewer days and dealing with pressures to drink. Leaflets and drink diaries may be provided.
- Empathetic style – the underpinning component.
- Self-efficacy. The practitioner expresses optimism in the person's ability to change and tries to strengthen his self-efficacy through motivational enhancement.

The Scottish Intercollegiate Guidelines Network (2004) also stresses the importance of helping the person to decide whether his goal is abstinence or moderation and what the latter might mean in practice. Once a practitioner feels comfortable with using the FRAMES model, the areas outlined can be covered in very brief exchanges when time is at a premium or extended somewhat if the situation allows.

Education, employment, social work and criminal justice settings also present opportunities for brief interventions. However, further work is needed to evaluate effectiveness and methods of implementation in these locations (Raistrick, Heather and Godfrey, 2006).

### Drug use

There is a paucity of research into the effectiveness of brief interventions with drug users but two major studies (Humeniuk, Dennington and Ali, 2008; Madras et al., 2009) do suggest that it has considerable potential to reduce consumption within this group too.

### Smoking

Brief interventions with people who smoke are offered primarily by staff in health settings but there is potential for practitioners in a wide range of disciplines to raise the issue of cessation in a more systematic way. National Institute for Health and Care Excellence guidance (NICE, 2006), aimed at medical staff, recommends:

- encouraging those who are not yet ready to stop to think about doing so and to seek help when they feel inclined to do so. The issue should be discussed with the person on an annual basis.
- referring those who want to stop to specialist smoking cessation services.
- Cessation rates increase when nicotine replacement therapy or pharmacotherapies are used in combination with behavioural interventions (Sutherland, 2002).
- offering pharmacotherapy, if the practitioner is qualified to do this, to those who do not want to be referred to specialist services.

Ryder et al. (2001, p. 119) and Sutherland (2002) both note that the percentage increase in smoking cessation rates after a brief discussion with a GP is low. However, when these take place with large numbers of patients, the gains at the population level are very significant.

## Concluding comments

As Robson (2009, p. 210) says, 'the minimal requirement in the "treatment hierarchy" is risk reduction'. But this is not just a minimal, limited intervention; it should be an essential, ongoing component of brief and long-term engagement. While people with significant problems of dependency are likely to benefit from more comprehensive interventions, specific harm reduction services, less intensive treatment and brief interventions can have major beneficial impacts on large sections of the substance-using population for low per capita costs.

### RESOURCES

- Copeland, J., Frewen, A. and Elkins, K. (2009). *Management of Cannabis Use Disorder and Related Issues: A Clinician's Guide.* Available at: http://ncpic.org.au/ncpic/news/ ncpic-news/pdf/management-of-cannabis-use-disorder-and-related-issues-a-clinicians-guide.

- Exchange Supplies. The following guide for people who inject can be purchased in hard copy or accessed free of charge from the Exchange Supplies website: www.exchangesupplies.org:
  Preston, A. and Derricott, J. (undated). *The Safer Injecting Handbook* (7th edition).
- Health Scotland. A suite of materials for practitioners delivering brief interventions for alcohol use is available at: www.healthscotland.com/documents/3273.aspx.
- A wide range of harm reduction leaflets and other resources for practitioners, service users and the wider public are available from:
  www.substance.org.uk
  www.exchangesupplies.org
- The following site provides information about steroids and image enhancing drugs: www.siedsinfo.co.uk.

# CHAPTER 10

# Pharmacological Treatments

KEY THEMES

- From stabilisation to relapse prevention, drugs can be prescribed for various purposes.
- Pharmacological options are only available for some substances and some types of problematic use.
- In certain circumstances, detoxification is a critical step.
- The effectiveness of pharmacotherapy is enhanced if it is used in conjunction with psychosocial and recovery-orientated interventions.
- Effective inter-agency working is crucial.

## Pharmacotherapy: a central intervention for some

It is safe to assume that ever since humans discovered substances, they have used remedies to ameliorate the negative consequences of using them. However, drug treatments for substance problems have a somewhat chequered history. Chemicals as bizarre as strychnine and hydrochloric acid have been used to treat alcohol problems in the past (Drummond, 2002), and heroin, when first synthesised, was thought to be non-addictive and was used to treat morphine dependence (Gossop, 2007, p. 132)! The controversies surrounding methadone are described in Chapter 6. Nevertheless drugs can save the lives of people with substance problems and augment their efforts to deal with their difficulties. Practitioners who are not in the health professions need an understanding of the uses to which pharmacological treatments can be put. Detailed knowledge of how the drugs act or their side effects is not necessary. This chapter describes the main options.

It is now well accepted that the contribution of pharmacotherapy is crucial but, on its own, limited; pharmacotherapy should always be combined with psychosocial interventions and, if the person is interested, engagement with recovery-orientated activities (NTA, 2012a; Raistrick, Heather and Godfrey, 2006, p. 127). Close collaboration between medical and non-medical staff is, therefore, essential if the person is to achieve her goals. Single shared assessments and joint care plans are central to this. Gone should be the day when medical professionals make radical changes to prescribing regimes without liaising with the other practitioners involved.

## The purposes of pharmacotherapy

Drug therapy can be used for various purposes including:

- substitution;
- facilitating detoxification;
- reducing the likelihood of relapse;
- relieving substance-related physical and mental health problems.

These categories may overlap and, in some instances, drugs which fulfil one purpose can also serve another. A person might employ nicotine patches as she reduces her cigarette consumption and then continue to use them for a period after achieving abstinence. In this example, the patch acts as a substitute to aid smoking cessation and then helps to prevent relapse.

### Substitution

Substitution can reduce harm, buy time and help create stability. It offers an immediate and tangible response, thus encouraging people into treatment; once there, additional interventions can be offered. Substitute prescribing for opiate users (known as opiate replacement or substitution therapy) can remove the relentless pressure to obtain the funding to simply ward off withdrawals; in a more settled space, the person can start to address the other issues affecting her. For some, substitution is a first step towards the goal of a life without drugs, prescribed or otherwise; for others, long-term use of a substitute (maintenance prescribing) allows a normal life to be lived, just as insulin does for diabetics. Substitution therapy does not, however, resolve the issue of physical dependence.

As well as replacing an illicit street drug with a legal and pure alternative, substitution allows a risky method of ingestion (injection) to be changed to a safer one (oral consumption). Nicotine replacement therapy (NRT) is another example of changing the drug delivery method; in fact, NRT is a misnomer as nicotine itself is not being replaced but rather ingested via a different route. With patches, inhalers and gum, nicotine is still delivered but without the dangers of tobacco smoke. Substitute prescribing or alternative delivery systems are not available for many substances, alcohol included. Substitution remains a controversial approach, particularly as an intervention for heroin users. At the heart of such debates are fundamental disagreements about the priority that should be afforded to different goals. Is stabilisation and improved health the objective or should complete abstinence take precedence? Supporting the person herself to take responsibility for such decisions renders such arguments less relevant.

### Detoxification

For many people with substance problems, detoxification is not an issue: the drugs they use or the ways they use them do not lead to physical dependence.

For some, fear of withdrawals is a barrier to progress; however, many people do detoxify from time to time only to lapse back into use. Avoiding relapse is, perhaps, the greatest challenge. This underscores the importance of detoxification being part of a package of therapeutic and supportive measures. Preparation for detox is also essential; the person must feel ready to face the challenge of coping without a pharmacological crutch. The psychological and environmental factors supporting the person's substance use need to be addressed, and her recovery capital strengthened, before detoxification takes place.

In some circumstances, detoxification takes place on a slow reduction basis over a considerable period of time (often called tapering); in others, slow reduction is followed by a rapid process in the final stages; in yet others, it is achieved over a short period. However, detoxification is not always planned; for example, a physically dependent drinker may find herself detoxed during an emergency admission to hospital. Such situations demand that efforts are made quickly to put the building blocks of recovery in place. It is also important to bear in mind that a person may be physically dependent on more than one substance. If detoxification is undertaken in the community, support from close family can be invaluable.

## Opiates

### Opiate substitution

Methadone and buprenorphine (common brand name Subutex) are the substitutes most commonly used in the UK for maintenance and detoxification for opiate dependence. How do they compare?

Methadone acts in a broadly similar way to heroin; both are agonists. Methadone is slow acting, has little euphoric effect and dulls perception to some degree. It is normally prescribed in liquid form, which makes supervision of consumption relatively easy, and it is taken once daily. Some people experience unpleasant side effects. Risk of overdose is significant if methadone is used with other central nervous system depressants such as heroin, alcohol or benzodiazepines.

BOX 10.1 AGONISTS AND ANTAGONISTS

Agonists are substances which bind to, and trigger, particular receptors in the brain which are normally activated by naturally occurring neurotransmitters. For example, opiates replicate the effects of endorphins. An agonist mimics the effects of another substance.

Antagonists block particular receptor sites, preventing either naturally occurring neurotransmitters or agonists from having an effect. Some may also knock these off the receptor sites. Naltrexone is an opiate antagonist; opiates will have no effect if used after it has been taken.

In contrast to methadone, buprenorphine is both an agonist and an antagonist. Buprenorphine, therefore, both provides the effect of opiates and partially prevents any opiates used on top from latching on to the receptors. It is prescribed in tablet form and dissolved under the tongue (sublingual), which makes supervision of consumption difficult. It is taken daily initially, but once the person has stabilised this may be reduced to every couple of days. It provides less opiate-type effect than methadone and clarity of perception is maintained, making it attractive to people in employment. Overdose risk exists, but less so than for methadone, and it is easier to withdraw from buprenorphine. It is more expensive than methadone. A tablet combining buprenorphine and naloxone (brand name Suboxone) is marketed as a deterrent to injecting buprenorphine (Reckitt Benckiser, 2013). Naloxone is poorly absorbed if taken sublingually. Thus if Suboxone is taken sublingually as directed, the naloxone does not compromise the effects of the buprenorphine in a major way. However, if Suboxone is injected, the naloxone does limit the effectiveness of buprenorphine, precipitating a level of withdrawal. Some people do experience side effects with both buprenorphine and Suboxone.

Both methadone and buprenorphine are introduced via a process known as titration. Low levels are prescribed initially and then increased to the point where the person feels comfortable and is not experiencing withdrawals.

Whilst service user choice is fundamental, methadone remains the standard substitute for opiates in the UK (NICE, 2007b), with buprenorphine being considered when assessment identifies factors such as:

- a short history of dependence;
- the person experiences problems tolerating methadone;
- the person is considering detoxification in the foreseeable future;
- the person is at high risk of overdose;
- hazardous alcohol use. (NHS Fife, 2011)

There is the danger that people being prescribed opiate substitutes will compensate for the absence of the intoxicating effects of heroin by bingeing on other substances, particularly alcohol. This makes the ongoing monitoring of the use of all substances essential.

## BOX 10.2 HEROIN PRESCRIBING: BACK TO THE FUTURE

Historically, the so-called British system involved continuing to prescribe morphine or heroin to those unable to contemplate coming off these drugs, but this fell out of favour and methadone became the first line of response (see Chapter 4). From the 1990s onwards, Canada and some European countries, including England, have undertaken heroin assisted treatment trials. The purpose of these has been to evaluate whether providing injectable heroin under close supervision on a maintenance basis for people who have not responded to methadone and other interventions can improve outcomes. The results have been broadly positive, although this is not a cheap option (Strang, Groshkova and Metrebian, 2012). Heroin assisted treatment is now provided in some European countries but, as of 2013, this option had not been made widely available in the UK.

## Opiate detoxification

The stomach cramps, nausea and flu-like symptoms of opiate withdrawal are caused by over-activity in the central nervous system as it reacts to the removal of the depressant effects of opiates. Even when slow, step-by-step reduction is not the chosen approach, it is desirable that the person decreases consumption before detoxification takes place. Many people detoxify rapidly from opiates without medical help ('cold turkey') but this should not be attempted if the person has physical or mental health problems or is pregnant. Keeping the mind occupied, maintaining high fluid levels but avoiding caffeine, eating little but often and using over-the-counter medications for digestive discomfort and aches and pains all help the process (Drugs Action, 2010).

Medically supervised detoxification can take place quickly or via slow, stage-by-stage reduction (tapering). In many instances, transfer onto methadone or buprenorphine will be encouraged initially, with reduction of the substitute then taking place. As it is easier to come off buprenorphine than methadone, people may switch from methadone to this in the final stages. Tapering of the dose and the timing of reductions should be set at levels that do not leave the individual experiencing significant withdrawal symptoms. Dihydrocodeine, another agonist, is sometimes used for detoxification.

Various drugs, which do not act as substitutes, are available to lessen the symptoms. Lofexidine is one such drug and it is sometimes used when a person is going through the final stages of detoxification; it is also recommended as an option for detoxification for younger people and those with low levels of dependence (Department of Health (England) and the devolved administrations, 2007, p. 57). Various other drugs are prescribed to reduce sleeplessness, diarrhoea and abdominal pain.

Rapid supervised detoxification from opiates is available in the UK in some private clinics. Such procedures, which take place over a few days, involve heavy sedation or complete anaesthesia, with withdrawal being precipitated by the use of an antagonist such as naltrexone. It is important to ensure that people who choose this option are well supported medically and socially in the immediate aftermath as some level of withdrawal discomfort may continue for a period.

Other opiates, codeine and tramadol being examples, can lead to physical dependence. Detoxification, rather than maintenance, is encouraged and is usually achieved by gradual supervised reduction (Merrill, 2002).

## Drugs to reduce the likelihood of relapse to opiates

The opiate antagonist naltrexone is used by some to prevent relapse. It is normally prescribed as a tablet but has been used in implant and slow-release injectable forms. If an abstinent person uses heroin on top of naltrexone, they will experience no opiate effects. This can strengthen a commitment to abstinence but is dependent on compliance; it is easy to avoid taking a tablet. People have even been known to remove their implants! There are risks. Humans are not logical and people have taken heroin on top of naltrexone and, on experiencing no effect, have taken more; as the naltrexone has worn off, heroin overdose has occurred. Naltrexone does not impact on cravings. Gossop (2006, p. 9) notes that the high cost, along with limited enthusiasm for it among service users and significant drop-out rates among those prescribed it, means that naltrexone has not proved to be a radical advance. However a meta-analysis by Adi et al (2007) suggests that naltrexone can have a modest positive impact on relapse rates, at least in the short term, and psychosocial and other treatments can improve compliance. Naltrexone also has a role to play with people with alcohol problems (see below).

## Alcohol

### Alcohol detoxification

With no substitute for alcohol available, the physically dependent person must face detoxification at some stage. Care must be taken because of the risks alcohol presents in withdrawal (see Chapters 2 and 7). As it is essential that all practitioners consult colleagues in the health profession when involved with people considering alcohol detoxification, the following is provided for background information only.

It is feasible to detoxify from alcohol by carefully reducing the amount consumed over a period of time (tapering), thereby preventing significant withdrawals from occurring. However, the intoxicating effects of alcohol can undermine determination to continue with this method. If a person has a low level of physical dependence, immediate cessation without medication is unlikely to present great risks. As a broad guide, this should only be attempted if:

- consumption is less than 15 units a day for men and 10 units a day for women;
- there is no history of epilepsy, seizures or delirium tremens;
- the person displays no signs of withdrawals and is not drinking to stave these off;
- when the person's pattern is one of bingeing, the episode has lasted less than a week and consumption is lower than 20 units a day. (SA, 2011; Scottish Intercollegiate Guidelines Network, 2004)

Drinking plenty of fluids to counteract dehydration is essential and a warm bath can ease the discomfort. It is important that someone keeps an eye on the person.

When withdrawal symptoms feature or consumption has been excessive over a period, supervised medicated detoxification is always indicated. In most cases, this can be undertaken in the community with monitoring by health professionals or on a day-patient basis. Support from family or friends is invaluable. To prevent seizures, the benzodiazepine chlordiazepoxide (brand name Librium) or diazepam are prescribed on a reducing basis. Inpatient detoxification is necessary if certain factors apply, including when:

- the person is experiencing delirium tremens or seizures or has a history of these complications;
- the person has experienced multiple previous detoxifications;
- there is a pattern of polydrug use;
- there are acute health or psychiatric problems, including risk of suicide;
- social supports are lacking;
- a woman is pregnant;
- the person is older. (Dar and Cherian, 2012; Raistrick, Heather and Godfrey, 2006, p. 129)

### Vitamins

People who drink excessively can suffer from thiamine (vitamin B1) deficiency. This is because they often eat erratically and because alcohol utilises thiamine as it metabolises in the body. Lack of thiamine can lead to Wernicke's encephalopathy. Wernicke's often develops suddenly and its classic symptoms are vision and memory problems, confusion and impaired coordination, but all of these do not necessarily occur. It is a medical emergency which, unless treated, can lead to permanent brain damage (Korsakoff's syndrome) or death. To reduce the likelihood of Wernicke's encephalopathy, thiamine, along with other vitamins, is administered as part of the detoxification process. It is also given to people who are drinking heavily; it is essential that people continue to take vitamins as prescribed. Wernicke's can be successfully treated. Korsakoff's can be halted, and improvements can occur in some cases, if the person receives thiamine, maintains a good diet and abstains; the same is true for alcoholic dementia, a separate condition (Alzheimer's Society, 2012).

### Drugs to reduce the likelihood of relapse to alcohol

Disulfiram (commonly known by the brand name Antabuse), normally taken in tablet form, inhibits the breakdown of alcohol in the body leading to a build-up of acetaldehyde; this causes vomiting, facial flushing, accelerated heartbeat and headache. The extreme discomfort that follows drinking on top of disulfiram discourages relapse. Reviewing the evidence, Raistrick, Heather and Godfrey (2006, p. 130) conclude that disulfiram can be effective in combating relapse but supervised administration is necessary to reduce non-compliance.

Naltrexone and acamprosate act on the central nervous system to reduce cravings and the desire to drink but exactly how they do this remains unclear. Both score highly in the Mesa Grande (Miller and Wilbourne, 2002), confirming that they are useful additions to the armoury of treatments for alcohol problems. Neither of these drugs normally presents problems if a person drinks when taking them. Indeed Raistrick, Heather and Godfrey (2006, p. 134) suggest that naltrexone, particularly, is effective in helping people to curtail further drinking when a lapse has occurred.

---

CASE ILLUSTRATION 10.1

**Alcohol detoxification**

Vanessa (52) lives with her husband. A social drinker for most of her life, her alcohol consumption began to increase when she was made redundant two years ago and her son emigrated with his family. She has been drinking a bottle of vodka a day for the last six months and suffers withdrawal symptoms every morning. She has decided that she must stop drinking completely.

- What issues should be considered when drawing up a plan for her detoxification?
- What services might be involved?
- How would you help her prepare for detoxification and its aftermath?
- What might her GP prescribe to facilitate detoxification and, subsequently, what pharmacological options might reduce the likelihood of Vanessa relapsing?

---

# Psychostimulants

Stimulants are often used on an episodic basis as the accumulation of disagreeable consequences results in people taking breaks. Unlike alcohol or opiates, detoxification is much less of an issue. The biggest challenge is to help the person to avoid relapse when the unpleasant memories of use have faded and the desire for the rapid rewarding effects of these drugs returns. Research has been undertaken into pharmacological treatments, especially for cocaine, but effective drugs are proving elusive (Pierce et al., 2012).

## Psychostimulant substitution

While cocaine has been prescribed historically, amphetamine continues to be made available to some whose use of this drug is particularly problematic. The practice is controversial and is not supported by national guidance (Department of Health (England) and the devolved administrations, 2007, p. 61). Nevertheless Newcombe (2009) argues that there is evidence to suggest that prescribing dexamphetamine for longer term, heavy amphetamine users can encourage people to enter and remain in treatment, provide the opportunity to give them access to other recovery services and reduce the harms. As the effects of dexamphetamine are relatively short lived, very regular doses are necessary, making adequate supervision unworkable (Merrill, 2002, p. 161). Research into the use of dexamphetamine and other stimulants as substitutes for cocaine has produced inconclusive or negative results (EMCDDA, 2007, p. 16).

### Psychostimulants: other pharmacological options

Depression, anxiety, sleep disturbance and, in some instances, temporary psychosis accompany the come-down from bouts of stimulant use. Tranquillisers and other drugs are sometimes prescribed to reduce these symptoms. Antidepressants are also sometimes used for cocaine and amphetamine users but selective serotonin re-uptake inhibitors should only be prescribed if the person is abstinent (Department of Health (England) and the devolved administrations, 2007, p. 62). The risk of suicide should be assessed and hospitalisation may be necessary if a person experiences a more serious psychotic episode.

Most research into drugs to discourage relapse among cocaine users has reported inconclusive outcomes (EMCDDA, 2007, p. 16). Interestingly, one drug which does appear to have a positive impact is disulfiram (Antabuse). It is not clear whether this is because of how it acts within the central nervous system or because abstinence from alcohol may reduce the cues for cocaine use, alcohol and cocaine often being consumed together (Gossop and Carroll, 2006). In addition, Ashton (2001) notes that disulfiram has been shown to reduce cocaine use among people on opiate substitution therapy.

## Benzodiazepines

### Benzodiazepines: detoxification

While some people binge on benzodiazepines, the ready availability of illicit supplies frequently leads to persistent use, often as part of a poly-substance cocktail, and physical dependence can follow. Dependence on prescribed benzodiazepines is also an issue. As the value of maintenance prescribing of benzodiazepines is questionable (Department of Health (England) and the devolved administrations, 2007, p. 60), detoxification by tapering use is the course normally advocated. The risks benzodiazepines present in withdrawal (see Chapters 2 and 7) demand that this takes place under medical supervision. The standard procedure is to prescribe diazepam, which is longer acting than some other benzodiazepines and so promotes stability, on a slow reducing basis normally over a period of months. There are protocols for the rate of reduction. As people are prescribed benzodiazepines to deal with anxiety and related problems, and often use them illicitly for similar reasons, it is essential that psychosocial interventions are available when a person decides to detoxify.

### BOX 10.3 PHYSICAL DEPENDENCY: MORE THAN ONE SUBSTANCE

NICE (2007c) recommends that, in community settings, consideration is given to detoxification from alcohol or benzodiazepines prior to detoxification from heroin or other opiates.

# Nicotine

### Nicotine substitution

Public health authorities have encouraged the use of nicotine replacement therapies (NTR), such as gum, patches and inhalers, as a bridge towards abstinence. However, interest in using NTR on a maintenance basis for people who have been unable to quit has been growing. The risks have yet to be adequately evaluated but they are accepted as being much lower than for continued smoking (Shields, 2011).

### Nicotine: detoxification and drugs to prevent relapse

While withdrawal from nicotine without pharmacotherapy is commonplace, NRT (nicotine replacement therapy) and two drugs, varenicline (common brand name Champix) and bupropion (common brand name Zyban) are often used. Varenicline and bupropion are prescription-only drugs in the UK and both act on the central nervous system. The normal process is to start treatment a short time before the proposed cessation date and then continue with the regime for up to three months afterwards to reduce the likelihood of relapse. With NRT, staged reduction of the dose usually takes place after cessation. There is considerable evidence to support the use of these options for detoxification and for helping people to remain off tobacco, at least in the medium term (Eisenberg et al., 2008; Woolacott et al., 2002).

# Vaccines

Vaccines are a radical and intriguing possibility. They are being trialled for various substances but technical challenges remain. They act by preventing drugs from latching onto the receptors in the central nervous system. Vaccines raise practical and ethical issues:

- Who should be vaccinated? For example, should a nicotine vaccine be made available only to those unable to stop smoking by other means or should all babies receive this?
- When identification of those with a genetic predisposition to develop problems with particular classes of drugs becomes more advanced, should babies in risk groups be vaccinated? Would this be ethical when substance use is often not problematic and the development of difficulties is as much about learning and social context as genetic endowment?
- Would vaccination simply lead a person to change to another drug to achieve euphoria or deaden psychological pain?

**The dilemma of vaccines**

In addition to problems for the individual, excessive drinking causes harm to others and to wider society. If a vaccine for alcohol becomes a reality, do you think it should be used and, if so, for whom? What are your reasons?

## Concluding comments

New pharmacological approaches are often heralded as breakthroughs that will transform the treatment landscape. However, this is unlikely to ever be the case as the medical and neurological aspects of substance use are only elements of a complex phenomenon which also involves human personality, learning, choice and environmental influences. For many, pharmacotherapy is not necessary; for some, it is an essential intervention at particular points but one whose efficacy is enhanced when it is part of a holistic programme. Our rapidly increasing knowledge of genetics and neurology will bring a greater range of options in the future.

## RESOURCES

- Department of Health (England) and the devolved administrations (2007). *Drug Misuse and Dependence: UK Guidelines on Clinical Management* (commonly known as the 'Orange Book'). Available at: www.nta.nhs.uk/uploads/clinical_guidelines_2007.pdf.
- Exchange Supplies. The following guides for service users can be purchased in hard copy or accessed free of charge from the Exchange Supplies website: www.exchangesupplies.org:
  Preston, A. (undated). *The Methadone Handbook* (11th edition).
  Preston, A. and Malinowski, A. (undated). *The Detox Handbook* (8th edition).
- National Institute for Health and Care Excellence. There is NICE guidance on various aspects of working with substance problems, including pharmacotherapy: www.nice.org.uk/.

# CHAPTER 11

# Interventions: Specific Approaches

## KEY THEMES

- **Cognitive behavioural therapy** (CBT) is a core psychosocial intervention used with people with substance problems. **Contingency management** and **community reinforcement** are also based on behavioural principles.
- **Mutual aid groups**, such as Alcoholics and Narcotics Anonymous, have now been joined by other communities. There has been increasing interest in aligning these options more closely with formal services as part of the recovery agenda.
- **Controlled drinking** remains controversial; it is also often confused with reduced alcohol consumption, a different concept.
- Whilst the interventions for **stimulant users** are broadly similar to those employed with people who use opiates and other substances, a somewhat different mode of working is required with this group.
- Practitioners need to feel confident to engage with people experiencing problems with **new psychoactive substances** and **club drugs**.

## The foundations of effective interventions

This catch-all chapter explores particular interventions and modes of working. Throughout, the tenets governing effective interventions, outlined in Chapter 6, should be borne in mind. These are:

- A positive therapeutic alliance between service user and practitioner is essential.
- Research has established which interventions achieve the best outcomes but has not identified any one of these as being the most effective.
- The interventions shown to be effective do not help everyone.
- Better results are achieved when more than one intervention is used. (Gossop, 2006; Raistrick, Heather and Godfrey, 2006)

The cycle of change (see Chapter 5) can help to decide what combination of interventions is appropriate at which point, with reviews leading to adjustments to the care plan. For a person with a heroin problem, interventions might progress as follows:

- Stage one: motivational interviewing and harm reduction.
- Stage two: stabilisation using pharmacotherapy.
- Stage three: continuing pharmacotherapy and contingency management; relapse prevention utilising CBT.
- Stage four: continuing pharmacotherapy and involvement in recovery activities.

## Cognitive behavioural therapy (CBT)

Although often referred to as a single intervention, CBT is two overlapping modalities based on learning theories (see Chapter 3):

- Cognitive therapies are based on the notion that it is not experiences themselves which influence our moods and behaviour but how we interpret them. We appraise events, a process characterised by Sheldon (2011, p. 172) as holding 'internal "conversations"' using cognitive frameworks built on previous experiences. Helping a person to challenge these appraisals when they are unrealistic or unhelpful can improve mood, increase self-efficacy and influence behaviour.
- Behavioural interventions are grounded in learning theories. Associations and cues, reinforcement and punishment, along with modelling and wider cultural influences, all shape our habits. Just as we have learned, so we can relearn. Various methods can be used to help a person to abstain from use or learn to use in a harm-free manner. Exposing a person in controlled ways to situations and other cues associated with his substance taking can also be employed to eradicate the desire to use.

Whilst a clinical psychologist might apply a highly structured programme, a key worker might explore with a person how she views her drug taking and ways of altering her behaviour based on the principles of CBT without calling it this. Gossop (2011) has described CBT as a 'broad church' which encompasses a cluster of similar approaches. CBT's popularity is supported by numerous studies demonstrating that it can be an effective element in addressing certain mental health difficulties (Sheldon, 2011), offending behaviour (McGuire, 2007; Whyte and McNeill, 2007, p. 170) and substance problems (Carroll and Onken, 2005; Dutra et al., 2008; Raistrick, Heather and Godfrey, 2006), including smoking cessation (Perkins, Conklin and Levine, 2008; Sykes and Marks, 2001).

The following are key features of CBT:

- It focuses on how the person thinks and behaves in the present. It is assumed that current patterns have developed through prior learning and experiences but how and why these have developed is of limited interest. Unresolved childhood difficulties, past abuse or trauma may, therefore, have to be addressed separately using different therapeutic approaches.
- Goals are agreed, time scales are set and then progress is measured. CBT fits well, therefore, with the 'assess, plan, do, review cycle'.

- The person and the practitioner explore the thoughts which precipitate cravings or substance use and address how these might be restructured.
- Strategies are developed, and then implemented, to help the person behave differently in specific, problematic situations.
- The practitioner and service user work in partnership on specific tasks, with a strong emphasis on the service user taking responsibility for following through agreed activities. Homework between sessions is an important component.
- As work progresses, the person is encouraged to apply what has been learned across all aspects of his life (generalisation).

### Cognitive restructuring

Based on the principle that an event triggers a thought which, in turn, generates an emotional response, Ellis developed his famous ABC model (Activating event; Belief system; Consequences) (Ellis et al., 1997). Unrealistic or unnecessarily negative 'internal conversations' (the belief system) influence mood and actions in unhelpful ways, as the simple case outlined in Case Illustration 11.1 shows.

---

**CASE ILLUSTRATION 11.1**

**Cognitive appraisals**

Two people are facing a problematic meeting. Both have recently stopped smoking.

| | Activating event | Belief system | Consequences |
|---|---|---|---|
| Jim | Impending meeting | 'I can't cope with this' | Anxiety; feeling overwhelmed; strong desire for cigarette |
| Jenny | Impending meeting | 'I can deal with this challenge' | Confidence; low risk of relapse |

Beliefs are the difference between these two people. The emotional responses to these beliefs are likely to influence how they behave.

---

Ellis suggests that we often link the consequences directly to the activating event without considering the role of the belief system. In Case Illustration 11.1, Jim may attribute his agitation and desire for a cigarette to the impending meeting when, in fact, his belief system is the culprit. The purpose of therapy is to help the person to become more aware of how his cognitive frameworks dictate unhelpful or unrealistic thoughts and then learn ways to restructure these. Altered thinking has the potential to change emotional responses and behaviour. Faced with the meeting, Jim could think differently: 'I will feel anxious but I know I'll manage; a cigarette isn't the answer.'

Burns (1990, p. 8) and Ellis et al. (1997, p. 25) identify various types of unhelpful thinking including:

- 'All or nothing' responses. 'I can't stop smoking dope, so I might as well smoke all the time.'
- 'Emotional reasoning'. Here the person views feeling as the only reality in a situation. 'I can't enjoy going out without drinking.'
- 'Discounting the positive'. This describes the tendency to exaggerate negative possibilities at the expense of more positive evidence. The person will often use the word 'but'. 'Yes, I've stayed away from coke before but I always start again.'
- 'Awfulising' (also called catastrophising). Here the person is prone to attribute the worst possible outcome to experiences. 'I shared a needle once last month; I'm bound to have got hepatitis.'
- 'Overgeneralisation'. The person makes the assumption that because there was a negative experience in one situation, this will inevitably reoccur in other circumstances. 'I started drinking at the last party I went to, so that's my social life over.'

For people with substance problems, a particular trap is what Beck et al. (1993, p. 35) call 'permission-giving thoughts'. These allow the person to rationalise the desire to use, thus making the impending act acceptable: 'I deserve a blowout, given what I've had to deal with.'

Cognitive approaches tend to be associated with the implications of negative interpretations but, as we will see when we consider relapse (see Chapter 12), unrealistic optimism, too, can be a problem. The risks lurking in thoughts such as 'A joint won't hurt; I won't go back to using every day' are obvious.

Our cognitive frameworks tend to create tunnel vision; we fail to see all the options open to us in a given situation. The practitioner's task is to prompt the person to look beyond habitual responses. One method of doing this is to use a questioning technique known as guided discovery (Socratic questioning). Open and closed questions are used to help a person to challenge his assumptions in order to become conscious of thought processes and aware of different ways of viewing issues (Beck et al., 1993, p. 103). The person is encouraged to test the validity of his thoughts. Judicious summarising is an important feature of the approach. Ellis et al. (1997, p. 27) recommend the use of three types of question to help a person challenge unhelpful thinking:

- *Addressing illogicality*: 'Why do you think that one night's drinking is the end of the world?'
- *Emphasising reality*: 'But didn't you say that nothing terrible happened that night?'
- *Questioning the value of unconstructive thoughts*: 'How does believing that you're a failure help you?'

Jarvis et al. (2005, p. 131) suggest that the starting point is to ask the service user to pinpoint recent examples of where substance use occurred or when a negative mood put the person at risk. These are Ellis's negative consequences.

Guided discovery is then used to lead back to the event that triggered the problem and the thought processes in between.

In the following example, Mike intended to take his son swimming on Friday after work but got very drunk instead:

*Practitioner*: Mike, why did you get drunk?

*Mike*: Work had been difficult. I made a mistake with the orders; I'm hopeless.

*Practitioner*: As you left work, what did you think?

*Mike*: To hell with this, I'll go to the pub. Then I'll take my son swimming.

*Practitioner*: So it was the problem at work that led to the drinking?

*Mike*: Yes.

*Practitioner*: When you got to the bar, how many did you think you would have?

*Mike*: Oh, just one, and then I'd leave.

*Practitioner*: So why didn't you?

*Mike*: Well, I got talking to this guy and suddenly it was too late to go to the pool. Then I thought 'I've blown it again', and felt guilty, so I got drunk.

*Practitioner*: Let's go back over this, Mike. You told me last week that your boss was praising you, so this problem can't have been that serious.

*Mike*: Yes, but I never get the orders right.

*Practitioner*: Never?

*Mike*: Well, I sometimes get them right.

*Practitioner*: So if you'd stopped and thought that you do the job well most of the time, you might not have got so angry with yourself. If you hadn't got so wound up, what do you think would have happened?

*Mike*: I'd have gone home.

*Practitioner*: When later you thought you had blown it, what else could you have done other than go on drinking?

*Mike*: Well, I could have gone home, said sorry I was late and arranged to take him swimming the next morning.

*Practitioner*: Did you want to get drunk at that point?

*Mike*: No! [pause]. Well, maybe I did think that it would be a nice idea.

*Practitioner*: And was it?

*Mike*: Not when I got home or the next day, it wasn't.

*Practitioner*: Tell me if I've got this right, Mike. If you had stepped back and seen the problem at work as a minor one, you wouldn't have felt annoyed with yourself or gone to the pub. Having got there, you convinced yourself that you had blown it big time, when, in fact, the situation still wasn't too problematic. But by then you were giving yourself permission to go on drinking.

*Mike*: I suppose that's right.

The whole interaction has been an exploratory process with Mike and the practitioner working together to analyse two sequences:

**First sequence**

| *Activating event* | *Belief system* | *Consequences* |
|---|---|---|
| Problem at work | Mike thinks he is incompetent – discounting the positive | Frustration; anger; goes to pub. |

**Second sequence**

| *Activating event* | *Belief system* | *Consequences* |
|---|---|---|
| One drink | All or nothing thinking | Guilt; gets drunk |

In both sequences, we can see that Mike failed to seriously consider other ways of looking at the events; he was also was experiencing permission-giving thoughts. Note, too, how initially in the interaction he linked the consequences directly to the event by blaming his drinking on the problem at work without considering the role that thinking played. The practitioner's strategy was to encourage Mike to:

- become more aware of his thought processes and to understand the importance of the role these play;
- test out the reality of his thinking;
- become aware of the alternatives in any situation.

The next step is to encourage Mike to undertake homework which will sharpen his awareness of his belief system. A commonly used tool is a diary recording thoughts and reactions. There are numerous examples of these – indeed practitioners and service users can design individualised versions – but all should be designed to highlight thinking and moods which increase risk. Analysing the diary becomes part of each session.

### Behavioural programmes

The reader will have noticed that behaviour change and cognitive work are often inseparable and, indeed, working with both aspects of CBT together is often the most appropriate approach. Behavioural methods can involve complex schedules of rewards and punishments or cue exposure aimed at extinguishing old behaviours or establishing new ones. Such techniques are the preserve of behavioural psychologists and the like. What is of interest to practitioners from other disciplines is how to use more generalised methods, but ones which are based on similar principles.

The care plan should lay out how behaviour needs to change to enable the goals identified to be achieved. Just as goals must belong to the person, so decisions about what needs to change and how best to do this must be made by the person. Motivation to stay the course will depend on this ownership. To say this is not to downplay the role of the practitioner in providing information, challenging assumptions and suggesting options. Key elements include:

- an emphasis on *behaviour change as a learning process*.
- *individualised and specific targeting*. 'How do I avoid using cocaine?' is not the right question; 'How do I avoid using cocaine when I go out with friends to clubs on a Saturday night?' is.
- *learning by doing*. Educationalists such as Race (2012) emphasise the importance of experiential learning, feedback and reflection as a continuous process. A person can learn through practice to deal with cravings, avoid problematic situations, refuse substances, become more assertive and substitute constructive activities for drug use.
- *rehearsal and role play*. These can be used in the safety of the counselling room before new behaviours are tested in the real world. Feedback and reflection become the basis for the subsequent counselling session, with a diary again being a helpful tool. Learning involves trial and error and so relapse is viewed as part of the process rather than a catastrophe (see Chapter 12).
- *positive reinforcement*. Unless the person experiences advantages, then he is unlikely to persist. Some changes bring automatic rewards, such as improvements in physical wellbeing, but in other circumstances rewards may need to be consciously introduced. Positive, but realistic, praise from practitioner or family members for progress made, the use of money saved to indulge in pleasurable pursuits and the replacement of substance taking with satisfying activities can all make the effort worthwhile. The latter is particularly important. Substance use is often a time-consuming business. The negative reinforcement of no longer experiencing certain problems may be insufficient to sustain change in the face of boredom. Rewards need to follow soon after progress has been made. Using money saved to take a partner away next weekend has a stronger reinforcing effect than the promise of a holiday in a year's time.
- *making alterations in the environment* to help maintain changed behaviour.

If challenges are successfully met, self-efficacy will grow and the influences of the substance-using cues and stimuli will diminish. As progress is made, the emphasis switches from embedding new behaviour to preventing relapse. Examples of the practical application of the behavioural aspects of CBT are given in the chapter on relapse (Chapter 12).

## Contingency management

Contingency management is the name used to describe the structured use of rewards to encourage compliance or reinforce desired behaviours. It is supported by the National Institute for Health and Clinical Excellence (NICE, 2007a) as an adjunct to other interventions. It is used for targeted purposes such as:

- reinforcing abstinence;
- discouraging people from using illicit drugs on top of prescribed substitutes;
- increasing engagement with other medical procedures such as testing for blood-borne viruses.

Obviously, drug-testing regimes need to be in place to gauge compliance with abstinence or substitute prescribing goals. Various types of rewards can be employed including:

- vouchers which support recovery – for example, free passes to community facilities;
- small cash incentives;
- allowing people to take methadone home rather than visiting the pharmacy daily.

In the USA, some schemes have involved people who comply entering a lottery for prizes (Witton, 2008).

Rewards are withheld for failure to achieve the desired outcome. The person needs to clearly understand the link between the goal and the rewards and consistency needs to be built into the system. The effects tend to weaken when the reward system ends and so there is a need to build positive reinforcements into the person's own environment to replace this (Carroll and Onken, 2005). Modern technology is making testing for alcohol consumption easier (Barnett et al., 2011) and so contingency management may be increasingly used with problem drinkers too.

Rewarding people for conforming remains controversial. Service users who had complied from the start might consider it unfair. In addition, testing and the rewards cost money (Witton, 2008).

### Community reinforcement approach (CRA)

CRA also utilises behavioural methods but widens their application to harness the potential of family, friends and factors in the environment to reinforce behaviour change. CRA involves structuring relationships and activities to support the person's goals. In short, it aims to build social and physical capital (see Chapter 5). It has proved to be effective in trials (Miller, Meyers and Hiller-Sturmhöfel, 1999).

Many people who use substances problematically spend much of their time, along with others of a like mind, involved in an activity which brings them benefits. The purpose of CRA is, as Harris (2007, p. 181) aptly puts it, to put 'competing sources of satisfaction' in place. Assessment identifies current relationships and activities which reinforce substance taking, and the action plan outlines options for replacing these with networks and pursuits which do not support this. The person should decide who should be in these social networks and what activities are likely to bring satisfactions to counteract the pull of continued use. One type of network simply provides non-using company (for example, an activity group); another is one that is consciously constructed for more direct therapeutic purposes. In the UK Alcohol Treatment Trial (UKATT) (Copello et al., 2002), a structured approach called Social Behaviour and Network Therapy was developed which involved service users identifying people, typically family and close friends, who were available to support their goals. A series of sessions followed during which network members agreed on how to encourage the person to maintain progress, work productively with others in the network and identify signs that the person was at risk of using. Consistent and constructive responses to relapse were established. Members also analysed how they could reduce any influences within the network, such as strained relationships, which might encourage drinking. The aim is for such networks to remain in place after the formal programme has ended. The project demonstrated that Social Behaviour and Network Therapy is as effective as motivational enhancement therapy, with which it was compared (UKATT Research Team, 2005). A variant on the network theme is the concept of the Circle of Care. A grouping of relatives, volunteers and professionals is chosen by the person to provide practical and emotional support on an ongoing basis (Johnston, 2013).

In addition to using social and familial reinforcement, central to CRA is helping the person to identify constructive and enjoyable activities as an alternative to substance use; these can include hobbies, volunteering or preparation for employment. Addressing barriers is an important element of the process. Preparatory skills training will be necessary if the person lacks the confidence or social competencies needed to become involved. Practical steps, such as accompanying the person initially or helping with transport, can facilitate engagement.

---

**CASE ILLUSTRATION 11.2**

### A CRA action plan

Frankie (58) had a history of dependent drinking; living alone, the pub was his social life. Following successful detoxification, he faced the challenge of maintaining abstinence without obvious support and with little to fill his day. The practitioner suggested that Frankie should approach his son, who lived nearby, and Frankie agreed to the involvement of a volunteer from the agency's Buddy Scheme. The four met and worked out a plan in which Frankie would meet with the Buddy for a coffee or a visit to the cinema twice a week and he would go to the football with his son at the weekends. The parties agreed that, if Frankie had been drinking when they met up, they would encourage him to stop but would not continue with the activity. In addition, Frank expressed an interest in joining a computer class and the Buddy agreed to go with him to the taster session. One of the problems Frankie faced was dealing with past drinking companions who brought alcohol round to his flat. The practitioner agreed to work with him on ways of politely refusing them entry.

---

Readers will have noticed that, in harnessing the potency of supportive social networks and constructive activities, CRA is tapping into the same mechanisms which are known to maintain unassisted change (see Chapter 5). Some of these same elements can also be found in mutual aid groups.

## Mutual aid groups and self-help resources

Mutual aid and formal treatment are increasingly seen as being complementary. Whilst mutual aid cannot provide pharmacotherapy, psychosocial interventions, access to accommodation or financial advice, formal treatment does not confer the benefits of long-term peer support or recovery-orientated social networks. Mutual aid groups provide one of the foundation stones of self-efficacy: learning from experienced peers.

## Mutual aid groups: 12-step approach

In the UK, the 12-step approach is rarely employed by practitioners in community-based services. However, because service users may already attend or might benefit from joining Alcoholics or Narcotics Anonymous or the like, or may wish to consider residential rehabs whose ethos is based on the 12 steps, it is important for practitioners to have an understanding of the principles and practices involved. An appreciation of the strengths and limitations of the 12-step movement, and other mutual aid groups, is essential if service users are to be helped to make informed choices.

Despite criticisms of the theoretical basis of the disease model (see Chapter 3) and its 'one size fits all' philosophy, Alcoholics Anonymous (AA) has spread worldwide to become the most successful self-help movement in history and has spawned offshoots such as Narcotics Anonymous (NA) and Cocaine Anonymous (CA). Many find that the disease model provides an explanation of their experiences and the movement offers significant practical benefits. Project Match (Project Match Research Group, 1997) proved a turning point in the search for evidence of effectiveness as the outcomes for 12-step facilitation, albeit delivered as a one-to-one therapy, were as good as for the interventions with which it was compared. Reviewing the evidence, Proude et al. (2009) conclude that participating in AA can benefit some people with alcohol problems, and Gossop (2006, p. 15) notes that combining attendance at 12-step groups with formal interventions can improve outcomes for drug users.

## 12-step groups (AA and sister organisations)

The founding fathers of AA established the principles on which all the 12-step fellowships are based. The following gives a flavour of what participation involves and what areas may cause service users concern.

- The disease model promotes the view that abstinence from all psychoactive substances is the only solution and so the 12 steps are not for those who have a different goal. A person does not have to be abstinent to attend but he needs to have a desire to achieve this. Those on prescribed substitutes are welcomed, although abstinence from all mood-altering substance is seen as central to full recovery (LM, 2007).
- The disease has no cure, so perpetual vigilance is the order of the day. Some people dislike the idea of defining themselves as life-long addicts who are always in recovery. Others find strength in accepting this self-image.
- Participants see themselves as belonging to a fellowship of recovering addicts; they do not view meetings as 'treatment'.

- Regular, long-term attendance at meetings is strongly encouraged. One of the greatest benefits is the support of a social network with a shared understanding of problematic use and with a culture supportive of abstinence (Kelly et al., 2012).
- There is no pressure to speak but participants need to feel comfortable being in a group.
- Newcomers are allocated to a sponsor, a member of the community with lengthy experience of recovery, who can provide support and guidance on the programme. Sponsors try to make themselves available 24 hours a day.
- Meetings are based on the importance of a person actively progressing through the 12 steps in his day-to-day living.
- The programme is infused with a spiritual, rather than religious, dimension. Interpretation of the concept of 'God' and a 'Higher Power' is left to the individual. Some members understand this as God in the religious sense, some as 'the collective therapy' of the fellowship (Alcoholics Anonymous, 2013) and others simply that willpower, on its own, has proved to be inadequate. This spiritual dimension does not appeal to everyone.
- A woman may feel uncomfortable if she finds herself in a minority and so may want to find a group in which there is gender balance. It has also been suggested (Grace and Galvani, 2010) that care needs to be taken regarding how steps 4 and 5 are interpreted by women who have been abused as these could reinforce feelings of shame and self-blame. In addition, a person who has been abused should not consider making amends to the perpetrator.
- Part explanation, part vision, part practical guidance, the 12 steps provide a comprehensive belief system. For some, it all makes sense, but others find they are unwilling to submit to the philosophy or adopt what is an all-encompassing programme.

I was once corrected by an AA member for suggesting that the core objective of the 12 steps is abstinence. It is not; the core objective is 'sobriety', a constructive and satisfying existence founded on abstinence. The model stresses that a person cannot cure himself of the disease but he can live a fulfilled life without taking substances.

## BOX 11.1 THE 12 STEPS

The following are the 12 steps; they are the same whatever the substance.

1. We admitted that we were powerless over our addiction, that our lives had become unmanageable.
2. We came to believe that a Power greater than ourselves could restore us to sanity.
3. We made a decision to turn our will and our lives over to the care of God as we understood Him.

4. We made a searching and fearless moral inventory of ourselves.
5. We admitted to God, to ourselves, and to another human being the exact nature of our wrongs.
6. We were entirely ready to have God remove all these defects of character.
7. We humbly asked Him to remove our shortcomings.
8. We made a list of all persons we had harmed and became willing to make amends to them all.
9. We made direct amends to such people wherever possible, except when to do so would injure them or others.
10. We continued to take personal inventory and when we were wrong promptly admitted it.
11. We sought through prayer and meditation to improve our conscious contact with God as we understood Him, praying only for knowledge of His will for us and the power to carry that out.
12. Having had a spiritual awakening as a result of these steps, we tried to carry this message to addicts, and to practise these principles in all our affairs.

Reproduced with the permission of Narcotics Anonymous UK.

In addition to the 12 steps, there are 12 traditions which lay out the principles which groups and individuals should adhere to; these include the purpose of the movement (reaching out to the still-suffering addict) and the importance of anonymity.

Many find no contradiction between involvement with services which use behavioural techniques and attendance at AA or NA. Perhaps this is because, in practice, 12-step approaches and behavioural interventions both work to broadly similar psychological principles despite their theoretical differences. In AA, there is a strong emphasis on recognising patterns of thinking which might precipitate relapse and learning from the experiences of others, coupled with strong reinforcement of abstinence. Slogans are used to strengthen central messages. These challenge thinking and encourage change, as the following examples demonstrate:

- *Cognitive slogans*: 'Stinking thinking leads to drinking'; 'Remember your last drunk'.
- *Behavioural slogans*: 'One day at a time'; 'Call your sponsor before, not after, you take the first drug'.

There is some evidence to suggest that certain types of people, for example those who are isolated, those with more severe problems, older individuals and those who are uncomfortable with uncertainty, are more likely to affiliate to AA (Proude et al., 2009; Williams, 2002).

The 12-step approach has particular implications for relapse (see Chapter 12) and separate groups are available for relatives (see Chapter 15).

**Mutual aid groups: SMART Recovery**

SMART Recovery, founded in 1994 in the USA, is gaining a foothold in the UK. As with the Anonymous fellowships, SMART Recovery espouses an abstinence-based, peer-led group format but there are radical differences in philosophy and practice. Indeed it was developed deliberatively as an alternative:

- The programme is based on behavioural theories and not on the disease model. It has no particular spiritual reference point.
- Groups are usually peer led, but by a facilitator who has been trained.
- Groups are open to people who have difficulties with gambling, eating and the like, in addition to those experiencing difficulties with substances.
- The programme involves four overarching themes: strengthening motivation; dealing with urges; handling thoughts, feelings and behaviour; developing a balanced lifestyle. Specific tools and exercises, derived from a type of CBT called Rational Emotive Behaviour Therapy, are employed.
- There is an emphasis on finding solutions to problems in the present rather than dwelling on historical experiences.
- Labelling is discouraged. It is acknowledged that, when people feel ready, they will move on: recovery is not seen as being dependent on life-long attendance.
- SMART Recovery works in close cooperation with professional services; these are encouraged to facilitate the establishment of new groups and provide accommodation for meetings.
- Online groups and forums are available. (SMART Recovery, 2013)

SMART Recovery is relatively new and a body of research into its effectiveness has yet to be established.

**Web-based forums and therapeutic sites**

A quick search of the Web will identify two very different kinds of user-focused sites. Firstly, there are those where people discuss their substance taking. These sites are not necessarily concerned with cessation or reduction in use but participants do often share negative experiences and offer each other harm reduction advice. Obviously, there is no guarantee that the information given is accurate. In addition, it is not known how far the existence of such sites encourages initiation or normalises use. Interestingly, some people who use these sites probably know as much about new psychoactive substances as government-sponsored scientists! Secondly, there are sites where people encourage and support each other's recovery. Practitioners might ask service users which sites they access as familiarity with the content may provide the basis for fruitful discussions.

There are also websites – some free and some that charge – which offer online substance problem counselling and programmes. These increase accessibility to treatment for those who have difficulties accessing services; they may also appeal to people who are reluctant to engage face to face.

## Local recovery groups and activities

The first decade of the twenty-first century saw the emergence of a growing range of local recovery groups offering mutual support and activities. Some of these emerged from existing voluntary organisations and others were set up independently. Practitioners should be in a position to provide information to service users about what they offer.

## Mutual aid groups: the role of the practitioner

Informed service user choice is at the heart of the person-centred approach and so practitioners should encourage people to consider engaging with mutual aid fellowships, substance-free social clubs or the growing range of recovery groups and activities. To be able to do this, practitioners need to have the confidence to discuss the options in their area knowledgeably. When practitioners actively support initial engagement with AA, participation is likely to increase (Proude et al., 2009) and it is reasonable to assume that the same holds for other recovery activities. The 12-step fellowship and SMART Recovery websites (see Resources the end of this chapter) provide information about what is involved and AA and NA welcome the attendance of practitioners at open meetings.

To encourage participation in mutual aid or recovery projects, the NTA (2013b) suggests that practitioners should:

- provide service users with leaflets or access to websites and talk through the implications of involvement;
- when a person expresses an interest, facilitate his initial attendance by supplying information about meetings or activities, providing transport or fares and arranging for him to be escorted;
- regularly discuss with the service user his experiences of involvement.

If a person finds that one particular option does not suit him, an alternative may prove more attractive.

---

ACTIVITY 11.1

**Introducing recovery options**
You are working with a 22-year-old man who is dependent on heroin.

- At what stage in the cycle of change would you introduce the topic of mutual aid groups and recovery activities? What are the reasons for your decision?
- How would you describe these options to him?

---

## Controlled drinking

The term 'controlled drinking' is subject to various interpretations. Saladin and Santa Ana (2004), for example, construe it as including any intervention with a non-abstinent goal, including brief opportunistic interventions. Here we will consider controlled drinking as it was originally conceived: a treatment approach that aims to help a person to adopt a new pattern of use which brings none of the problems which he was previously experiencing. Controlled drinking is problem-free drinking. It is a demanding option employing specific, individualised programmes. Controlled drinking is not just reduced drinking, which may or may not be free from harm.

While some of the heat has dissipated from the controversy surrounding controlled drinking (see Chapter 6), proponents of the disease model, and many in the general public, continue to see abstinence as the sole aim of treatment. However, including controlled drinking as an option brings advantages (Raistrick, Heather and Godfrey, 2006, p. 25):

- The availability of controlled drinking programmes can encourage into treatment those who find the idea of abstinence unattractive.
- Some people who relapse regularly when attempting to abstain may be able to adhere to a controlled drinking programme.
- Failure to sustain a controlled drinking programme makes it clear that abstinence should become the goal.

Heather (2009) argues that, for some people, controlled drinking should be seen as the most appropriate objective; it should not be considered solely as the default option for people who are unwilling or unable to maintain abstinence. Indeed, there is evidence to suggest that the outcomes for people with lower levels of dependence can be better when moderation, rather than abstinence, is the goal (Heather and Robertson, 1981; Raistrick, Heather and Godfrey, 2006).

### Who might be suitable for controlled drinking?

Although some people exhibiting higher levels of dependence do manage to moderate their drinking, as a broad rule those with shorter histories of problematic use and fewer problems are more likely to be suitable for controlled drinking. When discussing with a service user the choice of abstinence or controlled drinking, the following benchmarks should be considered:

- *The person's preferred option.* If abstinence is his choice, this should be accepted regardless of other criteria.
- *Physical health.* Certain medical problems, particularly those caused by alcohol use, make any continued drinking inadvisable. Checking with the person's GP that there are no physical or mental health issues that would preclude controlled drinking is an essential precaution.
- *Psychological wellbeing.* Abstinence is indicated when a person has significant mental health problems or cognitive impairment.
- *Past and present drinking patterns.* Lower levels of dependence and a shorter history of problematic use support controlled drinking as a possible option. The majority of candidates will, therefore, be in younger age

groups. If problem-free drinking has been maintained for periods in the recent past, it is more likely to be re-established in the future; conversely, an inability to exercise any restraint when drinking suggests that abstinence may be easier to achieve. Abstinence is advisable if a person has experienced regular or problematic withdrawal episodes.

- *Significant others.* Controlled drinking is more likely to work if supported by the person's partner. Their involvement in decisions regarding suitability and the development of the controlled drinking plan is essential.
- *Social and environmental circumstances.* Trying to moderate drinking will be difficult if a person's lifestyle, employment or peer group reinforces heavy drinking. Involvement in an abstinence-based recovery fellowship can lessen the isolation which pulling back from alcohol-related social activities brings.
- *Pregnancy.* Abstinence is the recommended option if a woman is pregnant or is trying to conceive. (Jarvis et al., 2005, p. 66; Scottish Council on Alcoholism, 1983; plus additions)

It is not uncommon for people to want to pursue a goal of moderation even when the assessment indicates that is inadvisable. Some people may decide on abstinence but their subsequent behaviour makes it is clear that they are reluctant to commit themselves to this. This presents a dilemma for the practitioner, but one which is hardly solved by refusing to work with the person. Coercion is unlikely to bear fruit. The first response should be to acknowledge the service user's position and then discuss with him the ways in which his drinking is harmful. Motivational interviewing may be helpful here. If the person remains unwilling to consider working towards abstinence, even in the longer term, Miller and Page (1991) suggest that a trial programme of controlled use may be the only constructive option. They recommend that this is undertaken with the service user's agreement that he will reconsider his position on abstinence if attempts at control fail. If moderation is achieved, it could be viewed as a form of harm reduction.

---

ACTIVITY 11.2

**Controlled drinking**

Which of the theories as to why people develop problems with substances, outlined in Chapter 3, support controlled drinking as a valid option for some people and which do not?

---

### Designing a controlled drinking programme

As was suggested in Chapter 7, there is merit in encouraging a person to become abstinent for a period of up to three months prior to deciding on his longer term drinking goal (Booth, 2006; Raistrick, Heather and Godfrey, 2006, p. 25; Scottish Council on Alcoholism, 1983). This provides space to reflect on the benefits of different options at a distance from drinking.

Controlled drinking is more likely to work if a radical approach is taken to all the factors which support current problematic consumption: simply trying to drink less with the other reinforcers still in place, such as frequenting the same bars, with the same people and at the same times, is less likely to succeed. Zinberg's 'drug, set and setting' (Zinberg, 1984) provides a framework for analysing the variables (see Chapter 1). Once this has been done, a completely new drinking regime can be constructed geared to avoiding the problems the person has experienced in the past. The plan should be designed by the person, along with his partner where appropriate, but under the guidance of the practitioner.

**Drug:**
- The units set should be within national guidelines.
- Spirits should be avoided.
- It may be helpful to substitute a favourite drink with one for which a taste has not been developed.
- Alternating alcoholic and soft drinks can curb consumption.

**Set:**
- Practitioner and service user should explore the cognitive processes which precede problematic use. Does the person drink heavily when feeling low? Are there particular times when pleasurable anticipation leads to excessive consumption? Having identified how mood influences current patterns of use, the person can design the plan to break the links between the two; for example, he might establish a rule of never drinking if feeling depressed. In the new regime, drinking should have a different 'psychological meaning'.
- The questions 'How often?' and 'At what times?' need to be addressed. Two evenings a week might be substituted for regular lunchtime and evening drinking.
- Solitary drinking is inadvisable.
- Speed of drinking is a factor.
- Eating before drinking helps limit consumption.
- The person should plan to fill the times previously taken up with drinking with enjoyable distracting activities.

**Setting:**
- The person needs to decide whether he should avoid old drinking venues and the company of drinking companions.
- Participating in the round system should be avoided. (Booth, 2006; Scottish Council on Alcoholism, 1983; with additions).

Each plan is unique to the individual. It should be written out, monitored and subject to regular review. Some flexibility may need to be built in but the intentions for each week should be written out in advance.

Behavioural techniques such as role playing refusal skills and sipping, not gulping, can be practised. Slips should be viewed as learning experiences and addressed in the same way as relapse on an abstinence programme (see Chapter 12).

CASE ILLUSTRATION 11.3

**A controlled drinking programme**

Following employment problems due to drinking, Joan (28) tried to abstain. She found that this curtailed her social life and a different pattern emerged: regular evening drinking ceased but weekend bingeing became the norm. At this point, she sought help. Assessment did not identify any factors which suggested that controlled drinking would be inadvisable.

Along with her practitioner, Joan analysed a typical weekend's drinking:

|  | **Friday** | **Saturday** |
|---|---|---|
| *Mood:* | Anticipation mid-afternoon | Washed out; desire for a drink to cure hangover |
| *Time:* | 5.30 p.m. until midnight | 6 p.m. until midnight |
| *Company:* | Work colleagues | Friends |
| *Place:* | Bars and clubs | Meals out/dinner parties |
| *Consumption:* | Wine and vodka (20 units) | Vodka before going out; wine (16 units) |
| *Consequences:* | Hangover; occasional regretted sexual encounters | Hangover; embarrassment following day |

Joan developed a plan which allowed her to maintain a full social life while keeping consumption within recommended limits. Her practitioner suggested that she pay particular attention to the triggers to consumption.

Joan's controlled drinking plan involved:

- taking a complete break from alcohol for a month;
- avoiding spirits; limiting consumption to three units per day; never drinking alone at home;
- telling her friends what her intentions were in the hope they would support her efforts;
- *Fridays*: home after work; light meal. Meet friends in bar at 7 p.m. – one unit of wine. Go to cinema or theatre. Two units of wine in bar afterwards. If going to clubs, not going out until 9 p.m. – three units of wine only.
- *Saturdays*: Soft drink before meal. Three units of wine with meal.

Joan agreed to use a diary to record the frequency, amount and circumstances of use and to meet with her practitioner fortnightly. While she failed to take a break from drinking, she implemented the rest of her plan immediately. Spirit drinking became a thing of the past but she struggled to keep consumption below eight units per evening. At the three-month review, she decided that she needed to break the cycle and decided not to go out for a few weekends. A further reduction in consumption followed. At the six-month review, she said that she was now adhering to her original plan, apart from on the occasional evening, and was happy with progress. She asked for continuing telephone contact with her practitioner.

## Working with stimulant users

The UK has not experienced the crack epidemic which blighted inner-city USA towards the end of the twentieth century and methamphetamine has not attracted a substantial following in Britain. Nevertheless, stimulant use is a constant, with different substances going in and out of fashion. Self-reported use of cocaine among adults (aged 16–59) in the past year increased in England and Wales from 0.6 per cent of the 16- to 59-year-old population in 1996 to 2.2 per cent in 2011/12, having peaked in 2008/9. However, over the same time, amphetamine use in the past year reduced from 3.2 per cent to 0.8 per cent. Self-reported ketamine use in the last year among adults remained stable at 0.6 per cent between 2008/9 and 2011/12. In respect of last-year use, powder cocaine was the most popular illicit drug after cannabis (Home Office, 2012b). It is too early to evaluate longer term trends in the use of the plethora of new stimulants such as mephedrone and naphyrone.

### Stimulants: varied populations

An interesting feature of stimulants, and one that has relevance for how services are provided, is how use extends through various social groupings. Clubbers use stimulants as recreational dance drugs and some people with high-octane, high-salary lifestyles see powder cocaine as an essential accessory, although price reduction has led to its more widespread use (Shapiro, 2010, p. 100). These two groups, mainly employed and with significant social capital, are less likely to be stigmatised as drug users. Polydrug use, particularly combining cocaine with alcohol, is common in these cohorts but injection is less likely. Patterns of use in these groups are not homogeneous. There are recreational users, who take stimulants to augment a night out, there are bingers and there are those who have crossed over into more compulsive and habitual use. All run the risks of the immediate health problems associated with stimulants, such as chest pains, nausea and breathing difficulties. These are more likely to take the person to an accident and emergency clinic or a GP's surgery rather than to a substance problems service; health settings bring opportunities for brief interventions and harm reduction advice (see Chapter 9). Even when use becomes habitual or bingeing becomes chronic, attracting people into treatment has proved challenging (Bottomley, 1999; Bottomley et al., 1997). Reasons for this include the following:

- Because persistent use leads to unpleasant distressing psychological and physical reactions, many people take regular breaks. Times prior to, or just after, cessation are when people often feel most in need of help and motivation can wane if they cannot access services quickly.
- Stimulant users may regard services as being for 'drug addicts', a stereotype with which they do not readily identify. They also see mainstream provision as being ill equipped to respond to their needs. Indeed, there is some justification in this view. The pressing need in the 1980s to orientate treatment towards harm reduction and substitute prescribing for injecting opiate users

to avert the potential catastrophe of HIV led to provision for stimulant users becoming the Cinderella of drug services. Reconfiguring service delivery to meet the needs of all substance users remains work in progress.

- For opioid users, substitute prescribing acts as a lure; most consider this option at some point. Services can offer no such incentive to stimulant users. Some agencies have provided complementary therapies for stimulant users as an inducement to engagement.
- Stimulant users who are sustaining employment and living within the mainstream may be concerned about confidentiality. They may also fear a criminal record. Such anxieties can be exacerbated by the paranoia associated with cocaine and amphetamine use.
- Cocaine users, in particular, may be loath to abandon a lifestyle which they find appealing but which strongly reinforces drug taking.

As well as those who use stimulants as their drug of choice, there are people with established problems with other substances, primarily heroin users, who also use these drugs. In addition, stimulants can provide the rush that those on methadone no longer experience. The circumstances of this cohort contrast sharply with those of the other groups of stimulant user; they are more likely to be experiencing all the effects of social disadvantage. With a history of injecting, they may take stimulants in this way too. Although many will already be involved with substance problems agencies, they may be unwilling to admit to their additional habits and services may not screen regularly for their use of other drugs. Finally, there are habitual crack users, a particularly marginalised group.

## Attracting stimulant users

Clear referral pathways need to exist in each area to encourage those who approach emergency services because of immediate health problems to consider help. Outreach and harm reduction initiatives in clubs and at concerts provide similar opportunities. But how can drug services themselves be made more attractive to stimulant users? Should separate provision be made or should existing services extend their repertoire of responses to meet the needs of all drug users? There is no evidence to favour one of these options over the other (Bottomley, 1999). The balance of particular drug problems in any given area, along with its geography, will dictate how services are configured but, to attract stimulant users, a number of steps need to be taken:

- The agency should publicise that it works with stimulant users.
- People approaching the service should be given reassurances about confidentiality.
- Rapid access to a specialist worker is needed; placing stimulant users on waiting lists will leave a service with few clients!
- Practitioners should be able to provide accurate information about the different types of stimulants.

- Practitioners should have a good understanding of the physical and psychological effects and the nature of the 'come down' experience. These differ somewhat depending on which stimulant is used. People enduring depression, anxiety, extreme tiredness or restlessness should be reassured and consideration should be given to providing complementary therapies.
- Regular contact via phone or texting can continue to provide reassurance and encourage people to remain engaged.
- Practitioners working with people with heroin problems should screen for use of other substances on an ongoing basis. (Bottomley, 1999; with additions)

### Interventions with stimulant users

Cravings and compulsive bingeing make controlled use exceedingly difficult and most stimulant users seeking help see abstinence as their desired goal (Bottomley, 1999; Malcolm, 2013). For those with the engrained difficulties, the research supports the use of the psychosocial interventions commonly used with other drug types (Baker, Lee and Jenner, 2004; EMCDDA, 2007; NTA, 2002). It should be noted that the evidence is based primarily on studies considering cocaine, crack or amphetamines. These interventions are:

- **Motivational interviewing.**
- **Cognitive behavioural therapy.** While use of CBT is supported by the research, studies suggest that it may be less effective with cocaine users with cognitive impairment (EMCDDA, 2007).
- **Community reinforcement.** Malcolm (2013) suggests that for those with comfortable lifestyles, mainly cocaine users, it is not low self-esteem that is a barrier to dealing with their use, it is low self-efficacy; with their social environments providing powerful reinforcement, they may find it difficult to contemplate change. However, for this group, family relationships and wider social networks may also be intact and can be harnessed to support change through implementing a community reinforcement approach.
- **Contingency management.**
- **Relapse prevention.**
- **Pharmacotherapy** (see Chapter 10). With no replacement therapies formally supported, pharmacotherapy is primarily limited to prescribing for symptoms following cessation, such as anxiety. The importance of this should not, however, be underestimated. Disulfiram (Antabuse) may help to reduce cocaine use.
- **Complementary therapies.** Research into the effectiveness of acupuncture is inconclusive (EMCDDA, 2007). However, therapies such as aural acupuncture, relaxation techniques, massage and sleep exercises have been found by practitioners to help people deal with the agitation and anxiety associated with stimulants (Malcolm, 2013). They also provide tangible responses, which may attract people into treatment.
- **Residential rehab.** Those with multiple difficulties and poor social supports may benefit from this option (NTA, 2002).

Practitioners should be sensitive to the psychological distress associated with stimulants and the potential risk of suicide. Arrangements should be in place for rapid referral to psychiatric services if mental health problems persist.

## New psychoactive substances and club drugs

A variety of responses are likely to be required to the wide range of new psychoactive substances which continue to emerge, but a body of evidence regarding what interventions are most likely to be effective has yet to appear (EMCDDA, 2012). However, given that these drugs can be categorised by their broad effects on the central nervous system, it would seem logical to adopt the same interventions used with traditional drugs which have similar implications for the user. New psychoactive substances are also likely to be found in the club scene where more established substances such as ketamine, ecstasy and GHB are used. With regard to club drugs, the NTA (2012b) notes that:

- the number of people who enter treatment because of problems with these is low;
- people often seek help following some kind of crisis related to use, usually involving health concerns;
- outcomes are good and this may be partly because many of those involved still have considerable social and personal capital.

Treatment of people experiencing problems with club drugs involves the same psychosocial interventions used with other groups with substance problems, such as motivational work and relapse prevention; however, there is a need to take into account aspects specific to particular drugs (NTA, 2012b). For example, GHB and GBL are depressants, which can lead to physical dependence, so medically supervised detox may be required and access to specialist urology services is needed for ketamine users experiencing bladder and other urinary problems. Unless evidence emerges to the contrary, a similar approach is likely to be taken to new psychoactive substances, with the same emphasis on combining the drug-specific elements with commonly used interventions. This demands that services keep abreast of the changing availability of drugs within their areas, no small challenge in a rapidly shifting landscape.

As has been noted, club drug users are mainly people with jobs and accommodation whose lives are not defined primarily by their substance use, and the same is likely to hold for those who experiment with new psychoactive substances. However, as with stimulant users, all these drugs may be taken by those who already have serious substance problems, and this can compound the difficulties of helping them to move on. In 2012, there was evidence that mephedrone, in particular, was being injected by some heroin users. In addition, some mephedrone users with no history of intravenous drug taking had started to inject the drug (Daly, 2012). Whether such trends are temporary or herald the beginning of a shift in drug preferences among the most vulnerable has yet to be seen.

## Concluding comments

This chapter reflects William Miller's optimism about the range of interventions which has been developed: 'The good news in addiction treatment is that we have a menu of evidence-based alternatives to try. If one thing is not working, try something else, or a combination of approaches' (Miller quoted in White, 2012). But this menu on its own is not enough. Wraparound services, such as accommodation, financial help and access to activities and employment, need to be in place. A service culture that supports a person-centred approach and which encourages people to take responsibility for their own recovery is a critical factor too.

## RESOURCES

- The following are examples of manuals and workbooks, broadly based on cognitive and behavioural principles, for work with service users. While their application in practice is not complex, a level of prior familiarisation/training is needed:

  NTA (2008). *The ITEP Manual: Delivering Psychosocial Interventions.* London: NTA. Available at: www.nta.nhs.uk/uploads/itep_routes_to_recovery_part2_180209.pdf. (NB: Material on the NTA website is scheduled to be transferred by 2014 to the PHE website or placed on the National Archive's website or similar.)
  NTA/COCA/Rugby House (2006), *Crack and Cocaine. Brief Intervention Programmes.* London: NTA. Available at: www.drugsandalcohol.ie/13628/1/NTA_brief_cocaine_ programme.pdf.
  Peets, V. (2004). *Meeting the Challenge. A Manual for Using Workbooks for Group and One-to-One Sessions with Drugs Users.*
  Peets, V. (2004). *Meeting the Challenge. Dealing with Heroin Addiction. A Workbook for Use by Individuals in One-to-One or Group Work Sessions.*
  Peets, V. (2004). *Meeting the Challenge. Dealing with Crack and Cocaine Addiction. A Workbook for Use by Individuals in One-to-One or Group Work Sessions.*
  (DrugScope publications are available from HIT www.hit.org.uk)

- Mutual aid fellowships. Details of meetings are available at:
  Alcoholics Anonymous: www.alcoholics-anonymous.org.uk.
  Narcotics Anonymous: www.ukna.org.
  Cocaine Anonymous: www.cauk.org.uk.
  Marijuana Anonymous: www.marijuana-anonymous.co.uk.
  Drug Addicts Anonymous: www.drugaddictsanonymous.org.uk.
  SMART Recovery: www.smartrecovery.org.uk.

- Skills Consortium. The Skills hub section of the Skills Consortium website provides links to numerous treatment guidance documents and manuals: www.skillsconsortium.org.uk/skillshub.aspx.

# CHAPTER 12

# Relapse Prevention, Endings and Follow-up Care

## KEY THEMES

- Relapse is commonplace but not inevitable.
- Helping people to avoid relapse or prevent a lapse from escalating are key interventions.
- The most commonly used approaches to relapse prevention are based on CBT.
- Reintegration into the community should be an ongoing strand of formal treatment.
- Endings are not always smooth and systematic follow-up procedures should be put in place.

## Perspectives on relapse

Even those with the most serious problems tend to reduce consumption or abstain for periods. Perhaps the biggest test of all is maintaining changed behaviour and not slipping back into old habits. This challenge is succinctly put by Mark Twain (undated): 'Giving up smoking is the easiest thing in the world. I know because I've done it thousands of times.'

It is not possible to consider relapse without leaning heavily on the work of G. Alan Marlatt. His application of cognitive and behavioural psychology to the challenge of relapse has led to the development of the most commonly used methods of helping people to tackle this troubling phenomenon. Relapse is a return to any behaviour which a person had succeeded in changing; therefore it is as applicable to controlled drinking as it is to abstinence. There is a tendency to view relapse in catastrophic terms, but Marlatt and Witkiewitz (2005) draw the helpful distinction between a 'lapse' (a minor breach) and a 'relapse' (a fuller return to previous behaviour). The purpose of relapse prevention is to help a person:

- to avoid a lapse;
- to prevent a lapse from escalating into a relapse.

The maintenance stage in the cycle of change can be seen as the continuous successful application of relapse prevention techniques. Relapse is a process rather than an event. Relapse does not just happen; certain factors put an individual at greater risk. Within the cycle of change, relapse has become characterised as recycling to an earlier stage (DiClemente, 2005). On the one hand, this may lead to the rapid re-establishment of maintenance; on the other, it can herald a return to precontemplation.

The cycle of change is based on research which shows that relapse and recycling are commonplace (Prochaska, DiClemente and Norcross, 1992). It does need to be stressed that not everyone lapses, although the reality of working through a substance problem is that steps backward are to be expected; this has led to addiction being conceptualised as a 'chronic relapsing condition'. The negative attitudes engendered by this phrase ignore what is known about unassisted change and fuelled the emergence of the recovery movement (see Chapter 6). Despite recycling being unexceptional, many do achieve a life beyond problematic use in due course (Best, 2010; Prochaska, DiClemente and Norcross, 1992).

### Why do people relapse?

Many people do tend to stop from time to time. Cessation can follow a deliberate decision, or imprisonment or hospitalisation may intervene; pregnancy can also act as a spur to stopping use (Massey et al., 2012). Having reached a point where a major hurdle has been negotiated, why do people find it hard to maintain what would seem to be progress? Factors associated with initial lapsing have been identified (Marlatt, Parks and Witkiewitz, 2002):

Personal factors:
- Negative emotions.
- Positive emotions.
- Feeling unwell or experiencing pain.
- Testing ability to control use.
- Impulses to use.

Interpersonal factors:
- Friction in relationships.
- Social pressures. This can involve direct invitations (for example, being offered substances) or being in situations where substances are being used.
- Use in social settings to enhance positive feelings.

Experiencing negative emotions is one of the most significant precursors to relapse (Marlatt and Witkiewitz, 2005). This highlights the fact that, whilst bringing obvious benefits, changing substance-using behaviour only goes so far in helping a person to resolve the problems she faces. Once the optimism associated with stabilisation and improved health has worn off, the realisation that major problems, such as debt and strained relationships, remain can lead to disillusionment. Indeed, change may throw into sharp relief difficulties that substance use masked. As time passes, the person may minimise the unpleasant aspects of substance taking and dwell on the pleasures (Marlatt, Parks and Witkiewitz, 2002). The threat inherent in the combination of disenchantment, positive expectancy from future use and the ready availability of substances is obvious.

Cues within the broader environment also present a risk. Living in an area with high levels of drug-related activities or in a house where other people smoke make maintaining change difficult. In Chapter 5, we saw how some people choose to move elsewhere to prevent a return to use. The ubiquity of cheap alcohol is a hazard. For many, substance taking is a communal activity and building a new social life is a necessity if change is to be maintained. Learning avoidance and refusal skills need to go hand in hand with efforts both to reduce the reinforcers in the environment and to build social capital.

However, the process of relapse involves more than the personal and inter-personal factors outlined above. People can experience negative emotions or strained relationships and not relapse. For relapse to occur, other factors need to be in play such as low self-efficacy, the person's belief that she cannot cope with the situation, often in tandem with the notion that a return to the old behaviour will bring benefits (Marlatt, Parks and Witkiewitz, 2002). Self-efficacy is, of course, built on prior experience. If a person has learned to recognise when she is at risk, has discovered how to manage problematic emotional states and has mastered techniques for dealing with testing situations, then self-efficacy will be strengthened. It will be bolstered further by every instance when a challenging situation has been successfully negotiated. However, Saunders (1994) makes the point that relapse is not always linked to deficits in coping at all. While it may be convenient for a person to ascribe a lapse to an inability to deal with problematic situations, the cause may be a desire to use again and a lack of motivation to maintain change.

It is important to consider two other processes which can be at work: seemingly irrelevant decisions and the abstinence violation effect.

## Seemingly irrelevant decisions

It is not uncommon for a practitioner to be faced with a demoralised service user saying, 'I don't know what came over me; I just started using again.' Yet something must have been different that day. An analysis of the period before a lapse often uncovers a series of small steps leading inexorably in one direction (Marlatt, Parks and Witkiewitz, 2002). Behind these steps lies an unacknowledged desire to use again (see Case Illustration 12.1).

> ### CASE ILLUSTRATION 12.1
>
> **Seemingly irrelevant decisions**
>
> Three months after a successful spell in rehab, Barry has started to have persistent thoughts about using heroin again. He dismisses these but finds that he is becoming increasingly moody. He argues with his father over very little and storms out of the house. With nowhere to go unless he returns to apologise, he visits the flat of someone he met in rehab and asks if he can stay, despite rumours that this man is using again. 'Of course you can,' says this acquaintance, 'and you're welcome to a little of this quality stuff.' Barry initially resists but then thinks, 'One hit won't hurt; it'll calm me down.'

> At each decision point, Barry chose the option that led towards the lapse. He has engineered a situation where there are no barriers to use. Helping a person to become aware of the course such thinking takes, and to learn how to break the chain, are central elements of relapse prevention.

## Abstinence violation effect

The abstinence violation effect describes a particular cognitive process that increases the likelihood of a lapse becoming a relapse (Marlatt, Parks and Witkiewitz, 2002). Having used, a person may feel that she might as well continue. This decision is one way of resolving the cognitive dissonance which can follow a lapse. The person feels uncomfortable because her self-image as someone who has resolved her substance problem is at odds with her resumption of use. This sense of discomfort is increased if the person blames herself for the lapse. To reduce this discomfort, two strategies are available to the person. She can:

- *Either* revert to behaving in line with her self-image by stopping again: 'I'm no longer a smoker; this is just an unfortunate slip.'
- *Or* align her self-image with the lapse, thus seeing herself again as a user: 'Even when I wasn't smoking, I knew I wouldn't manage to stay off for long.' This type of rationalisation increases the likelihood of continued use. (Barber, 2002, p. 134)

The challenge here is to help the person see through the thinking illustrated in the second response.

## The stages of relapse

Relapse tends to occur in a staged manner (see Figure 12.1):

*Stage 1*: Risk of relapse is heightened through personal or interpersonal factors. The substance also needs to be available at the crucial time.
*Stage 2*: If self-efficacy is high, with the person thinking that she can handle what she is facing, and this is not overridden by the desire to use, then the likelihood of relapse recedes. If self-efficacy is low, then relapse is more likely to happen.
*Stage 3*: A lapse occurs. Concerned about the consequences, the person may simply arrest the process. However, the abstinence violation effect, along with a desire to continue to use, increases the likelihood of a fuller relapse. (Marlatt, Parks and Witkiewitz, 2002)

## How belief can influence behaviour

A central precept of social learning theory is that we all have internal frames of reference built on past experience and knowledge. When faced with situations,

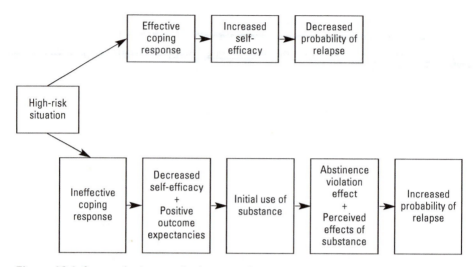

**Figure 12.1** Stages of relapse and relapse avoidance
*Source:* Marlatt, G. A. and Gordon, J. R. (1985) (reproduced with permission)

these cognitive constructs help us to make sense of what is happening to us. They shape what we expect to feel and influence how we will react (see Chapter 3). Adherents of the disease model believe that a lapse reactivates processes that have been lying dormant, including loss of control. Thus, 12-step interventions stress the importance of avoiding relapse at all costs, reinforcing this with slogans such as 'It's the first drink that gets you drunk'. Whilst this view of lapsing can strengthen resolve not to use, it also creates the expectation that any ingestion of the substance will inevitably undermine the ability to stop. A belief that the disease takes over can heighten the risk that a lapse will become a relapse. By way of contrast, those who understand problematic use as a learned behaviour may interpret a lapse as a mistake which can be quickly rectified; for them, the outcome is not determined by an inevitable process.

## Relapse prevention using CBT methods

A relapse prevention programme using cognitive and behavioural methods (see Chapter 11) aims to build self-efficacy by helping the person to:

- recognise moods and thought processes (personal factors) that increase risk and learn to deal with these;
- identify environmental and interpersonal factors and develop skills to deal with these;
- make changes to those aspects of her physical environment and social life which support continued problematic behaviour.

Practitioners new to the substance problems field may feel reluctant to broach the issue of relapse for fear that this may grant permission. Care when introducing the issue should remove the risk. Suggesting to a person who is maintaining change that relapse is to be expected is hardly helpful, but it is only sensible to equip the person for the challenges she will face. The matter might be introduced as follows: 'You have managed to make real changes; let's discuss ways of ensuring that you don't slip back.'

Discussing relapse can demystify it (Saunders, 1994, p. 166). If working to prevent a lapse is seen as a normal step in the recovery process, and relapse is not considered a taboo subject, then a person is less likely to drop out of treatment because of feelings of failure if problems do occur. Because potential risk situations are ubiquitous, Saunders suggests that helping a person to learn generalised coping skills may be the most appropriate approach. This is debatable, however. In CBT, there is an emphasis on addressing individual patterns of thinking and specific situations which the person finds problematic. Responses developed to deal with these successfully can then be applied more widely (generalisation).

### Dealing with unhelpful thinking

A guided discovery approach (see Chapter 11) can be used to examine the sequence of thoughts and events which occurred when a person has used in the recent past. This helps her to become aware of the links between moods and chains of thought and the risk of relapse. If she can recognise when she is taking seemingly irrelevant decisions or having permission-giving thoughts, then she can take action to reduce the likelihood of a lapse occurring. It is important to explain to the person that such thoughts and cravings are normal and that they usually pass quite quickly. Once a person can identify the thought processes that lead towards use, she can build a repertoire of techniques to deal with these such as:

- *learning to reframe negative thought patterns.* 'I always start smoking dope when I feel down' becomes 'Feeling down puts me at risk but by the next day I usually feel better.'
- *emphasising choice.* In any situation, various options will be always available; however, we may not be conscious of these at the time. A person may say, 'He bought me a beer, so I just had to drink it', but that is not the case. The alternatives may be socially sensitive and demand quick thinking but they certainly exist.
- *thought stopping.* The practitioner asks the person to imagine a situation when she was thinking about using. The practitioner says firmly 'Stop!' and then encourages the person to get into the habit of doing this for herself (Sheldon, 2011, p. 240).
- *distraction.* The person decides on a specific plan to take her mind off cravings or troubling thoughts when they occur. It might involve cooking a meal, watching television or going for a walk.
- *involving others.* The person can agree with a friend or relative that she will make contact when she feels at risk.
- *flash cards.* The person carries cards with reminders on them which she can refer to during difficult situations (Bennett, 2002). These can be specific

('Remember, cravings pass in an hour') or more generalised for use in various situations ('Think about what you risk losing').

### Addressing environmental risks

While some interpersonal risks cannot be foreseen, many can be predicted. Certain places or people will either bring the person into contact with substances or, through association, heighten the desire to use. Situations presenting predictable risks can be mapped and then plans developed to deal with these (see Case Illustration 12.2). The person may decide to avoid such situations where possible but learning refusal and other skills to deal with these is also essential. The person also needs to be prepared for the unforeseen, such as bad news which triggers a desire to use or the unanticipated meeting with someone offering drugs. The final stage is to build a lifestyle and a circle of friends which do not support substance using.

While the principles of relapse prevention are universal, each plan is unique, reflecting the risks the individual has identified.

---

**CASE ILLUSTRATION 12.2**

**Mapping environmental risks**

Mary has not used street drugs on top of her methadone prescription for two months but she still feels vulnerable. Along with her practitioner, she maps each week on a graph, identifying predictable risk times. For the coming week, she has singled out:

- *Tuesday morning* when she goes to the Department of Work and Pensions, where she will meet people she knows are still using.
- *Thursday afternoon* when she goes to the clinic, where again she may meet others with whom she has used in the past.
- *Friday night* when there is a dance at the local hotel. She wants to go to this but drugs are likely to be available and she associates the venue with past use.

She cannot avoid the first two scenarios, so she decides to ask her mother to go with her. Reluctantly, she feels that the dance is a step too far at this stage. By way of compensation, she decides to go to the cinema on Friday night with a non-using friend.

Consider the circumstances of a person you have worked with or someone you know who has a substance problem:

- In what situations is he/she at greatest risk of using?
- At what times of the week is he/she at most risk?

---

### Developing drink and drug refusal skills

Learning how to refuse is a core skill. The first step is to help the person to identify scenarios in which it might be necessary to refuse substances, and then to discuss with her how she feels at those times. Dealing with the emotional aspects is important.

The next stage is to plan how to refuse:

- *What does the person say?* She needs to decide what she feels comfortable with. With a friend she might be honest but with a stranger a white lie may be more appropriate ('I can't drink. I'm on medication'). If it is to be a white lie, it should be one chosen by the person.
- *How does the person say it?* Communicating the message firmly and unambiguously is essential. Verbal and non-verbal skills come into play here. 'No thanks, I'm drinking orange juice', said with eye contact and the palm of the hand raised forward, draws a clear line. 'Not at the moment, thanks', said with the head down, gives the impression that refusal is temporary and the person may be open to a further offer in due course.

Refusal skills can be modelled and then rehearsed using role play in the safety of the counselling room, or with a partner at home, before applying them in the real world. With every successful refusal, self-efficacy should grow.

---

CASE ILLUSTRATION 12.3

**A big breakfast relapse prevention plan**

Gerry (58) was referred to the service I was working in by his GP. Since leaving the army, where he trained as a chef, he had worked in hotels, moving on when the consequences of his drinking caught up with him. He had become a bout drinker, consuming large quantities of whisky during regular two-day binges. Health problems were hardening a determination to live differently. We discussed various strategies he could employ when the desire to drink was strong. However, distraction techniques, avoiding the corner shop and going for walks with his dog had no impact. One day he said: 'You know, if I'm in the mood and go to the shop when my stomach's empty, I've had it. But if I've eaten breakfast, I lose all interest in drink.'

A man with a substantial appetite, breakfast for Gerry was a generous fry-up. This became the focus of his relapse prevention plan:

- Every evening, lay out food and frying pan.
- Put notices on doors saying 'breakfast'.
- After washing, start to cook immediately.
- Eat slowly; enjoy food; listen to the radio.
- Never leave the flat before eating.

Gerry was right; the binges decreased, then stopped.

Gerry's case illustrates the unique nature of every successful relapse prevention plan.

### Preventing a lapse becoming a relapse

If a lapse has occurred, the practitioner should frame this as a learning experience which happens to many people. Feelings of guilt and failure may well lead the person to exaggerate the consequences of the incident (catastrophising) and discount the progress that had occurred prior to the lapse. Self-efficacy will be reduced. The practitioner should try to help the person to put the lapse into the context of her longer term recovery journey. The person may again be experiencing ambivalence about use, with remorse offset by a desire to continue to use; in this case, motivational interviewing may be appropriate. The reasons for the relapse will help identify what other issues need to be addressed.

A controversial issue is whether ways of dealing with possible future lapses should be discussed with the person. Saunders and Allsop (1991, p. 87) note that some service users might be reluctant to discuss this as it could be interpreted as the practitioner suggesting that relapse is inevitable. This is a risk, but Saunders and Allsop suggest approaching it using the fire drill analogy: it is hoped that a fire will not happen but preparations need to be in place should it occur. Marlatt, Parks and Witkiewitz, (2002) recommend helping a person to be ready to act as follows should she lapse:

1   Stand back and interrupt the developing process. What is happening should be viewed as an alarm signal.
2   Implement a prepared plan, such as leaving the situation and immediately contacting a supportive friend.
3   Consciously replace feelings of failure with thoughts that the lapse need go no further and that past progress can be reinstated. It is essential that the person attempts to undermine the abstinence violation effect.
4   Carry a card with simple instructions and the numbers of people to phone.

Finally, if a fuller relapse does occur and the person has reverted to precontemplation or contemplation stages, then reassessment and readjustments to the care plan are likely to be necessary. Motivational work may be required again and different approaches may be indicated.

If the person is receiving an opiate substitute, this should be reviewed in the light of lapses both for safety reasons and, if prescribing is to continue, to ensure that this is at the optimum level to reduce the likelihood of continuing use of street heroin.

ACTIVITY 12.1

**Planning to avoid relapse**
Cat (44) has abstained from drinking for four months. She is keen to attend the wedding of her niece but is concerned that she might relapse. How would you go about helping her?

## Endings and follow-up care

Given that recovery is a halting journey for many, it is important that the door to further treatment episodes is kept wide open. It is, therefore, surprising that aftercare planning and follow-up care is given a low priority by many agencies (Keene, 2010, p. 66); even more remarkable is how little there is in the literature on the topic of endings. 'Follow-up care' is used here to describe what is provided after a more intensive period of treatment has been completed or if a person drops out of the service.

### Endings

Ideally, a case should close when a person is stable, has learned ways of avoiding relapse, has built a supportive social network and has addressed the negative reinforcers in her environment. Of course, endings often do not occur like that. Some people relapse and do not return. Others may drift away without mutual decisions being taken to close the case. Although it should not be assumed that people who drop out always fare badly, the outcomes tend to be poorer than for those who remain in treatment (Stark, 1992). Systematic responses to missed appointments and the provision of continuing contact should be routine.

## BOX 12.1 KEY QUESTIONS WHEN SERVICE ARRANGEMENTS CHANGE

Before levels of contact are significantly reduced or the case is closed, or when a service user drops out, certain questions should be addressed:

- What risks still exist for the service user? Is action needed to address these?
- What are the implications for significant others of any changes in arrangements? Do they need to be contacted? When a service user has responsibility for children, the ramifications must be considered (see Chapter 14).
- Do other agencies need to be consulted?

### Follow-up care

It has been a major theme of this book that, from the earliest stages of engagement, consideration should be given to helping a person to strengthen his recovery capital. Wraparound services dealing with accommodation, employment and financial issues should go hand in hand with work to create an environment that supports an altered lifestyle. People should be given information about self-help and recovery groups and encouraged to consider these. However, there is also evidence that providing formal follow-up care can consolidate changes made and limit the repercussions of relapse (McKay et al., 2009; Raistrick, Heather and Godfrey, 2006, p. 113). Arrangements for this should be an integrated part of the service offered (Jarvis et al., 2005, p. 238) and should be discussed with the person at an early stage.

It is good practice to offer a further appointment immediately after any sessions are missed. A lapse or a simple missed appointment can lead to feelings of failure or embarrassment which a friendly offer of renewed contact can dispel. If there is no response to this communication, a further attempt a month or so later may bear fruit.

While some people will need little additional input after the more intensive phase of treatment has ended, the only way to identify individuals who do need further help is by maintaining contact for a period. Arrangements for planned follow-up care can include scheduled appointments or agreed telephone contacts. Texting and email increase the options. Contact is more likely to be maintained if:

- *systems are assertive*. For example, it is better to offer a specific appointment than a general invitation to get in touch.
- *the agency is persistent*.
- *reminders are sent* if appointments were arranged some time earlier.
- *communication is personalised* and motivational wording is used. ('I hope volunteering at the community centre continues to go well but if you have had any problems we can discuss them next week').
- *contact continues* over a significant period of time. (Ashton and Whitton, 2004)

Careful but systematic probing may be needed to overcome any resistance people may have to admitting to ongoing problems. Scott and Dennis (2009) suggest that follow-up should involve screening for problems, feedback and motivational approaches. If it is discovered that relapse has occurred, harm reduction measures should be implemented, followed by reassessment and re-entry into treatment (Keene, 2010, p. 184).

---

**ACTIVITY 12.2**

**Follow-up systems**
Consider a substance problem service which you have had contact with. What follow-up systems are in place and how effective do you think these are?

---

In a review of McKay's work, Ashton (2009) argues that the evidence supporting continuing care challenges the current orthodoxy in the UK regarding people with drug problems. The recovery agenda places a heavy emphasis on moving people on from treatment; however, when people are struggling to reintegrate, formal support on a longer term basis may well be necessary.

## Concluding comments

Relapse prevention is a central intervention. It should go hand in hand with ensuring that the person's environment and social network help to maintain the changed behaviour. It is also essential that services provide barrier-free pathways to re-engagement with formal treatment should this again prove necessary.

### RESOURCES

- Jarvis, T., Tebutt, J., Mattick, R. and Shand, F. (2005). *Treatment Approaches to Drug and Alcohol Dependence. An Introductory Guide* (2nd edition). See Part III, 'Maintaining Change'.
- Marlatt, G. and Donovan, D. (eds) (2005). *Relapse Prevention: Maintenance Strategies in the Treatment of Addictive Behaviors* (2nd edition).
- NTA/University of Birmingham (2008). *Routes to Recovery Part 5. The BTEI Exiting Treatment Manual: Mapping Achievable Goals.* Available at: www.nta.nhs.uk/uploads/ itep_routes_to_recovery_part5_240309.pdf. (This is an example of a relapse prevention/maintenance manual for use with service users.)
  (NB: Material on the NTA website is scheduled to be transferred by 2014 to the PHE website or placed on the National Archive's website or similar.)
- Skills Consortium. The Skills Hub section of the Skills Consortium website provides links to treatment guidance documents and manuals, including those dealing with relapse prevention: www.skillsconsortium.org.uk/skillshub.aspx.

PART III

# Specific Populations

# Psychological Distress and Substance Problems

- The relationship between psychological distress and substance use is multifaceted.
- People with co-occurring psychological and substance problems are also more likely to experience a range of other social and personal difficulties.
- Trying to help people experiencing both types of problem can be particularly challenging.
- It is critical that both substance problem and mental health services in each area are structured so as to provide a coordinated approach.

## Dual diagnosis: an unhelpful term?

The co-occurrence of mental health and substance problems is commonly called 'dual diagnosis', but this label is problematic. Dual diagnosis suggests that it is possible to determine a discrete group of people who are experiencing both such difficulties. However, the often episodic nature of both mental health and substance problems, along with the pitfalls of defining both, makes distinct categorisation difficult. Galvani (2012, p. 183) raises the risk of double stigmatisation and questions the medicalisation that the name implies. With its emphasis on two issues, the term 'dual diagnosis' risks minimising other problems, such as poor physical health or the social consequences of use. While some people can be clearly defined as experiencing 'mental illness', the broader concept of 'psychological distress' will also be used here; it captures more accurately the wide range of uncomfortable mental states that can precede or follow the use of substances.

## The links between psychological distress and substance problems

It is axiomatic that the ingestion of substances and psychological functioning are inextricably intertwined (Galvani, 2012, p. 181). The very reason we take psychoactive substances is to interfere with the chemistry of the central nervous system to our advantage. We may want to elevate mood, deaden pain, reduce our inhibitions or view the world in a different way. Such interference can, of course, have unwanted consequences.

Psychological distress may be transitory, particularly when it is the result of the specific effects of a drug or cessation of use, or it may be longer lasting. The latter can bring with it additional problems of social functioning and presents the greater challenge to services. It would be wrong, however, to minimise the somewhat different risks associated with the former.

Lehman (adapted by Rorstad and Checinski, 1996) describes the following four ways in which psychological distress and use of substances are related.

### Problematic substance use which follows psychological distress

A person experiencing psychological problems may start to use substances to cope with the discomfort. The very effectiveness of such self-medication, at least in the short term, can lead to escalating use and growing reliance on the drug. As we saw in Chapter 3, this is one of the theories as to why people develop problems with substances. For example, a person who hears voices might use cannabis to try to reduce the impact of these or a person might start to drink to reduce the symptoms of post-traumatic stress. Use might then become persistent and problematic. Some drugs can compound psychological distress. Alcohol's capacity to initially lift mood by dampening inhibitions is soon overtaken by its depressant effect on the central nervous system; continued or regular heavy drinking will simply make a depressed person more depressed. It is important to note that while practitioners may consider that substance taking is inadvisable for those suffering more serious psychological distress, that is not necessarily how such people view the situation. Interviewing individuals diagnosed with schizophrenia, Asher and Gask (2010) found that a number identified benefits in illicit drug use such as lessening the apprehension associated with hearing voices or the belief that substances enabled them to outmanoeuvre the tormentors behind these. Many in the sample considered that prescribed medication and illicit substances served similar purposes for them. This is a good example of how 'problematic' use is in the eye of the beholder, at least to a certain degree. The other side of the coin is that drugs or alcohol can exacerbate symptoms or provoke a recurrence of these. It should be noted that substances may compromise the effectiveness of drugs prescribed for mental health problems or intensify their side effects (Alcohol Focus Scotland, undated). A further dimension is that people can become dependent on the drugs prescribed to deal with psychological difficulties; the history of prescribing benzodiazepines for anxiety and sleeping problems illustrates this.

### Substance use leading to psychological distress or impaired mental functioning

The potential effects of substance use can be broken down into four categories:

- *Consequences of use on mood and cognitive functioning.* The price of the pleasurable effects of substance use can be fairly short lived, but distressing, psychological experiences. These include the LSD 'bad trip', blackouts following excessive drinking and the paranoia and anxiety associated with the use of stimulants.

■ *Psychological problems associated with cessation of use (abstinence syndromes).* Various conditions are associated with this. The florid hallucinations and delusions typical of delirium tremens (see Chapter 7) can also occur following abrupt cessation of benzodiazepine or barbiturate use (Rorstad and Checinski, 1996). The psychotic states that can follow longer term use of cocaine and amphetamines can persist for a period after cessation.

■ *Long-term damage to the functioning of the brain.* It has long been known that some substances can have detrimental effects on the brain. With others, the implications are less clear. Ecstasy is a case in point, with sensationalist headlines warning of the consequences of use. However, the implications of occasional or regular ecstasy use still remain uncertain. Halpern et al. (2011) failed to identify significant mental impairment in a group of ecstasy users. However, they also noted that, despite methodological problems, a number of meta-analyses do suggest that some cognitive deficiencies may result. Regular use of cocaine may be implicated in structural changes in the brain (Ersche et al., 2011) and smoking tobacco in cognitive deterioration (Dregan, Stewart and Gulliford, 2012). However, much is still not known regarding the implications of the use of many substances on cognitive functioning, motor control and ageing or whether such changes are permanent if a person stops using. What is well understood are the risks of Wernicke's encephalopathy, Korsakoff's syndrome and alcoholic dementia inherent in chronic drinking (see Chapter 10).

■ *The association between use and the development of specific psychiatric conditions.* A question which continues to perplex is whether use of substances can cause or trigger specific longer term psychiatric conditions, as opposed to damage to the brain or shorter-lasting syndromes. LSD is a classic example. The psychotic episodes that can follow use appear not dissimilar to those experienced by people diagnosed with schizophrenia and, in the popular mind, it was thought that a link existed. Long-term problems of a psychotic nature are uncommon but have been recorded and it may be that LSD can act as a trigger for an underlying condition (Shapiro, 2010). Because of its ubiquitousness, the drug that has caused most concern is cannabis (see Box 13.1).

## BOX 13.1 CANNABIS AND MENTAL HEALTH

Some people do experience transitory distress such as confusion and panic attacks following cannabis use but what is less clear is the relationship between cannabis use and more enduring mental health problems. Pointing to the uncertainties in the evidence, the Advisory Council on the Misuse of Drugs (ACMD, 2008) concluded that:

- the great majority of cannabis users do not develop psychotic illnesses;
- cannabis can exacerbate symptoms, or precipitate relapse, in individuals already suffering from schizophrenia;
- there is a small increased risk of people who have used cannabis in adolescence developing schizophrenia-like conditions;
- extent of use may be relevant;
- a genetic influence may need to be present;
- a link between cannabis use and the development of anxiety, bipolar disorder or depression is unproven.

### Both problems without apparent connections

It is possible for someone to have difficulties with substances and experience impaired psychological wellbeing without any apparent connections between the two.

### Problematic substance use and psychological distress with a shared origin

Both sets of difficulties may be linked back to a particular experience. For example, a person who has suffered serious injuries might come to depend on cannabis to control the pain but might also experience depressive episodes because of reduced mobility.

## Co-occurring problems, multiple difficulties

The hurdles which people who experience more persistent co-occurring psychological and substance problems face are greater, and the outcomes across a range of indicators are poorer, than for people with only one of these difficulties (Crome et al., 2009; NICE, 2011a). Non-compliance with prescribed medication or care plans, early withdrawal from services and increased likelihood of hospitalisation or admission to institutions are all issues. There is a greater probability that people with co-occurring problems will experience poor physical health. They are also more likely to offend or encounter social problems including homelessness and unemployment and their circumstances are likely to create considerable stress for their families. There is a strong connection between suicide and substance problems. There are links between aggressive behaviour, problematic substance use and mental health difficulties, particularly when the latter are of a psychotic nature (Crome et al., 2009; Soyka, 2000).

---

**CASE ILLUSTRATION 13.1**

**The problem of compliance**

Following an industrial accident which left him unable to work, Colin moved in with his father who lived in an isolated village. Quite lengthy periods of abstinence were interspersed by week-long episodes of heavy drinking. He told me that he experienced mood swings and regular panic attacks which left him unable to leave the house. He said he would like to receive help for his psychological problems but, because of the panic attacks, he felt unable to travel on the bus to the nearest hospital without first taking tranquillisers. I spoke to his GP, who was sympathetic but said that she was unwilling to prescribe because of Colin's history of misusing, or selling, his medication. She did, however, arrange for a psychologist to come to the local surgery to see him there. On the appointed date, Colin was drinking and failed to attend.

## Prevalence

Estimates of prevalence vary considerably because of difficulties such as achieving consistency in classifying problems; nevertheless, there is agreement that co-occurring problems are commonplace:

■ Summarising the evidence, the Scottish Executive (2003b) estimated that, at a maximum, 75 per cent of clients of drug services and 50 per cent of patients with alcohol problems had mental health issues and 40 per cent of people diagnosed with mental health difficulties had problems with substances.
■ Research by Weaver et al. (2003) across four urban areas found that, over the previous year, 44 per cent of people involved with community mental health services described using substances detrimentally and 75 per cent of users of drug services and 85 per cent of people attending alcohol services had exhibited mental health problems.

What is highly relevant for how services are delivered is that Weaver et al. (2003) suggest that, in their study, only 24 per cent of people using drug services and 38 per cent using alcohol services who were experiencing mental health problems would meet the thresholds for acceptance by community mental health teams (CMHT). This is reflected in an American study which showed that the most common causes of psychological distress among people with alcohol and drug problems in treatment settings were anxiety, affective disorders and antisocial personality, the types of difficulty seen as a lower priority by mental health services than psychotic disorders (Regier et al. cited in Gilvarry, 1998, p. 114). Conversely, Weaver et al. (2003) noted that most patients of CMHTs with drug problems would be considered low priority by drug services because they were using cannabis, tranquillisers and sedatives rather than class A drugs. The authors consider that the potential for cross-referral of patients of CMHTs with alcohol problems might be somewhat higher. The implications for this will now be considered.

## How services are provided

The research by Weaver et al. (2003) demonstrates that the population with coexisting problems is extensive. This suggests that, however services are structured in a particular area, both substance problems and mental health practitioners need to acquire a level of competence in each other's disciplines: there are simply too many people involved for onward referral in all cases to be practical.

Historically it was often thought that one problem had to be resolved before the other could be addressed. In addition, the compartmentalisation of mental health and substance problems services led to people with co-occurring problems either only receiving help for one of their difficulties or falling between disciplines and receiving no help at all. Sequential approaches, accessing a service to deal with one problem before transferring to a different specialism to address the other issue, and parallel models, dealing with the two problems simultaneously but by separate services acting in comparative isolation, have fallen out of favour. These modes of delivery have been criticised for leading to fragmented care (El-Mallakh, 1998), with confusion in care planning, perpetuation of differences in treatment philosophy and limited cross-fertilisation of knowledge and skills. People can find themselves being passed backward and forward between services, based in different locales, with dissimilar perspectives and ways of operating. The specialist multidisciplinary team is one model for reducing such difficulties, especially for people with more serious mental health problems. However, it has proved difficult to find evidence that this achieves superior outcomes (Cleary et al., 2007). Also the level of resources required for separate specialist teams means that access will always be limited to those with the most complex problems. The following approach is currently favoured in both England and Scotland (Department of Health, 2002; Scottish Government, 2007); broadly similar models operate in Wales (Welsh Government, 2013) and Northern Ireland (MindWise, 2013), with the same emphasis on person-centred treatment and care pathways:

- People with more severe mental health problems co-occurring with difficulties with substances should be the responsibility of mental health services. They should be supported under the Care Programme Approach, which provides formal, structured responses to need and risk for people with complex psychological difficulties. People with more severe difficulties will benefit from long-term engagement. They are likely to present problems of case management, such as erratic compliance and behaviour and high levels of relapse, which demand tolerance and persistence on the part of services.
- Models for delivery should be developed to best meet the needs of each geographical area but planning should be a collaborative exercise between mental health and substance problem services. Where specialist dual diagnosis teams do exist, these should support mainstream mental health services and not operate in isolation.
- Local protocols should include clear care pathways, along with shared assessment procedures and confidentiality policies.
- Practitioners should be aware of what their roles are and how their agencies fit into the mosaic of services in their areas. Practitioner competence and service capacity should be further developed in both disciplines. Substance problem workers should be trained to screen their service users

for both lower level psychological distress and more serious mental health problems. Mental health workers should be able to screen for substance problems. All parties should be trained to engage with the issues at a level commensurate with the roles their agencies play. Suicide prevention training should be a priority. Training should be delivered, at least in part, on a multidisciplinary basis.

- Service users and carers should be involved in designing provision (Turning Point, 2007).

The Centre for Mental Health, DrugScope and the UK Drug Policy Commission (2012) note that, whilst arrangements are improving, much remains to be done, particularly to meet the needs of people with 'lower level' psychological distress. 'Lower level' is really a misnomer as anxiety, depression, post-traumatic stress and the like erode quality of life and also heighten the risk of suicide. More comprehensive guidance is needed throughout the UK on how both mental health and substance problems services should best handle people experiencing lower level psychological distress. Guidance for practitioners involved in the Improving Access to Psychological Therapies (IAPT) programme outlines when people should be referred to substance problems services, along with the importance of cross-disciplinary consultation and training initiatives (IAPT, DrugScope and NTA, 2012). As both sets of practitioners use motivational, cognitive and behavioural approaches, the potential for interdisciplinary initiatives to improve responses to those with co-occurring substance problems and psychological distress short of serious mental health problems is considerable.

---

ACTIVITY 13.1

**Service coordination**
How are services for people with co-occurring problems structured in the area where you work or where you have been on placement?

---

## Assessment, care planning and interventions

The principles of assessment, care planning and interventions are essentially the same as for people without co-occurring problems (see Chapter 7). The literature puts particular emphasis on a non-judgemental and empathetic approach, the engagement phase, the involvement of carers and relatives and the need to consider impacts on social functioning (Scottish Government, 2007). What is of particular importance is practitioner confidence, clear pathways and interdisciplinary cooperation, along with an understanding of the complexities and the need for patience borne of realistic expectations about outcomes.

Practitioners in mental health services should screen all patients to ascertain whether problematic use of substances is an issue and, where indicated, fuller assessment should follow. Guidance has been produced for Improving Access to Psychological Therapies teams on working with people with substance problems (DrugScope and NTA, 2012). What follows is written from the perspective of practitioners in drug and alcohol services. Because of the ubiquitous nature of co-occurring problems, substance problems practitioners should assume that all service users are experiencing some level of psychological distress until it becomes clear that this is not the case.

## Assessment

Standard assessment of people with substance problems should, at a minimum, address the following:

- Is the person currently in contact with mental health services or is he consulting his GP regarding psychological problems? Is he being prescribed any medication for such problems? Has he received treatment in the past? If the answer to any of these is in the affirmative, then permission should be sought to contact the other agencies to ensure that a comprehensive assessment can be made and, if involvement is current, a multi-agency care plan can be devised.
- Is the person suffering from any form of psychological distress? Open questions should be used to encourage the person to describe his moods and feelings over the past few weeks. More structured questions can be used to ascertain how long the person has experienced difficulties and the nature of these. Substance problems staff should be trained to be able to differentiate between the various categories of mental health problems. People experiencing anxiety disorders, such as obsessive compulsive disorder, panic attacks, post-traumatic stress or various types of phobia will describe highly exaggerated responses to situations. These can include excessive fears of everyday situations, feelings of losing control and being overwhelmed, extreme guilt and physical symptoms such as sweating, diarrhoea, dizziness and raised heart rate or palpitations. People experiencing post-traumatic stress often have nightmares or flashbacks in which they relive the event. People will often try to avoid situations or encounters which risk triggering their symptoms. People who are depressed often express feelings of hopelessness and pessimism and can find it difficult to engage with activities; they may lose interest in everyday activities, food and sex. Periods of depression can be short lived or lengthy. Whilst the symptoms of anxiety disorders may appear to others to be highly irrational, those experiencing them tend to know this, despite feeling unable to control them. They remain orientated in reality. This is the feature which most clearly demarcates such problems from psychotic disorders, such as schizophrenia. These are characterised by hallucinations, such as hearing voices, or delusional thoughts which, during psychotic episodes, the person is inclined to interpret as reality. A person with bipolar disorder will exhibit moods which swing from phases of serious depression to periods marked by extreme elation, high energy levels, risky and irrational decision making and, sometimes, delusional thinking. Clues to problems can be picked up through observing behaviour as well as from what people describe. Body language, posture

and how a person presents himself should be noted. The content of speech can reflect the disordered and confused thought patterns people experience during psychotic episodes.

Psychological distress is not confined to people with conditions which meet formal diagnostic criteria. Many who approach substance problems services have histories of disrupted upbringings, fractured relationships or abuse which have led to feelings of depression, low self-esteem and pessimism about their ability to change.

- As has been noted, substance taking and cessation of use can both be associated with distressing states with strong similarities to the symptoms of particular types of mental health problems. If a person drinks excessively and complains of depression, but there is no evidence that depressive episodes occurred when he was abstinent or drinking moderately, then it is reasonable to assume that alcohol is the culprit. Similarly, the mood disorders and short-lived psychotic-type events associated with heavier and more persistent use or cessation of some stimulants may indicate nothing more than the effects of these drugs; the hallucinations which follow taking ketamine or LSD may be of a similar nature. However, it can take a period of time after use has stopped to ascertain whether this is the case. It is also important not to minimise the psychological distress of these shorter term episodes or the heightened risk of suicide that goes with them.
- Co-occurring problems increase the risk of suicide; use of substances can precipitate impulsive behaviour and certain drugs provide a ready method. The person should be asked whether he has a history of self-harm or attempted suicide and whether he has recently had thoughts of the latter. Far from reinforcing any ideas service users may have about harming themselves, discussing the issue with them in a sensitive way may bring relief and provide the opportunity to intervene (Hawkings and Gilbert, 2004). Feelings of depression, social isolation, risk-taking behaviour, previous attempts at suicide, stated intentions or specific plans regarding self-harm are all indicators of heightened risk (NHS Health Scotland, 2005, p. 28).
- People with co-occurring problems are more likely to exhibit aggressive behaviour than people with mental health problems only (Hawkings and Gilbert, 2004). A person's offending history can provide valuable information in this regard.
- Efforts should be made to include partners, parents or others close to the person in the assessment process unless there are reasons suggesting that this is not desirable. The information they supply may help to clarify the extent of the person's psychological distress and the risks it presents. Of equal importance is the opportunity that engagement with significant others brings to find out whether they need help for themselves in coping with the challenges of living with someone with co-occurring problems (see Chapter 15).
- Although the relationship between a person's psychological distress and problematic use of substances can be obvious, and inform how the case should be managed, this is often far from the case. An inability to readily disentangle the connections should not be allowed to impede implementing immediate risk reduction measures.

- Psychological distress is often episodic; in addition, some people develop sophisticated ways of hiding their unhappiness or the symptoms of specific conditions through fear of stigma or a desire to soldier on regardless. This underscores the importance of assessment being an ongoing process.

If serious immediate risks are identified, these will demand a speedy response such as referral to the GP or to emergency health or psychiatric services. The person may need to be accompanied and given continuing reassurance. Urgent action is needed when the person is:

- displaying psychotic symptoms, even if these seem likely to be drug induced;
- threatening self-harm or suicide;
- experiencing withdrawals from depressants such as alcohol, benzodiazepines, GHB or GBL or barbiturates, whether or not more florid psychological disturbance is present.

When handing the person on to the care of others, it is important that the concerns are clearly articulated; it is best to put these in writing. This also holds if it is necessary to call the police or an ambulance. Where relevant, a person's relatives should be advised of the actions taken.

### Care planning

As normal, the principle of establishing short- and longer term goals applies (see Chapter 7). Goals should belong to the individual and realistic judgements should be made regarding the likely pace of change. Shorter term goals should include normal substance problem harm reduction measures. Issues to consider include the following:

- If a person is experiencing serious mental health problems, such as incapacitating depression, severe mood swings or psychotic symptoms which cannot be attributed to recent substance use, then referral to mental health services is indicated. As has been noted, the case will then be led by those services although the substance problem agency may continue to have a role. The referring agency should support the person until the psychiatric assessment process has begun.
- When a person is experiencing lower levels of psychiatric distress, decisions need to be made as to which services best meet their various needs. For some, reductions in their problematic use, along with general counselling for issues such as low self-esteem and helping the person to come to terms with past experiences, may mean that referral to mental health services is unnecessary. For others, more specialist psychological inputs can mean that substance problems practitioners are working alongside GPs, community psychiatric nurses, practitioners in IAPT teams or bereavement counsellors. In such instances, all agencies should be party to the care plan and a lead practitioner to coordinate care should be agreed. In some circumstances,

the substance problems worker might consider that a referral to an agency providing psychiatric approaches is desirable but the person is unwilling to contemplate this. The service user may be anxious about going to yet another service or feel he only wants to receive help from the person he already feels comfortable with. In such a situation, substance problems practitioners may need to seek supervision from someone in the mental health field.

- As substance use can aggravate psychological distress and also interact negatively with prescribed drugs, people with co-occurring problems should consider abstinence. NICE (2011b) recommends this specifically for people with alcohol problems and significant mental health difficulties. Of course, the person may not find abstinence acceptable, in which case goals will switch to controlled drinking or to harm minimisation and reduction in use.
- Because of alcohol's effects on mood and cognitive functioning, NICE (2011b) recommends that a period of around a month following abstinence should elapse before a decision is taken as to whether specific mental health interventions are needed.
- Early consideration should be given to putting wraparound services in place when social isolation, unstable accommodation, poor self-care and the like are issues.
- Where relevant, the process of care planning should include carers or other significant adults. If they need support for themselves, it may be best to develop a separate care plan for them (see Chapter 15).
- If the person has a history of aggressive behaviour, measures should be put in place to reduce the risks to significant others and to practitioners.

### Interventions

Moves to support people with coexisting problems in a holistic manner and to adopt more integrated approaches only began to occur in the 1990s, so it is unsurprising that uncertainties remain regarding what interventions are the most effective. Galvani (2012, p. 202) notes that evidence has been found to support motivational interviewing and CBT. However, Jarvis et al. (2005, p. 283) consider that cognitive interventions are of limited value for people with cognitive impairments or psychosis and they suggest that behavioural programmes and relapse prevention are more appropriate. Hawkings and Gilbert (2004) suggest that, for people with severe mental health problems, research does not support any specific psychosocial interventions as being the most effective in reducing substance use or improving mental wellbeing. This would seem to indicate that, until further work is undertaken, the best approach lies with the same evidence-based interventions used with people without co-occurring problems, along with pharmacotherapies and specific programmes for mental health problems where these are indicated.

Residential rehab may be an appropriate option when a person finds it difficult to achieve any stability in the community or has poor social supports and unsettled accommodation. However, it is important to consider from the outset the challenges of reintegration back into the community. NICE (2011a) recommends that people with psychosis should not be excluded from staffed or residential accommodation by virtue of either their substance or mental health problems. However, case managers will need to ensure that a particular project can both meet the person's needs and cope with the challenges he might present. Long-term residential care will be needed for some people with Korsakoff's syndrome.

Recovery, with its emphasis on optimism, resilience and personal growth despite the persistence of problems, is now a well-developed concept in the mental health field and is increasingly shaping how substance problems services are structured (see Chapter 6). This approach, along with the growth of recovery activities and support groups, may have much to offer people with more enduring co-occurring problems in the future (Crome et al., 2009).

---

CASE ILLUSTRATION 13.2

**Co-occurring problems**

Following a warning at work for poor performance, Andy (29) approached the community-based substance problems service where you work. His wife came with him for that first appointment but since then he has attended on his own. He has reduced his heavy cannabis use but his drinking remains excessive (60 units a week). Having hinted that he is a worrier, he now tells you that he has been having irrational thoughts for years. 'I keep thinking I'm going mad,' he says, 'but alcohol and dope calm me.' He describes various ways in which he fears that he might be hurting people and the elaborate checks he undertakes to reduce his anxiety.

Consider all the options for taking Andy's case forward.

---

## Concluding comments

Despite co-occurring problems being commonplace among people presenting to both mental health and substance problems services, and not withstanding various strategy documents outlining the importance of local planning and interdisciplinary working, responses remain underdeveloped (Galvani, 2012, p. 194). There is no doubting the testing nature of work with people with co-occurring problems, but the challenge of providing effective services across the whole country has been avoided for too long.

RESOURCES

- Mental health problems and their treatment. Introductory information is available at: MIND: www.mind.org.uk.
  Royal College of Psychiatrists: www.rcpsych.ac.uk/expertadvice/problemsdisorders.aspx.
- Crome, I., Chambers, P., Frisher, M., Bloor, R. and Roberts, M. (2009). *The Relationship between Dual Diagnosis: Substance Misuse and Dealing with Mental Health Issues.* Available at: www.scie.org.uk/publications/briefings/files/briefing30.pdf.

- NICE (2011). *Psychosis with Existing Substance Misuse.* www.nice.org.uk/guidance/ CG120.
- Rassool, G. H. (2001). *Dual Diagnosis: Substance Misuse and Psychiatric Disorders.*
- Watson, S. and Hawkings, C. (2007). *Dual Diagnosis. Good Practice Handbook.* Available at: www.nmhdu.org.uk/silo/files/dual-diagnosis-good-practice-handbook.pdf.

# CHAPTER 14

# Children Affected by Parental Problems

KEY THEMES

- Major policy initiatives have ensured that the wellbeing of children is now a priority for services working with adults with substance problems.
- Effective inter-agency working is essential to ensure that children's needs are met and that they are protected from harm.
- Developing best practice regarding children affected by parental substance use remains a work in progress for services providing for adults with alcohol or drug problems.

## Children affected

The phrase 'children affected' is used here to describe any child or adolescent for whom an adult with a substance problem has responsibility, whether or not that adult is a blood relative. Public concern has tended to centre on child protection but it is also essential to take into account unmet or compromised needs too when considering how parental or carer substance use impacts on children. The welfare of children has become a universal responsibility. It is a requirement for all services for adults and for children, whether in the statutory, voluntary or private sectors, to consider whether parental/carer substance use is an issue on a case-by-case basis. What follows focuses on practice from the perspective of services for adults with substance problems, but the principles are applicable across the board.

### Children affected come to the fore

Until the turn of the millennium, only a minority of projects for adults with substance problems paid much regard to the implications of their service users' behaviour for any children for whom they might be responsible. An increasing understanding of the potential risks which parental substance problems can cause, along with instances when services had failed to protect children where parental/carer substance use was an issue, triggered a change in approach. A number of systemic deficiencies were identified: limited joint working involving adult and children's services; confidentiality policies which were interpreted as restricting the transmission of information relevant to the protection of children; inadequate training in child protection and children's issues in adult services and a parallel lack of knowledge about substance issues in children's services (ACMD, 2003). In addition, specialisation had encouraged a limited focus. This problem was tellingly summarised in one report into the death of a baby where parental substance use was identified as a factor (O'Brien, Hammond and McKinnon, 2003, p. 6): 'Many concerned professionals did their best for this family, but too many operated from within a narrow perspective without full appreciation of the wider picture.'

In 2003, two seminal and complementary documents, 'Getting our Priorities Right' (Scottish Executive, 2003a) and 'Hidden Harm' (ACMD, 2003), were published with the aim of addressing the shortcomings in practice. These highlighted:

- the need for a cultural shift in services for adults to ensure that practitioners engage with the issue of children's welfare in every case;
- the importance of inter-agency working at both the planning and operational levels;
- the benefits of early intervention to prevent crises;
- the value of ensuring that parents get ready access to good quality services.

These documents acted as the catalyst for major improvements and led to local multi-agency planning forums producing protocols for how services in their areas should respond to children affected. Child protection is now seen as 'everyone's business', although this remains an evolving agenda.

While research has documented the risks, and the voices of children are increasingly being heard, the concealed nature of much problematic use hampers attempts to determine the number of children affected. The ACMD (2003) estimated that a maximum of 360,000 children in the UK had a drug-using parent but not all these were living with that parent. In England in 2011/12, 34 per cent of adults in treatment for drug problems were living with children (NTA, 2012d). Estimating the numbers affected by parental alcohol problems is even more difficult, with figures ranging from less than one million to over two million (Murray, 2006). If the numbers experiencing significant harm at any given time are simply unknown, what is not in doubt is that this is a serious and widespread social problem.

### Children affected: not just risks, needs too

Parental substance problems can seriously impact on the physical and psychological wellbeing of children and compromise their development. However, it would be wrong to assume that all such children receive inadequate parenting or emerge from their childhoods scarred (Kroll and Taylor, 2013; Velleman and Templeton, 2007). Galvani (2012, p. 87) stresses that what is important is not the use of drugs or alcohol as such but the implications of that use for parenting skills and capacity. The type of potential difficulties which the children of parents with substance problems face alter somewhat with age and there is a danger in assuming that the implications for older children are less serious because the risk of physical harm has reduced. While ensuring that children do not come to immediate harm is given the highest priority, substance problems practitioners should also remain alive to whether or not children's developmental needs are being met. Potential risks start with pregnancy (see Box 14.1).

Younger children may be at risk of:

- physical neglect (poor diet; safety issues such as hazards in the home or having access to drugs or paraphernalia);
- physical/sexual abuse;
- emotional neglect/lack of stimulation (preoccupation with substance use leaving parents 'unavailable' to their children);
- forming poor attachments;
- erratic supervision;
- exposure to criminal behaviour.

Other problems can emerge as children grow older including:

- self-blame: children may feel responsible for the situation;
- emotional effects such as anger, embarrassment, feelings of isolation and anxieties about their parent's welfare;
- behavioural or educational difficulties;
- the adoption of roles inappropriate to their age, such as trying to manage the household, looking after their young siblings or acting as carers for their intoxicated or ill parents;
- becoming concerned that they, too, will develop problems with substances, a fear not without foundation as the risk for these children is heightened. (Cleaver, Unell and Algate, 1999; Hart and Powell, 2006; Scottish Executive, 2003a)

The implications of parental problems may be different for each child in a family. A 12-year-old may be able to leave the house to avoid the return of his intoxicated father whereas his five-year-old sister cannot do this. One child may display greater resilience than another.

When children are facing serious difficulties, it is often the case that other problems, in addition to parental substance use, are present. It can be difficult to disentangle drug and alcohol taking from the effects of poverty, isolation and social disadvantage (Templeton et al., 2006). The risks to children are greater when family relationships are marked by discord and domestic violence (Cleaver, Unell and Algate, 1999; Templeton et al., 2006). Because of these other factors, a reduction in problematic substance use by the parents may not necessarily lead to improvements in a child's situation. More research is needed into whether having a step-parent with a substance problem increases the risk.

Protective factors have been identified; these can reduce, but do not eliminate, the risks:

- the presence of one consistent, caring adult (including a non-using parent, older sibling, grandparent or another close family member);
- the substance-using parent receiving treatment;
- the maintenance of activities and rituals within the family;
- consistent attendance at nursery or school;
- involvement in out-of-school pursuits;
- understanding and vigilant teachers;
- social workers, health service staff or the like who can consistently monitor the situation and provide help as required. (Cleaver, Unell and Algate, 1999)

## BOX 14.1 PREGNANCY

The implications for the unborn child of some substances are well evidenced (alcohol, nicotine); for others they are less clear (cannabis, hallucinogens). As well as the potential effects of a particular drug, factors such as the quantities used, the method of ingestion, how long it has been used for and what point in the pregnancy it was taken can all influence the level of risk. In addition to substance use, the effects of disadvantage on a woman, such as poor housing, inadequate diet and a history of health problems, can also influence the progress of a pregnancy (Whittaker, 2011). The following are examples of some potential associations (Whittaker, 2011):

- *Alcohol*: low birth weight; miscarriage; fetal alcohol spectrum disorder (FASD). FASD is a possible consequence of excessive maternal drinking and covers both fetal alcohol syndrome (FAS) and fetal alcohol effect (FAE). Children born with FAS, a rare condition, have developmental impairments, permanent brain defects leading to memory, learning and behavioural problems and physical abnormalities including facial deformities. Children with fetal alcohol effect have less pronounced cognitive deficits and behavioural difficulties; it is more common (May and Gossage, 2013). If alcohol is consumed at very modest levels and bingeing is avoided, then the risks are very low but the importance of providing clear, unambiguous advice led the Department of Health (2008b) to advise women to avoid alcohol if pregnant or trying to conceive.
- *Nicotine*: low birth weight; miscarriage; sudden infant death syndrome; respiratory problems in childhood.
- *Opiates*: low birth weight; premature birth; neonatal abstinence syndrome (baby experiences withdrawals following birth).
- *Benzodiazepines*: maternal dependence can lead to neonatal abstinence syndrome.

Pregnancy and its aftermath are managed under local multi-agency protocols and substance problems practitioners should maintain close contact with maternity services.

Where there are concerns about the ability of the parents to manage a baby, multidisciplinary case conferences will be arranged early in the pregnancy and close to the birth to consider options. Arrangements should also cover the situation when a male service user has a partner who is pregnant, even if she does not have a substance problem herself.

## Children affected: the role of substance problems practitioners

There are some projects which provide specialist interventions for parents with substance problems and their children together and there are teams staffed by both childcare and substance problems practitioners. However, in the majority of instances where concerns about children have been identified, the parents will remain involved with services for adults and the responsibility for the childcare aspects will lie with social services or dedicated children's organisations. Most substance problems practitioners are not qualified to undertake comprehensive child or parenting assessments but they should be trained to be able to:

- discuss parenting issues with their service users;
- screen the implications of their service users' substance use for children they are responsible for;
- recognise situations where immediate child protection procedures must be instigated;
- know when it is necessary to contact childcare agencies to ensure that children are receiving services to meet their needs;
- act as part of a multidisciplinary response when a number of services are involved.

All agencies for adults with substance problems should have child protection policies in place and a manager with responsibility for this area of work to provide guidance to staff and maintain close links with statutory children's services.

### BOX 14.2 MANAGING PROFESSIONAL CONFLICTS

It is to be expected that the contrasting perspectives of substance problems practitioners and childcare workers will lead to differences of opinion. This often reflects the fact that the pace at which adults change does not necessarily match the time scales within which it is essential to provide a child with a stable living situation. A substance problems practitioner might argue that circumstances have improved because the parent is stabilising on methadone; the childcare worker may say that the situation remains unsettled. Both are right and it is for the case conference manager or the like to make the final judgement as to whether the parents have the capacity to consistently meet the children's needs.

An area of continuing concern is that deficiencies in training mean that childcare social workers still lack the skills and confidence to engage effectively with families where drugs and alcohol are an issue (Forrester and Harwin, 2011).

## Adult services: screening and monitoring

Adult services should work within local protocols. The following takes an overview of the issues. Little attention has been paid to the process of engaging service users in discussions about the children they are responsible for. Some parents may avoid treatment services for fear of the implications for their children (Potts, 2005; Roberts and Nuru-Jeter, 2010) but the extent of this is not known. What is obvious is that sensitivity and empathy are prerequisites for reducing the anxieties that parents will inevitably feel. If a parent seeking help for her substance problem feels under threat, then she is unlikely to return and an opportunity to both help her and ensure the wellbeing of the children will be lost. Two crucial issues need to be considered:

1  *Timing*. During a first appointment, a service user will be preoccupied with her own circumstances. She will be anxious, uncertain as to how to present her situation and perhaps experiencing a level of withdrawal; she will, however, be 'motivated about something' (Thorley, 1980). She will make a judgement as to whether it is worth continuing contact based on how far she thinks that 'that something' has been both heard and addressed. If the practitioner appears to be more interested in her children at this stage then she is less likely return. Care with timing is needed.
2  *How the issue is presented*. Empathy is the key. Compare these two approaches:

> 'We need to know what is happening with your children because drug taking can be really harmful to kids.'

> 'Parenting is stressful and drug taking can add to the stress. Tell me, how are you managing with two children?'

The response to the first is likely to be defensiveness; the reaction to the second is more likely to be a willingness to talk.

Adult services need to obtain the following information related to children to allow judgements to be made:

- Factual details: names, age, relationships.
- Involvement of other professionals and services: GP, health visitor, social worker, nursery, school.
- Who lives in the accommodation and who else has close involvement with the family.
- Whether there is statutory involvement with any members of the household.
- The circumstances in which substance use takes place and whether this, or the availability of substances or paraphernalia, could pose risks.
- Any other factors in the living situation which might be detrimental to children.

It is important to verify information provided by parents with third parties, such as a reliable relative or professionals already involved with the family. If it is part of the agency's remit, home visiting will help build a clearer picture. In respect of younger children, the health visitor, often trusted and with ready access to the home, can be a key figure.

---

**CASE ILLUSTRATION 14.1**

**Parental problems**

Jackie (24) and Calvin (27) both binge drink regularly and take various drugs when these are available. When intoxicated, they argue and Calvin can become physically aggressive. Jackie is pregnant and has a son, Aaron (4), from a previous relationship.

Jackie gives various reasons to the nursery for Aaron's regular absences and the staff there have noticed that he can be quite withdrawn. They know that Jackie is pregnant. The midwife is concerned about Jackie's reluctance to discuss her general poor health and the fact that, despite home visits, she has never seen Calvin. Neither the nursery staff nor the midwife know that the couple drink and use drugs.

What action, if any, do you think that the nursery manager and midwife should take given what they know?

---

When children's services, statutory or otherwise, are already involved because of concerns or the need for additional services, substance problems practitioners should make contact and maintain links with these. Both parties should share information about any changes in the adult's or children's circumstances. If no such services are involved, substance problems practitioners should:

- Decide whether referral to children services for fuller assessment is required because of possible risks or unmet needs. It should be stressed that what adult services can normally carry out is screening, not assessment.
- Continue to engage with the service user on the issue of parenting, if referral is not considered necessary. It may be appropriate to provide information about agencies which support families and encourage the service user to consider using these. Screening should be ongoing and liaison with other parties involved should be maintained. If the adult's circumstances change, the implications of this for the children should be considered.
- Contact maternity services if a woman is pregnant or a male substance user has a partner who is pregnant even if she does not have a substance problem herself. Adult services should not assume that maternity services are already aware that drug or alcohol use is an issue.
- Before taking a decision to close the case, consider the implications for the children and discuss these with any childcare agencies involved.

It goes without saying that child protection procedures should be initiated if it is thought that any child is facing an immediate significant risk.

## BOX 14.3 ADULT SERVICES: LIMITS, DILEMMAS AND CONFIDENTIALITY

How far an adult service engages with the issue of children affected will depend on its specific remit. The responsibilities and limitations of each service should be agreed with local commissioners. Needle exchanges provide an example of services whose engagement with this issue will be circumscribed. Needle exchange practitioners must be alive to potential risks to children and can provide opportunistic advice. However, it could prove counterproductive if they attempted to systematically screen for issues beyond the service's core function.

Where these limitations do not apply, substance problems practitioners should routinely seek permission to liaise with other services involved with the family. What should happen if this is not forthcoming? If a child, or an adult considered to be vulnerable, is clearly at risk, then the service user's wish for confidentiality must be overridden. If immediate risk is not an issue but uncertainties exist, then the reasons for the service user's refusal should be fully discussed with her. If she still has misgivings, a judgement needs to be made as to whether the parent's wishes should be overruled.

Despite being aware of the bounds of confidentiality, a service user may still interpret the sharing of information against her wishes as a breach of trust. The best the practitioner can do is to clearly and sensitively explain the reasons for the action being taken and continue to ensure a service is offered to the adult, whatever her reaction.

### Children affected: interventions

To avoid situations researching crisis points, early and planned responses addressing the needs of all family members are desirable (Kroll and Taylor, 2013). Encouraging adults to enter and remain in treatment is essential as these are protective factors for children (NTA, 2012d). Risks can wax and wane, however. Changes, such as a mother struggling to adapt to a prescribed substitute or alterations in family relationships, should prompt a further assessment of the implications for the children. A recovery-oriented approach, addressing the needs of each family member, should be adopted. In certain circumstances, it will be judged necessary to remove the children from parental care. When this is not the case, a number of options present themselves:

- If the children do not require specialist services, then monitoring their development by the mainstream services, such as the nursery or school, will run in tandem with parental/carer treatment.
- In some areas, there are specialist projects for families in which substance use is an issue. These provide intensive inputs combining play therapy, parenting programmes and family support. Generic family centres and the like may work closely with substance problems services as part of an integrated package of care. Where families are experiencing a range of problems in addition

to substance use, it is critical that the appropriate wraparound services are in place. Velleman and Templeton (2007) stress that focusing on reducing aggressive behaviour and familial conflict, and working with parents to help them learn to manage their children in consistent and caring ways, can be as important to the wellbeing of children as working with parents to alter their substance use.

- Family therapy involving older children may be of value.
- Even when older children are involved in whole-family approaches, consideration should be given to providing advice and guidance for them on an individual basis. In certain circumstances, work can involve enabling the young person to adjust to the unhappy fact that her mother or father has not changed their behaviour. Counselling can help a young person to address feelings of guilt and low self-esteem and learn to develop her own interests and relationships despite ongoing difficulties in the home. Specialist mentoring schemes help isolated adolescents to engage with mainstream activities. There are online forums for young people affected, such as the one provided by Children of Addicted Parents and People.
- Some children may benefit from involvement in young carers projects. Group work can reduce the feelings of isolation they so often experience (Harbin, 2000).
- Alateen coordinates self-help meetings for the teenage children of problem drinkers. It is part of Al-Anon and so its theoretical base is the disease model.
- A very small number of residential rehabs admit families.
- Kinship carers, such as grandparents or other close family members, can provide invaluable assistance through practical help and taking the children at times of stress. Children's services should ensure that they are well supported.

Whatever arrangements are put in place, continuous liaison between services in the context of an agreed, inter-agency care plan is critical to ensure the well-being of the children.

In addition to encouraging the substance-using parent to remain in treatment and maintaining close inter-agency working, an analysis of the literature (Dawe, Harnett and Frye, 2008) identifies the importance of:

- paying particular attention to the process of engagement because of the parental mistrust of authority;
- parents being party to setting the goals;
- tackling factors in the family's environment which erode parenting capacity, in addition to addressing parenting skills themselves;
- building on the positives in the family's situation;
- multifaceted and intensive responses involving staff with small caseloads;
- adapting approaches to individual families' circumstances.

CASE ILLUSTRATION 14.2

**Engaging with the issue of children's welfare**

Ben has sought help from the substance problems agency you are working for. He binges on cocaine and alcohol. He has a son aged two and his wife is pregnant.

- How would you go about raising the issue of the family's wellbeing with Ben?
- What information would you need to allow you to judge what the risks are and whether the family's needs are being met?
- What other agencies would you consider contacting?

## Concluding comments

The wellbeing of children is now a central consideration for practitioners working with adults with alcohol or drug problems and inter-agency working between adult and children's services has improved significantly. Despite this sea change, much remains unclear or unresolved. The numbers of children on whom parental drug or alcohol use is having a serious impact is unknown. In policy terms, parental drug use continues to receive a higher profile than parental alcohol problems. Some adult services, particularly those offering street-based or immediate access provision, face dilemmas as how best to engage with the agenda without alienating their clientele. Stigma and a fear of losing their children may well keep some parents from engaging with treatment services. There are no easy solutions to some of these quandaries but a wider range of early intervention services supporting families where substance use is an issue is needed.

## RESOURCES

- Glover, M. (2010). *Drugs, Alcohol and Parenting. A Workbook for Parents.* For use directly with parents.
- Hart, D. and Powell, J. (2006). *Adult Drug Problems, Children's Needs. Assessing the Impact of Parental Drug Use.* A toolkit for use by practitioners in a wide range of disciplines.
- Kroll, B. and Taylor, A. (2003). *Parental Substance Misuse and Child Welfare.*
- Whittaker, A. (2011). *The Essential Guide to Problem Substance Use During Pregnancy* (updated edition).
- Useful websites/online resources:
  Alateen. Information is available on the Al-Anon website: http://al-anonuk.org.uk.
  Children of Addicted Parents and People: www.coap.org.uk/frontpage.
  Alcohol and Families. Toolkits to support children affected are available on this site for use by different disciplines: www.alcoholandfamilies.org.uk/index.htm.

# CHAPTER 15

# Significant Others: Adults

- A person's substance problem often has serious implications for the wellbeing of other adult family members and close friends; family structures can be altered profoundly.
- The involvement of 'significant adults' in the treatment of the person with the substance problems can improve outcomes. However, it is essential that the needs of such adults are also considered separately.
- Services to support significant adults remain underdeveloped.

## Significant adults

The somewhat cumbersome phrase 'significant adults' refers to anyone within the immediate circle of a person with a substance problem whose wellbeing is negatively affected. This includes parents of young people with substance problems, partners/spouses, siblings and anyone with a close attachment. The needs of significant adults are beginning to receive greater attention but services remain underdeveloped and inadequately resourced.

### Significant adults: their needs come first

Significant adults are often keen to be involved in the treatment of the person with the substance problem. They can be instrumental in encouraging the person to seek help, they can provide support during and after the process and their participation can improve outcomes (Evans, 2010; Jarvis et al., 2005). However, such involvement should not take priority over considering what significant adults need for themselves; it is this which we will consider first.

For too long, substance problems have been conceptualised as a problem for the individual and for wider society, rather than a family predicament (Velleman, 2010). Ironically, much is known about the difficulties substance use can cause for significant adults and its implications for family functioning. Work to accurately estimate the number of adults affected is at an early stage (Copello, Templeton and Powell, 2010b) but it is very significant.

## Drugs and alcohol: the impact on significant adults

Velleman (2010) notes that historically, particularly in the USA, significant adults were viewed through the lens of pathology; the cause of the individual's substance problem was interpreted as being located, partially at least, in the inadequacies of other family members and malfunctioning relationships. In short, significant adults were often blamed. Modern theories as to why people develop substance problems challenge such a paradigm. The bio-psycho-social model suggests that, while family influences can play a part for some people, the reasons why people develop substance problems are multifaceted (see Chapter 3). Significant adults can behave in seemingly unhelpful ways and family relations may be skewed but, more often than not, these are the result of the substance problem, not its cause.

It is often not the person's substance use per se that causes problems for family members but the various consequences of that use such as erratic conduct, criminal behaviour, impaired social functioning and endless crises. Significant adults can be adversely affected in a variety of ways (Adfam, 2009; Dorn, Ribbens and South, 1994):

■ Significant adults can experience an array of emotions. They may feel that their world is out of control. Anger is a frequent response, particularly if it is suddenly discovered that problematic use is occurring; this is often the case when parents find out one of their children is using drugs. Significant adults worry about the implications for their loved one, such as the risk of overdose, ill health or what the future may hold; they may also be fearful for their own or the family's safety, particularly if aggression follows use or illegal activity is involved. Family members may feel guilty and shoulder blame for the person's alcohol or drug use. The substance user may compound this by making accusations of this nature. Feelings of betrayal are common. Parents of a young user often experience disappointment and a sense of loss. Shame and stigma can add to significant adults' distress. They can find themselves on a roller coaster of emotions as the optimism engendered by each period of stability is dashed time and again by relapses. In addition to concerns about their substance-using offspring, parents can find themselves looking after their grandchildren, with the strain and stigma that this can cause.
■ Significant adults can face a number of practical problems. The financial costs of a person's habit or his inability to work can have a major impact on a family's wellbeing. Where use involves illicit drugs, some families have moved to try to avoid reprisals from dealers. Significant adults can be faced with a series of dilemmas. Should the person's debts be paid? Should they leave an intoxicated person alone? Should they clean up when a person is sick? Is telling those outside the immediate family a good idea?

The outcome of these uncertainties and pressures can be profound. Significant adults can suffer physical and mental ill health. Relationships can fracture. The substance problem and its consequences can mould all aspects of a marriage or domestic life; holidays may be cancelled and social lives abandoned. Non-using members of the family can fall out over how best to respond.

## BOX 15.1 SIBLINGS OF YOUNG SUBSTANCE USERS: HIDDEN HURT

If significant adults have been a neglected group historically, the siblings of young users have been completely overlooked in policy terms, yet they can experience the same gamut of emotions as their parents. They may protect or, conversely, reject their substance-using sibling. Parental preoccupation with their sibling's substance use may leave them feeling isolated and resentful as they wonder how to gain the attention of their mother and father. They may be left to their own devices, along with the risks that this entails. Parental disharmony and a fear of family breakdown can be constants in their lives (Dorn, Ribbens and South, 1994). There is an increased risk that siblings will also start using substances problematically (Barnard, 2005).

Work with families should always pay due attention to the circumstances of siblings. It is important to encourage parents to try to adopt an even-handed approach to all their children, however difficult this may be. Preservation of whole-family rituals, the maintenance of normal friendships and participation in out-of-home activities may all act as protective factors. Barnard (2005) suggests that siblings can benefit from mentoring and respite away from the home. In certain circumstances, their participation in family therapy is indicated.

How do individuals and families cope with this relentless strain? Orford et al. (2010b) identify three strategies that significant adults adopt. These are not necessarily discrete or permanent stances; they may overlap or change with time. Only those directly involved can judge whether their method of adaption is beneficial.

- *'Putting up with it'*. In this mode, the significant adult may be critical and refuse to cooperate with all the substance user's demands, but essentially he tries to live as best he can with the problem. Some may adopt a somewhat self-sacrificing role. Empathy for the user and a desire to help her, a sense of defeat or a wish to avoid the further erosion of relationships may be behind this method of coping. Copello et al. (2010a) note that this type of adaption is particularly associated with health problems for family members.
- *'Standing up to it'*. Here the significant adult adopts a proactive strategy and attempts to gain control. Efforts are made to prevent life from being determined by the substance user's demands and behaviour. Attempts are made to encourage the person to change. Measures may be put in place to try to reduce the harms to others. Orford et al. (2010b) describe this approach as trying to alter 'the rules of engagement'.
- *'Withdrawing and maintaining independence'*. A significant adult may cope by avoiding confrontation and disengaging to a degree. Effort is

concentrated on maintaining a life beyond the day-to-day trials of living with the person with the problem.

When significant adults attempt to get the substance user to alter her behaviour, a variety of strategies are employed. Buying drugs or alcohol in an attempt to control consumption, covering up for the person or, conversely, refusing to do so and making threats regarding the consequences of failure to change are common strategies. While adopting certain approaches can nudge the substance user towards altering her behaviour, such efforts, especially when applied inconsistently, often fail, leading to frustration and renewed efforts by the significant adult to impose change, a self-defeating spiral. In particular, if threats are not carried through, the user soon learns that she can continue with impunity.

**CASE ILLUSTRATION 15.1**

**Substance use and family dynamics**

Family life became overshadowed by Jack's periods of intoxication, absences and his lack of interest in Clare, his wife, and their son, Gareth; family finances began to suffer. When Clare's efforts to get Jack to change met with failure, she decided that she would ensure that the family did not disintegrate. She took a full-time job, made certain that Gareth was protected from the worst of his father's excesses and helped her husband to survive as severe dependency developed. She also sought advice from an alcohol counselling service. She found a strength and abilities she did not know she possessed. When Gareth was 16, Jack was hospitalised with alcohol-related health problems. He had reached a turning point; on discharge, detoxed and healthier, he committed himself to Alcoholics Anonymous. As he put alcohol behind him, Jack began to try to reinstate himself as the head of the family. Clare found that she still could not trust him; she also felt that the role she had come to occupy was now being challenged. What the couple had before Jack's drinking escalated no longer seemed to be there. Gareth started to resent his father efforts to re-establish a disciplinary role after years of what he saw as neglect. The couple decided to separate.

## Significant adults: assessment

A significant adult may seek help for himself, irrespective of whether the person with the substance problems has come forward, or he may accompany the user. He may not come forward initially but may be encouraged to do so as treatment of the person with the substance problem progresses. As we saw in Chapter 7, assessment of a person with a drug or alcohol problem should include gathering information about significant adults and screening for risk. The practitioner should discuss with the person with the substance problem the desirability of encouraging family members to seek help or of accompanying her to a future appointment unless this is inappropriate. Information can be provided to pass on to significant others about specific services for them and, in certain circumstances, a direct approach by the practitioner to one or more significant adults might be made. When both the person with the substance problem and one or more significant adults become involved with the same agency, a decision needs to be made as to whether they should be seen together or whether this could lead to effective engagement with all parties being compromised. The risk is that addressing the substance user's problems will take precedence over the significant adult's needs. A mixture of individual and joint sessions is an option. When relationships are fraught, separate appointments with different practitioners are likely to be necessary, initially at least.

The principles of engagement and assessment are universal. An empathetic, non-judgemental approach should underpin the process of helping significant adults to identify risks and needs. Questions that need to be addressed include:

- What is the nature of the substance problem?
- How is it affecting the significant adult who has sought help? This should include consideration of both health issues and psychological distress.
- How is it affecting other family members, including children?
- How has the functioning of the family as a whole changed?
- Are there any risks, such as concerns about children or domestic violence, which need to be addressed immediately (see Chapters 7 and 14)?
- What coping strategies has the person adopted? Are these proving helpful?
- What support does the person have and is this beneficial?
- Is the family facing other difficulties such as financial problems?

Orford et al. (2010a) suggest that presenting relationships in diagrammatic form can be helpful. This can be used to highlight the problems each person is experiencing and how they try to cope.

BOX 15.2 DIVERSITY

Orford et al. (2010b) suggest that there is a commonality of experience in living close to a person with a substance problem but that there are different family and cultural norms which cannot be ignored. Services for significant adults should be provided to accommodate an area's ethnic diversity. Options include establishing black or ethnic groups, employing specialist family support workers and ensuring a staff mix which reflects the local population (Adfam, 2009).

## Significant adults: care planning and interventions

Immediate risks to children will require a child protection response. Domestic abuse in all its forms will necessitate the development of a self-protection plan, which may involve enabling the person to access crisis accommodation or specialist counselling. Beyond such emergencies, NICE (2007a) suggests adopting a two-tier approach. The first stage is to provide a single session exploring the impact of the substance problem and discussing coping strategies. It is recommended that people should be given written self-help material and encouraged to attend support groups for partners or parents of people with substance problems. If this is inadequate, then the second stage consists of a more comprehensive response involving a number of sessions for individuals or families. This is similar to the 5-step method (Copello et al., 2010a). Focusing entirely on the needs of the significant adult, the 5-step method is a person-centred, present-orientated, problem-solving programme. Significant adults are viewed as 'ordinary people facing highly stressful circumstances' (Copello et al., 2010a) who can be helped to cope. Designed to be used in a wide variety of settings over five sessions, its flexibility allows it to be delivered in less. The steps are:

1 *Listening and exploring.* In this session the family member outlines the situation as he sees it and identifies the stresses he faces.
2 *Providing information.* The aim here is to help the person put his situation in context by filling in gaps in his knowledge regarding relevant substances, types of problem and the impact of these on others. If the substance user has just begun to engage with treatment, significant others may have unrealistic expectations about the pace of change or the role of treatment in the recovery journey.
3 *Coping.* This step involves the person exploring his ways of coping and the benefits and problems which these bring. Discussion then turns to other possible ways of responding and whether these might be more helpful. The practitioner does not present any particular coping method as superior but allows the person to decide which he thinks will work best for him. Yet again, the principle of the person owning the solutions applies. For some, coping may involve a partner separating from the substance user or parents putting a greater distance between themselves and their offspring. It does have to be acknowledged that family members can sometimes face impossible situations (see Case Illustration 15.2).
4 *Social support.* In this session, the person is encouraged to draw a diagram of his social network and then identify those within it who are supportive and those with unhelpful attitudes or behaviour. Ways of enhancing existing support, finding new sources of assistance and improving communication within the network are all considered. The purpose is to develop consistent approaches to the situation.
5 *Additional action.* The final step is to help the person decide whether he wants to join a self-help group or access services to help with other difficulties. It may be that the person with the substance problem is considering seeking help and the implications of this for the significant adult is a further issue for consideration.

> ### CASE ILLUSTRATION 15.2
>
> **Dilemmas for family members**
>
> Adhering to particular strategies for both self-protection and to put responsibility back to the person with the substance problem is no easy task. Doreen discussed with me how she intended to try to get Kyle, her 20-year-old son, to face up to the consequences of his drug use by adopting a plan not to rescue him from every tight corner he found himself in. No longer paying his drug debts for him was part of this strategy. The next time I visited she said:
>
> > 'I haven't seen him for a couple of days. Those men came round last night looking for him. When I told them I didn't know where he was, they said they'd smash the car windscreen if I didn't pay them £100.'
> > 'What did you do?,' I asked.
> > 'What do you think I did?,' she replied.

An issue which significant adults will want to discuss is how best to encourage the person with the substance problem to change. Initially it is important to help the person to understand that no one can control someone else's behaviour but that he can provide encouragement and support. What is important is for family members to make clear how the situation is affecting them and what they are prepared, and not prepared, to accept. A significant adult presenting his perspective calmly and rationally to the substance user may encourage her to consider altering her behaviour, particularly if she is in the contemplation stage and is experiencing growing ambivalence. As we saw in Chapter 5, marital strain, relationship problems and family issues are all factors that can precipitate change. When a significant other has decided to make his position clear, Smith (1995) suggests that he should:

- focus on the goal of encouraging the person to seek help;
- raise the issue after a bout, not while the person is using or is intoxicated;
- present concerns directly and without ambiguity;
- prevent the discussion from straying away from the core issue, namely the distress the significant adult is experiencing because of the substance use.

## BOX 15.3 MUTUAL AID GROUPS FOR SIGNIFICANT ADULTS

There is a range of support groups for family members. Some of these function independently and some are supported by treatment services, usually in the voluntary sector. There are also groups for family members, based on the disease model and 12-step principles, which are part of the 'Anonymous Movement'. (See the Resources section.)

As with mutual aid and recovery initiatives for people with substances problems, practitioners should give information to significant adults about what is available in their areas. They should encourage people to consider attending and assist them to do this if need be. Some find that involvement helps them make sense of their experiences, relieves guilt and provides invaluable long-term support; mutual aid groups do not appeal to everyone, though.

We will now turn to significant adults' involvement in treatment for the person with the substance problem.

## Significant adults: supporting the substance user

In addition to the contribution which significant adults can make to the design of services (NTA, 2008), there is evidence that their participation in the treatment of people with substance problems and their role in developing supportive networks can improve outcomes (Copello and Orford, 2002). The nature and state of their relationship with the substance user will dictate whether involvement is likely to be beneficial and the consent of all parties is obviously essential. For example, a young substance user might want to try to resolve his difficulties without the involvement of his parents. Friction between the parties or differing goals may make the direct involvement of significant adults problematic, initially at least. In these situations, separate workers, different services or self-help groups should be offered to significant adults.

Significant adults can help the person with the substance problem in a number of ways (NTA, 2008). These include:

- *encouraging the person into treatment.* Significant adults may motivate the substance user to seek help through firm but supportive approaches or by adopting the 'standing up to it' strategy (see above). Examples of the latter include developing consistent responses to the often erratic behaviour of the substance user and acting in ways which make it less likely that she can avoid the consequences of her use.
- *contributing to assessment.* Significant adults can confirm information given by the substance user as well as provide a different perspective on risk and need.
- *participating in care planning.* Joint decision making involving both the person with the substance problem and significant others can ensure that issues beyond the drug and alcohol use are included. It is important that a partner understands the implications of the goals being considered and endorses them. For example, the relationship will come under strain if a husband wants to try a controlled drinking programme and his wife considers abstinence to be the only acceptable goal.
- *monitoring pharmacotherapy.* Significant others can help medical professionals to supervise community detox. They can also encourage the person with the problem to comply with prescribing regimes.
- *supporting maintenance and managing relapse.* Once stabilisation has occurred, significant adults can reinforce progress by using rewards such as praise, demonstrating improved trust and joint participation in pleasurable

activities. Efforts to create a culture around the person which reinforces maintenance through building supportive relationships can be strengthened by using Social Behaviour and Network Therapy or other community reinforcement programmes (see Chapter 11). If relapse occurs or goals are not met, rewards can be withdrawn. It is necessary for significant adults to try to take a detached view of relapse and have measures in place to protect themselves where this is necessary.

■ *supporting recovery*. As an enduring part of the life of the person with the problem, significant adults can play a central role in supporting her to rebuild a social life away from substances and re-engage with normal social activities. Active encouragement to attend recovery groups can be given.

The families' recovery and the person's recovery can go hand in hand. Reviews of the evidence endorse the use of family therapy and behavioural couples therapy, when these have a focus on the substance problem (Copello and Orford, 2002; Raistrick, Heather and Godfrey, 2006, p. 109). These interventions present opportunities to address directly family members' differing perceptions of the situation and how roles have been affected. Participants can explore ways of improving communication, what adjustments in relationships are needed to reduce points of stress and how changes in behaviour can be positively reinforced. Practitioners, and it is often best for two to be involved, need to feel confident in undertaking this type of work. Because of the power dynamics at play, couples and family therapy are not suitable interventions where domestic abuse is a recent or current issue (London Borough of Camden, 2007).

---

**CASE ILLUSTRATION 15.3**

**A daughter's drug problem**

You work in a voluntary organisation providing services for both drug users and their families. Sandra and Bill approach the service asking for help to 'stop their daughter using heroin'. She is aged 19 and has been injecting for six months. She left university after the first year and has not worked since. They give her money to survive but she has also stolen from them. She stays sometimes with them and sometimes with friends. Sandra is suffering from anxiety and has an appointment to see her GP.

Describe what approach you would take and what your reasons are for this.

---

## Concluding comments

There is undoubted value in involving significant adults directly in work with the person with the substance problem, where appropriate, but consideration should first be given to what help they need for themselves. There remains a significant gap between what is known about the problems significant adults face and the level of service provision available in many areas. Too often their needs are not addressed or they are simply signposted to mutual aid groups without fuller consideration of what they feel might help them. Awareness and political commitment has led to the due prioritisation of children affected by parental substance problems; a similar paradigm shift, along with increased resources, is now needed if the difficulties significant others face are to be effectively addressed.

## RESOURCES

- This chapter is indebted to the work of Coppello, Templeton, Orford, Velleman and their associates. A special edition of the journal *Drugs: Education, Prevention and Policy* (December 2010, 17 s1) is devoted to their work and is recommended reading.
- Adfam (2009). *'We count too'. Good Practice Guide and Quality Standards for Work with Family Members Affected by Someone Else's Drug Problem* (2nd edition).
- Adfam provides DVDs and booklets for significant adults: www.adfam.org.uk/home.
- Harris, P. (2010). *The Concerned Other. How to Change Drug and Alcohol Users Through Their Family Members. A Complete Manual.*
- Mutual aid groups. Information about groups for significant adults is available as follows:
  *England.* Adfam: www.adfam.org.uk/home.
  *Scotland.* Scottish Families Affected by Alcohol and Drugs: www.sfad.org.uk.
  *Wales.* Wales Drug and Alcohol Helpline: www.dan247.org.uk/default.asp.
  *Northern Ireland.* Northern Ireland Public Health Agency:
  www.publichealth.hscni.net/publications/drug-and-alcohol-directories-services.
- 12-step groups for significant adults. Details of meetings are available at:
  Families Anonymous (for relatives and friends of people with drug problems): http://famanon.org.uk.
  Al-Anon (for relatives and friends of people with alcohol problems): www.al-anonuk. org.uk.

# CHAPTER 16

# Young People: Substance Use and Substance Problems

## KEY THEMES

- Experimentation with substances by young people is normal but not risk free.
- Ongoing problematic use of substances by young people is usually associated with other psychological or social problems.
- Dependence on substances, nicotine excepted, is rare among young people.
- Educational inputs and brief interventions will be adequate for many young people experiencing lower levels of harm.
- Interventions for adolescents with more ingrained problems are not dissimilar to those for adults; however, they should be adjusted for age and maturity and delivered by agencies specialising in this area of work.

## Young people's substance use

In this chapter 'young person' and 'adolescent' refers to teenagers up to the age of 18. After this point, young people with substance problems are more likely to engage with adult services.

Young people's substance use should be understood in the context of a particular phase in human growth and development and, as such, it differs to some degree from adults' involvement with tobacco, alcohol and drugs. Adolescence is characterised by paradoxes: insecurity and risk taking; assertiveness and a lack of confidence; rebellion and the need to conform to peer group norms. It is a time of experimentation and initiation into adult roles, a stage marked by excitement, confusion and making mistakes. In this heady and rapidly changing mix, use of substances has enormous symbolic importance for young people and for grown-ups alike (Ghodse, 2004). Compared with adults, young people are not excessive consumers but this does not prevent the regular eruption of moral panics regarding adolescent substance use. Stoked by a sensation-loving media, these are driven by fear of new drugs and anxieties about social decline, along with legitimate concerns about the wellbeing of the young. Despite these frequent alarms, the great majority of young people survive the particular pitfalls of adolescent use and emerge into adulthood with much the same substance-taking habits as their parents. While significant consumption among younger teenagers must raise concerns, use itself is not necessarily problematic. Nevertheless, adolescence is when the seeds of longer term difficulties can take root; this underscores the need for effective early intervention.

## Prevalence

At the end of the first decade of the twenty-first century, self-reporting population surveys and data from treatment agencies showed continuing and marked declines in substance use among young people. The ongoing survey of substance-using habits among 11–15-year-olds in England (Health and Social Care Information Centre, 2013b) showed that in 2012

- 4 per cent were regular smokers, a decline from a peak of 13 per cent in 1996.
- 43 per cent had tried alcohol. 10 per cent had used alcohol in the previous week, a reduction from 26 per cent in 2001.
- 17 per cent had ever used drugs, a reduction from 30 per cent in 2003, with 6 per cent using in the previous month. Cannabis was the most popular (8.2 per cent in the past year), with 3.6 per cent using volatile substances and 2.6 per cent taking stimulants, the third highest category, in the past year.

Similar declines have also occurred among younger teenagers in Scotland, although prevalence rates are higher (Ipsos MORI, 2011). Downward trends were also evident in 2011/12 in the under-18-year-old treatment population in England, which peaked in 2008–9. Cannabis problems continued to dominate but there were fewer cases where alcohol was the primary issue. Numbers being treated for substances such as amphetamines, solvents and mephedrone were quite low (NTA, 2012e). It should be noted, however, that first use of many illicit substances occurs during the later teenage years (Home Office, 2012b), as does increased alcohol consumption. Among young adults, poly-drug use is not uncommon, with alcohol, tobacco and cannabis to the fore (EMCDDA, 2009).

Although a substantial reduction in adolescent substance use has taken place, this needs to be balanced against estimates that, in England in 2012, 120,000 11–15-year-olds were regular smokers, 320,000 drank alcohol in the previous week and 200,000 had taken drugs in the previous month (Health and Social Care Information Centre, 2013b).

ACTIVITY 16.1

**Young adolescents and substances**
- List the factors which you think might make experimenting with alcohol and tobacco attractive to a 14-year-old? Do you think that these factors are different from those which might encourage adolescents to use illicit substances?
- Were you interested in substances at that age and, if so, why?

### Patterns and risks

Young people do not come to substances with a blank slate. They will have absorbed information and learned, through observation, how to use some substances and how people behave after taking them. Cultural and family influences will have shaped their perceptions of what is acceptable and unacceptable. The dizziness that often accompanies initial tobacco use or the oddly unappealing first taste of beer can make initial experiences disagreeable or disappointing, but there are rewards to be gained from persisting. Initiation is a rite of passage which may facilitate entry into a group of users or gain status with peers. Growing enjoyment of the effects of the substance and the thrill of participation in a forbidden activity can encourage more regular use, and then the reinforcing mechanisms of classical conditioning and operant learning will come into play (see Chapter 3). Of course, many will try a substance once or twice and find no reason to continue.

Experimentation and intoxication bring particular risks. The novice user will not know how much she can consume or, in some cases, how to use safely. This may mean no more than a sore head but it can lead to injury or the stomach pump. Death has been known to follow first-time use of some drugs, volatile substances and ecstasy being examples. Intoxication is associated with antisocial behaviour and cavalier attitudes towards sex. Immediate harms are not the only risks. Maturing organs are particularly susceptible to damage. As teenagers progress towards adulthood, they begin to know what substances they like and how they enjoy using them and a pattern of recreational use emerges; this is not risk free either. A need to boost confidence in social settings or enhance the party experience may lead to a measure of psychological dependence but physical dependence on drugs or alcohol is rare among young people. The exception to this is nicotine. Its ready availability and highly addictive nature leads to a steady stream of dependent youngsters.

Within the adolescent population, there are abstainers, experimenters and recreational users; many run risks from time to time, occasionally with catastrophic consequences, but most come to no serious harm. However, a significant percentage will go on to drink at levels detrimental to health, at least for periods of their adult lives. In addition, within this broader population is a group where more ingrained and problematic use of substances is already occurring. What characterises their circumstances?

### Substance problems, multiple difficulties

The bio-psycho-social framework integrating theories as to why people develop difficulties can help shed light on both the processes through which young people are initiated into substance taking and why some go on to use in harmful ways (see Chapter 3). Although demonstrating causal relationships is problematic, the connections between particular influences and the subsequent development of substance problems help to indicate which adolescents are most at risk (Lloyd, 1998). Factors identified (Galvani, 2012; Harris, 2013; McMurran, 1994) include:

- *kinship influences.* A familial culture in which use is customary and substances are tolerated normalises substance taking and provides opportunities for learning by modelling. Lack of clarity regarding roles within the family and what constitutes acceptable and unacceptable behaviour are also issues, as is interpersonal conflict.
- *peer impacts.* Initiation usually takes place in groups or with like-minded friends; the processes within such relationships then reinforce continuing use. However, McMurran (1994, p. 60) notes that this can be explained in two ways. The more experienced may induct the less experienced or young people may actively seek out others with similar predilections.
- *poverty and disadvantage.*
- *ready availability and easy access* to substances, along with social norms both in the young person's locale and nationally, which support use.
- *age of initiation.* Whilst it is difficult to disentangle the influence of this from the effects of adverse factors in the lives of young people, there does appear to be a link between early use and the development of substance problems at a later stage (Harris, 2013, p. 80). In particular, early use of nicotine or alcohol is associated with later problematic use of other drugs (McWhirter, 2008, p. 15).
- *psychological problems.*
- *behavioural characteristics.* Delinquency, poor educational attainment, truanting, school exclusion and rebellious attitudes, along with positive feelings towards use, put the individual at greater risk. What appears to be important, however, is the negative influence of a combination of these factors, rather than any one taken in isolation (McMurran, 1994, p. 67). Constellations of behaviours such as these suggest an attraction to risk taking and a disregard for consequences whose roots may lie in particular personality types (see Chapter 3). This clustering of issues is very important; it suggests that when a young person develops ongoing difficulties with substances she is likely to be coping with a number of parallel problems (Crome, 2004, p. 132). Three quarters of referrals of young people to specialist agencies in England in 2011–12 were experiencing problems additional to their substance use (NTA, 2012e).

Protective factors are similar to those which reduce the risks to children affected by parental substance problems and include:

- optimistic temperament;
- intellectual ability;
- attainment and feelings of self-esteem;
- a positive relationship with one consistent, caring adult;
- a supportive home life with consistent rules and familial attitudes opposed to deviant behaviour. (Effective Interventions Unit, 2004, p. 9; Williams, Gilvarry and Christian, 2004)

**A problem emerges and then subsides**

Trevor's parents still struggle to understand why it happened. Until he was 14, Trevor was a quiet boy who applied himself to school. Overnight, things changed. He missed classes, lost interest in education and became part of a group of adolescents who had a reputation for antisocial behaviour. He came home intoxicated quite regularly. The smell, along with traces of solvents on his jacket, indicated that it was not only alcohol that he was using. His behaviour also suggested that he took stimulants from time to time. Called to the school on a number of occasions and worried that Trevor might be arrested, his parents sought advice from a substance problems service for young people. This helped them to understand more about the nature of the risks involved, but their efforts to get Trevor to discuss the issues, let alone consider getting help, proved fruitless. The family endured a stressful period with the parents regularly arguing over how to respond. This phase lasted for around 18 months until Trevor left school. After a period of inactivity, he decided to go to college to pursue a course in animal husbandry, which he had shown an interest in when younger. A problem that had emerged without warning, and then escalated, subsided equally quickly. With a changed focus, a new peer group and a girlfriend, Trevor's life settled down. He still got drunk on the occasional Friday night, but no more so than other students, and his parents picked up no evidence of other drug use.

## The structuring of services

For obvious reasons, it is important that services for adolescents are separate from those for adults and are staffed by practitioners trained to work with children and young people. Services for young people are organised on a tier model similar to that developed for adults (see Chapter 6). The tiers provide interventions of increasing intensity and specialisation geared to ensuring that a young person receives inputs commensurate with her level of vulnerability (see Box 16.1)

BOX 16.1 THE TIER MODEL OF SERVICES FOR YOUNG PEOPLE

The tier model was originally developed by the Health Advisory Service (1996).

■ **Tier one**. Drug and alcohol education for all children takes place at tier one. In addition, one of the roles of universal services is to identify children and young people who require additional help. In many instances, generic staff in health, education or youth services will deal with concerns without the need for onward referral. If a young person presents at school suffering the after effects of a one-off solvent sniffing session, the school nurse, a discussion with the parents and the continuing guidance of a sympathetic teacher may be all that is required. When ongoing concerns are identified, the area's common assessment framework for children and adolescents is the door to specialist pathways.

- **Tier two.** The purpose of tier two initiatives is to try to reduce the risks presented by those identified as vulnerable so that they can remain within universal provision. Tier two practitioners will have the skills and knowledge to work with young people exhibiting a range of difficulties including antisocial behaviour, social isolation and substance use over and above occasional experimentation. Targeted group work in schools, youth advice centres, agencies providing specialist diversionary projects and youth offending teams all operate at tier two.

- **Tier three.** Services provided at this level are for adolescents whose use is persistent and problematic. Delivered by specialists, programmes are unlikely to focus solely on drugs and alcohol but substances will be a central element.

- **Tier four.** Only the very small number of young people presenting with multiple difficulties, such as co-occurring serious substance problems and psychological distress or physical dependence, reach tier four. Pharmacotherapy, intensive support and residential care are all options at this level, with multi-component packages delivered by health, psychiatric and specialist substance problems practitioners.

Thorough assessment and careful gate keeping, particularly between tiers two and three, should ensure that the more intensive and expensive interventions are reserved for those that need them. Providing interventions at the level appropriate to each young person safeguards against the risks inherent in labelling. There is remarkably little about this in the literature. Deviance theory suggests that if a young person who is in the early stages of using substances in a cavalier manner gains the impression that others see him as a 'druggie' or 'young alki', then he may begin to behave according to such definitions (Lloyd, 1998) (see Chapter 3). On the other hand, Harris (2013, p. 13) argues that failure to identify and address problematic use increases the likelihood of an adolescent being stigmatised and ostracised. These are not contradictory concerns; rather they underscore the importance of ensuring that the tier system works effectively.

The tier system works best in areas where clear care pathways are in place (see Figure 16.1). It will be noted that in this model, the Royal College of Psychiatrists (2012) recognises the particular vulnerability of young teenagers and recommends that any concerns regarding substance use by someone under the age of 15 should always lead to a comprehensive assessment.

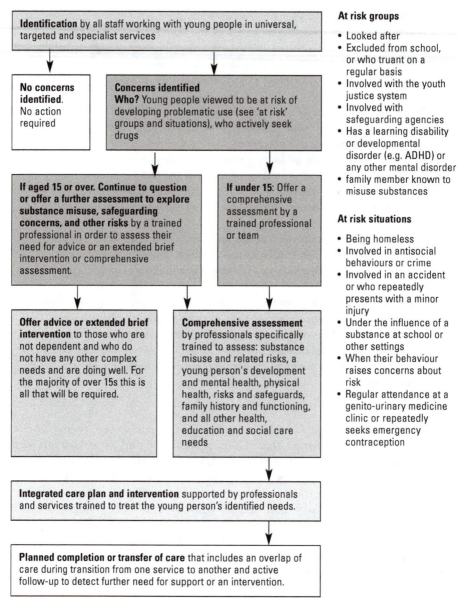

**Figure 16.1** Care pathways
*Source*: Royal College of Psychiatrists (2012) (reproduced with permission)

## Engagement, assessment and care planning

A major distinction between adolescents and adults is that the former rarely self-refer. In 2011–12, only 11 per cent of young people accessing services in England were referred by family, friends or themselves, with the great majority coming via youth justice, education or social care (NTA, 2012e). Substance use is likely to emerge as an issue because behaviour has been witnessed, offences have been committed or because social, educational or developmental progress is causing concern. In many instances, the young person will not consider her substance use to be a problem. A 15-year-old who is smoking cannabis and truanting from school is unlikely to view the situation in the same way as her teacher and worried parents; altering her substance use may be low on her list of priorities. Various steps can be taken to remove the barriers (Effective Interventions Unit, 2004):

- Where possible, young people should be given the choice of setting for initial contact with specialist services. For some, school may be the least threatening option; for others, a venue away from their day-to-day existence may feel safer. Care should be taken to create a welcoming atmosphere. Meeting some young people on their own territory may be necessary at first.
- Appointments should be at times convenient to the young person.
- If the young person wants to be accompanied by an advocate, this should be encouraged.
- Time should be taken to establish trust. The ability of practitioners to build empathetic relationships with young people is of overriding importance.
- Providing access to activities or facilities can be an inducement.

---

**CASE ILLUSTRATION 16.2**

**A challenging situation**

You work in a club providing sporting facilities for young people. Omar (aged 15) is a very promising footballer but his attendance at training has become erratic. It is rumoured that he is using cannabis and various other substances and you have seen evidence of mild intoxication.

- What do you think would be the best way of approaching him?
- What are your reasons for choosing this option?

---

Assessment of substance use should be one part of a fuller appraisal of the young person's needs. Unless it is inadvisable, parents should contribute to the process. The core issues to be addressed are the same for young people as for adults (see Chapter 7), but the NTA (2007) suggests that particular emphasis should be put on:

- how the young person views her substance use and what meaning it has for her;
- the other factors which are contributing to her difficulties. It is these, rather than the substance use, which the young person may be keen to address;
- the likelihood of polydrug use;
- psychological distress and any history of self-harm or overdose, deliberate or otherwise;
- regular use in the company of older and more experienced substance takers or the administering of drugs by others;

- risky sexual behaviour or sexual exploitation;
- dangerous substance-using practices such as excessive bingeing, injecting, using alone, using in hazardous environments and inhaling butane;
- the cultural context if the young person is from a minority community;
- the young person's abilities and the positive factors in the situation.

One model of assessment involves the potential domains for change in a young person's life being presented visually in the form of an outcome wheel. These domains include health, relationships, looking after self, antisocial behaviour, risk taking, substance use, education and employment and other key areas. The young person scores these, thus identifying the priorities for the action plan. This also provides a simple framework for measuring progress (Barnardos, 2010).

The first consideration is harm reduction and, in certain circumstances, statutory child protection procedures may need to be considered.

As we saw in Chapter 6, the goals of treatment for adults remain controversial and this is true for adolescents as well but in a somewhat different way. Should the goal for a young person be abstinence or should it be maintaining behaviour normal to her age group? Of course 'normal' is a relative concept and typical adolescent substance use is not entirely risk free. While it may be desirable to encourage a 13-year-old to completely refrain from drinking, what of her 16-year-old brother? He is unlikely to be dependent or have a lengthy history of problematic use and a goal of abstinence may well be highly unappealing to him. Discouraging excessive consumption or bingeing and helping him to learn to respect alcohol may be more realistic and less likely to lead to his dropping out of treatment. And what of cannabis? Refraining from any illegal behaviour may be the ideal but if many of his peers smoke from time to time, is a goal of reduced consumption and harm minimisation acceptable?

As most young people involved with services will be facing a range of difficulties, the effectiveness of treatment needs to be judged across a number of dimensions. Improved relationships, physical and psychological wellbeing, growth in self-esteem, decreased offending and reintegration into education or employment are as important as reductions in substance use. The NTA (2007) suggests that using the following hierarchy of goals can help structure the care plan:

- reducing substance-related health and social problems;
- reducing risk;
- reducing problems not related to substance use;
- achieving controlled or non-problematic use;
- abstinence from drugs that caused the main difficulties;
- abstinence from all drugs.

As has been noted, goals regarding alcohol may be somewhat different than those for drugs.

With the guidance of the practitioner, the young person should set his own goals. Roberts (2010) notes that many young people start to consider their use to be a problem when it becomes an obstacle to achieving other things they want, such as succeeding in education, finding a job or maintaining stable relationships. Identifying and focusing on such ambitions can build motivation.

## Interventions

The first decade of the twenty-first century saw a rapid expansion in the variety and number of services in the UK for young people with substance problems. However, studies into effectiveness have almost all been undertaken in North America and there is a pressing need to research interventions in the British context. Determining what influences reductions in problems presents a dilemma. Rapid developmental changes occur during adolescence and young people often grow out of troublesome behaviours (see Case Illustration 16.1). This raises the question as to whether positive outcomes are the consequence of treatment or of normal maturation.

Harris (2013, p. 166) notes that no treatments have been developed that are distinct from those used with adults, albeit they are delivered somewhat differently. In a review of the – mainly American – literature, Britton (2009) identified the following as being effective with young people:

- **Motivational interviewing** used either as a brief intervention or to facilitate involvement in more comprehensive programmes.
- **Cognitive behavioural therapy** both on an individual basis and as the foundation of group work; the latter provides particular opportunities for problem sharing, role playing, modelling and learning coping skills.
- **Multi-systemic therapy.** This takes an ecological approach by assessing how the young person's family, social and educational networks impact on her substance use and other problematic behaviours. Work is then undertaken with both the young person and with members of these networks to support behaviour change. Multi-dimensional family therapy, based on similar principles, is also supported by research (Liddle, 2010). This involves work with the young person and her parents separately before bringing them together for family sessions. Extra-familial agencies are co-opted as required.
- **Family involvement** both in formalised therapeutic programmes and in supporting work being undertaken with the young person.
- **Specialist residential facilities.** Research regarding the effectiveness of these is limited to studies from the USA. These suggest that some establishments achieve good outcomes but this is dependent on the nature of the regime. Residential options in the UK are very limited and tend to be reserved for those with the most complex needs.

The application of these interventions with adolescents differs in two fundamental ways from how they are used with adults. Firstly, they are adjusted to take account of the maturity and language development of the young people involved. For examples, games, quizzes, interactive exercises and the like, based on behavioural principles, are often used. With motivational interviewing, particular care is taken with the level of verbal communication. Secondly, the focus is usually not solely on substance use; indeed other issues often take precedence. Most services for young people are involved in addressing what can be summed up in one word: vulnerability. In the UK, services tend to use multi-component programmes involving motivational work, information giving, behaviour change and positive reinforcements for compliance. What distinguishes responses at tier two from those at tier three is the duration and intensity of the engagement.

The removal of practical barriers to engagement is particularly important for younger people and a number of measures can be used to facilitate treatment (Britton, 2009) such as:

- the provision of transport;
- help with problems such as finance and accommodation;
- advocacy;
- maintaining informal contact in addition to structured sessions.

Contingency management can reinforce compliance. The use of reward systems, such as providing outings or access to particular activities, is easier to put in place for young people than for adults because of the range of options which are likely to be attractive to them.

## BOX 16.2 TRANSITIONAL ARRANGEMENTS: A CAUSE FOR CONCERN

Referrals of people over the age of 18 are normally channelled to adult services. Adolescents involved with young people's services are usually considered for transfer to adult services when they reach that age, although flexibility is normally allowed in order to take account of maturity. Roberts (2010) has questioned these arrangements and has made the case for fresh thinking for young adults aged up to their mid-twenties. With polydrug taking becoming the norm among many younger users, Roberts argues that adult services, with their focus on dependent heroin use, are ill equipped to respond. In addition, the flexibility and holistic nature of the regimes for young people are more suitable for many young adults. However, simply extending the upper limit for such services is not the answer: programmes for 16-year-olds are obviously not suitable for 24-year-olds. Solutions include improving the capacity of adult services to respond to the younger poly substance-using cohort and the development of innovative services based on maturity and the nature of problematic use at particular age bands.

### Involving parents

Parental participation can improve the effectiveness of work with young people in a number of ways (Britton, 2009; McIntosh et al., 2006):

- It can enhance assessment by providing fuller information and an understanding of the culture in which the young person lives.

- Knowledge of the programme used allows parents to encourage compliance, reinforce positive behaviours and promote participation in activities supporting recovery.
- Parental involvement can help the young person to understand how her use impacts on others.
- Parents can be helped to cope with the stresses the situation brings (see Chapter 15). They can learn ways of handling the challenges their child's behaviour presents.
- Where parents themselves have problems with substances, they may be persuaded to access treatment or try to reduce its impact on their child.
- Parental views on the timing of case closure can be valuable.

The extent of involvement will depend on the circumstances of each case. Two issues do need to be taken into consideration. Firstly, in some situations relationships between the young person and his parents may be so poor, or parental behaviour so problematic, that their involvement may be counterproductive. Secondly, a young person may not want to share certain information with her parents, and vice versa, and care needs to be taken with the boundaries of confidentiality.

## Pharmacotherapy and young people

Pharmacotherapy is seldom needed for adolescents. Physical dependence on drugs or alcohol is uncommon in this age group and injecting is rare. Where pharmacotherapy is considered necessary, the same drugs are available for young people as for adults. However, the evidence for their effectiveness is based on trials with adults and most are not licensed for use with under 18-year-olds. This does not mean, however, that they cannot be used if deemed appropriate. If used with a young person, substitute prescribing is normally initiated with a view to planned reduction and abstinence within a fairly short period (Gilvarry and Britton, 2009).

## BOX 16.3 CONSENT TO TREATMENT

The legal position regarding whether a young person under 16 can give consent to treatment without the knowledge or agreement of parent or guardian is not the same throughout the UK although the broad principles are similar. The Fraser Guidelines apply in England, Wales and Northern Ireland and state that consent can be given by a young person without parental knowledge or agreement provided that:

- she is considered competent to do this. This means that she must fully understand what the intervention will entail and what its implications are;
- she cannot be persuaded to allow parents or guardians to be advised;
- without treatment, her physical or mental health will be impaired;

- treatment without parental consent is in her interests and she will continue to be at risk without it.

Fraser does not apply in Scotland, but the 'test of competency' does. Agencies working with young people should have policies in place which meet the legal requirements regarding consent and confidentiality.

If an adolescent says that she does not want parental involvement, the reasons for this should be fully explored with her and the potential benefits of parental participation outlined.

### Adolescents and tobacco

Among the substances that adolescents use, tobacco receives the least attention from a treatment perspective as it does not lead to intoxication or behavioural problems. However, young people who smoke regularly tend to experience poorer health than their non-smoking peers. In addition, the processes that lead to the wide range of health issues in adults start as soon as smoking becomes a habit, and early initiation increases the likelihood of various diseases occurring in later life (Woodhouse, 2004). It should not be thought that adolescents are uninterested in stopping. Among 11–15-year-olds in England who regularly smoke, around one third would like to give up and around two thirds had tried (Health and Social Care Information Centre, 2013b). This suggests that all services involved with adolescents should screen for tobacco use and be alive to opportunities to help those who want to stop.

There is a lack of evidence about what interventions might be effective with young people, although a Cochrane Review (Grimshaw and Stanton, 2006) suggests that multifaceted approaches incorporating, in particular, motivational enhancement, the stages of change and elements of CBT hold promise. This review did not support the use of pharmacotherapy or nicotine replacement therapy with adolescents, a finding endorsed by Kim et al. (2011).

Woodhouse (2004) notes that encouraging young people into treatment, sustaining their motivation and retaining them in programmes are all issues. This suggests that it may be worth drug and alcohol services for young people introducing the option of smoking cessation for their existing service users as they are already engaged in treatment. However, care with timing is needed to avoid the young person attempting to address more issues than she can cope with.

Interestingly, the young adolescents in the Health and Social Care Information Centre survey (2013b) stated that they were more likely to turn for help regarding cessation to family or friends, rather than other sources of advice. They also said that their main method of trying to stop was avoiding spending time with peers who smoked. These findings indicate that the involvement of families in programmes and encouraging diversionary activities may be worthwhile.

### Recovery and young people

Reintegration as a key component of recovery is as relevant for young people as it is for adults. Efforts to help the young person to engage with normal age-related activities and mainstream services should be a consistent theme throughout programmatic work. In addition to its role as a preventative measure for young people at risk, mentoring can help isolated or unconfident adolescents reintegrate. In a similar way, encouraging new interests and activities can be an important adjunct to structured work.

Aftercare is essential if change is to be maintained. Britton (2009) underlines the importance of monitoring and continuing support after more formal work has ended.

## Concluding comments

The range and quality of service provision for young people continues to improve; however, more research on what works best in the UK context is needed. In addition, the changing nature of substance use among older teenagers and young adults is exposing a gap in provision between existing services for adolescents and those for adults with problems. The solution to this lies in the development of a range of diverse and flexible models.

### RESOURCES

- Britton, J. (2009). *Young People's Specialist Substance Misuse Treatment: Exploring the Evidence*: www.nta.nhs.uk.
- Crome, I., Ghodse, H., Gilvarry, E. and McArdle, P. (eds) (2004). *Young People and Substance Misuse*.
- McWhirter, J. and Mir, H. (eds) (2008). *The Essential Guide to Working with Young People about Drugs and Alcohol*.
- NTA (2007). *Assessing Young People for Substance Misuse*: www.nta.nhs.uk.
- Royal College of Psychiatrists (2012). *Practice Standards for Young People with Substance Misuse Problems*: www.rcpsych.ac.uk.
- Smoking: NHS Choices, 'Under-18s Guide to Quitting': www.nhs.uk/Livewell/smoking/Pages/Teensmokersquit.aspx.
- Volatile substances: Re-Solv is a UK voluntary organisation providing training and resources: www.re-solv.org.
  (NB: Material on the NTA website is scheduled to be transferred by 2014 to the PHE website or placed on the National Archive's website or similar.)

# CHAPTER 17

# Offenders and Other Involuntary Service Users

- People may be channelled into treatment via workplace policies or the criminal justice system but voluntary service users are also often under pressure to change.
- The links between substance use and crime are complex; they are not a matter of simple cause and effect.
- Various points within the criminal justice system provide opportunities to engage with offenders with substance problems.
- Interventions used with involuntary service users are the same as those used with people who attend voluntarily; however, particular attention needs to be paid the processes of engagement and the negotiation of goals.
- The outcomes of treatment for involuntary service users and for people who engage of their own accord are similar.

## Voluntary and involuntary

When we consider the issue of coerced and involuntary service users, we again run into the problem of language. 'Involuntary' suggests that a person has no option, but this is rarely the case. The employee required to participate in an alcohol programme by his company or the offender placed on a community order with a condition of drug treatment do have a choice; neither is 'forced' to cooperate although there will be consequences for not doing so. A person who has been told by his partner that she will leave unless he addresses his substance use can feel as coerced as someone under a requirement from the court. Interpersonal factors, the pressure from friends or relatives to 'do something about it', are often motivators for seemingly voluntary service users (see Chapter 5). As Harris (2010, p. 14) suggests, it would be wrong to assume that those who approach services voluntarily can be neatly differentiated from those who are coerced to attend. Indeed, as awareness of the implications of substance problems for others has grown, the boundaries between voluntary engagement and some level of social control have become blurred. For example, a mother might seek help with a heroin problem but find that concerns about the implications for her children lead to the involvement of social services. A man coming forward to tackle his use of alcohol may be unable to avoid dealing with his aggressive behaviour towards his partner too. This can present an ethical minefield, with practitioners caught between supporting an individual's self-determination and protecting vulnerable third parties or safe-guarding the wider public good. The benefits to others are seen as justifying the use of control (Burman, 2004).

For ease of reference in this chapter, the word 'involuntary' will be used to depict someone who is formally required to attend for treatment and 'coercion' to describe the broader concept of applying pressure on a person to address his problem; both these imply consequences for failure to comply. These two concepts should not be confused with what Hough (1996) calls 'compulsory treatment', any attempt to force interventions on a person, an approach likely to contravene human rights.

## Engagement

Some coerced and involuntary service users will see treatment as an opportunity, despite the circumstances of their referral. Others, however, will enter the counselling room viewing their substance use as unproblematic or as something they have little inclination to address; they may be resentful or hostile and feel that they are being treated unfairly. In short, resistance presents a major challenge for the practitioner. To overcome this, particular attention must be given to the processes of engagement.

Writing from a social work perspective, Barber (1991, p. 47) describes two unhelpful approaches to this quandary:

- 'Casework by concessions'. The practitioner, insecure in a role that carries authority, gives in to the person's demands in the hope that this will lead to a consensual relationship. When this does not happen, the practitioner must draw a line in the sand, further undermining an already confused relationship.
- 'Casework by oppression'. The practitioner considers compliance to be the prime objective of engagement and focuses entirely on trying to impose this.

Believing that both of these are doomed to failure, Barber proposes a third way, 'casework by negotiation'. Trotter (2006) believes that what should be sought with involuntary service users is a balance between therapeutic engagement and control and a mutual understanding as to when the latter must take precedence. These two authors suggest that careful attention must be paid to:

- *providing factual information about the nature of the relationship* and giving the person the opportunity to express his feelings about this.
- *asking the person what his expectation of the referral is.* Thorley's maxim – 'for the patient to come to the doctor's surgery shows he is motivated about something' – is particularly pertinent here (Thorley, 1980). Helping each person to identify what that 'something' is, is critical. The person under a court order or the person referred by his employer may attend solely through fear of custody or dread of unemployment respectively but these are powerful motivators if they can be harnessed.

- *making explicit what is, and is not, negotiable.* The service user needs to be clear about whom progress is reported to, what is expected regarding attendance and engagement and the consequences of non-compliance. The process of ensuring the person understands inevitably emphasises the practitioner's authority and the relative powerlessness of the service user. Having done this, the discussion can then turn to what is negotiable; this gives some power back to the person and allows space for him to lay out his own agenda. For example, the principal objective when working with a person subject to a court condition to address an alcohol problem is to prevent reoffending; however, whether this is achieved through abstinence or controlled drinking may be negotiable. In addition, the person may want to include secondary objectives of his own such as help with being rehoused.
- *asking the person what his expectation of the practitioner is.* This further helps to clarify roles whilst empowering the service user and providing the opportunity to discuss the nature of responsibility.

In addition to the signing of any formal orders, providing leaflets which lay out the purposes of the relationship, what is not negotiable and the limits of confidentiality is important.

The process of engagement remains an interactional and client-centred one, albeit with clearly defined parameters. Throughout, the practitioner should be mindful that his role will influence how the person views him and what he will be prepared to bring to sessions (see Chapter 6).

The processes of working with people with substance problems are similar whatever the status of the case but the nature of the relationship differs in one fundamental way: work with voluntary service users is a process of collaboration whereas, with involuntary referrals, it is one of negotiation.

## Employee policies

The purpose of workplace drug and alcohol policies is to ensure that organisations run efficiently and maintain safety standards, whilst acknowledging that substance use can have a human cost. Policies should include whole workforce awareness-raising components (primary prevention) in addition to arrangements covering employees exhibiting problems (secondary prevention). A core feature of such policies is the option of referring an employee for counselling whose ability to carry out his job is impaired by substance use. This may be done informally or as part of disciplinary procedures. Counselling is usually undertaken by an external agency such as an occupational health or substance problems service. Employee policies should focus on work performance; it is not for employers to interfere in the private lives of employees. Some companies carry out random drug and alcohol testing, the offshore oil industry being one example. While the need to maintain the highest standards of safety is indisputable, testing remains controversial on human rights grounds, particularly because some substances can be detected a considerable time after last use.

### Engagement

Bert works in a warehouse. He attended a disciplinary hearing following instances of returning late from lunch smelling of alcohol. The panel decided to refer him to an alcohol counselling service with which the company has an agreement. As he enters the counselling room, Bert feels angry and humiliated.

*Practitioner:* Hello Bert. Tell me your understanding of why you are here.

*Bert:* Work sent me. It was unfair what happened. Others have been late too – they picked on me. I've worked hard for years and now they do this.

*Practitioner:* You are obviously angry.

*Bert:* I certainly am. If they think they're going to get me to go teetotal, they'd better think again.

*Practitioner:* What would you like to see as the outcome of our discussions?

*Bert:* Well, I don't want to lose my job. I mustn't lose it – my wife might leave.

*Practitioner:* So, if we can ensure that you don't get into trouble again at work, coming here will be worthwhile.

*Bert:* I suppose so.

*Practitioner:* How do you think you can avoid getting the sack?

*Bert:* I'll need to stay away from the pub at lunchtime.

*Practitioner:* Before we discuss that and how you view your drinking overall, I want to ask you what you expect from me.

*Bert:* Well, I don't want you phoning them behind my back or telling them everything I tell you.

*Practitioner:* That's something that worries everyone. Let me explain what the agreement with your company says that we both have to do. [Describes expectations regarding attendance, reporting arrangements and the boundaries of confidentiality.] Here's a leaflet which explains how it works. You will see that we put everything in writing and I don't speak to your boss on the phone without your agreement. Your boss doesn't want to know if you've stopped drink completely; he wants to ensure that there are no more problems at work. Have you any questions about this?

*Bert:* No. That's clear.

*Practitioner:* Before we discuss things in more detail, tell me whether I've picked up things correctly. You think that work has treated you unfairly. Also, you don't want to stop drinking. You're worried, though, that you might be sacked and that this would affect your marriage. You see stopping lunchtime drinking as the way to prevent this.

*Bert:* That's about right.

*Practitioner:* Now, before we work out a plan together, tell me about the incidents that led to the hearing.

Consider the following:

- Which of the principles of engagement outlined above has the practitioner applied?
- What issues are negotiable and which are not?
- There are elements of motivational interviewing in this exchange. Can you identify them?

## Substance problems and the criminal justice system

### Crime–substance connections

We will now turn from the principles of working with people coerced into treatment to considering the links between offending and substance use and how the criminal justice system responds.

It is often assumed that substance use causes crime and addressing the former will also substantially reduce the latter. However, just as the links between mental health and substance use are complex and diverse, so too are the connections between substance taking and crime; they are not a matter of simple causality. It is important to remember that crime is a construct; societies decide what behaviours should be made subject to the law. At one level, therefore, society designates what aspects of our relationship with substances should be criminalised. A new psychoactive substance may emerge, the manufacture and possession of which is not, at that stage, an offence. Concerns lead the government to placing it under the Misuse of Drugs Act 1971. This action, designed to protect the public, makes criminals of those who continue to use it whether or not it is affecting them adversely. In the same way, smoking in an enclosed public place is only an offence because we recently decided that it should be.

Crime and substance use are connected in various possible ways (Bennett, 2008; Bennett and Holloway, 2005; McMurran, 1994):

- Substance use may lead to crime. The obvious example of this is the dependent user who steals to maintain his habit. The same link exists when a person only behaves aggressively when intoxicated; this does not, however, indicate that the substance or its use 'caused' the aggression.
- Crime can lead to substance use. A criminal lifestyle may bring a person into regular contact with illicit drugs or provide the necessary funding for regular purchases. A variation on this relationship is the use of substances to facilitate a criminal act which the person has already decided to commit. For example, a housebreaker might always drink to steel himself for his work or football casuals might deliberately consume stimulants to get themselves in the mood for troublemaking.
- The criminal act is manufacture or supply, not possession for use or the consequences of consumption.
- The problematic use of substances and offending are both associated with a common factor. As we have seen in Chapter 3, some people exhibit a cluster of behaviours including risk taking, rebelliousness, delinquency and

substance taking. Various theoretical perspectives have been used to explain why this should be, including learning theories, deviance models and genetic predisposition. Another shared influence might be a lack of opportunity and poverty.

- A person might use substances and commit crime without there being any obvious link. For example, an accountant might use cocaine heavily at weekends and defraud his company without there being any connection.

What the reader will notice is that where these associations exist it is not necessarily the case that substance use itself is problematic.

## BOX 17.1 DRUG–CRIME CONNECTIONS: SOME STATISTICS

Substance use is a feature in the lives and the offending of very significant numbers of people involved in the criminal justice system.

- Using various sources, Kirby et al. (2011) compared self-declared drug use in the past 12 months in various groups: 3.1 per cent of the general adult population (aged 16–59) reported class A drug use in contrast to 35 per cent of arrestees (heroin, crack and cocaine only; aged 17+), 39 per cent of people sentenced to community penalties (aged 16+) and 53 per cent of prisoners (aged 18+). The same review found high levels of problematic alcohol use among offenders within the criminal justice system.
- A survey of 16–21-year-old offenders in custody in Scotland in 2007 (McKinlay, Forsyth and Khan, 2009), found that 79.6 per cent considered that alcohol had played a part in their previous offending, with 56.8 per cent blaming their current offence on drinking or drinking along with drugs; 36.3 per cent blamed alcohol on its own; 30.1 per cent blamed illicit drugs for their current offence but this was usually in association with alcohol; the drug most often taken with alcohol was diazepam. Only 9.7 per cent blamed illicit drugs on their own for their current offence. Both violence and violence involving a weapon was strongly associated with prior alcohol or alcohol and diazepam consumption. This link between violence and alcohol is endorsed by Martin et al. (2004) and McCoard et al. (2011). In contrast to this link between aggression and alcohol, class A drug users tend to commit acquisitive crimes to fund their habits. Boreham et al. (2006) found that the most commonly alleged offences among arrestees who had used heroin, crack and/or cocaine in the past 12 months were, firstly, shoplifting and, secondly, burglary. Research by Allen (2005) suggested that when use escalated, shoplifting, a crime which many had previously committed, increased and people also turned, reluctantly, to robbing people in public places.

It is important to stress that, contrary to popular myth, the majority of illicit drug users do not commit crimes other than the offence of possession (Turning Point, 2004).

### Drugs become central to crime reduction strategies

The law does not accept substance use as a defence but it does acknowledge that there can be connections between the two and that dealing with problematic substance use has the potential to reduce crime. The links between illicit drugs and crime became the focus of particular attention from the 1980s onwards for two reasons. Firstly, the UK was experiencing a wave of Class A drug use and all its associated problems. Secondly, the dominant paradigm within the justice system became risk reduction and the prevention of reoffending, rather than just deserts. If drug use could be tackled, crime would reduce and public safety would increase. Responses to people who offend became based on the risk-need-responsivity model (Bonta and Andrews, 2007). This approach is based on three key notions:

- The central objective is risk reduction, and the extent of intervention should reflect the level of risk which the individual offender presents.
- The target of interventions should be the factors in the person's life which support offending and which can be changed. These are called criminogenic needs and include antisocial attitudes, problematic family functioning, delinquent peer groups and use of substances.
- Interventions should be based on cognitive and behavioural principles and adapted to the person's learning style.

Although the risk-need-responsivity model has been subject to criticism (McNeill, 2009), it remains the basis for how people who offend are managed in the UK. The New Labour government, which came into power in 1997, made the reduction of crime, based on this model, a priority. With drug use being seen as an obvious criminogenic need, initiatives were introduced to intervene with drug-using offenders at various stages in the criminal justice system. This has led to 'treatment' becoming a central plank of the justice system. In policy terms, drugs became even more firmly defined as a law and order issue, albeit one with secondary health and social components. In England and Wales, particularly, very significant resources have been made available to address the drug issue via the justice system; so much so that concerns were expressed for a time that offenders could access treatment with ease and those who presented to their GPs voluntarily were left on waiting lists (Turning Point, 2004). This has ensured, though, that many have been channelled into treatment who might not have accessed it otherwise or who might not have done so until later in their substance-using careers. The blurring of treatment and justice is not without its problems, however. There is a danger that a person may be sentenced because of his substance use and receive a higher tariff penalty than his crime might otherwise merit. McSweeney et al. (2007) note the paradox of 'increasing the intrusiveness of punishment in the name of rehabilitation'. Net widening is a serious and ongoing issue for practitioners writing reports for the court, for sentencers and for policy makers.

In policy terms, the focus has been on the drug-using offender, with his alcohol-using counterpart receiving scant attention. However, as concerns about the detrimental effects of alcohol have risen up the political agenda, there is growing interest in the potential for the justice system to intervene further with alcohol-using offenders. Examples of this are specific practice guidance for probation staff in England and Wales (Ministry of Justice, 2010) and the introduction of the Alcohol Abstinence and Monitoring Requirement.

### Points of intervention across the justice system

While the condition in a probation order requiring an offender to address his substance use has a lengthy history, the range of options within the criminal justice system has increased markedly since the 1990s. Although the arrangements for intervening pre-trial and the sentences available to the courts vary between England and Wales, Northern Ireland and Scotland, the potential points for intervention are similar:

- *Arrest.* The options available include medical intervention to reduce the immediate risks posed by intoxication or withdrawals, the provision of information about services, drug testing and arrest referral, and restriction on bail schemes.
- *Diversion from prosecution.* In Scotland, arrangements are in place in many areas for the public prosecutor (the Procurator Fiscal) to refer people to drug and alcohol programmes when minor offences linked to use are alleged to have been committed. The Fiscal normally defers the decision to prosecute until the outcome of counselling is known. The person has the choice to go to court instead of participating in the scheme. With an entirely different legal basis, the conditional caution can be used in England and Wales for identical purposes.
- *Community-based disposals.* Specialist drug courts exist in some areas. Drug Rehabilitation Requirements involving testing have been introduced in England and Wales (in Scotland the Drug Treatment and Testing Order fulfils a broadly similar function). Community Orders (England and Wales), Community Payback Orders (Scotland) and Probation Orders (Northern Ireland) can contain specific drug or alcohol treatment requirements. Alcohol Abstinence and Monitoring Requirements, which target non-dependent offenders whose drinking contributed to their court appearance, involve regular testing and are being piloted in England. Drink driving programmes, run by a variety of agencies, are also available to the courts in some areas.
- *Prison.* Prison is not a drug-free – or, indeed, alcohol-free – environment but for some it can bring respite from the environmental pressures in the community, particularly for those opting to enter drug-free wings. Although inconsistencies remain between establishments, much has been done to try to coordinate the management of people with substance problems during their journey through a custodial sentence. Identification, pharmacotherapy, accredited drug and alcohol programmes, the availability of AA and Narcotics Anonymous groups and through-care arrangements to link people back into community services on their release all need to be part of

an integrated pathway within each prison. There is guidance on substitute prescribing in prison (Department of Health, 2010). A person who enters prison already receiving an opiate substitute, or who is stabilised on one in custody, should continue on that prescribing regime if he is serving a short sentence; he should be linked back into community prescribing services on his release. Those serving longer sentences are encouraged to work towards abstinence. Some people who have been detoxified in prison may be prescribed an opiate substitute prior to release if they are considered to be at significant risk of overdose after returning to the community.

## Intervention with involuntary service users

We have already noted that particular attention needs to be paid to the process of engagement. The interventions employed are the same for people who are coerced into treatment and those who engage voluntarily; what differs is the need to tailor these to the different context.

Trotter (2006) has developed a particular model for working with all involuntary service users, not just those with substance problems. Based on behavioural principles, it supports what he calls 'pro-social outcomes'. This involves using every opportunity to:

- *spot constructive behaviours or remarks and reward these*. Rewards can take various forms. Most often, they will involve verbal compliments. Other options include sharing positive comments written in case notes or taking tangible actions to make it easier for the person to comply, such as helping with transport. The practitioner can also make it clear that help provided for practical problems is a response to progress. It is important to link practical rewards directly to the desired behaviour. This is a form of contingency management.
- *model prosocial actions and statements*. Trotter emphasises the importance of the practitioner behaving in ways she would want the service user to behave, such as keeping appointments in a timely fashion and responding efficiently to issues. Prosocial statements might include commenting on the value of safety at work (employee referral) or the importance of treating children in particular ways (child protection referral).
- *challenge unhelpful remarks or actions*. The practitioner should not ignore antisocial conduct or comments reflecting undesirable attitudes. However, Trotter stresses the need to address these with care; criticism should be measured and outweighed by positive comments and rewards for prosocial behaviours.

Trotter's emphasis on addressing unhelpful thinking and employing approaches based on behavioural principles underpins the risk-need-responsivity model of working with offenders and dovetails neatly with the interventions which are known to work with people with substance problems. Motivational interviewing, too, has become a staple of work with people who offend.

Kirby et al (2011) suggest that working with offenders with substance problems is enhanced when:

- barriers to compliance are removed by helping with transport, ensuring flexibility regarding appointment times and sending appointment reminders;
- inter-agency working, particularly when a person progresses through various parts of the criminal justice system, is managed efficiently. Practical and personal support during the transition from custody back into the community is essential;
- punishment is balanced by incentives for compliance.

---

CASE ILLUSTRATION 17.2

**Intervening through the criminal justice system**

Jamal (19) came to the UK with his parents when he was ten. From the beginning he found it difficult to settle in a new country. He caused concerns at school and he has only ever had temporary low-paid jobs. He left home recently following months of arguing with his parents and he is sleeping on a friend's floor. For some years he has smoked cannabis daily but recently he has begun to try other substances. He has been found guilty of theft and possession of class A drugs. He has one previous conviction for possession. Jamal has a nonchalant air but, behind this, he is increasingly concerned that he is losing control of his substance use.

You are the probation officer writing the pre-sentence report:

- How do you think Jamal would view you?
- In what ways might he respond to your questions about his substance use?
- What do you think Jamal might hope would be the outcome of his engagement with you?

---

### Does involuntary treatment work?

The purpose of involuntary interventions is primarily to benefit third parties and therefore the measurement of success can prove problematic, as the following example demonstrates. An offender, who stole to pay for an expensive drug habit, might switch to heavy alcohol use. The objective of crime reduction might be met without any gain in the health or wellbeing of the person. Nevertheless, it is possible to draw conclusions about involuntary and coerced treatment. Evidence, primarily from the USA, suggests that it is as effective, and sometimes more so, in terms of compliance and outcomes when compared with those who attend voluntarily.

With regard to both mothers and pregnant women with substance problems, coerced treatment can improve retention in services and reduce consumption (Miller and Flaherty, 2000; Ondersma, Winhusen and Lewis, 2010). Against this needs to be set research and anecdotal evidence that some parents or pregnant women will go to great lengths to hide the extent of their problems or try to avoid services altogether for obvious reasons (Potts, 2005; Roberts and Nuru-Jeter, 2010).

Studies in the USA into the effectiveness of employee drug testing suggest that it can reduce accidents and consumption among occasional and chronic users; however, it may be that some drug users seek employment in organisations without such policies (French, Roebuck and Alexandre, 2004; Gerber and Yacoubian Jr, 2001). Roman and Blum (2002) note that, despite methodological limitations, research supports employee alcohol policies.

The greatest attention has been given to the involuntary treatment of drug users within the criminal justice system. McSweeney, Turnbull and Hough (2008) suggest that there are difficulties in researching this area and that the evidence of the effectiveness of interventions implemented via court or community settings is contradictory. However, the Drug Treatment Outcomes Research Study (DTORS), a major English initiative, found that treatment reduces drug-related offending and that levels of retention and positive outcomes were similar between those who entered treatment via criminal justice routes and those who were referred from other sources (Jones et al., 2009). This finding that treatment within the criminal justice system is as effective as interventions undertaken voluntarily is supported by others (Hough, 1996; McSweeney et al., 2007; NTA, 2012f). Breach of community orders remains a problem but so does dropout from voluntary treatment. However, because the numbers of people who offend are so much greater than the numbers who enter treatment under court orders, the impact of involuntary treatment on rates of crime overall is always going to be low (McSweeney et al., 2007).

Research into how best to identify and work with alcohol users in the criminal justice system is more limited (McCoard et al., 2011). There is considerable interest in how best to screen for this group and whether brief or more comprehensive interventions are more effective (Ashton, 2012b).

## Concluding comments

On the one hand, some people enter treatment entirely voluntarily and, on the other, some are formally mandated to attend. However, for a great many, various degrees of coercion have led them to the door of services. The evidence suggests that coerced or involuntary treatment can be as effective as voluntary engagement. Many questions remain, however. Further consideration needs to be given as to whether different counselling styles are, indeed, needed in these differing contexts. In addition, McSweeney et al. (2008) suggest that some initiatives within the criminal justice system appear to be more effective than others and therefore more research is needed to inform future policy direction.

## RESOURCES

■ Bennett, T. and Holloway, K. (2005). *Understanding Drugs, Alcohol and Crime.*

- Kirby, A., McSweeney, T., Turnbull, P. and Bhardwa, B. (2011). *Engaging Substance Misusing Offenders: A Rapid Review of the Substance Misuse Treatment Literature.* Available at: www.icpr.org.uk/.
- McMurran, M. (2006). 'Drug and Alcohol Programmes: Concept, Theory, and Practice'. In C. Hollin and E. Palmer (eds), *Offending Behaviour Programmes: Development, Application and Controversies.*
- Trotter, C. (2006). *Working with Involuntary Clients: A Guide to Practice* (2nd edition).

# Appendix: Validated Questionnaires

There are number of validated instruments. The following are included as examples of those used with people who drink.

## AUDIT and SADQ-C

AUDIT and SADQ-C serve somewhat different purposes:

- AUDIT is an initial screening tool which readily picks up hazardous, harmful and dependent drinking, but it does not explore the latter in depth. It is normally used either for mass or targeted screening in generic settings, such as accident and emergency departments and GP surgeries, or as part of initial triage in specialist services. Lower scores suggest brief interventions and higher scores fuller assessment.
- SADQ-C focuses on physical dependence and is used primarily by specialist services to gauge the level of this when problematic use has already been identified.

## AUDIT

**The Alcohol Use Disorders Identification Test: Interview Version**

Read questions as written. Record answers carefully. Begin the AUDIT by saying "Now I am going to ask you some questions about your use of alcoholic beverages during this past year." Explain what is meant by "alcoholic beverages" by using local examples of beer, wine, vodka, etc. Code answers in terms of "standard drinks'. Place the correct answer number in the box at the right.

1.  How often do you have a drink containing alcohol?

    (0) Never [Skip to Qs 9–10]
    (1) Monthly or less
    (2) 2 to 4 times a month
    (3) 2 to 3 times a week
    (4) 4 or more times a week ☐

6.  How often during the last year have you needed a first drink in the morning to get yourself going after a heavy drinking session?

    (0) Never
    (1) Less than monthly
    (2) Monthly
    (3) Weekly
    (4) Daily or almost daily ☐

2. How many drinks containing alcohol do you have on a typical day when your are drinking?

(0) 1 or 2
(1) 3 or 4
(2) 5 or 6
(3) 7, 8, or 9
(4) 10 or more ☐

3. How often do you have six or more drinks on one occasion

(0) Never
(1) Less than monthly
(2) Monthly
(3) Weekly
(4) Daily or almost daily
*Skip to Questions 9 and 10 if Total Score for Questions 2 and 3 = 0* ☐

4. How often during the last year have you found that you were not able to stop drinking once you had started?

(0) Never
(1) Less than monthly
(2) Monthly
(3) Weekly
(4) Daily or almost daily ☐

5. How often during the last year have you failed to do what was normally expected from you because of drinking?

(0) Never
(1) Less than monthly
(2) Monthly
(3) Weekly
(4) Daily or almost daily ☐

7. How often during the last year have you had a feeling of guilt or remorse after drinking?

(0) Never
(1) Less than monthly
(2) Monthly
(3) Weekly
(4) Daily or almost daily ☐

8. How often during the last year have you been unable to remember what happened the night before because you had been drinking?

(0) Never
(1) Less than monthly
(2) Monthly
(3) Weekly
(4) Daily or almost daily ☐

9. Have you or someone else been injured as a result of your drinking

(0) No
(2) Yes, but not in the last year
(4) Yes, during the last year ☐

10. Has a relative or friend or a doctor or another health worker been concerned abut your drinking or suggested you cut down?

(0) No
(2) Yes, but not in the last year
(4) Yes, during the last year ☐

Record total of specific items here ☐

*If total is greater than recommended cut-off, consult User's Manual.*

*Source*: Babor, T., Higgins Biddle, J., Saunders, J. and Monteiro, M. (2001) (reproduced with permission).

*Note*: In the UK, a standard drink is one unit of alcohol (half pint of regular beer, lager or cider; two thirds of one small glass of wine (125 ml); a single measure of spirits).

## Interpretation

A score of between 8 and 15 indicates that the person has a medium level of problematic use and a score of 16 and above indicates serious difficulties. Babor et al. (2001), while emphasising the importance of exercising professional judgement in parallel with AUDIT, suggest that:

- brief interventions are likely to be appropriate for people scoring between 8 and 15;
- less intensive treatment, followed by monitoring, may be appropriate for people scoring between 16 and 19;
- people scoring more than 20 will need comprehensive treatment.

## SADQ-C

---

**Severity of Alcohol Dependence Questionnaire: Form C**

Please answer all the following questions about your drinking by circling your most appropriate response:

**During the past <u>six months</u>:**

1. The day after drinking alcohol, I woke up feeling sweaty.
   Never or Almost Never        Sometimes        Often        Nearly Always        ☐

2. The day after drinking alcohol, my hands shook first thing in the morning.
   Never or Almost Never        Sometimes        Often        Nearly Always        ☐

3. The day after drinking alcohol, my whole body shook violently first thing in the morning if I didn't have a drink.
   Never or Almost Never        Sometimes        Often        Nearly Always        ☐

4. The day after drinking alcohol, I woke up absolutely drenched in sweat.
   Never or Almost Never        Sometimes        Often        Nearly Always        ☐

5. The day after drinking alcohol, I dreaded waking up in the morning.
   Never or Almost Never        Sometimes        Often        Nearly Always        ☐

6. The day after drinking alcohol, I was frightened of meeting people first thing in the morning.
   Never or Almost Never        Sometimes        Often        Nearly Always        ☐

7. The day after drinking alcohol, I felt at the edge of despair when I awoke.
   Never or Almost Never        Sometimes        Often        Nearly Always        ☐

8. The day after drinking alcohol, I felt very frightened when I awoke.
   Never or Almost Never        Sometimes        Often        Nearly Always        ☐

9. The day after drinking alcohol, I liked to have an alcoholic drink in the morning.
   Never or Almost Never        Sometimes        Often        Nearly Always        ☐

10. The day after drinking alcohol, in the morning I always gulped my first few alcoholic drinks down as quickly as possible.
   Never or Almost Never        Sometimes        Often        Nearly Always        ☐

11. The day after drinking alcohol, I drank more alcohol in the morning to get rid of the shakes.
   Never or Almost Never        Sometimes        Often        Nearly Always        ☐

12. The day after drinking alcohol, I had a very strong craving for an alcoholic drink when I awoke.

    Never or Almost Never     Sometimes     Often     Nearly Always     ☐

13. I drank more than a quarter of a bottle of spirits a day (OR 1 bottle of wine OR 4 pints of regular beer).

    Never or Almost Never     Sometimes     Often     Nearly Always     ☐

14. I drank more than a half of a bottle of spirits a day (OR 2 bottles of wine OR 8 pints of regular beer).

    Never or Almost Never     Sometimes     Often     Nearly Always     ☐

15. I drank more than one bottle of spirits a day (OR 4 bottles of wine OR 15 pints of regular beer).

    Never or Almost Never     Sometimes     Often     Nearly Always     ☐

16. I drank more than two bottles of spirits a day (OR 8 bottles of wine OR 30 pints of regular beer).

    Never or Almost Never     Sometimes     Often     Nearly Always     ☐

**Imagine the following situation:**

1. You have HARDLY DRUNK ANY ALCOHOL FOR A FEW WEEKS.
2. You then drink VERY HEAVILY for TWO DAYS.

HOW WOULD YOU FEEL THE <u>MORNING AFTER</u> THOSE TWO DAYS OF HEAVY DRINKING?

17. I would start to sweat.

    Not at all     Slightly     Moderately     Quite a Lot     ☐

18. My hands would shake.

    Not at all     Slightly     Moderately     Quite a Lot     ☐

19. My body would shake.

    Not at all     Slightly     Moderately     Quite a Lot     ☐

20. I would be craving for a drink.

    Not at all     Slightly     Moderately     Quite a Lot     ☐

    **Total score**     ☐

**Scoring**

Never or Almost Never = 0     Sometimes = 1     Often = 2     Nearly Always = 3

Not at all = 0     Slightly = 1     Moderately = 2     Quite a Lot = 3

If questions 17 to 20 are not used, the total for questions 1 to 16 should be multiplied by 1.25.

*Source*: Stockwell, T. and Sitharthan, T. (1991).

## Interpretation

20 or less = low dependence
21 to 30 = moderate level of dependence
31 and above = severe dependence (Jarvis et al., 2005, p. 24)

Careful consideration should always be given as to whether medical supervision of alcohol withdrawal is necessary when the score approaches a moderate level of dependence. The SADQ-C score should not be used on its own to make this judgement but as one of a number of indicators (see Chapter 10).

# References

ACMD (Advisory Council on the Misuse of Drugs) (1998). *Drug Misuse and the Environment*. London: HMSO.

ACMD (2003). *Hidden Harm – Responding to the Needs of Children of Problem Drug Users*. www.gov.uk/government/uploads/system/uploads/attachment_data/file/120620/hidden-harm-full.pdf.

ACMD (2008). *Cannabis: Classification and Public Health*. London: Home Office.

ACMD (2012). *Recovery from Alcohol and Drug Dependence: An Overview of the Evidence*: www.gov.uk.

Adfam (2009). *'We count too'. Good Practice Guide and Quality Standards for Work with Family Members Affected by Someone Else's Drug Problem* (2nd edn). London: Adfam.

Adi, Y., Juarez-Garcia, A., Wang, D., Jowett, S., Frew, E., Day, E., Bayliss, S., Roberts, T. and Burls, A. (2007). 'Oral naltrexone as a treatment for relapse prevention in formerly opioid-dependent drug users: a systematic review and economic evaluation'. *Health Technology Assessment*, 11 (6).

Alcohol Academy (2010). *Cocaethylene: Responding to Combined Alcohol and Cocaine Use*. www.alcoholacademy.net.

Alcohol Concern (2002). *Alcohol Misuse among Older People*. www.alcoholconcern.org.uk/publications/factsheets.

Alcohol Focus Scotland (undated). *What Is Dual Diagnosis?* Leaflet. Glasgow: Alcohol Focus Scotland.

Alcoholics Anonymous (2001). *The Big Book*. www.alcoholics-anonymous.org.uk.

Alcoholics Anonymous (2013). *Frequently Asked Questions*. www.alcoholics-anonymous.org.uk.

Allen, C. (2005). 'Links between heroin, crack cocaine and crime. Where does the street fit in?'. *British Journal of Criminology*, 45 (3), 355–72.

Alzheimer's Society (2012). *What Is Korsakoff's Syndrome?* Fact sheet. www.alzheimers.org.uk.

ASH (2012a). *Key Dates in the History of Anti-Tobacco Campaigning*. www.ash.org.uk (accessed 14 September 2012).

ASH (2012b). *Smoking in Cars*. www.ash.org.uk.

ASH (2012c). *Smoking and Health Inequalities*. www.ash.org.uk (accessed 16 September 2012).

ASH (2013). *Smoking Statistics: Who Smokes and How Much*. www.ash.org.uk.

Asher, C. and Gask, L. (2010). 'Reasons for illicit drug use in people with schizophrenia: qualitative study'. *BMC Psychiatry*, 10, 94.

Ashton, M. (2001). 'Antabuse reduces cocaine and alcohol use among opioid maintenance patients'. *Drug and Alcohol Findings*, Issue 6. London: Drug and Alcohol Findings.

Ashton, M. (2004a). 'Confident kids … like to party'. *Drug and Alcohol Findings*. London: Drug and Alcohol Findings. http://findings.org.uk/docs/Ashton_M_30.pdf.

Ashton, M. (2005a). 'Can we help?'. *Drug and Alcohol Findings*, Issue 12. London: Drug and Alcohol Findings.

Ashton, M. (2005b). 'The motivational hello'. *Drug and Alcohol Findings*, Issue 13. London: Drug and Alcohol Findings.

Ashton, M. (2008). *The new abstentionists*. www.drugscope.org.uk/Documents/PDF/Good%20Practice/Ashton_M_30.pdf.

Ashton, M. (2009). *Continuing Care Research; What We Have Learned and Where We Are Going*. www.findings.org.uk/count/downloads/download.php?file=McKay_JR_18.txt.

Ashton, M. (2010). *Residential Rehabilitation: The Best Route to Recovery?* http://findings.org.uk/count/downloads/download.php?file=hot_resrehab.hot.

Ashton, M. (2011). *Why Are Some Treatment Services More Effective Than Others?* http://findings.org.uk/count/downloads/download.php?file=tr_org.hot.

Ashton, M. (2012a). 'Beg to differ'. *Druglink*, March/April 2012. London: DrugScope.

Ashton, M. (2012b). *Alcohol Screening and Brief Interventions in Probation*. http://findings.org.uk/count/downloads/download.php?file=McGovern_R_2.txt.

Ashton, M. and Whitton, J. (2004). 'The power of the welcoming reminder'. *Drug and Alcohol Findings*, Issue 11. London: Drug and Alcohol Findings.

Babor, T., Higgins-Biddle, J., Saunders, J. and Monteiro, M. (2001). *AUDIT. The Alcohol Use Disorders Identification Test* (2nd edn). http://whqlibdoc.who.int/hq/2001/who_msd_msb_01.6a.pdf (accessed 10 July 2013).

Baker, A., Lee, N. and Jenner, L. (eds) (2004). *Models of Intervention and Care for Psychostimulant Users* (2nd edn). www.health.gov.au.

Baldacchino, A. (2012). *Overdose Risk Information Project (ORION): Implication for Prevention Policies in Europe*. Presentation at European Parliament on 28 November 2012. http://orion-euproject.com.

Bamber, S. and White, W. (2011). *Dialogue I: Recovery-Orientated Methadone Maintenance*. www.williamwhitepapers.com.

Bandura, A. (1977). *Social Learning Theory*. Englewood Cliffs: Prentice Hall.

Bandura, A. (1998). 'Self-efficacy'. In V. Ramachaudran (ed.), *Encyclopaedia of Human Behavior*, vol. 4. New York: Academic Press.

Bandura, A. (2008). 'The reconstrual of "free will" from the agentic perspective of social cognitive theory'. In J. Baer, J. Kaufman and R. Baumeister (eds), *Are We Free? Psychology and Free Will*. Oxford: Oxford University Press.

Bandura, A., Ross, D. and Ross, S. (1961). 'Transmission of aggression through imitation of aggressive models'. *Journal of Abnormal and Social Psychology*, 63, 575–82.

Barber, J. (1991). *Beyond Casework*. Basingstoke: Macmillan.

Barber, J. (2002). *Social Work with Addictions* (2nd edn). Basingstoke: Palgrave Macmillan.

Barnard, M. (2005). *Drugs in the Family. The Impact on Parents and Siblings*. www.jrf.org.uk.

Barnardos (2010). Personal correspondence between the author and Barnardos in Aberdeenshire.

Barnett, N., Tidey, J., Murphy, J., Swift, R. and Colby, S. (2011). 'Contingency management for alcohol use reduction: a pilot study using a transdermal alcohol sensor'. *Drug and Alcohol Dependence*, 118 (2–3), 391–9.

Beck, A. (1989). *Cognitive Therapy and the Emotional Disorders*. London: Penguin.

Beck, A., Wright, F., Newman, C. and Liese, B. (1993). *Cognitive Therapy of Substance Abuse*. New York: Guilford Press.

Becker, H. (1997). *Outsiders: Studies in the Sociology of Deviance* (new edn). New York: The Free Press.

Becker, J. and Duffy, C. (2002). *Women Drug Users and Drugs Service Provision: Service-level Responses to Engagement and Retention*. DPAS Briefing Paper 17. London: Home Office.

Beddoes, D., Sheikh, S. Khanna, M. and Francis, R. (2010a). *The Impact of Drugs on Different Minority Groups: A Review of the UK Literature. Part 1: Ethnic Groups.* www.ukdpc.org.uk.

Beddoes, D., Sheikh, S., Khanna, M., and Francis, R. (2010b). *The Impact of Drugs on Different Minority Groups: A Review of the UK Literature. Part 2: Lesbian, Gay, Bisexual & Transgender (LGBT) Groups.* www.ukdpc.org.uk.

Bennett, P. (2002). 'Behavioural and cognitive behavioural approaches to substance misuse treatment'. In T. Petersen and A. McBride (eds), *Working with Substance Misusers. A Guide to Theory and Practice*. London: Routledge.

Bennett, T. (2008). 'Drug use and criminal behaviour'. In H. Shapiro (ed.), *The Essential Student Reader on Drugs*. London: DrugScope.

Bennett, T. and Holloway, K. (2005). *Understanding Drugs Alcohol and Crime*. Maidenhead: Open University Press.

Berridge, V. and Edwards, G. (1982). *Opium and the People: Opiate Use in Nineteenth-Century England*. London: St Martin's Press.

Best, D. (2010). *Digesting the Evidence*. Glasgow: Scottish Drugs Recovery Consortium.

Birmingham Drug and Alcohol Action Team (2012). *Safer Injecting*. www.bdaat.co.uk/page.php?pid=48&mid=52 (accessed 23 December 2012).

Blank, M. (2002). 'A suitable case for treatment: an introduction to British drug policy'. In T. Petersen and A. McBride (eds), *Working with Substance Misusers: A Guide to Theory and Practice*. London: Routledge.

Blocker, J. (2006). 'Did prohibition really work? Alcohol prohibition as a public health innovation'. *American Journal of Public Health*, 96 (2), 233–43.

Blomqvist, J. (2002). 'Recovery with and without treatment: a comparison of resolutions of drug and alcohol problems'. *Addiction Research and Theory*, 10 (2), 119–58.

Bonta, J. and Andrews, D. (2007). *Risk-Need-Responsivity Model of Offender Assessment and Rehabilitation 2007–06*. www.publicsafety.gc.ca/index-eng.aspx.

Booth, P. (2006). 'Idiosyncratic patterns of drinking in long-term successful controlled drinkers'. *Addiction Research and Theory*, 14 (1), 25–33.

Boreham, R., Fuller, E., Hills, A. and Pudney, S. (2006). *The Arrestee Survey Annual Report: Oct 2003–Sept. 2004*. London: Home Office.

Bottomley, T. (1999). 'Life in the slow lane: are we serious about services for stimulant users?' *Druglink*, May/June 1999. London: DrugScope.

Bottomley, T., Carnwath, T., Jeacock, J., Wibberley, C. and Smith, M. (1997). 'Crack cocaine – tailoring services to user need'. *Addiction Research*, 5 (3), 223–34.

Bremner, J., Southwick, S., Darnell, A. and Charney, D. (1996). 'Chronic PTSD in Vietnam combat veterans: course of illness and substance abuse'. *American Journal of Psychiatry*, 153 (3), 369–75.

Bretteville-Jensen, A. (2011). 'Illegal drug use and the economic recession – what can we learn from existing research?' *International Journal of Drug Policy*, 22 (5), 353–9.

Britt, E., Hudson, S. and Blampied, N. (2004). 'Motivational interviewing in health settings: a review'. *Patient Education and Counseling*, 53, 147–55.

Britton, J. (2009). *Young People's Specialist Substance Misuse Treatment: Exploring the Evidence*. www.nta.nhs.uk/uploads/yp_exploring_the_evidence_0109.pdf.

Burman, S. (2004). 'Revisiting the agents of social control role: implications for substance abuse treatment'. *Journal of Social Work Practice*, 18 (2), 197–210.

Burns, D. (1990). *The Feel Good Handbook*. New York: Plume.

Carroll, K. and Onken, L. (2005). 'Behavioral therapies for drug abuse'. *American Journal of Psychiatry*, 162 (8), 1452–60.

Centers for Disease Control and Prevention (2012). *Smoke-Free Policies Improve Health*. www.cdc.gov (accessed 16 September 2012).

Centre for Mental Health, DrugScope and the UK Drug Policy Commission (2012). *Dual Diagnosis: A Challenge for the Reformed NHS and for Public Health England*. www.centreformentalhealth.org.uk/pdfs/dual_diagnosis.pdf.

Chau, D, Walker, V., Pai, L. and Cho, L. (2008). 'Opiates and elderly: use and side effects'. *Clinical Interventions in Aging*, 3 (2), 273–78.

Cherry, K. (2013). *Pavlov's Dogs*. http://psychology.about.com/od/classicalconditioning/a/pavlovs-dogs.htm (accessed 15 July 2013).

Clark, M. (2011). 'Conceptualising addiction: how useful is the construct?' *International Journal of Humanities and Social Science* (Special Issue September 2011), 1 (13), 55–64.

Cleary, M., Hunt, G., Matheson, L., Seigfried, N. and Walter, G. (2007). *Psychosocial Interventions for People with Both Severe Mental Illness and Substance Misuse*. The Cochrane Library. http://onlinelibrary.wiley.com/cochranelibrary/search.

Cleaver, H., Unell, I. and Algate, J. (1999). *Children's Needs – Parenting Capacity. The Impact of Parental Mental Illness, Problem Alcohol and Drug Use and Domestic Violence on Children's Development*. London: The Stationery Office.

Clinical Training Institute (2013). *Pocket Guide for Motivational Interviewing*. www.motivationalinterviewing.info/resources/CTI_MI_Pocket_guide.pdf (accessed 19 July 2013).

Cloud, W. and Granfield, R. (1994). 'Natural recovery from addiction: treatment implications'. *Addictions Nursing*, 6 (4), 112–16.

Cloud, W. and Granfield, R. (2001). 'Natural recovery from substance dependency: lessons for treatment providers'. *Journal of Social Work Practice in the Addictions*, 1 (1), 83–104.

Copeland, J., Frewen, A. and Elkins, K. (2009). *Management of Cannabis Use Disorder and Related Issues: A Clinician's Guide*. http://ncpic.org.au/ncpic/news/ncpic-news/pdf/management-of-cannabis-use-disorder-and-related-issues-a-clinicians-guide.

Copello, A. and Orford, J. (2002). 'Addiction and the family: is it time for services to take note of the evidence?' *Addiction*, 97 (11), 1361–3.

Copello, A., Orford, J., Hodgson, R., Tober, G. and Barrett, C. (2002). 'Social behaviour and network therapy: basic principles and early experiences'. *Addictive Behaviors*, 27 (3), 345–66.

Copello, A., Templeton, L., Orford, J. and Velleman (2010a). 'The 5-step method: principles'. *Drugs: Education, Prevention and Policy*, 17 (s1), 86–99.

Copello, A., Templeton, L. and Powell, J. (2010b). 'The impact of addiction on the family: estimates of prevalence and costs'. *Drugs: Education, Prevention and Policy*, 17 (s1), 63–74.

Crome, I. (2004). 'The process of assessment'. In I. Crome, H. Ghodse, E. Gilvarry and P. McArdle (eds), *Young People and Substance Misuse*. London: Gaskell.

Crome, I., Chambers, P., Frisher, M., Bloor, R. and Roberts, D. (2009). *The Relationship between Dual Diagnosis: Substance Misuse and Dealing with Mental Health Issues*. Social Care Institute for Excellence Research Briefing 30. www.scie.org.uk.

Daly, M. (2009). 'Commercial breakdown'. *Druglink*, September/October 2009. London: DrugScope.

Daly, M. (2012). 'Drone strike'. *Druglink*, November/December 2012. London: DrugScope.

Dar, K. and Cherian, R. (2012). 'Seize the moment'. *Druglink*, September/October 2012. London: DrugScope.

Davidson, R. (2002). 'Cycle of change: ideas, issues and implications'. *Drugs: Education, Prevention and Policy*, 9 (1), 7–14.

Davies, J. (2006a). 'Addiction from the outside in'. *Druglink*, November/December 2006. London: DrugScope.

Davies, J. (2006b). 'The waltz of addiction'. *Druglink*, November/December 2006. London: DrugScope.

Davies, J. (2011). 'Mind the gap'. *Druglink*, September/October 2011. London: DrugScope.

Dawe, S., Harnett, P. and Frye, S. (2008). 'Improving outcomes for children living in families with parental substance misuse: what we know and what we should do'. *Child Abuse Prevention Issues* No. 29. www.aifs.gov.au/nch/pubs/issues/issues29/issues29.html.

Degenhardt, L., Bruno, R. and Topp, L. (2010). 'Is ecstasy a drug of dependence?' *Drug and Alcohol Dependence*, 107 (1), 1–10.

Department for Education and Skills (2006). *What to Do if You Are Worried That a Child Is Being Abused*. www.gov.uk/government/publications/what-to-do-if-youre-worried-a-child-is-being-abused.

Department of Health (2002). *Mental Health Policy Implementation Guide: Dual Diagnosis Good Practice Guide*. London: Department of Health.

Department of Health (2008a). *Smokefree England – One Year On*. London: Department of Health.

Department of Health (2008b). *Pregnancy and Alcohol*. London: Department of Health.

Department of Health (2010). *Updated Guidance for Prison Based Opioid Maintenance Prescribing*. www.nta.nhs.uk.

Department of Health (2013). *Smokefree*. http://smokefree.nhs.uk/quit-tools/calculate-the-cost.

Department of Health (England) and the devolved administrations (2007). *Drug Misuse and Dependence: UK Guidelines on Clinical Management*. www.dh.gov.uk/publications.

DiClemente, C. (2005). 'Conceptual models and applied research: the ongoing contribution of the transtheoretical model'. *Journal of Addictions Nursing*, 16, 5–12.

Dorn, N., Ribbens, J. and South, N. (1994). *Coping with a Nightmare. Family Feelings about Long-Term Drug Use* (revised edn). London: ISDD/Adfam.

Downs, W. and Harrison, L. (1998). 'Childhood maltreatment and the risk of substance problems in later life'. *Health and Social Care in the Community*, 6 (1), 35–46.

Dregan, A., Stewart, R. and Gulliford, M. (2012). 'Cardiovascular risk factors and cognitive decline in adults aged 50 and over: a population-based cohort study'. *Age and Ageing*, 42 (3), 338–45.

Drink and Drug News (2011). 'The recovery position'. *Drink and Drug News* (June 2011). Ashford: C. J. Wellings.

Drugs Action (2010). *DIY Detox and Recovery Support Book*. Aberdeen: Drugs Action.

DrugScope (2009a). *Ecstasy*. www.drugscope.org.uk/resources/drugsearch/drugsearch pages/ecstasy.

DrugScope (2009b). *DrugScope Street Trends Survey 2009*. www.drugscope.org.uk/ Media/Press+office/pressreleases/Street_drug_trends_2009.

Drummond, C. (2002). 'Pharmacological approaches to excessive drinking and alcohol dependence'. *Expert Review of Neurotherapeutics*, 2 (1), 119–25.

Dutra, L., Stathopoulou, G., Basden, S., Leyro, T., Powers, M. and Otto, M. (2008). 'A meta-analytic review of psychosocial interventions for substance use disorders'. *American Journal of Psychiatry*, 165 (2), 179–87.

Edwards, G. (2005). *Matters of Substance. Drugs: Is Legalization the Right Answer – Or the Wrong Question?* London: Penguin.

Edwards, G., Anderson, P., Babor, T., Casswell, S., Ferrence, R., Giesbrecht, N., Godfrey, C., Holder, H., Lemmens, P., Makela, K., Midanik, L., Norstrom, T., Osterberg, E., Romelsjö, A., Room, R., Simpura, J. and Skog, O.-J. (1994). *Alcohol Policy and the Public Good*. Oxford: Oxford University Press.

Effective Interventions Unit (2004). *Young People with, or at Risk of Developing, Problematic Substance Misuse. A Guide to Assessment.* Scottish Executive: Effective Interventions Unit.

Eisenberg, M., Filion, K., Yavin, D., Bélisle, P., Mottillo, S., Joseph, L., Gervais, A., O'Loughlin, J., Paradis, G., Rinfret, S. and Pilote,L. (2008). 'Pharmacotherapies for smoking cessation: a meta-analysis of randomized controlled trials'. *Canadian Medical Association Journal*, 179 (2), 125–44.

Eliason, M. and Hughes, T. (2004). 'Treatment counselors' attitudes about lesbian, gay, bisexual and transgendered clients: urban vs rural settings'. *Substance Use & Misuse*, 39 (4), 625–44.

Ellis, A., Gordon, J., Neenan, M. and Palmer, S. (1997). *Stress Counselling: A Rational Emotive Behaviour Approach*. London: Cassell.

El-Mallakh, P. (1998). 'Treatment models for clients with co-occurring addictive and mental disorders'. *Archives of Psychiatric Nursing*, 12 (2), 71–80.

EMCDDA (European Monitoring Centre for Drugs and Drug Addiction) (2007). *Treatment of Problem Cocaine Use: A Review of the Literature.* www.emcdda.europa.eu.

EMCDDA (2009). *Polydrug Use: Patterns and Responses*. www.emcdda.europa.eu.

EMCDDA (2012). *Annual Report 2012*. www.emcdda.europa.eu.

EMCDDA (2013a). *Countries*. www.emcdda.europa.eu/countries (accessed 23 July 2013).

EMCDDA (2013b). *Data: Statistical Bulletin 2013*. www.emcdda.europa.eu/stats13.

EMCDDA (2013c). *European Drug Report 2013*. www.emcdda.europa.eu.

Ersche, K., Barnes, A., Jones, P., Morein-Zamir, S., Robbins, T. and Bullmore, E. T. (2011). 'Abnormal structure of frontostriatal brain systems is associated with aspects of impulsivity and compulsivity in cocaine dependence'. *Brain*, 134 (7), 2013–14.

European Commission (2013). *Income Distribution Stats*. http://epp.eurostat.ec. europa.eu/statistics_explained/index.php/Income_distribution_statistics.

Evans, V. (2010). 'The role of families'. In J. Barlow (ed.), *Substance Misuse. The Implications of Research Policy and Practice*. London: Jessica Kingsley.

Exchange Supplies/The Alliance (2004). *Substitute Prescribing: The User's View*. DVD. Dorchester: Exchange Supplies.

Festinger, L. (1957). *A Theory of Cognitive Dissonance*. Stanford: Stanford University Press.

Fiorentine, R., Nakashima, J. and Anglin, M. (1999). 'Client engagement in drug treatment'. *Journal of Substance Abuse Treatment*, 17 (30), 199–206.

Flemen, K. (2013). 'Psychoactive challenge'. *Drink and Drug News* (May 2013). Ashford: C. J. Wellings.

Forrester, D. and Harwin, J. (2011). *Parents Who Misuse Drugs and Alcohol. Effective Interventions in Social Work and Child Protection.* Chichester: John Wiley.

French, M., Roebuck, M. and Alexandre, P. (2004). 'To test or not to test: do workplace drug testing programs discourage employee use?' *Social Science Research*, 33 (1), 45–63.

Galvani, S. (2012). *Supporting People with Alcohol and Drug Problems. Making a Difference.* Bristol: Policy Press.

Gartner, C., Hall, W., Vos, T., Bertram, M., Wallace, A. and Lim, S. (2007). 'Assessment of Swedish snus for tobacco harm reduction: an epidemiological modelling study'. *Lancet*, 369 (9578), 2010–14.

Gerber, J. and Yacoubian Jr, G. (2001). 'Evaluation of drug testing in the workplace: study of the construction industry'. *Journal of Construction Engineering and Management*, 127 (6), 438–44.

Ghodse, H. (2004). 'Introduction'. In I. Crome, H. Ghodse, E. Gilvarry and P. McArdle (eds), *Young People and Substance Misuse*. London: Gaskell.

Gilvarry, E. (1998). 'Psychiatric perspective'. In R. Robertson (ed.), *Management of Drug Users in the Community*. London: Arnold.

Gilvarry, E. and Britton, J. (2009). *Guidance for the Pharmacological Management of Substance Misuse amongst Young People.* www.nta.nhs.uk.

Gleitman, H. (1995). *Psychology* (4th edn). London: Norton.

Good Drugs Guide (2013). *Mixing.* www.thegooddrugsguide.com/heroin/mixing.htm (accessed 13 July 2013).

Gossop, M. (2006). *Treating Drug Misuse Problems: Evidence of Effectiveness.* London: NTA.

Gossop, M. (2007). *Living with Drugs* (6th edn). Aldershot: Ashgate.

Gossop, M. (2011). 'Behaviourism, cognitive therapy and CBT'. Podcast on *Film Exchange on Drugs and Alcohol.* www.fead.org.uk.

Gossop, M. and Carroll, K. (2006). 'Disulfiram, cocaine, and alcohol: two outcomes for the price of one'. *Alcohol and Alcoholism*, 41 (2), 119–20.

Grace and Galvani, S. (2010). 'Care or control? A way forward. *Drink and Drug News* (15th March 2010). Ashford: C. J. Wellings.

Grimshaw, G. and Stanton, A. (2006). 'Tobacco cessation interventions for young people'. *Cochrane Database of Systematic Reviews*, 4. www.thecochranelibrary.com/view/0/index.html.

Guardian (2009). 'Jacqui Smith slaps down drugs adviser for comparing ecstasy to horse riding'. *The Guardian* online, 9 February 2009. www.guardian.co.uk.

Halpern, J., Sherwood, A., Hudson, J., Gruber, S., Kozin, D. and Pope Jr, H. (2011). 'Residual neurocognitive features of long-term ecstasy users with minimal exposure to other drugs'. *Addiction*, 106 (4), 777–86.

Hammersley, R. and Dalgarno, P. (2013). *Trauma and Recovery amongst People Who Have Injected Drugs within the Past Five Years. Executive Summary.* Glasgow: Scottish Drugs Forum.

Harbin, F. (2000). 'Therapeutic work with children of substance misusing parents'. In F. Harbin and M. Murphy (eds), *Substance Misuse and Child Care. How to Understand, Assist and Intervene When Drugs Affect Parenting.* Lyme Regis: Russell House.

Harris, P. (2007). *Empathy for the Devil.* Lyme Regis: Russell House.

Harris, P. (2010). *The Concerned Other. How to Change Drug and Alcohol Users Through Their Family Members. A Complete Manual.* Lyme Regis: Russell House.

Harris, P. (2013). *Youthoria.* Lyme Regis: Russell House.

Hart, D. and Powell, J. (2006). *Adult Drug Problems, Children's Needs. Assessing the Impact of Parental Drug Use*. London: National Children's Bureau.

Hasin, D., Aharonovich, E., Liu, X., Mamman, Z., Matseoane, K., Carr, L. and Li, T.-K. (2002). 'Alcohol dependence symptoms and alcohol dehydrogenase 2 polymorphism: Israeli Ashkenazis, Sephardics, and recent Russian immigrants'. *Alcoholism: Clinical and Experimental Research*, 26 (9), 1315–21.

Hawkings, C. and Gilbert, H. (2004). *Dual Diagnosis Toolkit. Mental Health and Substance Misuse*. London: Turning Point and Rethink.

Health Advisory Service (1996). *Children and Young People Substance Misuse Services: The Substance of Young Needs*. London: HMSO.

Health and Social Care Information Centre (2012). *Smoking, Drinking and Drug Use among Young People in England in 2011*. www.hscic.gov.uk.

Health and Social Care Information Centre (2013a). *Statistics on Alcohol: England, 2013*. www.hscic.gov.uk.

Health and Social Care Information Centre (2013b). *Smoking, Drinking and Drug Use among Young People in England in 2012*. www.hscic.gov.uk.

Heather, N. (2009). 'Nick Heather on controlled drinking and the relationship to harm reduction'. Podcast on *Film Exchange on Drugs and Alcohol*. www.fead.org.uk.

Heather, N. and Robertson, I. (1981). *Controlled Drinking*. London: Methuen.

Heather, N. and Robertson, I. (1997). *Problem Drinking* (3rd edn). Oxford: Oxford University Press.

Hecksher, J. (2001). *Living without Drugs – Behaviour Change and Identity Change*. Presented to The International Conference: Behaviour Change in Addictions: Where to Now? Paisley, September 2001.

HM Government (1998). *Tackling Drugs to Build a Better Britain*. London: The Stationery Office.

HM Government (2010). *Drug Strategy 2010. Reducing Demand, Restricting Supply, Building Recovery: Supporting People to Live a Drug Free Life*. www.gov.uk.

Hoffman, J. (1990). 'The historical shift in the perception of opiates: from medicine to social menace'. *Journal of Psychoactive Drugs*, 22 (1), 53–62.

Home Office (2012a). *The Government's Alcohol Strategy*. Norwich: The Stationery Office.

Home Office (2012b). *Drug Misuse Declared: Findings from the 2011/12 Crime Survey for England and Wales (CSEW)* (2nd edn). www.gov.uk/government/publications.

Hopper, E. (1995). 'A psychoanalytical theory of "drug addiction": unconscious fantasies of homosexuality, compulsions and masturbation within the context of traumatogenic processes'. *International Journal of Psychoanalysis*, 76 (Pt6), 1121–42.

Hough, M. (1996). *Drug Misuse and the Criminal Justice System: A Review of the Literature*. London: Home Office.

House of Commons Science and Technology Committee (2011). *Alcohol Guidelines. Eleventh Report of the Session 2011–12*. www.parliament.uk.

Hughes, T., McCabe, S., Wilsnack, S., West, B. and Boyd, C. (2010). 'Victimization and substance use disorders in a national sample of heterosexual and sexual minority women and men'. *Addiction*, 105 (12), 2130–40.

Humeniuk, R., Dennington, V. and Ali, R. (2008). *The Effectiveness of a Brief Intervention for Illicit Drugs Linked to Alcohol, Smoking and Substance Involvement Screening Test (ASSIST) in Primary Health Care Settings: A Technical Report of Phase III Findings of the WHO ASSIST Randomized Controlled Trial*. www.who.int/substance_abuse/activities/assist/en/.

Hurcombe, R., Bayley, M. and Goodman, A. (2010). *Ethnicity and Alcohol: A Review of the Literature*. www.jrf.org.uk.

Hutchinson, R. (1998). *Aleister Crowley: The Beast Demystified*. Edinburgh: Mainstream Publishing.

IAPT, DrugScope and NTA (2012). *Improving Access to Psychological Therapies: Positive Practice Guide for Working with People Who Use Drugs and Alcohol*. www.iapt.nhs.uk/silo/files/iaptdrugandalcoholpositivepracticeguide.pdf.

IAS (Institute of Alcohol Studies) (2013). *Older People and Alcohol. Factsheet*. www.ias.org.uk.

International Opium Convention (1912). *International Opium Convention*. www.worldlii.org/int/other/LNTSer/1922/29.html.

Ipsos MORI (2011). *Scottish Schools Adolescent Lifestyle and Substance Use Survey (SALSUS) National Report 2010*. www.drugmisuse.isdscotland.org/publications/local/SALSUS_2010.pdf.

Jarvis, T., Tebutt, J., Mattick, R. and Shand, F. (2005). *Treatment Approaches to Drug and Alcohol Dependence. An Introductory Guide* (2nd edn). Chichester: John Wiley.

Johnston, L. (2013). 'Wrap around service'. *Druglink* (January/February 2013). London: DrugScop).

Jones, A., Donmall, M., Millar, T., Moody, A., Weston, S., Anderson, T., Gittins, M., Abeywardana, V. and D'Souza, J. (2009). *The Drug Treatment Outcome Research Study (DTORS). Quantitative Study: Summary Report*. www.dtors.org.uk/QuantitativeStudy.apx.

Judge, M. (2012). 'Entry point'. *Drink and Drug News* (December 2012). Ashford: C. J. Wellings.

Keene, J. (2010). *Understanding Drug Misuse*. Basingstoke: Palgrave Macmillan.

Kelly, J., Hoeppner, B., Stout, R. and Pagano, M. (2012). 'Determining the relative importance of the mechanisms of behavior change within Alcoholics Anonymous: a multiple mediator analysis'. *Addiction*, 107 (2), 289–99.

Keogh, P., Reid, D., Borne, A., Weatherburn, P., Hickson, F., Jessop, K. and Hammond, G. (2009). *Wasted Opportunities*. www.sigmaresearch.org.uk/files/report2009c.pdf.

Kerr, A. (1999). 'American dream'. *New Scientist*, 27 November 1999.

Kessel, N. and Walton, H. (1965). *Alcoholism*. Harmondsworth: Penguin.

Khan, K. (2002). 'Culture before client'. *Druglink* (November/December 2002). London: DrugScope.

Khantzian, E. (1995). 'Causes of substance abuse: psychological (psychoanalytic) perspective'. In J. Jaffe (ed.), *Encyclopaedia of Drugs and Alcohol*. New York: Macmillan.

Khantzian, E. (1997). 'The self-medicating hypothesis of substance use disorders: a reconsideration and recent applications'. *Harvard review of Psychiatry*, 4 (5), 231–44.

Kim, Y., Myung, S.-K., Jeon, Y.-J., Lee, E.-H., Park, C.-h., Seo, H. and Huh, B. (2011). 'Effectiveness of pharmalogical therapy for smoking cessation in adolescent smokers: meta-analysis of randomized controlled trials'. *American Journal of Health-System Pharmacy*, 68 (3), 219–26.

Kirby, A., McSweeney, T., Turnbull, P. and Bhardwa, B. (2011). *Engaging Substance Misusing Offenders: A Rapid Review of the Substance Misuse Treatment Literature*. www.icpr.org.uk/.

Know the Score (2012). *Amyl Nitrite*. http://knowthescore.info (accessed 23 December 2013).

Kroll, B. and Taylor, A. (2003). *Parental Substance Misuse and Child Welfare*. London: Jessica Kingsley.

Kroll, B. and Taylor, A. (2013). *Interventions for Children and Families Where There Is Parental Drug Misuse*. Department of Health. http://dmri.lshtm.ac.uk/pdfs/Kroll%20summary.pdf (accessed 13 August 2013).

Lemert, E. (1967). *Human Deviance, Social Problems and Social Control*. Englewood Cliffs: Prentice Hall.

Levine, J. (1995). *Introduction to Alcoholism Counseling: A Bio-Psycho-Social Approach* (2nd edn). London: Taylor and Francis.

Liddle, H. (2010). 'Treating adolescent substance abuse using multidimensional family therapy'. In J. Weisz and A. Kazdin (eds), *Evidence-based Psychotherapies for Children and Adolescents* (2nd edn). New York: Guilford Press.

Light, A. and Torrance, E. (1929). 'Opium addiction: VI. The effects of abrupt withdrawal followed by readministration of morphine in human addicts with special reference to the composition of the blood, the circulation and the metabolism'. *Archives of Internal Medicine*, 44 (1), 1–16.

Light, J. (2010). 'Alcohol licensing, crime and disorder'. In M. Herzog-Evans (ed.), *Transnational Criminological Manual*. Nijmegen: Wolf Legal Publishing.

Lloyd, C. (1998). 'Risk factors for problem drug use: identifying vulnerable groups'. *Drugs: Education, Prevention and Policy*, 5 (3), 217–32.

LM (2007). Private correspondence between author and NA member LM.

London Borough of Camden (2007). *Refining the Routes. Domestic Violence and Substance Misuse: Policies Procedures and Protocols for Partnership Work in Camden*. www.camden.gov.uk/ccm/content/policing-and-public-safety/domestic-violence/file-storage-items/refining-the-routes---domestic-violence-and-substance-misuse-policies-procedures-and-protocols-for-partnership-work-in-camden-.en;jsessionid=B03FA7BB72F46004DCC24B5E4A898F23.

Madras, B., Compton, W., Avula, D., Stegbauer, T., Stein, J. and Clark, H. (2009). 'Screening, brief interventions, referral to treatment (SBIRT) for illicit drug and alcohol use at multiple healthcare sites: comparison at intake and six months later'. *Drug and Alcohol Dependence*, 99 (1–3), 280–95.

Malcolm, K. (2013). Personal correspondence with the author.

Marlatt, G. and Donovan, D. (eds) (2005). *Relapse Prevention: Maintenance Strategies in the Treatment of Addictive Behaviors* (2nd edn). New York: Guilford Press.

Marlatt G., Parks, G. and Witkiewitz, D. (2002). *Clinical Guidelines for Implementing Relapse Prevention Therapy*. Illinois Behavioral Health Management Project. www.bhrm.org/index.htm.

Marlatt, G. and Witkiewitz, D. (2005). 'Relapse prevention for alcohol and drug problems'. In G. Marlatt and D. Donovan (eds), *Relapse Prevention: Maintenance Strategies in the Treatment of Addictive Behaviors* (2nd edn). New York: Guilford Press.

Martin, S., Maxwell, C., White, H. and Zhang, Y. (2004). 'Trends in alcohol use, cocaine use, and Ccrime: 1989–1998'. *Journal of Drug Issues*, 34 (20), 333–59.

Massey, S., Neiderhiser, J., Shaw, D., Leve, L., Ganiban, J. and Reiss, D. (2012). 'Maternal self concept as a provider and cessation of substance use during pregnancy', *Addictive Behaviors*, 37 (8), 956–61.

May, P. and Gossage, J. (2013). *Estimating the Prevalence of Fetal Alcohol Syndrome: A Summary*. http://pubs.niaaa.nih.gov/publications/arh25-3/159-167.htm (accessed 14 August 2013).

Mayer, J. and Timms, N. (1970). *The Client Speaks*. London: Routledge and Keegan Paul.

McCoard, S., Skellington Orr, K., McKellar, J., Paterson, C. and Scott, G. (2011). *Scoping Study of Interventions for Offenders with Alcohol Problems in Community Justice Settings.* www.ohrn.nhs.uk/resource/policy/InterventionsforOffenders Alcohol.pdf.

McGuire, J. (2007). 'Programmes for probationers'. In G. McIvor and P. Raynor (eds), *Developments in Social Work with Offenders.* London: Jessica Kingsley.

McIntosh, J., MacAskill, S., Eadie, D., Curtice, J., McKeganey, N., Hastings, G., Hay, G. and Gannon, M. (2006). *Evaluation and Description of Drug Projects Working with Young People and Families Funded by Lloyds TSB Foundation.* www. scotland.gov.uk.

McIntosh, J. and McKeganey, N. (2002). *Beating the Dragon: The Recovery from Dependent Drug Use.* Harlow: Pearson Education.

McKay, J., Carise, D., Dennis, M., Dupont, R., Humphreys, K., Kemp, J., Reynolds, D., White, W., Armstrong, R., Chalk, M., Haberle, B., McLellan, T., O'Connor, G., Pakull, B. and Schwarzlose, J. (2009). 'Extending the benefits of addiction treatment: practical strategies for continuing care and recovery'. *Journal of Substance Abuse Treatment,* 36 (2), 127–30.

McKeganey, M., Neale, J. and Robertson, M. (2005). 'Physical and sexual abuse among drug users contacting drug treatment services in Scotland'. *Drugs: Education, Prevention and Policy,* 12 (3), 223–32.

McKinlay, W., Forsyth, A. and Khan, F. (2009). *Alcohol and Violence amongst Young Male Offenders in Scotland (1979–2009).* www.sps.gov.uk.

McLellan, T., Grissom, G., Zanis, D., Randall, M., Brill, P., O'Brien, C. and Charles, P. (1997). 'Problem–service 'matching' in addiction treatment: a prospective study in 4 programs'. *Archives of General Psychiatry,* 54 (8), 730–5.

McMurran, M. (1994). *The Psychology of Addiction.* London: Taylor and Francis.

McMurran, M. (1995). *Motivational Interviewing: A Strategic Counselling Approach.* Video and literature. Market Harborough: Insight Video Graphics.

McMurran, M. (2009). 'Motivational interviewing with offenders: A systematic review'. *Legal and Criminological Psychology,* 14, 83–100.

McNeill, F. (2009). *Towards Effective Practice in Offender Supervision.* www.sccjr.ac.uk/publications/towards-effective-practice-in-offender-supervision.

McSweeney, T., Stevens, A., Hunt, N. and Turnbull, P. (2007). 'Twisting arms or a helping hand? Assessing the impact of 'coerced' or comparable 'voluntary' drug treatment options'. *British Journal of Criminology,* 47 (3), 470–90.

McSweeney, T., Turnbull, P. and Hough, M. (2008). *The Treatment and Supervision of Drug-dependent Offenders. A Review of the Literature Prepared by the UK Drug Policy Commission.* www.ukdpc.org.uk.

McWhirter, J. (2008). 'Drug and alcohol use by young people; problems and policy responses'. In J. McWhirter and H. Mir (eds), *The Essential Guide to Working with Young People about Drugs and Alcohol.* London: DrugScope.

Merrill, J. (2002). 'Medical approaches and prescribing: drugs'. In T. Petersen and A. McBride (eds), *Working with Substance Misusers. A Guide to Theory and Practice.* London: Routledge.

Merton, R. (1968). *Social Theory and Social Structure.* Toronto: Collier-Macmillan.

Miech, R., Bohnert, A., Heard, K. and Boardman, J. (2013). 'Increasing use of nonmedical analgesics among younger cohorts in the United States: a birth cohort effect'. *Journal of Adolescent Health,* 52 (10), 35–4.

Millard, B. and Smith, K. (2011). 'Attitudes to drug-taking behaviour and location and source of obtaining drugs'. In K. Smith and J. Flatley (eds), *Drug Misuse Declared: Findings of the British Crime Survey 2010/11.* www.gov.uk.

Miller, N. and Flaherty, J. (2000). 'Effectiveness of coerced addiction treatment (alternative consequences); A review of the clinical research'. *Journal of Substance Abuse Treatment*, 18 (1), 9–16.

Miller, W. (1983). 'Motivational interviewing with problem drinkers'. *Behavioural Psychotherapy*, 11 (20), 147–72.

Miller, W. (2005). 'A message from Albuquerque'. *Alcohol and Drug Findings*, Issue 13. London: Drug and Alcohol Findings.

Miller, W., Meyers, M. and Hiller-Sturmhöfel, S. (1999). 'The community-reinforcement approach'. *Addiction Research and Health*, 23 (2), 116–21.

Miller, W. and Page, A. (1991). 'Warm turkey: other routes to abstinence'. *Journal of Substance Abuse Treatment*, 8 (4), 227–32.

Miller, W. and Rollnick, S. (eds) (2002). *Motivational Interviewing* (2nd edn). London: Guilford Press.

Miller, W. and Rollnick, S. (2009). 'Ten things motivational interviewing is not'. *Behavioural and Cognitive Psychotherapy*, 37, 129–40.

Miller, W. and Rollnick, S. (eds) (2013). *Motivational Interviewing* (3rd edn). London: Guilford Press.

Miller, W. and Wilbourne, P. (2002). 'Mesa Grande: a methodological analysis of clinical trials of treatments for alcohol use disorders'. *Addiction*, 97 (3), 265–77.

MindWise (2013). Personal correspondence with the author.

Ministry of Justice (2010). *NOM-S Alcohol Interventions Guidance Including Revised Guidance on Managing the Alcohol Treatment Requirement (ART)- Update of Annex B to Probation Circular 57/2005.* http://ranzetta.typepad.com/files/noms-alcohol-interventions-guidance.pdf.

Murray, S. (2006). 'Keeping it out of the Family'. *Drink and Drug News* (25 September 2006). Ashford: C. J. Wellings.

NAT (2013). *HIV and Injecting Drug Use.* www.nat.org.uk.

National Institute on Alcohol Abuse and Alcoholism (2007). *Alcohol Metabolism: An Update.* http://pubs.niaaa.nih.gov/publications/AA72/AA72.htm.

National Institute on Alcohol Abuse and Alcoholism (1999). *Brief Interventions for Alcohol Problems.* http://pubs.niaaa.nih.gov/publications/aa43.htm.

National Statistics for Scotland (2012). *Drug-related Deaths in Scotland in 2011.* www.gro-scotland.gov.uk.

Newcombe, R. (2009). *The Need for Speed: Substitute Prescribing to Amphetamine Users in Britain.* Presentation to National Drug Treatment Conference, London, March 2009. www.exchangesupplies.org/conferences/NDTC/2009_NDTC/presentations/russell_newcombe.html.

NHS (2013). *NHS Choices.* www.nhs.uk.

NHS Fife (2011). *Guidelines for Methadone Titration in Opioid Dependence.* www.fifeadtc.scot.nhs.uk.

NHS Health Scotland (2005). *Scotland's Mental Health. Manual.* Edinburgh: NHS Health Scotland.

NHS Scotland (2011). *Alcohol Brief Interventions Professional Pack Reprinted.* www.healthscotland.com/documents/3273.aspx.

NICE (National Institute for Health and Care Excellence) (2006). *Brief Interventions and Referral for Smoking Cessation.* www.nice.org.uk/.

NICE (2007a). *Drug Misuse. Psychosocial Interventions. Clinical Guidelines 51.* www.nice.org.uk/.

NICE (2007b). *Methadone and Buprenorphine for the Management of Opioid Dependence.* www.nice.org.uk/.

NICE (2007c). *Drug Misuse. Opioid Detoxification. Clinical Guidelines 52.* www.nice.org.uk/.

NICE (2009). *Needle and Syringe Programmes.* http://guidance.nice.org.uk/ph18.

NICE (2011a). *Psychosis with Coexisting Substance Misuse.* www.nice.org.uk/cg120.

NICE (2011b). *Alcohol-use Disorders: Diagnosis, Assessment and Management of Harmful Drinking and Alcohol Dependence.* www.nice.org.uk/CG115.

NICE (2013). *Tobacco: Harm-Reduction Approaches to Smoking.* http://guidance. nice.org.uk/PH45.

North West Evening Mail (2013). 'Evening Mail starts campaign to keep Cumbria safe from menace of legal highs'. *North West Evening Mail* online, 8 July 2013. www.nwemail.co.uk.

NTA (National Treatment Agency for Substance Misuse) (2002). *Treating Cocaine/Crack Dependence.* www.nta.nhs.uk.

NTA (2006a). *Models of Care for Treatment of Adult Drug Misusers: Update 2006.* www.nta.nhs.uk.

NTA (2006b). *Care Planning Practice Guide.* www.nta.nhs.uk.

NTA (2007). *Assessing Young People for Substance Misuse.* www.nta.nhs.uk.

NTA (2008). *Supporting and Involving Carers. A Guide for Commissioners and Providers.* www.nta.nhs.uk.

NTA (2009). *Diversity: Learning from Good Practice in the Field.* www.nta.nhs.uk.

NTA (2010). *Injecting Drug Use in England: A Declining Trend.* www.nta.nhs.uk.

NTA (2012a). *Medications in Recovery: Re-orientating Drug Dependence Treatment.* www.nta.nhs.uk.

NTA (2012b). *Club Drugs: Emerging Trends and Risks.* www.nta.nhs.uk.

NTA (2012c). *The Role of Residential Rehab in an Integrated Treatment System.* www.nta.nhs.uk.

NTA (2012d). *Parents with Drug Problems: How Treatment Helps Families.* www.nta.nhs.uk.

NTA (2012e). *Substance Misuse among Young People 2011–12.* www.nta.nhs.uk.

NTA (2012f). *The Impact of Drug Treatment on Reconviction.* www.nta.nhs.uk.

NTA (2013a). *Falling Drug Use: The Impact of Treatment.* www.nta.nhs.uk.

NTA (2013b). *Helping Clients to Access and Engage with Mutual Aid.* www.nta.nhs.uk/uploads/rr_facilitatingmutualaid_jan2013[0].pdf.

Nutt, D. (2009). 'Equasy – An overlooked addiction with implications for the current debate on drug harms'. *Journal of Psychopharmacology*, 23 (1) 3–5.

Nutt, D., King, L., Saulsbury, W. and Blakemore, C. (2007). 'Development of a rational scale to assess the harms of drugs of potential misuse'. *The Lancet*, 369 (9566), 1047–53.

Nutt, D., King, L. and Phillips, L. (2010). 'Drug harms in the UK: a multicriteria decision analysis'. *The Lancet*, 376 (9752), 1558–65.

O'Brien, S., Hammond, H. and McKinnon, M. (2003). *Report of the Caleb Ness Enquiry.* Edinburgh: Edinburgh and Lothians Child Protection Committee.

Office of National Statistics (2012). *General Lifestyle Survey Overview. A Report on the 2010 General Lifestyle Survey.* www.ons.gov.uk/ons/index.html.

Ondersma, S., Winhusen, T. and Lewis, D. (2010). 'External pressure, motivation, and treatment outcome amongst substance-using women'. *Drug and Alcohol Dependence*, 107 (2–3), 149–53.

Orange, A. (2013). *The Funny Spirituality of Bill Wilson and AA.* www.orange-papers.org/orange-funny_spirituality.html.

Orford, J. (2001). *Excessive Appetites: A Psychological View of Addictions* (2nd edn). Chichester: John Wiley.

Orford, J., Templeton, L., Velleman, R. and Copello, A. (2010a). 'Methods of assessment for affected family members'. *Drugs: Education, Prevention and Policy*, 17 (s1), 75–85.

Orford, J., Velleman, R., Copello, A., Templeton, L. and Ibanga, A. (2010b). 'The experiences of affected family members: a summary of two decades of qualitative research'. *Drugs: Education, Prevention and Policy*, 17 (s1), 44–62.

Pacula, R. (2011). 'Substance use and recessions: what can be learned from economic analyses of alcohol?' *International Journal of Drug Policy*, 22 (5), 326–34.

Parker, C. (undated). *Bird Lives*. www.birdlives.co.uk (accessed 8 July 2013).

Peele, S. (1983). *Out of the Habit Trap: Five Stages to Freedom*. http://peele.net/lib/trap.php.

Perkins, K., Conklin, C. and Levine, M. (2008). *Cognitive-Behavioral Therapy for Smoking Cessation. A Practical Guidebook to the Most Effective Interventions*. Abingdon: Routledge.

Peto, R., Darby, S., Deo, H., Silcocks, P., Whiteley, E. and Doll, R. (2000). 'Smoking, smoking cessation, and lung cancer in the UK since 1950: combination of national statistics with two case control studies'. *BMJ*, 321 (7257), 323–9.

Pierce, C., O'Brien, C., Kenny, P. and Vanderschuren, L. (2012). 'Rational development of addiction pharmacotherapies: successes, failures and prospects'. *Perspectives in Medicine*, 2 (6).

Plant, M. (2009). *Factsheet: Drinking Patterns*. www.alcoholconcern.org.uk.

Platt, J., Husband, S. and Taube, D. (1990–91). 'Major psychotherapeutic modalities for heroin addiction: a brief overview'. *International Journal of the Addictions*, 25 (12A), 1453–77.

Poe, E. A. (undated). *The Edgar Allan Poe Society of Baltimore*. www.eapoe.org/works/letters/p4811030.htm.

Potts, N. (2005). 'Problem drug use and child protection: interagency working and policies in Scotland'. *Infant* 6 (1), 189–93.

Preston, A. and Derricot, J. (1999). *The Safer Injecting Handbook* (2nd edn). Dorchester: Exchange.

Prochaska, J., DiClemente, C. and Norcross, J. (1992). 'In search of how people change: applications to addictive behaviors'. *American Psychologist*, 47 (9), 1102–14.

Project Match Research Group (1997). 'Matching alcoholism treatments to client heterogeneity: Project MATCH posttreatment drinking outcomes'. *Journal of Studies on Alcohol*, 58 (1), 7–29.

Proude, E., Lapatko, O., Lintzeris, N. and Haber, P. (2009). *The Treatment of Alcohol problems: A Review of the Evidence*. www.health.gov.au/internet/alcohol/publishing.nsf/Content/877AC32A7ADD8AEECA2576C00007B5C7/$File/evid.pdf.

Pycroft, A. (2010). *Understanding and Working with Substance Misusers*. London: Sage.

Race, P. (2012). *Ripples Model of Learning: Seven Factors Underpinning Successful Learning*. Presentation. http://phil-race.co.uk/most-popular-downloads.

Raistrick, D., Heather, N. and Godfrey, C. (2006). *Review of the Effectiveness of Treatment for Alcohol Problems*. London: NTA.

Reading, B. (2002). 'The application of Bowlby's attachment theory to the psychotherapy of the addictions'. In M. Weegmann and R. Cohen (eds), *The Psychodynamics of Addiction*. London: Whurr.

Reckitt Benckiser (2013). *Pharmaceutical. Suboxone*. www.rb.com/media-investors/category-performance/pharmaceutical.

Ritter, A. and Cameron, J. (2006). 'A review of the efficacy and effectiveness of harm reduction strategies for alcohol, tobacco and illicit drugs'. *Drug and Alcohol Review*, 25 (6), 611–24.

Roberts, M. (2010). *Young People's Drug and Alcohol Treatment at the Crossroads*. www.drugscope.org.uk.

Roberts, S. and Nuru-Jeter, A. (2010). 'Women's perspectives on screening for alcohol and drug use in prenatal care'. *Women's Health Issues*, 20 (3), 193–200.

Robson, P. (2009). *Forbidden Drugs*. Oxford: Oxford University Press.

Rohsenow, D., Corbett, R. and Devine, D. (1988). 'Molested as children: a hidden contribution to substance abuse?' *Journal of Substance Abuse Treatment*, 5 (1), 13–18.

Rolles, S. (2009). *After the War on Drugs: Blueprint for Regulation*. Bristol: Transform.

Roman, P. and Blum, T. (2002). *Workplace and Alcohol Problem Prevention*. http://pubs.niaaa.nih.gov/publications/arh26-1/49-57.htm.

Room, R. (1980). 'Treatment-seeking populations and larger realities'. In G. Edwards and M. Grant (eds), *Alcoholism Treatment in Transition*. London: Croom Helm.

Rorstad, P. and Checinski, K. (1996). *Dual Diagnosis: Facing the Challenge*. Guildford: Wynne Howard Publishing.

Royal College of Psychiatrists (2012). *Practice Standards for Young People with Substance Misuse Problems*. www.rcpsych.ac.uk.

Royal College of Psychiatrists and the Royal College of Physicians (2000). *Drugs: Dilemmas and Choices*. London: Gaskell.

Royal Society for the Encouragement of Arts, Manufactures and Commerce (2007). *Drugs- facing facts. The Report of the RSA Commission on Illegal Drugs, Communities and Public Policy*. www.thersa.org.

Ryder, D., Salmon, A. and Walker, N. (2001). *Drug Use and Drug-related Harm*. Melbourne: IP Communications.

SA (2011). Private correspondence between author and consultant psychiatrist SA.

Saladin, M. and Santa Ana, E. (2004). 'Controlled drinking: more than just a controversy'. *Current Opinion in Psychiatry*, 17 (3), 175–87.

Saunders, B. (1994). 'The cognitive-behavioural approach to the management of addictive behaviour'. In J. Chick and R. Cantwell (eds), *Seminars in Alcohol and Drug Misuse*. London: Gaskell.

Saunders, B. (1996). 'Are addictions inherited?'. In C. Wilkinson and B. Saunders (eds), *Perspectives in Addiction: Making Sense of Issues*. Perth WA: William Montgomery.

Saunders, B. and Allsop, S. (1991). 'Helping those who relapse'. In R. Davidson, S. Rollnik and I. MacEwan (eds), *Counselling Problem Drinkers*. London: Routledge.

Saunders, W. and Kershaw, P. (1979). 'Spontaneous remission from alcoholism: a community study'. *British Journal of Addiction*, 74 (3), 251–65.

ScotchWhisky.net (2012). 'Scotch Whisky Industry Now in a "Golden Age", Says Benriach's Walker'. News Release, 29 August 2012. www.scotchwhisky.net/news/index.php.

Scott, C. and Dennis, M. (2009). 'Results from two randomized clinical trials evaluating the impact of quarterly recovery management checkups with adult chronic substance abusers'. *Addiction*, 104 (6), 959–71.

Scottish Council on Alcoholism (1983). *Advanced Training Package on Controlled Drinking*. Glasgow: Scottish Council on Alcoholism.

Scottish Executive (2003a). *Getting Our Priorities Right: Good Practice Guidance for Working with Children and Families Affected by Substance Misuse*. www.scotland.gov.uk.

Scottish Executive (2003b). *Mind the Gaps. Meeting the Needs of People with Co-occurring Substance Misuse and Mental Health Problems*. www.scotland.gov.uk.

Scottish Executive (2004). *Young People with, or at Risk of Developing, Problematic Substance Use*. www.scotland.gov.uk.

Scottish Government (2007). *Mental Health in Scotland. Closing the Gaps – Making a Difference*. www.scotland.gov.uk.

Scottish Government (2008). *The Road to Recovery*. www.scotland.gov.uk.

Scottish Government (2009). *Changing Scotland's Relationship with Alcohol: A Framework for Action*. www.scotland.gov.uk.

Scottish Government (2012). *2011/12 Scottish Crime and Justice Survey: Drug Use*. www.scotland.gov.uk.

Scottish Intercollegiate Guidelines Network (2004). *The Management of Harmful Drinking and Alcohol Dependence in Primary Care*. www.sign.ac.uk/guidelines/fulltext/74/.

Sellman, D. (2010). 'The 10 most important things known about addiction'. *Addiction*, 105 (1), 6–13.

Shapiro, H. (ed.) (2008). *The Essential Student Reader on Drugs*. London: DrugScope.

Shapiro, H. (2010). *The Essential Guide to Drugs and Alcohol* (14th edn). London: DrugScope)

Sheldon, B. (2011). *Cognitive-Behavioural Therapy. Research and Practice in Health and Social Care* (2nd edn). London: Routledge.

Shields, P. (2011). 'Long-term nicotine replacement therapy: cancer risks in context'. *Cancer Prevention Research (Phila)*, 4 (11), 1719–23.

Siegal, S. (2001). 'Pavlovian conditioning and drug overdose: when tolerance fails'. *Addiction Research and Theory*, 9 (5), 503–13.

Skinner, B. (1953). *Science and Human Behavior*. New York: The Free Press.

Small, A., Kampman, K., Plebani, J., De Jesus Quinn, M., Peoples, L. and Lynch, K. (2009). 'Tolerance and sensitization to the effects of cocaine use in humans: a retrospective study of long-term cocaine users in Philadelphia'. *Substance Use and Misuse*, 44 (13), 1888–98.

SMART Recovery (2013). *SMART Recovery UK*. www.smartrecovery.org.uk.

Smedslund, G., Berg, R., Hammerstrøm, K., Steiro, A., Leiknes, K., Dahl, H. and Karlsen, K. (2011). 'Motivational interviewing for substance abuse'. *Cochrane Library*. www.thecochranelibrary.com/view/0/index.html.

Smith, K. and Flatley, J. (eds) (2011). *Drug Misuse Declared: Findings of the British Crime Survey 2010/11*. www.gov.uk.

Smith, R. (1995). *'How Can I Help?'* Booklet. Paisley: Renfrew Council on Alcohol.

Sobell, L., Cunningham, J. and Sobell, M. (1996). 'Recovery from alcohol problems with and without treatment: prevalence in two population studies'. *American Journal of Public Health*, 86 (7), 966–72.

Sobell, L., Ellingstad, P. and Sobell, M. (2000). 'Natural recovery from alcohol and drug problems: methodological review of the research with suggestions for future directions'. *Addiction*, 95 (5), 749–64.

Social Issues Research Centre (1998). *Social and Cultural Aspects of Drinking*. www.sirc.org/publik/social_drinking.pdf.

Soyka, M. (2000). 'Substance misuse, psychiatric disorder and violent and disturbed behaviour'. *British Journal of Psychiatry*, 176 (4), 345–50.

Stall, R. and Biernacki, P. (1986). 'Spontaneous remission from the problematic use of substances: an inductive model derived from a comparative analysis of the alcohol, opiate, tobacco and food/obesity literature'. *The International Journal of Addictions*, 21 (1), 1–23.

Stark, M. (1992). 'Dropping out of substance abuse treatment: a clinically orientated review'. *Clinical Psychology Review*, 12 (1), 93–116.

Stepping Stones (2013). *Bill's Story*. www.steppingstones.org/billsstory.html (accessed 15 August 2012).

Strang, J., Groshkova, T. and Metrebian, N. (2012). *New Heroin-Assisted Treatment.* EMCCDA Insights 11. www.emcdda.europa.eu/attachements.cfm/att_154996_EN_Heroin%20Insight.pdf.

Stuber, J., Galea, S. and Link, B. (2009). 'Stigma and smoking: the consequences of our good intentions'. *Social Service Review*, 83 (4), 585–609.

Substance Create (2013a). *Snort.* (Leaflet). www.substance.org.uk.

Substance Create (2013b). *Swallow.* (Leaflet). www.substance.org.uk.

Sullivan, T. and Farrell, A. (2002). 'Risk factors'. In C. Essau (ed.), *Substance Abuse and Dependence in Adolescence.* Hove: Brunner-Routledge.

Sutherland, G. (2002). 'Current approaches to the management of smoking cessation'. *Drugs*, 62 (Suppl 2), 53–61.

Sweat, N. (1952). *The "whiskey speech".* http://en.wikipedia.org/wiki/Noah_S._Sweat.

Sykes, C. and Marks, D. (2001). 'Effectiveness of a cognitive behavioural self-help programme for smokers in London, UK'. *Health Promotion International*, 16 (3), 255–60.

Templeton, L., Zohhadi, S., Galvani, S. and Velleman, R. (2006). *"Looking Beyond Risk". Parental Substance Misuse: Scoping Study.* www.scotland.gov.uk.

Thom, B. and Green, A. (1996). 'Services for women: the way forward'. In L. Harrisson (ed.), *Alcohol Problems in the Community.* London: Routledge.

Thorley, A. (1980). 'Medical responses to problem drinking'. *Medicine* (3rd Series), 35, 1816–22.

Tobacco in Australia (2013). *International Comparisons of Smoking Prevalence.* www.tobaccoinaustralia.org.au.

Trotter, C. (2006). *Working with Involuntary Clients: A Guide to Practice* (2nd edn). London: Sage.

Trueman, J. (2009). *Detox Your Finances: The Ultimate Book of Money Matters for Women.* London: Allison and Busby.

Turning Point (2004). *Routes to Treatment: Drugs and Crime.* London: Turning Point.

Turning Point (2007). *Dual Diagnosis: Good Practice Handbook.* www.turning-point.co.uk/media/170796/dualdiagnosisgoodpracticehandbook.pdf.

Twain, M (undated). *Good Reads.* www.goodreads.com.

Uhl, G. (1995). 'Genetic Factors'. In J. Jaffe (ed.), *Encyclopaedia of Drugs and Alcohol.* Library: Macmillan Library Reference.

UK Drug Policy Commission (2008). *A Vision of Recovery.* www.ukdpc.org.uk.

UK Drug Policy Commission (2010a). *Getting Serious about Stigma: The Problem with Stigmatising Drug Users. An Overview.* www.ukdpc.org.uk.

UK Drug Policy Commission (2010b). *Drugs and Diversity: Ethnic Minority Groups. Learning from the Evidence.* www.ukdpc.org.uk.

UKATT Research Team (2005). 'Effectiveness of treatment for alcohol problems: findings of the randomised alcohol treatment trial (UKATT)'. *BMJ*, 331, 541.

Unal, B., Critchley, J. and Capewell, S. (2003). 'Impact of smoking reduction on coronary heart disease mortality trends during 1981–2000 in England and Wales'. *Tobacco Induced Diseases*, 1, 185.

Van Grundy, K. and Rebellon, C. (2010). ' A life-course perspective on the "gateway hypothesis"'. *Journal of Health and Social Behavior*, 51 (3), 244–59.

Velleman, R. (2010). 'The policy context: reversing a state of neglect'. *Drugs: Education, Prevention and Policy*, 17 (s1), 8–35.

Velleman, R. and Templeton, L. (2007). 'Understanding and modifying the impact of parents' substance misuse on children'. *Advances in Psychiatric Treatment*, 13, 79–89.

Waldorf, D. and Biernacki, P. (2008). *Natural Recovery from Heroin Addiction: A Review of the Incident Literature.* http://drugtext.org.

Ward, J., Henderson, Z. and Pearson, G. (2003). *One Problem among Many: Drug Use among Care Leavers in Transition to Independent Living.* London: Home Office.

Wardle, I. (2012). 'Five years of recovery: December 2005 to December 2010 – From challenge to orthodoxy'. *Drugs: Education, Prevention and Policy,* 19 (4), 294–8.

Weaver, T., Madden, P., Charles, V., Stimson, G., Renton, A., Tyrer, P., Barnes, T., Bench, C., Middleton, H., Wright, N., Paterson, S., Shanahan, W., Seivewright, N. and Ford, C. (2003). 'Comorbidity of substance misuse and mental illness in community mental health and substance misuse services'. *British Journal of Psychiatry,* 183 (4), 304–13.

Welsh Government (2013). *Service Framework to Meet the Needs of People with Co-occurring Substance Misuse and Mental Health Problems.* http://wales.gov.uk/?lang=en.

West, R. (2006). *Theory of Addiction.* Oxford: Blackwell.

White, W. (2011). 'States man'. *Drink and Drug News* (December 2011). Ashford: C. J. Wellings.

White, W. (2012). *The Psychology of Addiction Recovery: An Interview with William R. Miller.* www.williamwhitepapers.com.

Whittaker, A. (2011). *The Essential Guide to Problem Substance Use During Pregnancy* (updated edn). London: DrugScope.

WHO (World Health Organization) (2013a). *ICD 10 Mental and Behavioural Disorders Due to Psychoactive Substance Use.* www.who.int/substance_abuse/terminology/ICD10ClinicalDiagnosis.pdf (accessed 10 July 2013).

WHO (2013b). *Lexicon of Alcohol and Drug Terms.* www.who.int/substance_abuse/terminology/who_lexicon/en/.

WHO (2013c). *Global Health Observatory: Country Statistics.* www.who.int/gho/countries/en (accessed 13 July 2013).

Whyte, B. and McNeill, F. (2007). *Reducing Reoffending: Social Work and Community Justice in Scotland.* Edinburgh: Willan Publishing.

Wilkinson, R and Pickett, K. (2010). *The Spirit Level.* London: Penguin.

Williams, C. (2002). 'Twelve step approaches'. In T. Petersen and A. McBride (eds), *Working with Substance Misusers: A Guide to Theory and Practice.* Abingdon: Routledge.

Williams, R., Gilvarry, E. and Christian, J. (2004). 'Developing an evidence-based model for services'. In I. Crome, H. Ghodse, E. Gilvarry and P. McArdle (eds), *Young People and Substance Misuse.* London: Gaskell.

Witton, J. (2008). 'Contingency management: Factsheet 26'. *Druglink* (January/February 2008). London: DrugScope.

Woodhouse, K. (2004). 'Young people and smoking'. In I. Crome, H. Ghodse, E. Gilvarry and P. McArdle (eds), *Young People and Substance Misuse.* London: Gaskell.

Woolacott, N., Jones, L., Forbes, C., Mather, L., Sowden, A., Song, F., Raftery, J., Aveyard, P., Hyde, C. and Barton, P. (2002). 'The clinical effectiveness and cost effectiveness of bupropion and nicotine replacement therapy for smoking cessation: a systematic review and economic evaluation'. *Health Technology Assessment,* 6 (16), 245.

Yates, R. (2002). 'A brief history of British drug policy, 1950–2001'. *Drugs: Education, Prevention and Policy,* 9 (2), 113–24.

Zinberg, N. (1984). *Drug, Set, and Setting.* New Haven: Yale University Press.

# Index

Note: page references in **bold** indicate definition or extended examination.

5-step method, **221**
12 steps, 37, 87, 11, **164–6**, 168, 182
  see also Alcoholics Anonymous; Cocaine
    Anonymous

AA
  see Alcoholics Anonymous
ABC model Ellis), 157
abstinence, **7**, 36, 39, 83, 84, 164–7
  goal setting, **116–17**, 169–70, 175, 203, 234
  as smoking policy, 57, 138
abstinence violation effect, **181–2**, 186
abuse
  domestic, 94, 97, **112–13**, 117, 208, 224
  physical and sexual, **44–5**, 208
acamprosate, 150
acetaldehyde, 3–8, 150
  disulfiram causes build-up of, 150
  oriental flush, 38
action plan
  see care planning
acupuncture, 175
addict
  identity as, **34–5, 73–4**, 122
addiction, **3–6**, 17, 30, 35, 38, 85 ,179
  see also dependence
addictive personality, 44
administration of substances
  see ingestion of substances
adulteration
  see 'cutting' drugs
adolescents
  see young people's substance use
advertising substances, 15, 57, 62, 63
affordability of substances
  see cost of substances
Afganistan, 51
aftercare
  see follow-up care
age
  implications of, 15, 23,52, 69

restrictions on purchase, 53, 57, 62
  see also children and young people, older
    people
aggressive behaviour, 25, 196, 201, 203, 214,
    245
  see also abuse; crime
agonists, **146–7**, 148
Aids
  see HIV
Al-Anon, 214
Alateen, 214
alcohol, 8, **9**, 15, 19–20, 25, 32, **35–7**,38, 69, 89,
    **106**, **109–10**, 194, 195, 197, 202, 203,
    209, 227, 234, 245, 247, 250
  controlled drinking, **83**, 116–17, **168–72**,
    178, 203, 223, 242
  detoxification, **149**
  harm reduction, **132–5**
  interventions, **116–17**, **141**, **139–40**,
    149–151, 184–5, **152–6**
  minimum unit pricing, 25, 64
  licensing, 17, 50–1, **63–4**, 56, 65, 134, 247
  pharmacological treatments, **149–51**
  pregnancy, **209**
  dangers in withdrawal, 21, **108**, 202
Alcohol Abstinence and Monitoring
    Requirement, 247
alcoholic, 44, 83
  concept of, 3, 4, 17, 30, 37
  dementia, 9, 150, 30
  identity as, 34
  see also disease model
Alcoholics Anonymous (AA), **35–7**, 83, 87,
    **164–6**
alcoholism
  see disease model
ambivalence, **70–1**, 75, 77, 101, 110, **121–2**,
    **125–6**, 186
  regarding control of alcohol, 64
America
  see USA

amounts, 19
  assessment of, 105, **106–7**
amphetamines, **12**, 21, 59, 195, 227
analgesics, 10
anomie, 33
Antabuse (disulfiram), 150, 152, 175
antagonists, **146–7**, 148
anthrax, 20
antidepressants, 13
antisocial behaviour, 25, 38, 64, 228, 234
  see also crime
anxiety, 152, 197, 199, 200
  related to substance use, 11–12, 152, 175,
    195
arrest, 140, 247
ascorbic acid (vitamin C), 136
aspirin, 10
assessment, 95, **100–15**, 139, 223, 252
  children affected by parental problems,
    **211–13**
  children and young people, 231, **232–4**
  psychological distress, **199–202**
  significant adults, **219–20**
AUDIT (assessment questionnaire), 104, 141,
  **252–4**
availability of substances, 24, **31**, 53, 62, 64,
  229

barbiturates, 9–10
  dangers in withdrawal, 21, 108, 202
barriers
  to engagement, 96, 98, 233, 236, 249
  to recovery, 8, 74, 105, 110–11, 163
behavioural theories of problematic use
  see learning theories of problematic use
benefits of use
  acknowledging benefits, 127
  economic, 51
  in medicine, **51**
  personal, **18**, 43, 66, 162, 180, 194
benzodiazepines, **10**, 23
  detoxification, **152**
  pregnancy, 209
  risks in withdrawal, 21, **108**, 202
Benzo Fury, 14
benzylpiperazine (BZP), 14
Best, George, 49
bipolar disorder, 200
  and cannabis, 196
bingeing, 6, 109, 147, 149, 209, 234
  on stimulants, 26, 173, 175
bio-psycho-social theory of problematic use,
  **47–8**, 217, 228

black and minority ethnic communities, 34, 52,
  96, **97–8**, 220
Black Mamba, 14
black market, 24, 25, 52, 53, 63
blackouts
  excessive drinking, 195
blood borne viruses, 22, 88, 135, 136, 137
  see also hepatitis
BME communities
  see black and minority ethnic communities
Bobo doll, 42
Bolivia, 50
brain, 8–9, 15, 22, 23, 39, 146
  damage to, 150, 195, 209
  see also central nervous system
'brain disease'
  addiction as, 38
brief interventions, 86, **132**, 134, **140–2**, 173,
  231, 25–4
British system (drug control), 55, 59, 147
buprenorphine (Subutex), 88, **146–7**, 148
bupropion (Zyban), 11, 153
BZP (benzylpiperazine), 14

caffeine, 12, 20, 21, 53, 148
Canada
  heroin prescribing, 147
cannabis, **13**, 59, 107, 234
  alternative model for regulation, **62–3**
  cafes, 63
  as gateway drug, 46
  interventions, **139**, 140
  mental health, 13, 19, 194, **195–6**, 197
  potential therapeutic benefits, 6, 13, 51
  pregnancy, 209
  use among young people, 227
cannabinoids
  synthetic, 14
care planning, 100, 104, 105, 110, 111, **114–19**,
  125, 140, 141, 155–6, 160, 186
  children affected by parental problems, **214**
  children and young people, **232–5**
  involuntary service users, **242**
  psychological distress, 200, **202–3**
  significant adults, **220–2**, 223
Care Programme Approach, 198
carers
  children as, 208, 214
  kinship, 214
  see also significant adults
cathinones, 14
CBT
  see cognitive behavioural therapy

central nervous system, 5, **8–9**, 15, 21, 22, **38–9**, 153

Champix (varenicline), 153

change (nature of), **67–78**, 87, 92, 122

    unassisted, **68–74**

    see also cycle of change, maintaining change, recovery (capital)

Charles II and coffee houses, 52

'chasing' heroin, 11, 22, 136, 137

children affected by parental problems, 25, 57, 61, 72, 82, 92, 96, 112, **206–15**, 200

    interventions, 213–14

    protective factors, **208–9**

    prevalence, 207

    risks, **208**

    role of adult services, **210–13**

children and young people's substance use

    see young people's substance use

Children of Addicted Parents and People, 214

China

    opium wars, 55

Chinese

    Oriental flush, 38

    immigrants, 52

chlordiazepoxide (Librium), 10, 150

Christians use of wine, 51

chronic relapsing condition, 77, 179

Churchill, Winston, 54

Circle of Care, 163

cirrhosis

    see liver

citric acid, 136

classes of drugs

    see Misuse of Drugs Act 1971

classical (Pavlovian) conditioning, 23, **39–40**, 228

closure of cases

    see endings

club drugs (dance drugs), 60, 173

    interventions, **176**

coca, 50–1

cocaethylene, 11

cocaine, 9, **11–12**, 21, 22, **26–7**, 60, 107, 136–7, 151–2, **173–6**, 195

    see also stimulants

Cocaine Anonymous, 164

codeine, 10, 148

coerced into treatment

    see involuntary treatment

coffee, 12, 52

    see also caffeine

cognitions, **41–42**

    see also cognitive behavioural therapy

cognitive behavioural therapy (CBT), **87**, 139, **154–61**, 175, **182–86**, 203, 235, 238

cognitive dissonance, 70, 73, 181

collaborative working

    see inter-agency working

Community Payback Orders, 247

community reinforcement approach (CRA), **162–3**, 175, 224

complimentary therapies, 174, 175

compulsory treatment, 241

    see also involuntary treatment

conditional caution, 247

confidentiality, 91, **103**, 174, 198, 237

    children affected by parental problems, 103, 206, **213**

    limits of, **103**, 242

confrontation, **91**, 122, 218

consent

    to share information, 103

    to treatment, 223, **237–8**

contingency management, **161–2**, 175, 236, 248

controlled drinking, **83**, 116–17, **168–72**, 178, 203, 223, 242

    assessment for, **169–70**

    controversies, **83**

    definition, **168–9**

    programmes, **170–2**

controlled drugs

    see Misuse of Drugs Act 1971

control of substances

    see social policy

cost of substances, **33**, 58, 62, 63, 65, 107

    alcohol minimum unit pricing, 25, 64

couples therapy, 122, 224

    see also marital therapy

crack cocaine, 11, 27, 107, 137, 173, 174–5

cravings, 5, **7**, 38, 109, 149, 175

    dealing with, 58, 72, 75, 86, 150, 157, 161, 183–4

crime, 24–5, 33, 52, 57, 61, 84, 112–13, 156, 208, **244–8**

    links with substance use, **244–5**

    see also criminal justice system

criminal justice system, 55, 63, **244–8**, 250

    substances as criminal justice issue, 55, 6, 64

    see also crime

criminogenic needs, 246

crises and change, **71–2**, 77, 176

cues, 16, 39, 40, 156, 161, 180

    see also triggers

cultivation of drugs, 59, 62

cultural factors influencing use, 15, **24**, 30, **31–5**, **50–2**, 64
'cutting' drugs, 20, 106–7
cycle of change, **75–7**, 130, 179
    use in assessment, **110**, 125, 155

dance drugs
    see club drugs
Dangerous Drugs Act 1920, 55
DANOS, 99
Davies, D.L., 83
decriminalisation, 62–3
Defence of the Realm Act (regulations 1916), 55
delirium tremens (DTs), 109, 149–50, 195
demand reduction, **53**, 57–58,64
denial, 4, 7, 36, 91, 122
dependence, **3–6**, 38, 60, 74, 104, 145, 169, 252–6
    physical, **5–6**, 21–2, 26–7, 105, **108–10**, **145–50**, 152, 176, 228 231, 237
    psychological, **5–6**, 26–7, 228
    see also addiction, *under names of substances*
depressant drugs, 8, **9–10**, 21, 45, 108
    dangerous in withdrawal, 108, 202
    overdose, 23, 146
    see also *under names of substances*
depression, 108, 199, 200–1, 202
    effect of substances, 11, 152, 175, 194, 201
deprivation
    see social disadvantage
detoxification, 4, **7**, 21, 86, 109, 117, 118–19, **145–6**, 152, 248
    alcohol, **149–51**
    benzodiazepines, **152**
    GHB/GBL, 176
    nicotine, **153**
    Opiates, **148**
deviance theory, **34–5**, 74, 231
diaries, 105, 141
diazepam, 10, 150, 152, 245
    see also benzodiazepines
dihydrocodeine, 11, 148
disease model
    see theories of problematic use
disulfiram (Antabuse), 150, 152, 175
diversionary activities, 231, 238
    risks of, 54
diversion from prosecution, 247
diversity see also BME
domestic abuse
    see abuse
dopamine, 9

drink driving legislation, 53, 134
drinking
    see alcohol
'drug, set and setting' (Zinberg), 8, 14, 19, 47, 171
drug courts, 247
Drug Rehabilitation Requirements, 247
drug testing, 162, 247, 250
Drug Treatment and Testing Order, 247
Drug Treatment Outcomes Research Study (DTORS), 250
drugs
    definition **4–5**, **8–9**, **14–16**
    social policy, 24, **53–7**, **59–63**, 65, **84–5**, **246–7**
    see also *under names of substances*
DTORS (Drug Treatment Outcomes Research Study), 250
DTs
    see delirium tremens
dual diagnosis
    see psychological distress

ecstasy (MDMA), **12**, 18, 19–20, 21, 51, 228
    mental health risks of, 12, 195
education
    regarding substances, 53, 57, 226, 230–1
empathy, **89–90**, 126, 211
employee policies, 240, **242–4**
    effectiveness of, 249–50
    interventions, **248–9**
endings, 94, 178, **187–8**, 237
energy drinks, 21
engagement (facilitating engagement), 47, **89–92**, **95–6**, **101–2**, 115, 163, 168
    BME communities, **97–8**
    involuntary referrals, **241–2**
    parents, **211**
    stimulant users, **174–5**
    women, **96–7**
    young people **232–3**, **236**
England, 173, 246
    adolescent use, 227
    alcohol policy, 64
    blood borne virus rates, 133
    children affected prevalence, 207
    court disposals, 247
    Fraser guidelines, 237
    heroin prescribing, 147
    mental health services, 198
environment, 43, 75, 180
    influence on change, **71–2**, 110–11, **161–3**
    influence on use, 8, **14–16**, **31–3**, 35

relapse, 182, 184
risks, 19, 23, **24–5**
epidemics, 32, 55, 58, 60, 66
epilepsy
see seizures
escape coping, 44
ethnic communities
see black and minority ethnic communities
European countries
challenge to unit pricing of alcohol, 64
heroin prescribing, 147–8
European Union
directives on tar levels, 58
evidence (methods of obtaining), 82–3
expectation regarding use, 8, 14–15, 21, 180,
182

family's involved in treatment of
an adult, 84, **103**, 146, 150, **162–3**, 175, 216,
**222–4**
a young person, **235**, **236–8**
family therapy, 214, 218, 224, 235
fashion in use, 51, 173
fetal alcohol spectrum disorder, **209**
five step method, **221**
flash cards, 183
follow-up care, 82, 140, **187–8**, 239
four Ls (Roizen), 26
FRAMES (acronym), 141
Fraser guidelines, 237–8
freebase (cocaine), 107
French drinking habits, 24

gateway theory, **45–6**, 138
GBL (gammabutyrolactone)
see GHB
genes, 38
see also genetic theories
genetic theories
see theories of problematic use
geography (availability of substances), 50–1
Getting our Priorities Right, 207
GHB (gammahydroxybutyrate), 9, **10**, 110, 137,
176
risks in withdrawal, 21, **108**, 202
Global Commission on Drug Policy, 62
goal setting
see care planninhg
Great War, 55
Greece
HIV increase, 133
group work, 214, 231, 235
guided discovery, 158–9, 183

Hague International Opium Convention, 55
hallucinogens, 8, **12–13**, 14, 33, 52, 59, 209
also see under names of substances
harms, **18–28**
see also under names of substances, individual
chapters in Part I I I Special Populations
harmful use (WHO definition), **6**, 18–19, 141,
252
harm reduction
as individual intervention, 101, **116**, **132–9**,
174, 202, 234
as social policy, **53**, 55, 58, 59, 60, 61, 84
hazardous use (WHO definition), **6**, 19, 141, 252
Health Act 2009, 57
hepatitis
A and B, 137
C, 61, 107, 133
see also blood borne viruses
heroin, **10–11**, 19–20, 22, 23, 54, 59–60, 68,
106, **109**, **136**
interventions, 87, **88**, **146–9**, 152, 155, 175,
186, 245
pregnancy, 209
prescribing, 63, **147–8**
see also opiates
Hidden Harm, 207
HIV, 60, 61, 84, 97, 107, 133, 174
comparative rates, 133
Holland
drug policy, 61
cannabis cafes, 63
human growth hormones, 137

image-enhancing drugs, 22, 137
Improving Access to Psychological Therapies,
199
infections, 20, 107, 136
information
providing to service users, 112, **115**, **134–7**,
168, 187, 212, 221, 241
ingestion of substances
methods of, 14, 19, **22**, 34, 46, 209
harm reduction, 133, **135–138**, 145
initiation into use, 31, 58, 167, 228, 229, 238
injecting, **22**, 60, 123, 174, 176
harm reduction, 134, **135–7**, 145, 147
risks, 22, 23, 108, 234
see also individual drugs
injecting rooms, 63
inter-agency working, 95, 100, **103**, 115, 144,
198, 249
regarding children affected by parental
problems, 206–7, 209, **210**, 212–214

Internet
  diaries on, 105
  information from, 134
  forums and therapeutic sites, 167, 168, 214
  sales of drugs, 63, 65
involuntary treatment, 115, **240–51**
  criminal justice system, 246–8
  employee policies, 242–4
  evidence of effectiveness, 249–50
  interventions, 248–9
Iranian revolution, 60
Islam
  prohibition, 17
isolation (social)

Japanese
  Oriental flush, 38
Jellinek's types of alcoholism, 36–8
Jewish people
  alcohol use, 31, **32**
junkie
  stereotype, 4

ketamine, 8, **13**, 173, 176, 201
khat, 52
Kinder eggs, 107
kinship carers, 214
Koreans
  Oriental flush, 38
Korsakoff's syndrome, 19, 150, 195, 204

labelling, **73–4**, 122, 167, 231
  theory, **34–5**
  see also stigma
lapse
  see relapse
lead professional, 115
learning theories of problematic use, **39–43**,
    156, **160–1**, 245
legal highs
  see new psychoactive substances
legalisation debate, 61, **62**
legislation, 16, 53, 55, 61
  alcohol licensing, 63, 134
  Dangerous Drugs Act 1920, 55
  Defence of the Realm Act (regulations
    1916), 55
  drink driving legislation, 53, 134
  Health Act 2009, 57
  Licensing Act 2003, 64
  minimum unit pricing alcohol, 25, 64
  Misuse of Drugs Act 1971, 8, 17, **59–60**,
    103

Pharmacy Act 1868, 54
Tobacco Advertising and Promotion Act,
    2002, 57
Tobacco and Primary Medical Services
    (Scotland) Act 2010, 57
lesbian, gay, bisexual and transgender
    community, **97**
less intensive treatment, 86, **132**, **139–40**,
    254
LGBT
  see lesbian, gay, bisexual and transgender
      community
Librium (chlordiazepoxide), 10, 150
licensing
  alcohol, 63, 134
  models for drugs, 62
  see also legislation
Licensing Act 2003, 64
liver, 5, 8–9, 11, 15
  damage, 9, 15, 19, 23, 24, 26, 56, 108
  function test, 107
lofexidine, 148
loss of control, 36–7, 38, 182
LSD, 12, 13, 24, 51
  psychological distress, 195, 201
lung cancer, 19, 57, 58

maintaining change, **71–4**, 111, 161, 162–3,
    **178–86**, 223–4, 239
  see also cycle of change
manuals, **94–5**, 123
mapping tools, 95, 105, 184
marital therapy, 139
  see also couples therapy
matching, 89
maturation out of problematic use, **69**, 235
MDMA
  see ecstasy
menstrual cycle, 15, 108
mental health
  see psychological distress
mentoring, 214, 218, 239
mephedrone, 14, 173, 176, 227
methadone, 10–11, 61, 63, **84–5**, 88, 109,
    **146–7**, 148
methamphetamine, 12, 173
methoxetamine, 14
methylphenidate (Ritalin), 11
Mexico
  drug trafficking, 25
  native people's peyote, 51
minimum unit pricing alcohol, 25, 64
misuse, **8**

Misuse of Drugs Act 1971, 8, 17, **59–60**, 103
mixing substances, 14, **21–2**, 23, 135
  see also overdose, polydrug use
modelling, 235, 248
  learning by, 42, 156, 229
moral panics, 52, 226
morphine, 10, 20, 54, 144, 147
motivation, **70–1**, 77, **101**, 121, 160, 173, 180,
    235, 238
  see also motivational interviewing
motivational interviewing, 71, 86, 101, **121–31**,
    139, 175, 203, 235, 248
  effectiveness of, 124
  essence of, **123–4**
  ethical concerns about, 124–5
  principles of, 126
  self motivational statements, 127
  when not appropriate, 110, 125
multi-agency working
  see inter-agency working
multi-systemic therapy, 235
  see also family therapy
mushrooms, 12–13
Muslims, 51
mutual aid groups, 73, 74, 83, 85, **163–8**, 187,
    221, 224
  role of practitioner, 168, 222–3, 224
  for significant adults, **222–3**

Naloxone, 135, 147
Naltrexone
  opiate antagonist, 146, 148–9
  reduce cravings for alcohol, 149, 150–1
naphyrone, 14, 173
narco-states, 25
Narcotics Anonymous, 71, 164, 247
needle, 136
  exchanges, 133, 134, 136, 213
  habit, 20
neonatal abstinence syndrome, 209
neurobiology, **38–9**
  see also central nervous system
neurotransmitters, 5, 9, **27**
New Labour
  crime reduction agenda, 61, 246
new psychoactive substances, **7**, 11, **13–14**, 20,
    60, 65, 107, 167
  interventions, **176**
nicotine
  see tobacco
nicotine replacement therapy
  see substitute prescribing
nitrazepam, 10

Northern Ireland
  Fraser guidelines, 237
  mental health services, 198
  court disposals, 247
Norway
  snus, 138
novice user, 228

obsessive compulsive disorder, 13, 200
offenders
  see crime
older people, 15, 23, 52, 69, 108, 138, 166
operant conditioning, **40–1**, 43, 69, 228
opiates, **10–11**, 45, **54–6**, 59, 108, 117, **146–9**,
    152
  detoxification, **148**
  harm reduction, **134–8**
  pregnancy, 209
  substitution therapy, **88**, 117, 145, **146–7**,
    133, 186
  see also under names of substances
opioids
  see opiates
opium, 54–6
Oriental flush, 38
outcomes (measuring)
  interventions, **82**, 234
  predicting, 86
  social policy, **56–7**
outlets (sales), 62–3
outreach, 97, 98, 133, 134, 135, 174
overdose 20, **23**, 24, 105, 146, 147, 223, 248
  reducing risk of, 134, **135**, 137
  see also individual drugs

packaging
  of cigarettes, 57
  alternative drug regulation, 62, 63
painkillers (prescribed), 65, 105
pain reducing drugs, 8, **10–11**, 21, 23
  see also under names of substances
panic attacks, 200
  cannabis, 13, 195
Papago people, 15
paracetamol, 10, 20, 136
paranoia
  related to substance use, 11–12, 108, 174,
    195
parental substance problems
  see children affected by parental problems
passive smoking, 57, 58
Pavlovian conditioning
  see classical conditioning

peer group influences, 31, 42, 46, 170, 226, 229
peer support, 85, 96
  see also mutual aid groups
permission giving thoughts, 158, 160, 183
pethidine, 10
peyote, 51
pharmacological treatments, 86, **144–54**, 223
  alcohol, **149–50**
  benzodiazepines, **152**
  nicotine, 142, **153**, 238
  opiates, **146–7**
  stimulants, **151–2**
  young people, **237**, 238
  see also substitute prescribing
Pharmacy Act 1868, 54
phenethylamines, 14
phobias, 200
physical abuse
  see abuse
piperazines, 14
polydrug use **7**, 21, 65, 106, 150, 173, 227, 233
  see also mixing substances
post traumatic stress, 45, 199, 200
  see also trauma
poverty
practitioner skills, **89–94**, 123–4, 140
pregnancy, 96, 106, **108**, 109, 148, 150, 170,
  208, **209**, 212, 249
prescription drugs, 65, 194, 196, 203
  and psychological distress, 108, 203
  see also under names of substances
price of substances
  see cost of substances
prison, 135, 247–8
Probation Order, 247
prohibition, 17
  alcohol in USA, 56
  drugs, 59–62
Project Match, 89, 164
psychoanalytical
  interventions, 87
  theories of problematic use, **43–5**
psychological distress, 19, **107–8**, 117, 150,
  176, **193–205**, 220, 233
  interventions, 145, 169, **199–204**
  links with substance use, 44, **193–6**
  prevalence, **197**
  services, **197–9**
  see also under individual substance names
psychosis, 196, 200–1, 202, 203, 204
  drug induced, 12, 152, 195, 201, 202
psychostimulants
  see stimulants

Public Health England, 61
purity of drugs
  see 'cutting' drugs

questions, types of
  closed, 92–3, 101, 113, 127, 158
  leading, 93, 127, 158, 200
  open, 93, 101, 127

Rand report, 83
Rastafarians, 52
rational choice (moral) model of problematic
  use, **46–7**
Rational Emotive Behaviour Therapy, 167
rebellion
  substance use as, 33–4, 52, 59
recapping
  see summarising
recession
  effects on substance use, 65
recovery, 8, 60, 61, **84–5**, 133, 144, 164, 167,
  204, 224
  capital, 72, **73**, 77, 86, **110–11**, 146, 187
  movement, 77, **84–5**, 179
  unassisted, **67–74**
  and young people, 239
recovery groups
  see mutual aid groups
recreational use, **7**, 51, 173, 228
reframing (technique), 126, 127
refusal skills, 72, 76, 171, 176, 180, **184–5**
rehab
  see residential rehab
relapse, **7**, 75, 77, 146, 161, **178–86**, 188,
  223–4
  pharmacological treatments to prevent, 145,
  148–9, 150–1, 152, 153
  prevention, 43, 72, 75, 87, 95, 110, 175,
  **182–6**, 203
relatives
  see significant adults
religion
  influences cultural attitudes, 51
  as part of recovery, 72
reproductive health, **108**, 138
residential rehab, 87, 89, **117–8**, 164, 175, 203,
  214
resistance to change, 91, 101, 122, 126, 127,
  241
reviews of cases, 86, 101, 103, 116, 155
risk-need-responsivity model (criminal justice),
  246, 248

risks of use, **18–28, 134–9, 194–6, 228,** **144–5**
  to children, **207–9**
  to significant adults, **217–18**
  see also under names of substances
Ritalin (methylphenidate), 11
ritual of substance taking, 40
'rock bottom', 36, 122
Roisen's four Ls, 26
role play, 96, 161, 171, 185, 235
Rolleston Committee, 55
Romania
  HIV increase, 133
Russia
  HIV rates, 133

SADQ-C (assessment questionnaire), 104, 109, **252, 254–6**
same sex counsellors, 97
schizophrenia, 194, 200
  possible links with substance use, 19, 195–6
schools
  see education
Scotland, 25, 51
  adolescent use, 227
  alcohol policy, 64
  Fraser guidelines, 238
  mental health services, 198
  court disposals, 247
seemingly irrelevant decisions, **180–1,** 183
seizures (in withdrawal), 21, 108, 109, 149–50
selective serotonin uptake inhibitors, 152
self efficacy, 42, **71, 126,** 141, 161, 164, 180, 181, 182
self help groups
  see mutual aid groups
self medication, 44, 194
self motivational statements, 127
  see also motivational interviewing
service culture, **95–8**
sexual abuse
  see abuse
sexual and reproductive health, **108,** 138
sex work, 96, 108
siblings
  effects on, 25, 216, **218**
significant adults, 87, 103, 163, 199, 203, **216–25**
  5-step method, 221
  involvement in service design, 199, 223
  involvement in treatment of substance user, 216, 222, **223–4**
  meeting own needs, **216–23**

single shared assessment, 103, 104, 144
slogans
  Alcoholics Anonymous, 166, 182
SMART criteria (acronym), 115
smart drugs, 65
SMART Recovery, 167, 168
smoking
  see tobacco
snorting drugs, 11, 19, 137
snuff, 11, 51
snus, 138
Social Behaviour and Network Therapy, **162–3,** 224
  see also community reinforcement approach
social disadvantage, 30, 31, **33,** 60, 73, 174, 208, 209, 229
social learning theory, **42–3,** 69, 181
social policy
  alcohol, **63–4**
  drugs, **59–61**
  historical, **54–6**
  judging effectiveness of, **56–7**
  methods of control, **52–4**
  tobacco, **57–8**
social networks, 72, 162–3, 164, 175, 223, 235
sociological theories of problematic use **31–5**
Socratic questioning (see guided discovery)
solvents
  see volatile substances
Somali people
  khat, 52
speedball, 22
speed
  see amphetamines
spontaneous change
  see unassisted recovery
stabilisation
steroids, 5
  injecting, 22, 136–7
stigma, 4, **34–5, 73–4,** 85, 173, 193, 217, 231
  see also labelling
stimulants, 8, **11–12,** 14, 21, 45, 117, 227
  come down (withdrawal), 11, 152, 175
  harm reduction, **134–7**
  interventions, **173–6**
  pharmacological treatments, **151–2**
  psychological distress, 152, 175, 176, 195, 201
  prevalence, 173
  see also under names of substances
stimulus control, 76
strain theory applied to problematic use, **33–4**

Suboxone, 147
substance
substances
substitute prescribing, 138, 145, 237, 248
    controversies, 61, **84–5, 88**
    for opiates, **88**, 117, 145, **146–7**, 133, 186
    for stimulants, **151**
    for tobacco, 142, 145, **153**, 238
Subutex (buprenorphine), 88, **146–7**, 148
suicide
    prevention, 108, 199
    risk of, 150, 152, 176, 196, 199, 201, 202
summarising (technique), 90, 104, 127, 158
supply reduction, **53**, 56, 57, 64
Sweden
    drug policy in, 61
    snus, 138

tanning agents, 137
taxation of substances, 53, 57, 62
temazepam, 10
temperance movement, 56
Temporary Class Drug Orders, 60
testing
    see drug testing
Thatcher government
    harm reduction, 60
    recession, 65
theories of problematic use, **29–49**
    bio-psycho-social theory, **47–8**, 217, 228
    disease model, 7, **35–7**, 83, 87, 122, 164,
        169, **182**
    gateway theory, **45–6**, 138
    genetic theories, 23, 35, **37–9**, 245
    learning (behavioural) theories, **39–43**, 156,
        **160–1**, 245
    psychoanalytical theories, **43–5**
    rational choice (moral) model, **46–7**
    sociological theories, **31–5**
therapeutic alliance, 86, **89–91**, 155
thiamine (vitamin B1) deficiency, 150
Thorley, Anthony, 101, 211, 241
    model, **26–7**, 105
thought stopping, 183
tier model of services
    for adults, **98–9**
    for children, **230–1**
titration, 147
tobacco, **11**, 19, 21, 22, 35, 44, 52, 74, 195, 228,
    229
    harm reduction, 53, 58, 133, **138**
    interventions, **142**, 145, **153**, **238**
    passive smoking, 25, 57, 58

pregnancy, 209
    social policy, 53, 56, **57–8**
Tobacco Advertising and Promotion Act 2002,
    57
Tobacco and Primary Medical Services
    (Scotland) Act 2010, 57
tolerance, **5**, 23, 24, 109, 135
    see also under names of substances
tramadol, 148
Transform, 62
Transtheoretical model
    see cycle of change
trauma, 105, 117, 156
    see also post-traumatic stress
treatments
    see under individual interventions
triage, 95, 96, **102**
triggers, 7, 105, 121, 184
    for change, **71–2**
twelve steps
    see 12-steps

UK Alcohol Treatment Trial (UKATT)
    see Social Behaviour and Network Therapy
unassisted recovery, **68–74**
unintended consequences
    social policy, 53–4
USA
    international control of drugs, 55
    native people's peyote, 51
    prescription painkillers, 65
    prohibition (alcohol), 56
Vietnam war, 32
user involvement, 71, 96, **135**

Valium
    see diazepam
varenicline (Champix), 153
vicarious learning, 42
Vietnam
    US soldiers and heroin, 31–2
vitamin C (ascorbic acid), 136
vitamins, 150
volatile substances, 7, 8, **10**, 227, 228

Wales, 173, 246
    alcohol policy, 64
    court disposals, 247
    Fraser guidelines, 237
    mental health services, 198
websites
    see Internet
welcoming gesture, **102**, 233

Wernicke's encephalopathy, 150, 195
Wilson, Bill, 36
Winehouse, Mitch, 3
withdrawals, **5**, 6, **20–1**, 41, 108, 145, 202, 209,
    256
  alcohol, **109**
  benzodiazepines, 110
  GHB/GBL, 110
  opiates, **109–10**
  substances dangerous in withdrawal, 21,
    **108**, 202
  see also detoxification
women, 34, 149
  services, **96–7**, 165
  risks, 15, 23, 108, 112–13
  see also pregnancy

workplace policies
  see employee policies
wraparound services, 85, 99, 117, 177, 187,
    203, 214

young people's substance use, 23, **226–39**
  assessment and care planning, **232–5**
  interventions, **235–9**
  prevalence, 227
  protective factors, **230**
  risks, **228–9**
  services, **230–2**

Zinberg's 'drug, set and setting', 8, 14, 19, 47,
    171
Zyban (bupropion), 11, 153